HAWAII BY SEXTANT

An In-depth Exercise in Celestial Navigation

Using Real Sextant Sights

and Logbook Entries

DAVID BURCH
&
STEPHEN MILLER

STARPATH®

www.starpathpublications.com

ISBN 978-0-914025-18-4

Published by

Starpath Publications

3050 NW 63rd Street, Seattle, WA 98107

www.starpathpublications.com

10   9   8   7   6   5   4   3

Acknowledgements (Past, Present, and Future)

Early work on the transcription from the original logbook and organization of the sight data were carried out by Starpath Instructor Robert Reeder.

The layout and design of the book and the immense task of accurately rendering the plots into accurate graphics was carried out by Tobias Burch. We cannot thank him enough for his skill and patience, and creative solutions to several layout challenges.

And once again we have benefited from the sharp eye of Starpath Instructor Larry Brandt. His review of the text led to valuable improvements. Lanny Petitjean also provided a productive review of parts of the text.

We are especially indebted to Stan Klein, developer of the software program *Celestial Tools*. His careful review of the work form solutions led to several improvements and corrections.

But despite the excellent help we have had so far, we offer thanks in advance for response from readers on the analysis and alternative solutions. This text contains over 30,000 digits, eighty percent of which depend upon preceding computations, as well as over 1,800 hand- drawn line segments whose direction must be accurate to 1º and length to 1 mm. Regardless of our efforts, it is statistically impossible that every one is correct. Your confirmations, corrections, or suggestions will be very much appreciated. Authors' contact and book resources are at starpath.com/HBS.

Contents

Abbreviations Used	
a-Lat	assumed latitude
a-Lon	assumed longitude
a-value	altitude intercept (difference between Hc and Ho)
C	course (in most cases assumed to be CMG)
cel nav	celestial navigation
CMG	course made good
Dec	declination
DR	dead reckoning
DR-Lat	latitude of the DR position
DR-Lon	longitude of the DR position
dsd	double second difference (Pub 229)
fix	a lat-lon position determined by cel nav or piloting
GMT	Greenwich Mean Time (same as UTC)
Hc	calculated height or altitude (from sight reduction)
HE	height of eye
Ho	observed height or altitude
Hs	sextant height or altitude (read directly from the sextant)
IC	index correction
Lat	latitude
LHA	local hour angle
LL	lower limb
log	odometer of miles through the water
Lon	longitude
LOP	line of position
meter	3.28 ft
PDT	Pacific Daylight Time (ZD=+7)
rfix	running fix
S	speed (in most cases assumed to be SMG)
SMG	speed made good
sunline	sextant sight of the sun reduced to an LOP on the plotting sheet
T	True (direction relative to north)
UL	upper limb
UTC	Universal Coordinated Time
WT	watch time
Z	azimuth angle
ZD	zone description
Zn	azimuth

For extra resources, news, and support of this book, as well as contact with the authors, see starpath.com/HBS

Introduction

Overview

This book presents an exercise in ocean navigation carried out by celestial navigation alone. It is intended for those who wish to practice their skills in navigation that they have learned from other sources.

This is not a book on basic celestial navigation.

This book assumes you have learned cel nav basics from another source, and we provide here the best way we can think of for you to master what you have learned, and gain the confidence that you can navigate an ocean passage by cel nav alone if you chose to or had to.

It is based on a real voyage using the actual sextant sights taken, along with the logbook of dead reckoning between sights. The successful completion of this exercise becomes in effect the successful navigation of an ocean crossing.

The voyage was from Victoria, BC to Maui, HI in July of 1982. The vessel was taking part in the Victoria to Maui Yacht Race at a time when celestial navigation was not only required, it was the only option. The vessel was a 41' sloop (*SV Passages*) with an average speed of 6.3 kts over the 2,800-mile voyage.

All times, unless specified otherwise, are Watch Times (WT) with zone description ZD = +7. Any reference to GMT refers to Universal Time, with UTC = WT +ZD = WT + 7h.

Unless otherwise stated, height of eye = 9 ft, watch error = 0 sec, and index correction = 0.0'.

This was the last voyage we made by pure celestial navigation, without any electronic aids. In principle, Radio Direction Finding was allowed, but it was not needed at the departure and there were no dependable stations at the destination, so this was not used.

The voyage begins with a last visual fix off Cape Flattery, WA (in the old days, called taking our departure), after transiting 75 nmi of the Strait of Juan de Fuca and entering the ocean. The destination was Lahaina on Maui, HI, which is just under 2,400 miles to the southwest as the crow flies–the great circle route–but rather farther when sailing around local and global wind patterns. In this voyage a total of about 2,800 miles was sailed.

There is a total of 38 sight sessions over a 17-day voyage, with each session including 3 to 10 sights-a total of 227 recorded sights, making up 27 celestial fixes of various kinds.

Each day's navigation is summarized at the beginning of the day, and then again after the fix has been achieved. In all cases, the DR was started anew from the most recent fix. There are no adjustments for ocean currents needed, nor for leeway-which is not to say the vessel was not affected by currents; it is just that we did not have enough data at the time to justify any such corrections.

The exercise is presented in several parts, and working through the voyage will require referring back and forth among them as needed. The days of the voyage are marked in a gray band for quick location; the individual problems are numbered sequentially from the start of the voyage, and to further assist in organization, each sextant sight session is given a unique Sight Session number. Thus on July 10th, we have one problem (No. 8), which is made up of two Sight Sessions (#13 and #14).

Logbook

The logbook lists daily entries of log readings and courses steered. The log reading is the odometer for the trip, recording the total number of miles sailed through the water. Each time a position fix was achieved, the DR position was shifted to the fix position and the DR track continued on from that new position. Before doing the sight reduction of each position fix, it will be necessary to plot out the DR track from the time of the last fix to determine the DR position at the time of the new sight session. Normally the logbook would record the compass course on each heading, but to simplify matters a bit, we have converted the compass headings to true headings for each entry. (In this voyage in 1982 the magnetic variation changed from 21.3°E at departure to 11.1°E in Hawaii, but those corrections have already been applied.)

Although there are multiple entries on most days, there are frankly not as many as would be best practice. I became much more diligent on subsequent voyages with more logbook entries. If no one else would enter the logbook, I would do it myself, as it does not take long to appreciate how valuable it is. This exercise demonstrates that in some cases. It is often a challenge to get crew to enter the logbook.

Section of the Logbook					
	Date	Time PDT	Log	Course T	Speed kts
21	8-Jul	0000	698	175	7.1
22		0800	755	165	6.4
23		1011	769	170	6.8

Notes on the Logbook

The left column just numbers the entries for reference only. In this case, on July 8 at 0000 PDT, the trip log read 698.0 nmi and the boat either turned to, or stayed, on course 175 T. (We do not know which without seeing the earlier log entry. We can certainly make a log entry without changing course, but we must make one when we do change course.)

Then 8h later at 0800, the log read 755.0 and we turned to course 165T. Thus our DR track will show a leg that is 57 mi long (755-698) in direction 175, then the track will angle off 10° to 165 and the next leg will be 14 mi long (769-755), at which point it turns 5° back to course 170.

The speeds recorded here are speed made good (SMG) on the leg listed. That is, between 0800 and 1011 (2h 11m = 2.183h) we traveled by log 14 nmi (769-755), so our SMG = 14/2.183 = 6.41 kts. This SMG can be used to estimate DR positions in between the log book entries.

In this book the word mile and nautical mile are the same (as it is on the boat) and we use watch time (WT) to enter the logbook and record the sights, again just as we would do on the boat. Watch time in this case was Pacific Daylight Time, which is 7 h earlier than UTC, ie UTC = WT + 7h. This is the same throughout the voyage, which is the recommended system, as opposed to changing ship's time during a voyage.

This logbook only records logs to the nearest whole mile. That was the way I did it on this voyage, but at this point I am not sure why. *We should definitely record logs to nearest tenth of a mile.* Cel nav is not pinpoint nav, but we do not want to throw away any information we can easily obtain, even if it may not be fully accurate to the tenth.

Navigation Sights

This section presents each of the daily sextant sights in tabular form, along with a few brief notes. In each case the actual sextant reading (Hs) is given for the corresponding time of the sight, which is listed as both WT and UTC. You will use the former in coordinating with the logbook, and the latter for the cel nav sight reductions. In almost all cases, we tried to take multiple sights of each body used with the intention of averaging them in some way to obtain the best value for a single sight. This is standard good procedure. It is always better to take multiple sights of the same two or three bodies than to take just one or two sights each of many bodies.

There are various ways to evaluate the several sights of the same body. We recommend what we call the Fit Slope Method described in the Analysis section. There are other methods, and if you are using a calculator or computer program for the analysis, it may have an option built into it. A simple, but less efficient, method is just to plot all of them and judge for yourself which is representative of the set, or use all of them in concluding where the fix should be. The Automatic Advancement of LOPs method we describe in the Analysis may help with this.

Each set of sights offers a proposed practice problem. You can navigate the passage as you see best, but solving the fixes at the suggested problem times will offer an easier comparison with the solutions provided.

And to illustrate that the real world is not always like a classroom exercise, we start right out with an unusual sight combination—a running fix from a morning sight of Venus, being the only thing visible in a cloudy sky, and a sun sight taken shortly after sunrise.

Table Selections

To work the exercises you will need the *Nautical Almanac* data for the times underway in 1982, which are presented in the Tables Selection at the back of this book. This does not include the Increments and Corrections tables, which are the same from year to year and can be obtained from any almanac of any year. If you do not have access to an outdated or current *Nautical Almanac*, you can download a set of Increments and Corrections from starpath.com/HBS, which offers several other documents of interest to navigators.

Solutions

Because this book is intended as a self-guided training exercise, the solutions are presented in depth, in several formats. A DR track of the full voyage is presented in multiple pages, so the plotted celestial lines of position (LOP) can be shown plotted as they might be in your own work. Depending on how you do the DR and what assumed position you end up using, your plots could look somewhat different from these, but the fix positions should be the same, if we end up choosing the same sights to reduce.

Numerical solutions by computation are also given, as well as full solutions using tables alone. The latter include all almanac data used, along with each step of the sight reduction, presented in the Starpath Workforms. If you care to use these, there is a blank one at the back of the book, or you can download a pdf from starpath.com/HBS

We also include in the plotting part of the solutions a section of the last nautical chart used as we leave the coast and move on to plotting sheets for the ocean, as well as the nautical chart we move onto at the end of the voyage as we finally leave the plotting sheets for the approach to land.

What you will Need

To customize the exercise to your own style of celestial navigation, you will need a set of Sight Reduction Tables. You can use any set of tables you like.

Alternatively, you can do the sight reduction and dead reckoning with a calculator or computer program. There are numerous commercial versions, as well as quite a few free ones online as a download. See also starpath.com/calc.

You will also need Universal Plotting Sheets and plotting tools, both are available at starpath.com or other online and local outlets. There are also high-resolution plotting sheets online that can be downloaded and printed.

If you are accustomed to using workforms for sight reduction, you can use any form you prefer. We have included copies of the Starpath workforms in the Appendix that you can reproduce and use if you choose to. We use these forms to present the detailed, step by step solutions, but you can use any forms you choose.

Procedures

To navigate this voyage, do as you would do underway. Start by setting up a universal plotting sheet that puts your first known position in the top right corner (we are headed SW).

Then use the logbook data to plot out your DR track to the times of the first and second sights. The two sets of sights taken about three and a half hours apart, make up the first celestial fix of the voyage, which is the first position fix for more than a day.

At each fix, compare your fix location with what your DR would have been for that time or log reading. That is, if you get a fix at say 1422 WT, but the sights that made up the fix were based on a DR at 14:02, then DR from 1402 up to 1422 so you can make a careful comparison of how good your DR was at the time of the fix. Do this for each fix and save the results. In each case compute or get from a plot, the range and bearing from the DR to the Fix and enter these into the answer sheet provided.

A main goal of ocean navigation is to learn how well you can do DR, so you are prepared to navigate intelligently if you are stuck with nothing but DR to go by. By making

and logging the DR to Fix difference for every fix taken you learn how well you are doing.

In the actual voyage, DR was done with log readings and courses, and then the average speeds made good (SMG) were computed from the times and log readings of sequential positions. The Logbook lists these SMGs, which can be used with the times listed to compute the DR positions.

For each set of sights, refer to the Logbook to get the course and speed of each leg. You will need this for the sight reductions and the running fixes. To simplify record keeping (and your self grading!) use the logbook format provided to fill in your answers and carry out the fixes at the times requested of each session that leads to a fix. You can use any form of sight reduction, books, calculator, or computer.

An important part of the exercise is to keep a clear, organized plot of your work on Universal Plotting Sheets. All of your DR plotting and cel nav LOPs can be plotted on them. If there is any question about how to lay them out, then take a quick peek at the answers to get a hint.

When you reach the bottom of a page, set up a new one, starting at the top, with where you left off at the bottom. For each set of sights, look ahead to the next pages of the book to be sure you have all the sights for that sight session.

You will see here a wide variety of celestial fixes. They are not all the textbook variety, because one has to deal with what is there, not just what we might wish for. However, this is a real voyage that was indeed navigated by exactly this data. We were sailing from 48 North, so even in the summer it was cloudy and bad weather for a while. As we got further south, there were more clear skies so we could do better navigation with star and planet sights.

One pervasive theme, however, is to take as many sights as you can and then average them. In most cases, you can improve the accuracy by evaluating the sights and then removing the ones that are most likely in error. In this exercise, however, as it was in the real voyage without Loran or GPS, you will not know for sure that you did it right until you progress to the next set of sights and check that your DR is now better or worse than it was.

We use the terms fix and running fix (rfix) throughout, but since almost all sight sessions include multiple sights, essentially all fixes are running fixes, so these terms mean the same thing in this context.

Standing Exercises

Beyond the regular exercises, which usually take the form of asking for a fix at a particular time, you can also carry out nearly daily exercises that are not crucial to the navigation but help understand the process of cel nav underway.

An example of that would be to predict the time that sights will become available for the given date and location and when they will no longer be available in the morning or evening. These are the times of civil and nautical twilight in the evening and the reverse in the morning. A few of these are specifically asked for, but this is a question that would come up every day. Or we might ask: how much do these times vary over such a voyage? That you can learn by looking them up.

Likewise, for each of the evening or morning sight sessions, you can also compare how long we were taking sights compared to how long we had according to these predictions. As a rule in practical cel nav, you generally use all the time you have, but you have here the perfect way to check what really took place.

Another example of a standing exercise would be to predict, by whatever method you have learned, what would be the best triad of celestial bodies to use for a fix in each of the situations, and then compare that to what was actually taken. Again, a couple samples are asked for, but the question comes up every night. And again: how does this change over a voyage of this length and duration?

Another thing you can ask yourself at the end of each sight session after you establish your position, is what is the desired or shortest course to our destination, or more realistically, to our next waypoint. Crossing the ocean in a sailboat is rarely point to point navigation. We have to follow the wind. But since it is such a long trip, we do not know where the wind will be when we get halfway there, so we have to make some guesses bases on climatic behavior for July.

This route usually calls for sailing around the Pacific High, with a corner at about 31.5N, 140W, near the former location of the last weather ship in the Pacific, called *November (30N, 140W)*. Ocean charts we sailed on at the time of this voyage (1982) still showed a big N at that location, long after the ship was retired in 1974. The location is a pure coincidence, but it made an easy waypoint to keep in mind. Put another way, the vast majority of the boats that have won the Victoria to Maui Yacht Race have gone within 100 miles of that location on their way across the Pacific.

Thus for practice you can ask yourself, what is course to that waypoint and our SMG in that direction for points north of there, and then once we get close or past that region, what is then the course and SMG to the destination at Pailolo Channel, the entrance to Lahaina, which is our destination. The SMG in the direction of a specific waypoint is called the waypoint closing velocity (WCV).

In such a long passage, it is tempting to think about our WCV to the destination right from the beginning, but that can be very misleading. It could be that early in the voyage we could indeed make good progress in that direction, but doing so from early in the voyage could drive us right into the middle of the Pacific High, with no wind at all, and once that happens it is very difficult to correct it. Thus the prudent route is go the way you are most likely to have good wind, and not get suckered into the direct route, at least not for more than a day or so. Every race there are numerous boats that try it. Periodically one sneaks through with grand success. More often it leaves the navigator with only visions of glory and a very poor showing.

You can plot out the full route to watch your progress on chart 530, which can be downloaded as a free pdf BookletChart, nicely divided into letter size pages for printing. Then paste them together for a full chart. See starpath.com/getcharts. Or just make a series of Placemarks for your fixes in Google Earth and save them. A sample of that is given and explained at starpath.com/HBS along with a gpx file of the fixes that can be loaded into any echart program or Google Earth. WCV data as described above is presented in the Solutions.

There is much to be learned from the data in this exercise!

Philosophy

There is no rush in the process. You can take your time. You can even maintain real time by spending as much as a full day on each position fix. One of the facts of life when relying on cel nav alone is it takes some time to get it done properly. It is not uncommon at all to spend an hour or more to analyze a set of sights to come up with the best fix, and if a mistake is made along the way, this can stretch out more. But the beauty of cel nav is, if you do make a mistake, you will eventually discover it, so you can go back over your work to find it.

Remember if you rule out blunders, which will show up because you have multiple sights, then an individual sight done properly should typically not be wrong by more than a couple miles, maybe a bit more in bad conditions. So when you see sights disagreeing by more than 5 or 10 miles, then something is clearly wrong, either with the analysis or with the sight. Most errors in analysis cause even larger discrepancies.

With that in mind, you have a philosophical choice. When you decide where you are, you can evaluate it as likely right and just carry on till the next day's sights, or doubt it, and go back over the work. Or you can peek ahead to the solutions, and correct yourself as you proceed.

Choose whichever approach seems the best way to learn or enjoy the venture. Not looking at the answers at all obviously provides the biggest challenge, and most closely matches the real world experience of navigating across the ocean with nothing but celestial navigation and dead reckoning.

Bon Voyage!

The Ocean Route

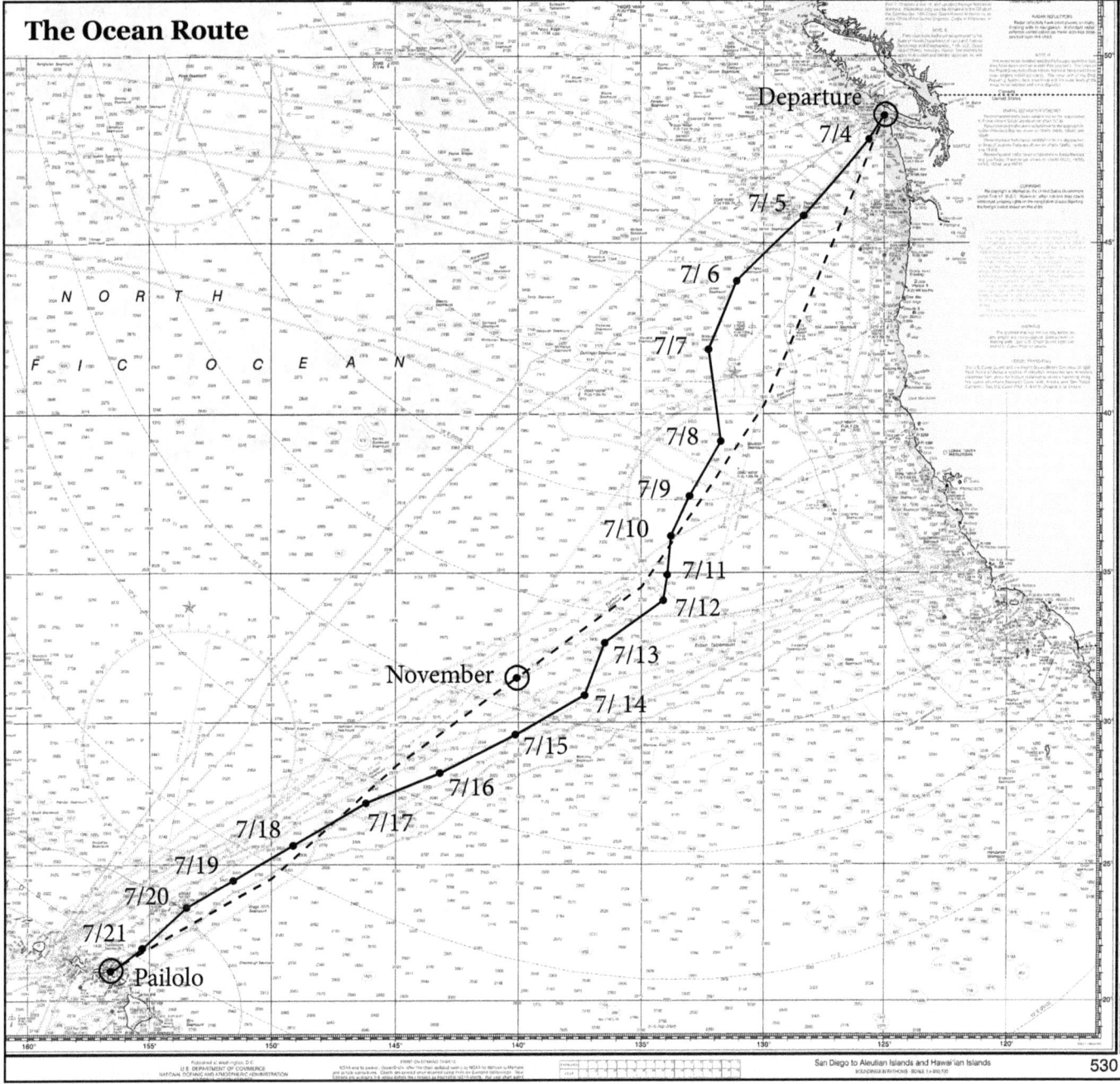

Map of the Ocean Route. *The dashed line is the average route of boats that have won the Vic-Maui Yacht Race, presumably implying the best sailing route to Hawaii from the Pacific NW. Starting from our departure, SW of Tatoosh Is, a key waypoint along the way is called November, in honor of the lightship that was stationed near there. Pailolo is our destination, the entrance to the channel, about 10 miles out from the finish line. The route that we took, and you will navigate, is marked with the 1200 PDT position for each day. These positions were found by DR from the nearest fix. Usually the last gibe into the Pailolo Channel and the run to the finish line is a challenging part of the route, but more a tactical and sailing issue than ocean navigation. It is, however, extremely important to not go lax on the navigation on that last leg. There are numerous hazards along the way, close on the Maui side.*

The preparatory exercise for the ocean navigation is to confirm the values listed in the table below, using both great circle (GC) and rhumb line (RL) computations. An online computer solution is at starpath.com/calc.

Waypoint	Location			GC Range and Bearing	RL Range and Bearing
Departure	48° 23' N, 124° 45' W				
November	31° 30' N, 140° 00' W	↓	↓	1227.2 @ 219.9T	1230.3 @ 214.6T
Pailolo	21° 07' N, 156° 38' W		↓	2238.4 @ 234.4T	2253.0 @ 223.4

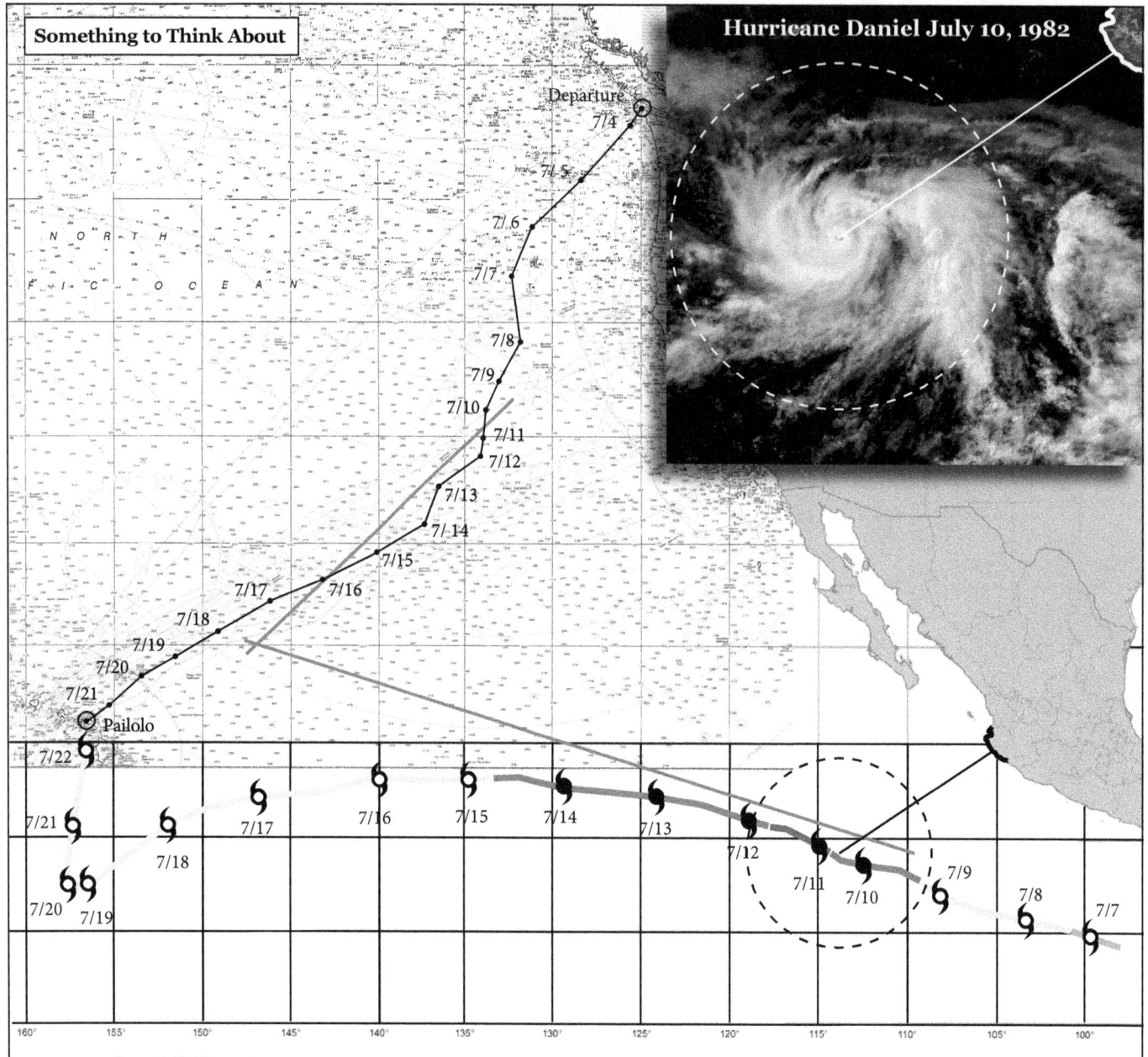

Hurricane Daniel July 10, 1982

What was going on south of us. *There is always something to think about on an ocean passage, but we had a bonus on this one. From July 12th onward, we had the threat of Hurricane Daniel. We were on a collision course most of the voyage, which was rather worse than it looks here, because the normal path of such storms is to curve north. Thus we had both good luck and bad luck. The bad luck was most Eastern Pacific Hurricanes do not go all the way to Hawaii (only roughly 1 every 5 years), so it was rare to occur at all; the good luck was this one did not curve away from the equator and go north and meet us. Normally they would either dissipate or turn north before reaching the longitude of November. Solid symbols are hurricane force winds. Daniel peaked at about 100 kts on the 11th (purple segment). Red section (7/9 to 7/15) is hurricane; yellow is tropical storm; green is tropical depression (7/7). Open symbols are tropical storms.*

We did, nevertheless, both get to Maui at about the same time! When Daniel turned north and ran up the Alenuihaha Channel and dissipate on the east side of Maui the winds were down to 30 kts or so. We did sail in violent rain and 40-kt squalls on the approach, which was likely influenced by the storm to the south.

We just lost a day or so of sunny skies once in Hawaii, but it could have been very serious underway. Sometimes tropical storms that curve north approaching Hawaii get caught in a deep dip of the winds aloft that captures them, and not only pulls them right up our track line here, but intensifies them as well. The three worst storms to ever hit the Pacific Northwest began in that manner. It is valuable for all mariners in the tropics to review what the NWS calls the 34-kt Rule and the Mariner's 1-2-3 Rule. We have a link at starpath.com/HBS.

Logbook

Inland Part of the Route

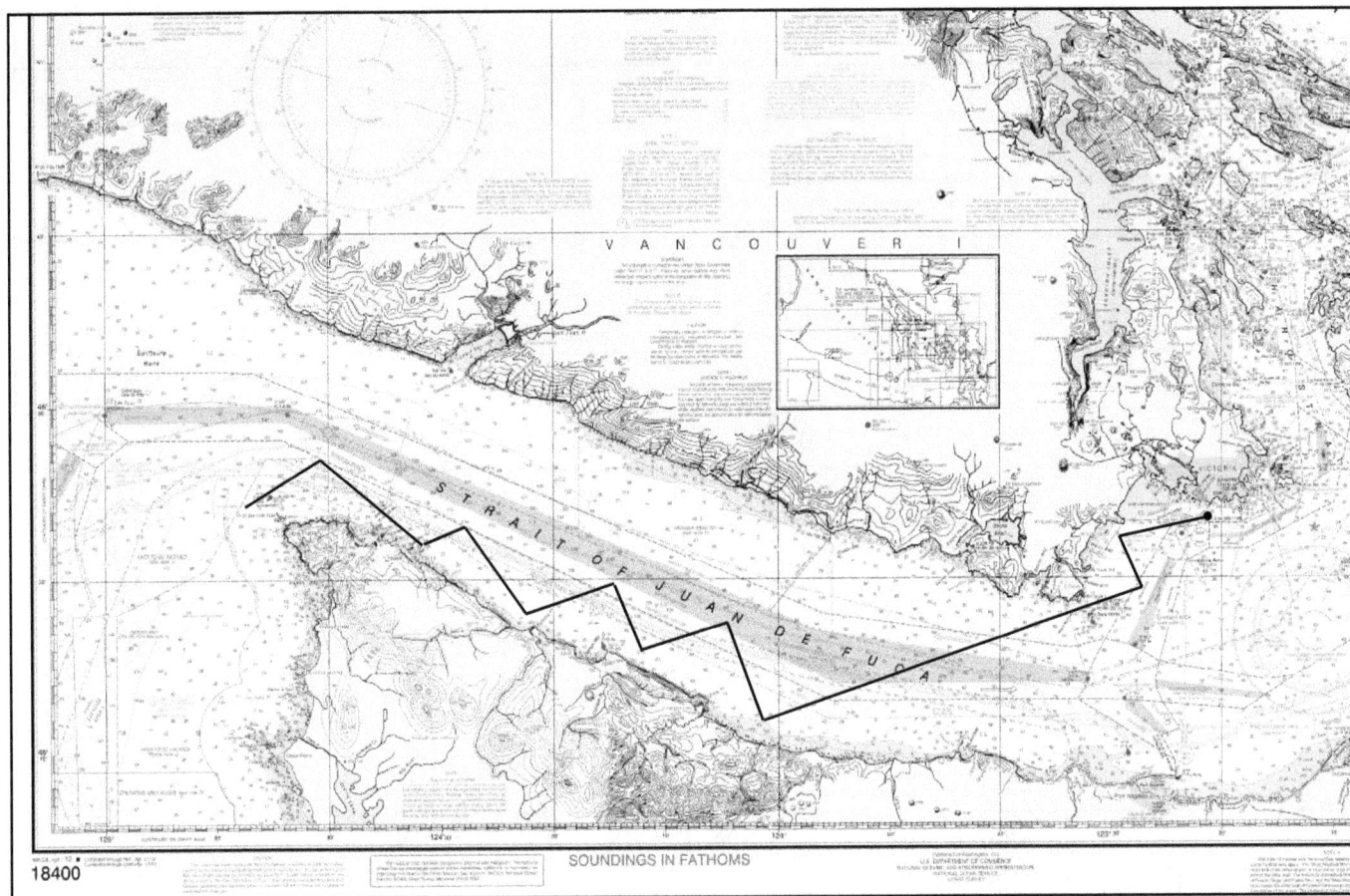

The First Leg of the Victoria to Maui Race. *We do not have records of the precise route taken from Brotchie Ledge, just outside Victoria, BC, the start of the race, out to the ocean, but the above is a typical sailing route, going through Race Passage and straight across the Strait, tacking against building westerlies. In this voyage the leg shown above took about 17 hours. From a geometric point of view, the distance to Maui is essentially the same if you entered the ocean from the Canadian side of the Strait, but this is nevertheless the most common route because a key tactical goal is to get south as soon as possible.*

Note on the Problem Times in the Logbook

The fix times asked for in the problems and listed in the Logbook are chosen as the last sight of each sight session. This is done simply for consistency. When reducing a set of sights underway, you can advance them to any time you choose within the set of times—or even outside of that period. For best results, however, each sight of a session should be advanced or retarded to the common time you choose, using course and speed during the sights. If you choose a time other than that of the last sight, then you will need to DR from that time to the time of the last sight to compare with the answers given.

On the other hand, you can navigate the trip however you see fit, and just use the solutions given for these times as a guideline. In the end, we should all end up with more or less the same track across the ocean, regardless of the details of how the sights were analyzed.

Daily Ocean Entries*

#	July	WT	Log	C	S	Comments
1	4	0400	75	274	7.0	Departure: 48° 23' N, 124° 45' W
2	4	0500	82	220	7.7	
3	4	1247	142	267	5.3	
4	4	1609	160	222	7.0	
5	5	0000	215	222	7.0	
6	5	0504	250	197	6.0	
7	5	0844	272	197	7.0	After P1 FIX
8	5	1335	306	267	7.0	
9	5	2200	365	226	7.0	
10	6	0000	379	226	7.0	
11	6	0534	418	209	5.4	
12	6	1046	446	200	7.3	
13	6	1527	480	188	7.3	After P2 FIX
14	7	0000	539	188	7.3	
15	7	0832	599	180	6.5	
16	7	1400	634	176	6.4	After P3 FIX
17	8	0000	698	176	6.4	
18	8	1009	769	169	6.7	
19	8	1307	789	156	6.5	After P4 FIX
20	8	2021	836	256	6.0	
21	9	0000	858	256	6.0	

Notes (Please refer to the plots for further clarification of the logbook interpretation)

(1) First column just numbers the entries this sheet; no nav significance.

(2) Column 2 is the date; column 3 is the time, WT = PDT (ZD = +7).

(3) All courses True; speeds in knots.

(4) Px labels Problem x, which marks the times of the position fixes.

(5) We only have log data to the nearest mile for this passage, but good practice would call for keeping log records accurate to the tenth of a mile.

(6) A new DR track begins with each new position fix.

See also important information on the logbook entries given in the Introduction.

#	July	WT	Log	C	S	Comments
22	9	0811	907	222	6.7	
23	9	1325	942	197	6.0	After P5 FIX
24						P6 LAN
25	9	2159	992	197	5.7	After P7 FIX
26	10	0000	1003	197	5.7	
27	10	0500	1032	276	5.7	
28	10	1334	1082	210	4.8	After P8 FIX
29	11	0000	1132	210	4.8	
30	11	0605	1161	197	4.0	After P9 FIX
31	11	1110	1181	230	3.3	After P10 FIX
32	12	0000	1222	230	3.3	
33	12	1445	1271	230	7.0	
34	12	1645	1285	235	5.7	After P11 FIX
35	13	0000	1326	235	5.7	
36	13	0642	1364	205	5.5	After P12 FIX
37	13	1019	1384	165	6.0	
38	13	1500	1412	170	6.3	
39	13	1741	1429	205	6.1	After P13 FIX
40	14	0000	1467	205	6.1	
41	14	1418	1554	260	7.5	After P14 FIX
42	15	0000	1627	260	7.5	
43	15	0728	1682	260	7.5	
44	15	0832	1690	240	7.5	
45	15	0917	1696	240	8.1	After P15 FIX
46	15	1052	1709	233	7.4	
47	15	1338	1730	245	7.7	After P16 FIX
48	16	0000	1809	245	7.7	
49	16	0714	1865	247	7.7	After P17 FIX
50	16	2213	1981	243	7.8	After P18 FIX

#	July	WT	Log	C	S	Comments
51	17	0000	1995	243	7.5	
52	17	1128	2081	243	6.8	
53	17	1450	2104	240	7.4	
54	17	1611	2114	240	8.6	
55	17	2000	2147	240	8.5	P19 DR
56	18	0000	2181	240	7.4	
57	18	0740	2238	242	7.3	
58	18	1121	2265	242	6.9	After P20 FIX
59	18	2240	2343	232	6.3	After P21 FIX
60	19	0000	2351	232	6.3	
61	19	0753	2401	238	5.8	After P22 FIX
62	19	2241	2487	230	5.3	After P23 FIX
63	20	0000	2494	230	5.3	
64	20	1227	2560	228	4.3	After P24 FIX
65	20	1520	2572	217	5.7	After P25 FIX
66	20	2240	2614	232	7.6	After P26 FIX
67	21	0000	2624	232	7.6	
68	21	0831	2689	232	7.6	After P27 FIX

Navigation Sights

Daily Sight Data

July 4

This is the start of the ocean navigation. We had, however, already sailed some 75 miles out the Strait of Juan de Fuca from back in Victoria, BC, which we left at 1100 the previous day. It has taken 17hr to get here in everything from light easterlies to strong westerlies, to flat calm. Here we are leaving land, and heading slowly out into the ocean, but weather and other factors will soon force us onto a more southerly course. Refer to the logbook for course and speed at the various sight times. This last visual piloting fix was about 0.7 mi SW of Tatoosh Island Light, at Cape Flattery, WA. Thus we take and record our *departure*, the official name for the last land-based fix of an ocean voyage.

Date: July 4, 1982

Fix Time: 0400 WT, Fix Log: 0075

Fix Position 48° 23.0'N, 124° 45.0' W

July 5

We start with an unusual running fix between Venus and the Sun, dawn to mid-morning, which were the only sights available in cloudy skies. Venus just peeked out of the clouds long enough for a few quick sights. It was not certain at the time whether or not we would see the sun that day at all, but we did. There was a cold front moving east over us that morning at about 20 kts. Seas about 7 ft, according to notes on Sights #2.

Sights #1	Date: July 5, 1982	Body: Venus
WT	UTC	Hs
05:03:58	12:03:58	12° 06.5'
05:06:24	12:06:24	12° 29.0'
05:09:27	12:09:27	13° 00.0'

Sights #2	Date: July 5, 1982	Body: Sun LL
WT	UTC	Hs
08:41:22	15:41:22	26° 54.5'
08:43:55	15:43:55	27° 24.0'
08:45:38	15:43:58	27° 41.0'
08:47:30	15:47:30	28° 03.0'

Problem 1

1A. Find a running fix at 0844 on July 5, enter it in the logbook, then from there DR to the time of the next sights (Sights #3) using logbook data.

1B. Find the WT of Nautical Twilight, Civil Twilight, and Sunrise for July 5, 1982 at 46N, 127 W. What was the stage of the twilight for the Venus sights done above, and how long after sunrise were the sun sights taken?

> **Reminder. For all sights in the book:**
> Height of Eye = 9 ft
> Index Correction = 0
> Watch Error = 0
> Zone Description = +7, ie UTC = WT +7h

July 6

In cloudy skies, there were no further sights on July 5 during the day nor evening and night, only DR. The next sights were sunlines in midmorning on July 6, which were then combined with afternoon sunlines for a running fix. Check the logbook for the C and S needed to complete the running fix. Logbook notes for second set read "rough swells."

Sights #3	Date: July 6, 1982	Body: Sun LL
WT	UTC	Hs
10:44:16	17:44:16	46° 25.0'
10:45:56	17:45:56	46° 42.3'

Sights #4	Date: July 6, 1982	Body: Sun LL
WT	UTC	Hs
15:20:50	22:20:50	61° 14.4'
15:22:56	22:22:56	60° 35.0'
15:26:57	22:26:57	60° 31.0'
15:28:42	22:28:42	60° 13.4'

Problem 2

2A. Which of these sights is clearly bad and can be discarded? (See Analysis section.) **2B** Find a running fix at 1527 on July 6, enter it in the log book, then from there DR to the time of the next sights using logbook data.

July 7

Again, our only navigation for this day is a running fix from the sun. Cloudy in rough seas. Get DR data from the logbook.

Sights #5	Date: July 7, 1982	Body: Sun LL
WT	UTC	Hs
08:27:41	15:27:41	21° 10.6'
08:29:34	15:29:34	21° 33.8'
08:30:47	15:30:47	21° 44.0'
08:32:28	15:32:28	22° 00.6'
08:33:40	15:33:40	22° 12.6'
08:35:00	15:35:00	22° 28.4'

Sights #6	Date: July 7, 1982	Body: Sun LL
WT	UTC	Hs
14:00:05	21:00:05	70° 38.5'
14:01:06	21:01:06	70° 38.2'
14:03:40	21:03:40	70° 32.6'

Problem 3

3A. Find a fix at 1400 on July 7, enter it in the log book, then from there DR to the time of the next sights using logbook data.

Next we prepare for evening twilight sights. After you get your afternoon running fix, figure the time of evening twilight when you would do your star sights (Problem **3B**) and then compute the DR position at that time (Problem **3C**), and then figure what the 3 best bodies would be for a fix. List the bodies, heights and bearings (Problem **3D**). As it turns out, we did not get to do star sights that night, but this is the type of preparation needed. We repeat this exercise later when we do indeed get to take sights.

July 8

This was a period of bad weather. We were sailing to weather in 20 or so kts of wind, hence again there is no celestial except a running fix from the sun. Be sure to keep track of the range and bearing from DR to Fix to monitor the quality of the DR. With few sights, accurate DR is crucial.

Sights #7	Date: July 8, 1982	Body: Sun LL
WT	UTC	Hs
10:09:35	17:09:35	40° 35.5'
10:11:06	17:11:06	40° 53.4'
10:12:04	17:12:04	41° 05.0'

Sights #8	Date: July 8, 1982	Body: Sun LL
WT	UTC	Hs
13:03:32	20:03:32	70° 35.0'
13:04:33	20:04:33	70° 42.4'
13:07:23	20:07:23	70° 54.0'

Problem 4

Find a fix at 1307 on July 8, enter it in the log book, then from there DR to the time of the next sights using logbook data.

July 9

On this day we get a lot more navigation done. A running fix from AM to Noon, and then another quick set of sunlines for an afternoon running fix; and then in the evening twilight we get our first star-planet fix.

Sights #9	Date: July 9, 1982	Body: Sun LL
WT	UTC	Hs
10:32:45	17:32:45	44° 22.6'
10:35:06	17:35:06	44° 45.9'
10:36:28	17:36:28	45° 01.5'
10:37:33	17:37:33	45° 15.5'
10:40:26	17:40:26	45° 50.2'

Sights #10	Date: July 9, 1982	Body: Sun LL
WT	UTC	Hs
13:21:55	20:21:55	72° 53.7'
13:23:02	20:23:02	72° 58.1'
13:24:55	20:24:55	73° 08.4'
13:26:22	20:26:22	73° 17.2'

Problem 5

5A. In sights #9, one of the sunlines is definitely bad. Which one was it?

5B. Remove the bad sight and then find a running fix at 1325 on July 9, enter it in the logbook, then from there DR to the time of the next sights using logbook data.

We do an LAN series about 30 minutes later, so we can double check the DR position. Normally we would not take another set of sunlines so close to the first set, but this is good practice since we have almost missed the peak. A plot of the data will help find the peak.

Sights #11	Date: July 9, 1982	Body: Sun LL
WT	UTC	Hs
13:53:13	20:53:13	74° 23.1'
13:54:41	20:54:41	74° 21.8'
13:55:56	20:55:56	74° 23.3'
13:57:44	20:57:44	74° 23.3'
13:58:51	20:58:51	74° 19.8'
14:01:01	21:01:01	74° 17.8'

Problem 6

6A. Solve for Lat by LAN using Sights #11.

6B. Is there any hope of getting an rfix from the data in Sights #11?

Now we get to our first evening star sights. Be sure to check the log for the proper courses taken during this day of navigation. Normally we would take sights of 3 bodies, but these two bright bodies were the only ones available at the time.

Sights #12a	Date: July 9, 1982	Body: Jupiter
WT	UTC(July 10)	Hs
21:44:32	04:44:32	39° 37.9'
21:49:54	04:49:54	39° 11.3'
21:55:34	04:55:34	38° 44.5'

Sights #12b	Date: July 9, 1982	Body: Vega (49)
WT	UTC(July 10)	Hs
21:47:41	04:47:41	49° 40.0'
21:53:07	04:53:07	50° 42.2'
21:59:07	04:59:07	51° 46.6'

Problem 7

Find a fix at 2159 on July 9 and compare to the DR position at that time. Note we had good navigation throughout the day, so we should not be off much this evening.

July 10

Back to running fix from the sun, AM to PM. This is in principle the most efficient type of rfix, in that you get the most separation in bearing in the shortest time.

Sights #13	Date: July 10, 1982	Body: Sun LL
WT	UTC	Hs
10:55:29	17:55:29	48° 04.3'
10:56:57	17:56:57	48° 20.2'
10:58:45	17:58:45	48° 46.2'

Continued next page.

| 11:02:02 | 18:02:02 | 49° 24.5' |
| 11:04:43 | 18:04:43 | 49° 57.4' |

Sights #14	Date: July 10, 1982	Body: Sun LL
WT	UTC	Hs
13:31:36	20:31:36	74° 27.9'
13:33:03	20:33:03	74° 33.8'
13:34:46	20:34:46	74° 42.0'

Problem 8

Find a fix at 1334 July 10 and compare to the DR position at that time.

July 11

Our first morning twilight star sights. Note that the sights were rotated to insure a fix. Starting with Vega and then coming back and ending with Vega.

Sights #15a	Date: July 11, 1982	Body: Vega (49)
WT	UTC	Hs
05:37:48	12:37:48	38° 40.5'
05:42:36	12:42:36	37° 47.3'
05:48:16	12:48:16	36° 42.4'
06:07:16	13:07:16	33° 12.8'
06:09:51	13:09:51	32° 45.1'

Sights #15b	Date: July 11, 1982	Body: Polaris (58)
WT	UTC	Hs
05:40:21	12:40:21	35° 53.3'
05:45:03	12:45:03	35° 57.5'

Sights #15c	Date: July 11, 1982	Body: Venus
WT	UTC	Hs
06:03:41	13:03:41	14° 50.3'
06:05:19	13:05:19	15° 10.5'
06:08:31	13:08:31	15° 47.8'

Problem 9

Find a fix at 0605 July 11 and compare to the DR position at that time.

Later in the morning, we get another fix from the sun and moon. Our Logbook noted that we could not see this daytime moon below 7°, even in a crystal clear sky. Thus we will ask you to look up the age/phase of the moon to think on that.

Sights #16a	Date: July 11, 1982	Body: Moon UL
WT	UTC	Hs
11:03:44	18:03:44	07° 46.7'
11:05:16	18:05:16	07° 32.0'
11:08:06	18:08:06	07° 01.0'

Continued next page.

Sights #16b	Date: July 11, 1982	Body: Sun LL
WT	*UTC*	*Hs*
11:10:23	18:10:23	50° 28.0'
11:11:21	18:11:21	50° 40.6'

Problem 10

10A. What was the phase, waxing or waning, and age of the moon in these sights?

10B. Find a fix at 1110 July 11 and compare to the DR position at that time.

July 12

Some practice sights to combine with a single sight for a (weak) running fix. Sights #17 by crew member with a plastic sextant. One quick sight by David (#18) when sun peaked out briefly, so we get a running fix.

Sights #17	Date: July 12, 1982	Body: Sun LL
WT (corrected)	*UTC*	*Hs*
14:42:15	21:42:15	75° 10.0'
14:43:30	21:43:30	75° 00.4'
14:44:28	21:44:28	74° 54.7'
14:45:57	21:45:57	74° 44.4'

Sights #18	Date: July 12, 1982	Body: Sun LL
WT	*UTC*	*Hs*
16:45:20	23:45:20	52° 55.4'

Problem 11

Find a fix at 1645 July 12 and compare to the DR position at that time. Remember that any one good sight is better than none, but multiple sights is always preferred if possible.

July 13

Early dawn sights of Venus, Moon, and unidentified 2nd magnitude body, bearing about 350T. Earliest sights had a weak sight horizon. Logbook noted the impression that the quality of the sights increased as the sky became lighter and the horizon became more clear.

Sights #19a	Date: July 13, 1982	Body: unknown
WT	*UTC*	*Hs*
06:00:18	13:00:18	23° 00.7'
06:02:55	13:02:55	22° 50.2'

Sights #19b	Date: July 13, 1982	Body: Venus
WT	*UTC*	*Hs*
06:17:00	13:17:00	14° 37.5'
06:19:57	13:19:57	15° 14.4'
06:23:45	13:23:45	15° 59.6'

Continued next page.

Sights #19c	Date: July 13, 1982	Body: Moon LL
WT	UTC	Hs
06:29:35	13:29:35	52° 38.9'
06:31:27	13:31:27	52° 51.4'
06:41:32	13:41:32	53° 47.9'
06:42:22	13:42:22	53° 52.8'
06:43:50	13:43:50	53° 59.6'
06:45:33	13:45:33	54° 08.9'

Problem 12

12A. Identify the unknown body in Sights 19a. **12B** Compare the sight time of this body with the time of nautical twilight. **12C**. Are these sights consistent with the Moon and Venus sights?

12D. Find an rfix at 0642 July 13, and compare to the DR position at that time.

We then carried on and got an afternoon running fix from the Sun. Both set of sights by a crew member.

Sights #20	Date: July 13, 1982	Body: Sun LL
WT	UTC	Hs
15:00:41	22:00:41	74° 13.1'
15:03:34	22:03:34	73° 48.4'
15:05:31	22:05:31	73° 30.8'
15:06:44	22:06:44	73° 15.8'
15:08:26	22:08:26	72° 58.0'

Sights #21	Date: July 13, 1982	Body: Sun LL
WT	UTC (July 14)	Hs
17:40:11	00:40:11	42° 17.4'
17:40:52	00:40:52	42° 16.5'
17:41:37	00:41:37	42° 06.1'
17:42:12	00:42:12	42° 02.3'
17:43:02	00:43:02	41° 53.8'

Problem 13

Find a rfix at 1741 July 13 and compare to the DR position at that time.

July 14

Bastille Day! We are again faced with the realities of navigation by cel nav alone. When it is socked in, or nearly so, you end up on the deck with sextant and watch at hand, just waiting for a shot of the sun. Sometimes with the filters in you can get a sight of the sun disk, even when to the naked eye it looks just like a bright patch.

On this day there was almost a chance for a set of LAN sights, but it ended up with only two quick sights possible, a few minutes apart, which by chance happened to be just either side of LAN. So we will get a good latitude and maybe a fix.

This will take special care in the sight reduction, because we will have to interpolate Pub 229 for accurate azimuths. You will see the problem when you start to work it. It is also a very good example to show the value of doing sight reduction by calculation or computer, as that removes the interpolations that must be done with tables alone.

Below are the only two sights for this cloudy day. In the Solutions section where the workforms are presented, we have added a note on the interpolation of Z needed for Zn.

Sights #22	Date: July 14, 1982	Body: Sun LL
WT	UTC	Hs
14:15:06	21:15:06	80° 57.7'
14:18:32	21:18:32	80° 55.4'

Problem 14

14A. Determine the two azimuths as carefully as possible, which will require triple interpolations if using tables for sight reduction. This problem has an expanded solutions sheet to show the process.

14B. Then make an expanded plotting sheet (30' per parallel, rather than the standard 60'), plot the two lines, and advance the 1415 line to the 1418 line to see if we might get an estimate of our Lon. The Lat should be good. Normally we would not hope for such an rfix on sights this close in time, but since the sights are high and spanning LAN, we have some modest hope. Again, when this is all we have, we need to get as much information from the data as we can.

July 15

The next day we got luckier, with a daylight moon sight. Dawn to mid-morning running fix of the Moon and Sun, with a course change in between.

Sights #23	Date: July 15, 1982	Body: Moon LL
WT	UTC	Hs
07:28:04	14:28:04	55° 33.7'
07:29:29	14:29:29	55° 51.8'
07:30:51	14:30:51	56° 05.6'

Sights #24	Date: July 15, 1982	Body: Sun LL
WT	UTC	Hs
09:15:55	16:15:55	20° 51.8'
09:17:01	16:17:01	21° 05.1'
09:17:48	16:17:48	21° 15.0'
09:19:15	16:19:15	21° 34.6'

Problem 15

15. Find a sun-moon rfix at 0917 July 15. With a course change between the sights we need to advance over the course and distance made good between the two sights. Compare the result to the DR position at that time.

We then carry on with another running fix in the afternoon from two sets of sunlines. Second set of sights by a crew member.

Sights #25	Date: July 15, 1982	Body: Sun LL
WT	UTC	Hs
10:52:26	17:52:26	41° 20.4'
10:53:58	17:53:58	41° 40.0'
10:55:30	17:55:30	41° 59.7'
10:56:21	17:56:21	42° 10.7'

Continued next page.

Sights #26	Date: July 15, 1982	Body: Sun LL
WT	UTC	Hs
13:37:07	20:37:07	75° 52.8'
13:38:05	20:38:05	76° 05.4'
13:40:47	20:40:47	76° 34.0'
13:41:45	20:41:45	76° 41.6'
13:43:27	20:43:27	76° 59.2'

Problem 16

Find a rfix at 1338 July 15 and compare to the DR position at that time.

July 16

Morning twilight fix of Deneb, Venus, and the Moon. Logbook says "sky very obscured; sea rough." Then a side note saying (of the Venus sight) "time may be wrong." So this is not very strong navigation, but we work with what we have.

Sights #27a	Date: July 16, 1982	Body: Deneb (53)
WT	UTC	Hs
06:55:50	13:55:50	47° 23.0'

Sights #27b	Date: July 16, 1982	Body: Venus
WT	UTC	Hs
06:58:30	13:58:30	15°56.0'

Sights #27c	Date: July 16, 1982	Body: Moon LL
WT	UTC	Hs
07:14:25	14:14:25	42° 06.8'
07:15:37	14:15:37	42° 23.6'
07:17:22	14:17:22	42° 45.0'

Problem 17

Find a fix at 0714 July 16 and compare to the DR position at that time.

No daytime sun navigation, but we do get an evening twilight fix from Jupiter and Vega.

Sights #28a	Date: July 16, 1982	Body: Jupiter
WT	UTC (July 17)	Hs
21:53:55	04:53:55	48° 56.0'
21:54:45	04:54:45	48° 50.5'
21:56:47	04:56:47	48° 40.0'
21:58:17	04:58:17	48° 32.7'
21:59:17	04:59:17	48° 27.0'

Continued next page.

Sights #28b	Date: July 16, 1982	Body: Vega (49)
WT	UTC	Hs
22:08:40	05:08:40	46° 08.7'
22:11:18	05:11:18	46° 38.2'
22:13:00	05:13:00	46° 57.6'
22:16:14	05:16:14	47° 33.9'

Problem 18

Find a fix at 2213 on July 16 and compare to DR.

Our logbook at this point had this note in it: "The reason for precomputing twilight sights is not so you can start earlier for a longer sight time, but so you can start earlier with a better horizon. In some conditions of visibility, you can separate the swells from the true sea horizon better, the earlier you start." This is not often a problem for daylight sights.

July 17

No celestial navigation done this day.

Problem 19

Refer to the Logbook. What is your DR position at 2000? As a plotting exercise, see how accurate you can get. Assume you are starting at 27° 58.0'N, 144° 32.0' W at time 2213 on 7/16 (log 1981). Then we ask for the DR position at 2000 on 7/17 following logbook entries. Detailed answer is on page 34.

July 18

Dawn to late morning running fix of Venus and Sun. This is similar to what we had at the start of the trip. Venus is a blessing because it is so bright, and we are lucky that it is still about 10° different in bearing from the sun. Recall it was more like 14° two weeks earlier.

Sights #29	Date: July 18, 1982	Body: Venus
WT	UTC	Hs
07:40:22	14:40:22	18° 26.2'
07:41:48	14:41:48	18° 43.0'
07:43:18	14:43:18	19° 03.8'
07:44:52	14:44:52	19° 24.3'
07:46:11	14:46:11	19° 42.5'

Sights #30	Date: July 18, 1982	Body: Sun LL
WT	UTC	Hs
11:20:20	18:20:20	38° 54.3'
11:21:11	18:21:11	39° 06.0'
11:22:23	18:22:23	39° 23.6'

Problem 20

Refer to the Logbook for Course and Speed to find the DR position, and then find a Fix at 1121 on July 18 and compare with DR.

Then that evening, a twilight fix of Vega and Alkaid.

Sights #31a	Date: July 18, 1982	Body: Vega (49)
WT	*UTC (July 19)*	*Hs*
22:23:10	05:23:10	44° 35.0'
22:25:33	05:25:33	45° 02.6'
22:37:30	05:37:30	47° 22.5'

Sights #31b	Date: July 18, 1982	Body: Alkaid (34)
WT	*UTC*	*Hs*
22:30:42	05:30:42	60° 21.5'
22:34:19	05:34:19	59° 58.3'
22:35:47	05:35:47	59° 47.8'
22:40:14	05:40:14	59° 14.0'

Problem 21

Refer to the Logbook for Course and Speed to compute DR, and then find a fix at 2240 on July 18 and compare with DR.

July 19

Morning star sights. This is a day of many sights; as we want to do the best we can, whenever we can. This is a 3-body fix, with extra sights of Polaris added in.

Sights #32a	Date: July 19, 1982	Body: Polaris (58)
WT	*UTC*	*Hs*
07:26:19	14:26:19	25° 29.5'
07:28:04	14:28:04	25° 28.8'
07:33:33	14:33:33	25° 33.0'

Sights #32b	Date: July 19, 1982	Body: Vega (59)
WT	*UTC*	*Hs*
07:36:33	14:36:33	18° 13.8'
07:37:50	14:37:50	18° 03.2'
07:39:17	14:39:17	17° 44.8'
07:41:16	14:41:16	17° 24.8'
07:44:09	14:44:09	16° 49.0'

Sights #32c	Date: July 19, 1982	Body: Capella (12)
WT	*UTC*	*Hs*
07:46:58	14:46:58	30° 20.8'

Sights #32d	Date: July 19, 1982	Body: Venus
WT	*UTC*	*Hs*
07:44:56	14:44:56	16° 39.8'
07:50:34	14:50:34	17° 52.4'
07:52:06	14:52:06	18° 11.8'
07:53:18	14:53:18	18° 28.4'
07:54:43	14:54:43	18° 43.4'
07:56:00	14:56:00	19° 02.2'

Problem 22

Find a fix at 0753 on July 19 and compare to the DR at that time.

No sun sights during the day, but more stars at evening twilight. One of Jupiter, and one of an unidentified magnitude 1 star, bearing about 090 T.

Sights #33a	Date: July 19, 1982	Body: Jupiter
WT	UTC (July 20)	Hs
22:18:54	05:18:54	51° 57.0'
22:19:37	05:19:37	51° 51.9'
22:20:58	05:20:58	51° 43.8'
22:21:37	05:21:37	51° 40.6'

Sights #33b	Date: July 19, 1982	Body: unknown
WT	UTC	Hs
22:36:35	05:36:35	23° 34.3'
22:37:55	05:37:55	23° 52.0'
22:39:34	05:39:34	24° 14.7'
22:41:10	05:41:10	24° 36.2'

Problem 23

23A. Identify the star sighted.

23B. Then find a fix at 2241 on July 19 and compare to the DR at that time.

July 20

Running fixes throughout the day. First from two morning sun sight sessions.

Sights #34	Date: July 20, 1982	Body: Sun LL
WT	UTC	Hs
09:42:06	16:42:06	12° 57.5'
09:42:47	16:42:47	13° 06.9'
09:43:23	16:43:23	13° 14.7'
09:44:07	16:44:07	13° 23.9'
09:45:00	16:45:00	13° 35.4'
09:45:39	16:45:39	13° 44.0'

Sights #35	Date: July 20, 1982	Body: Sun LL
WT	UTC	Hs
12:25:34	19:25:34	49° 30.2'
12:26:20	19:26:20	49° 41.7'
12:27:45	19:27:45	49° 59.6'
12:29:04	19:29:04	50° 18.4'
12:30:41	19:30:41	50° 40.0'

Problem 24

Find a fix at 1227 on July 20 and compare to the DR at that time. Then we will carry on with more sun navigation on this day.

About 3h after the last running fix we get a chance for a LAN sight for Lat. Notice that with our watch time set at ZD = +7, LAN occurs about 1520. We have sailed pretty far west with our watch still set on PDT. This is never a problem in navigation; it is much better to have noon be at some time later toward the end of the trip than to risk possible errors and other complexities that comes about when changing it.

Sights #36	Date: July 20, 1982	Body: Sun LL (LAN)
WT	*UTC*	*Hs*
15:11:40	22:11:40	86° 25.6'
15:12:50	22:12:50	86° 34.9'
15:14:35	22:14:35	86° 44.9'
15:15:45	22:15:45	86° 53.2'
15:16:58	22:16:58	86° 58.1'
15:18:30	22:18:30	87° 02.6'
15:20:20	22:20:20	87° 05.2'
15:21:00	22:21:00	87° 05.2'
15:21:50	22:21:50	87° 03.2'
15:22:45	22:22:45	87° 02.2'
15:23:40	22:23:40	86° 59.2'
15:25:05	22:25:05	86° 51.7'
15:26:33	22:26:33	86° 44.8'
15:27:35	22:27:35	86° 37.9'
15:28:40	22:28:40	86° 28.8'

Problem 25

25A. Find Lat by LAN.

25B. Find Lon by LAN. Plot Hs vs. WT to find the central point of the curve and from that determine the Lon at LAN. (This is an exercise alone. We do not recommend this procedure for routine navigation.) You may find some sights that are not consistent with the others.

Next we will prepare for evening star-planet sights on July 20. After you get your LAN fix:

25C. Figure the time of evening twilight when you would do your star sights. (Use halfway between Civil and Nautical.)

25D. Find your DR position at that time.

25E. Figure what the 3 best bodies would be for a fix at that time, from that position. List the 3 body names, heights and bearings.

Later that evening we do indeed get some sights, but these may or may not have been the same ones that we predicted as the best. It all depends on the conditions we find when we go on deck at that time.

At evening twilight we get another star-planet fix.

Sights #37a	Date: July 20, 1982	Body: Jupiter
WT	*UTC (July 21)*	*Hs*
22:03:59	05:03:59	54° 40.2'
22:05:54	05:05:54	54° 30.0'
22:06:48	05:06:48	54° 26.1'
22:08:19	05:08:19	54° 19.6'
22:10:26	05:10:26	54° 08.8'

Continued next page.

Sights #37b	Date: July 20, 1982	Body: Vega (49)
WT	*UTC*	*Hs*
22:19:25	05:19:25	41° 15.4'
22:22:42	05:22:42	41° 54.0'
22:23:55	05:23:55	42° 08.6'
22:25:56	05:25:56	42° 32.0'
22:27:12	05:27:12	42° 45.2'

Sights #37c	Date: July 20, 1982	Body: Altair (51)
WT	*UTC*	*Hs*
22:35:24	05:35:24	22° 44.8'
22:37:08	05:37:08	23° 09.0'
22:38:19	05:38:19	23° 23.2'
22:40:06	05:40:06	23° 49.0'

Problem 26

Find the fix at 2240 on July 20 and compare to DR.

July 21

We are getting close to sighting land. This could be our last chance for a good fix. We do a set of morning star sights. Usually in star sight sessions we add Polaris whenever we have time to do it because it takes no pre-computation. Just set your sextant to your latitude and look north. But in this case it was woven right into the set of all sights, which were alternated in time to get the best fix.

Sights #38a	Date: July 21, 1982	Body: Polaris (58)
WT	*UTC*	*Hs*
07:51:02	14:51:02	22° 58.2'
07:53:38	14:53:38	22° 57.2'
08:09:14	15:09:14	23° 00.7'
08:11:00	15:11:00	22° 58.2'

Sights #38b	Date: July 21, 1982	Body: Capella (12)
WT	*UTC*	*Hs*
07:55:12	14:55:12	28° 50.2'
07:56:34	14:56:34	29° 03.2'
08:01:40	15:01:40	29° 55.6'
08:15:25	15:15:25	31° 55.2'

Sights #38c	Date: July 21, 1982	Body: Vega (49)
WT	*UTC*	*Hs*
08:04:41	15:04:41	12° 54.2'
08:06:50	15:06:50	12° 26.5'
08:15:25	15:15:25	10° 56.1'

Continued next page.

Sights #38d	Date: July 21, 1982	Body: Venus
WT	*UTC*	*Hs*
07:58:24	14:58:24	14° 57.0'
08:29:44	15:29:44	21° 46.7'
08:30:48	15:30:48	22° 01.4'
08:31:37	15:31:37	22° 11.8'
08:33:38	15:33:38	22° 37.7'

Problem 27

27A. Which of these sights is bad... ie really bad; clearly a blunder?

27B. Plot all sights as Hs vs WT, then fit lines to each body (see Analysis, Auto Rfix). From this we can determine the Hs at 08:10, which was common to all sights. This then is equivalent to a simultaneous sight of all bodies.

27C. Find the fix at 0831 on July 21 and compare to DR. Estimate the accuracy of this final celestial fix.

27D. What is the range and bearing to waypoint Pailolo?

This was the end of the celestial navigation according to the logbook, although we had another 135 miles to go before tying up at the dock. The log reading at Lahaina Roads was 2824.3.

27E. Subract 75 miles from that log reading (to account for the inland run out to the ocean), then compare that to the great circle (GC) distance computed at the beginning of the voyage to see how much farther we sailed than the direct, shortest route.

The Boat

"PASSAGES" — Sail No. 59450 — Islander 40, LOA: 39.5'. Corinthian Seattle Yacht Club, Owner/Skipper: G. Bell, Crew: D. Burch, T. Clark, J. Taylor, W. Harvey-Smith, P. Fredrickson, J. Green, D. Bawden.

This is the image that appeared in the Vic-Maui Yacht Race brochure for 1982. It is still online. The boat owner and skipper was Dick Bell, now an active member of the Seattle Yacht Club. The Doug Petersen-designed yacht is still actively sailing in the Pacific Northwest under a new owner. Paul Fredrickson is a naval architect specializing in super yacht design. We have sadly lost contact with the other crew members.

Solutions

Instructions

The solutions are presented in several formats to facilitate checking answers worked by various means.

Recording and Checking Answers

You can use the main Logbook as a place to record answers, or there is an optional, printable answer form at starpath.com/HBS. There is a Logbook with detailed answers at the end of this section.

One option is to work the exercises without looking at the answers at all. Instead, you judge the quality of your own fix each time, and if that seems reasonable, just carry on with the DR to the next set of sights, and see then how well you are doing. This could be an instructive approach, and in this case you would just refer to the answers if there appears to be some mistake that you cannot find.

On the other hand, it could be even more valuable to know there must be some mistake in your analysis, and try again till it works out. Once you get underway on your own real voyage, there is obviously no answer sheet to refer to.

Computed Solutions

These results are typical of what you would get doing the sight reduction with a calculator or computer program. For this type of solution you do not need to choose an Assumed Position, but can do the sight reduction directly from a DR position of your choice.

For the solutions listed, the DR position often corresponds to the time of the sight used for a sample workform sight reduction. The choice of DR (unless way wrong) does not affect the final computed values if the course and speed are correct.

All intercepts shown have taken the course and speed into account at the times of the sights. The fix shown with this data is a running fix taking all sights into account, weighted according to the size of the a-value relative to the average of all a-values for a particular body (least squares).

An asterisk (*) marks the sample sight that was chosen for the workform solution. It was intended to represent the average, but it might not be the optimum choice in all cases. If you analyze them carefully, you may find a better choice to represent the set, and may well end up with a better fix when plotting than we show in the plots.

Plots of the computed solutions are in Appendix 4. In some cases, the best fix would call for removing some of these sights as discussed in the Analysis section. These plots are just to show the relative lay of the LOPs for each fix.

Sample Workform Solutions

The workform solutions use Publication 229 and the Starpath Workforms, given in Appendix 2. Only a sample is shown from the usual set of several. The course and speed shown in the form are usually the ones that would be used to advance the lines for a running fix. Often the course changed right after the last sight of a session.

Keep in mind, these are presented in a *solutions* section. You can decide which sights to do, in which manner, from the sight data itself, without looking at any of these sample solutions. These forms simply give you a way to practice sight reduction using real sight data if you care to. They are samples only, *not necessarily the best or most representative sight of the session in each case.* In principle you could get a better fix by choosing the best average sight by the Fit Slope Method we illustrate in the Analysis section. A form of that method was used in the actual voyage to choose the best sights for a fix.

The starting time and date at the top of each workform in Box 1 is the watch time of the sight. It gets converted to UTC before moving into Box 2 of the form. The Sights session number is given as well.

Plotted Workform Solutions

This section is the main results of the navigation. The lines of position from the cel nav sight reduction are plotted out on universal plotting sheets, along with the DR track before and after each sight session.

Your own plot may end up using different sights to represent each session, but they should look similar to these. That is, if you choose a different assumed position your lines will originate from different locations, and if you choose a different sight to represent the set, you may get a slightly different LOP, but it should be very similar, and the fix should be similar as well–though not exactly the same, and indeed your fix could be more accurate in some cases.

A key step to carry out after each fix has been found and plotted is to then measure the range and bearing from the DR position that corresponds to the time of the fix to the fix itself. This is the key information you get from each celestial fix. Record these in the logbook or a table of your own to compare with the ones we present. This tells you how good your DR is in the conditions at hand. If for any reason you lose the opportunity to take more cel nav sights, this tells you the accuracy of your DR as you proceed from there.

Computed Solutions

Unless otherwise noted, the DR positions are for the time of the sights marked by *, which are sights with work form solutions. See further notes in the Instructions.

Log 272	Problem 1	July 5

Sights #1

Venus—July 5, 1982
DR 46° 30'N, 127° 49'W

WT	a-value	Zn
05:03:58*	10.0 A	072.5°
05:06:24	10.3 A	073.4°
05:09:27	11.4 A	072.9°

Sights #2

Sun LL—July 5, 1982
DR 46° 09.0'N, 127° 58.0'W

WT	a-value	Zn
08:41:22	10.0 A	084.8°
08:43:55*	6.8 A	085.2°
08:45:38	7.6 A	085.5°
08:47:30	4.9 A	085.8°

▶ **Problem 1.** 0844 FIX using C197, S6.0
45° 51.5'N, 128° 06.4'W

Log 480	Problem 2	July 6

Sights #3

Sun LL—July 6, 1982
DR 44° 18'N, 131° 00'W

WT	a-value	Zn
10:44:16	1.8 A	104.4°
10:45:56*	1.8 A	104.8°

Sights #4

Sun LL—July 6, 1982
DR 43° 47'N, 131° 12'W

WT	a-value	Zn
15:20:50	15.7 A	229.1°
15:22:56	37.8 A	229.9° X
15:26:57*	8.2 A	231.4°
15:28:42	10.9 A	232.1°

▶ **Problem 2.** 1527 FIX using C200, S7.3
44° 05.0'N, 131° 11.9'W (omitting 1522 sight)

Log 634	Problem 3	July 7

Sights #5

Sun LL—July 7, 1982
DR 42° 12'N, 131° 55'W

WT	a-value	Zn
08:27:41	5.6 T	078.3°
08:29:34	8.4 T	078.6°
08:30:47	5.3 T	078.7°
08:32:28*	3.6 T	079.0°
08:33:40	2.6 A	079.2°
08:35:00	3.8 T	079.4°

Sights #6

Sun LL—July 7, 1982
DR 43° 36'N, 131° 55'W

WT	a-value	Zn
14:00:05*	2.1 A	185.3°
14:01:06	1.3 A	186.1°
14:03:40	3.4 A	187.9°

▶ **Problem 3.** 1400 FIX using C180, S6.5
41° 37.9'N, 131° 48.7'W

Log 789	Problem 4	July 8

Sights #7

Sun LL—July 8, 1982
DR 39° 24' N, 131° 40' W

WT	a-value	Zn
10:09:35*	29.3 T	092.8
10:11:06	29.6 T	093.0
10:12:04	30.1 T	093.2

Sights #8

Sun LL—July 8, 1982
DR 39° 05' N, 131° 36' W

WT	a-value	Zn
13:03:32	18.6 T	145.0
13:04:33	19.3 T	145.6
13:07:23*	12.7 T	147.4

▶ **Problem 4.** 1307 FIX using C169, S6.7
39° 04.6'N, 130° 56.7'W

Log 942	Problem 5	July 9

Sights #9

Sun LL—July 9, 1982

DR 37° 57' N, 132° 14' W

WT	a-value	Zn
10:32:45	12.0 T	095.1
10:35:06	7.7 T	095.5
10:36:28	7.2 T	095.7
10:37:33*	8.5 T	095.9
10:40:26	9.3 T	096.4

Sights #10

Sun LL—July 9, 1982

DR 37° 44' N, 132° 30' W

WT	a-value	Zn
13:21:55	5.5 T	152.8
13:23:02	3.9 T	153.6
13:24:55*	4.5 T	155.0
13:26:22	6.2 T	156.1

▶ **Problem 5**. 1325 FIX using C222, S6.7
37° 42.7' N, 132° 18.6'W

Log 945	Problem 6	July 9

Sights #11

Sun LL—July 9, 1982

DR 37° 22.8' N, 131° 52' W

WT	a-value	Zn
13:53:13	1.2 T	179.7
13:54:41	0.0 T	181.0
13:55:56	1.9 T	182.1
13:57:44	3.0 T	183.6
13:58:51	0.5 T	184.6
14:01:01	1.0 T	186.5

▶ **Problem 6**. 1355 LAN Lat using C197, S6.0
Lat = 37° 43.8'N

Reminder

Plots of the computed solutions
are in Appendix A4.

Log 992	Problem 7	July 9

Sights #12

Jupiter—July 9, 1982

DR 36° 56.5' N, 132° 32' W

WT	a-value	Zn
21:44:32*	9.9 A	202.5
21:49:54	11.0 A	204.1
21:55:34	9.1 A	205.8

Vega (49)—July 9, 1982

DR 36° 56.5' N, 132° 32' W

WT	a-value	Zn
21:47:41	4.5 T	071.0
21:53:07	4.9 T	071.4
21:59:07*	0.9 T	071.8

▶ **Problem 7**. 2159 FIX using C197, S6.0
37° 06.5'N, 132° 32.1'W

Log 1082	Problem 8	July 10

Sights #13

Sun LL—July 10, 1982

DR 36° 34' N, 133° 32' W

WT	a-value	Zn
10:55:29	22.7 T	096.8
10:56:57	21.1 T	097.1
10:58:45	25.6 T	097.4
11:02:02*	24.7 T	098.0
11:04:43	25.7 T	098.5

Sights #14

Sun LL—July 10, 1982

DR 36° 32' N, 133° 46' W

WT	a-value	Zn
13:31:36	18.4 T	154.5
13:33:03	17.0 T	155.7
13:34:46*	16.9 T	157.1

▶ **Problem 8**. 1334 FIX using C263, S4.5
36° 22.9'N, 133° 17.8'W

Log 1161	Problem 9	July 11

Sights #15

Vega (49)—July 11, 1982

DR 35° 17' N, 134° 05' W

WT	a-value	Zn
05:37:48	13.0 A	294.5
05:42:36*	12.7 A	294.9
05:48:16	14.6 A	295.3
06:07:16	15.0 A	296.9
06:09:51	14.4 A	297.1

Polaris (58)—July 11, 1982

WT	a-value	Zn
05:40:21	0.7 A	000.8
05:45:03*	2.8 T	000.7

Venus—July 11, 1982

WT	a-value	Zn
06:03:41	11.3 T	073.3
06:05:19*	12.4 T	073.5
06:08:31	12.3 T	074.0

▶ **Problem 9**. 0605 FIX using C210, S4.8
35° 15.3'N, 133° 47.9'W

Log 1181	Problem 10	July 11

Sights #16

Moon UL—July 11, 1982

DR 35° 01' N, 133° 56' W

WT	a-value	Zn
11:03:44	2.9 A	253.5
11:05:16	0.5 A	253.8
11:08:06*	0.3 T	254.2

Sun LL—July 11, 1982

WT	a-value	Zn
11:10:23*	0.1 A	097.5
11:11:21	0.7 T	097.7

▶ **Problem 10**. 1110 FIX using C197, S4.0
35° 02.4'N, 133° 55.4'W

Log 1285	Problem 11	July 12

Sights #17

Sun LL—July 12, 1982

DR 34° 00' N, 135° 20' W

WT	a-value	Zn
14:42:15	15.5 A	215.1
14:43:30	16.0 A	216.1
14:44:28	14.1 A	216.9
14:45:57*	13.7 A	217.9

Sights #18

Sun LL—July 12, 1982

DR 33° 51' N, 135° 32' W

WT	a-value	Zn
16:45:20*	18.7 A	261.4

▶ **Problem 11**. 1645 FIX using C230, S7.0
33° 55.4'N, 135° 10.1'W

Log 1364	Problem 12	July 13

Sights #19

Mag 2 Unknown Star—July 13, 1982

DR 33° 10' N, 136° 30' W

Determined to be Kochab (40)... and not usable

WT	a-value	Zn
06:00:18	0.7 A	346.4
06:02:55	3.5 A	346.5

Venus—July 13, 1982

WT	a-value	Zn
06:17:00	12.4 T	072.7
06:19:57*	14.0 T	073.1
06:23:45	13.7 T	073.6

Moon LL—July 13, 1982

WT	a-value	Zn
06:29:35	1.7 T	149.9
06:31:27	2.4 T	150.6
06:41:32	0.6 A	154.5
06:42:22*	0.2 A	154.7
06:43:50	1.4 A	155.3
06:45:33	1.1 A	155.9

▶ **Problem 12**. 0642 FIX using C235, S5.7
33° 15.0'N, 136° 17.5'W (Moon and Venus only)

Log 1429	Problem 13	July 13

Sights #20

Sun LL—July 13, 1982

DR 32° 29' N, 136° 20' W

WT	a-value	Zn
15:00:41	12.6 A	228.9
15:03:34*	9.4 A	230.7
15:06:44	10.6 A	232.6
15:08:26	11.2 A	233.5

Sights #21

Sun LL— July 13, 1982

DR 32° 13' N, 136° 17' W

WT	a-value	Zn
17:40:11	10.8 A	270.9
17:40:52	3.0 A	271.0
17:41:37*	3.9 A	271.1
17:42:12	0.3 A	271.1
17:43:02	1.7 T	271.2

▶**Problem 13**. 1741 FIX using C170, S6.3
32° 25.4'N, 136° 12.9'W

Log 1418	Problem 14	July 14

Sights #22

Sun LL—July 14, 1982

DR 30° 31' N, 137° 15' W

WT	a-value	Zn
14:15:06*	3.6 T	180.5
14:18:32*	3.7 T	185.6

▶**Problem 14.** 1418 FIX using C205, S6.1
30° 27.1'N, 137° 12.0'W

Log 1696	Problem 15	July 15

Sights #23

Moon LL—July 15, 1982

DR 30° 05' N, 139° 40' W

WT	a-value	Zn
07:28:04*	6.9 T	118.6
07:29:29	9.0 T	118.9
07:30:51	7.5 T	119.3

Sights #24

Sun LL—July 15, 1982

DR 30° 00' N, 139° 54' W

WT	a-value	Zn
09:15:55	0.9 A	076.6
09:17:01*	1.5 A	076.7
09:17:48	1.4 A	076.8
09:19:15	0.1 A	077.0

▶**Problem 15.** 0917 FIX using CMG250, SMG7.1
29° 48.4'N, 139° 51.9'W (Fix had a course change.)

Log 1730	Problem 16	July 15

Sights #25

Sun LL—July 15, 1982

DR 29° 42' N, 140° 03' W

WT	a-value	Zn
10:52:26*	0.8 A	086.7
10:53:58	1.2 A	086.8
10:53:30	1.4 A	087.0
10:56:21	1.4 A	087.1

Sights #26

Sun LL—July 15, 1982

DR 29° 29' N, 140° 24' W

WT	a-value	Zn
13:37:07	1.2 A	122.3
13:38:05*	0.8 T	122.9
13:40:47	0.1 T	124.6
13:41:45	2.7 A	125.2
13:43:27	3.1 A	126.4

▶**Problem 16.** 1338 FIX using C233, S7.4
29° 32.4'N, 140° 23.0'W

Log 1865	Problem 17	July 16

Sights #27

Deneb (53)—July 16, 1982

DR 28° 33' N, 142° 41' W

WT	a-value	Zn
06:55:50*	3.2 A	307.0

Venus—July 16, 1982

WT	a-value	Zn
06:58:30*	3.6 T	072.7

Moon LL—July 16, 1982

WT	a-value	Zn
07:14:25*	0.5 T	096.0
07:15:37	0.2 T	095.6
07:17:22	1.6 T	095.8

▶ **Problem 17.** 0714 FIX using C245, S7.7
28° 32.0'N, 142° 39.6'W

Log 1981	Problem 18	July 16

Sights #28

Jupiter—July 16, 1982

DR 27° 46' N, 144° 42' W

WT	a-value	Zn
21:53:55	14.7 A	201.6
21:54:45	16.1 A	201.9
21:56:47	16.4 A	202.6
21:58:17*	15.9 A	203.1
21:59:17	16.4 A	203.5

Vega (49)—July 16, 1982

WT	a-value	Zn
22:08:40	15.3 T	061.7
22:11:18	13.9 T	061.7
22:13:00*	13.4 T	061.8
22:16:14	11.8 T	061.8

▶ **Problem 18.** 2213 FIX using C247, S7.7
27° 57.8'N, 144° 31.8'W

Log 2147	Problem 19	July 17

▶ **Problem 19.** 17 July 1982
2000 DR 26° 41'N, 147° 16'W   (See page 34.)

Log 2265	Problem 20	July 18

Sights #29

Venus—July 18, 1982

DR 25° 55' N, 148° 44' W

WT	a-value	Zn
07:40:22	3.6 T	073.2
07:41:48	1.9 T	073.4
07:43:18*	3.4 T	073.5
07:44:52	3.7 T	073.6
07:46:11	4.9 T	073.7

Sights #30

Sun LL— July 18, 1982

DR 25° 43' N, 149° 10' W

WT	a-value	Zn
11:20:20	1.2 T	083.0
11:21:11*	1.5 T	083.1
11:22:23	3.0 T	083.2

▶ **Problem 20.** 1121 FIX using C242, S7.3
25° 51.7'N, 149° 08.9'W

Log 2343	Problem 21	July 18

Sights #31

Vega (49)—July 18, 1982

DR 25° 19' N, 150° 25' W

WT	a-value	Zn
22:23:10	1.2 A	059.6
22:25:33	1.6 A	059.6
22:37:30*	1.6 A	059.4

Alkaid (34)—July 18, 1982

WT	a-value	Zn
22:30:42	3.5 A	330.1
22:34:19	1.9 A	329.3
22:35:47	2.2 A	329.0
22:40:14*	4.4 A	328.0

▶ **Problem 21.** 2240 FIX using C242, S6.9
25° 15.0'N, 150° 25.9'W

Log 2401	Problem 22	July 19

Sights #32

Polaris (58)—July 19, 1982

DR 24° 39' N, 151° 15' W

WT	a-value	Zn
07:26:19	3.3 T	000.5
07:28:04*	2.4 T	000.5
07:33:33	6.0 T	000.5

Vega (49)—July 19, 1982

WT	a-value	Zn
07:36:33	4.0 A	305.1
07:37:50	0.3 A	305.1
07:39:17	2.5 A	305.1
07:41:16*	0.5 A	305.2
07:44:09	4.3 A	305.4

Capella (12)—July 19, 1982

WT	a-value	Zn
07:46:58*	5.5 T	049.6

Venus—July 19, 1982

WT	a-value	Zn
07:44:56	5.6 T	072.4
07:50:34	5.3 T	072.8
07:52:06	4.8 T	073.0
07:53:18*	5.8 T	073.1
07:54:43	2.4 T	073.2
07:56:00	4.5 T	073.3

▶**Problem 22.** 0753 FIX using C232, S6.3

24° 41.4'N, 151° 10.5'W

The DR for this computation is slightly different than the one used on the plots (24° 38', 151° 12'), but this does not change the final computed fix.

Log 2487	Problem 23	July 19

Sights #33

Jupiter—July 19, 1982

DR 23° 56' N, 152° 29' W

WT	a-value	Zn
22:18:54*	13.3 A	205.2
22:19:37	14.2 A	205.5
22:20:58	14.3 A	206.0
22:21:37	13.5 A	206.2

Unidentified Star Mag 1—July 19, 1982

WT	a-value	Zn
22:36:35	0.2 T	090.6
22:37:55	0.4 A	090.7
22:39:34	0.4 A	090.9
22:41:10*	0.8 T	091.0

▶**Problem 23.** 2241 FIX using C238, S5.8

24° 09.7'N, 152° 29.4'W

Log 2560	Problem 24	July 20

Sights #34

Sun LL—July 20, 1982

DR 23° 35' N, 153° 17' W

WT	a-value	Zn
09:42:06	3.4 T	072.9
09:42:47*	3.8 T	073.0
09:43:23	3.8 T	073.0
09:44:07	3.4 T	073.1
09:45:00	3.3 T	073.2
09:45:39	3.4 T	073.2

Sights #35

Sun LL —July 20, 1982

DR 23° 22' N, 153° 31' W

WT	a-value	Zn
12:25:34	9.8 T	085.2
12:26:20	10.8 T	085.2
12:27:45*	9.3 T	085.3
12:29:04	10.0 T	085.4
12:30:41	9.4 T	085.6

▶**Problem 24.** 1227 FIX using C230, S5.3

23° 06.7'N, 153° 18.7'W

Log 2572	Problem 25	July20

Sights #36

Sun LL—July 20, 1982

DR 23° 00' N, 153° 19' W

WT	a-value	Zn	
15:11:40*	0.1 T	142.7	
15:12:50	0.1 T	146.7	
15:14:35	2.0 A	153.3	?
15:15:45	0.3 A	158.1	
15:16:58	0.9 A	163.5	
15:18:30*	1.1 A	170.8	
15:20:20	0.5 A	179.9	
15:21:00	0.3 A	183.2	
15:21:50	1.2 A	187.3	
15:22:45	0.1 A	191.8	
15:23:40	0.1 A	196.1	
15:25:05	1.1 A	202.4	
15:26:33	0.6 T	208.4	
15:27:35	0.9 T	212.2	
15:28:40	0.2 T	216.0	

▶**Problem 25.**

Sights reduced from DR = LAN fix

LAN-Lat = 23° 17.3

LAN-Lon = 153° 31' ± 4'

1520 FIX from all sights using C228, S4.3
 23° 17.6'N, 153° 31.2'W

Log 2614	Problem 26	July 20

Sights #37

Jupiter—July 20, 1982

DR 22° 44' N, 153° 58' W (2240)

WT	a-value	Zn
22:03:59	4.9 A	199.2
22:05:54	6.2 A	200.0
22:06:48	5.8 A	200.3
22:08:19*	4.9 A	201.0
22:10:26	5.0 A	201.8

Vega (49)—July 20, 1982

WT	a-value	Zn
22:19:25	2.4 A	057.6
22:22:42	2.2 A	057.6
22:23:55	1.1 A	057.6
22:25:56	2.0 A	057.5
22:27:12*	3.7 A	057.5

Altair (51)—July 20, 1982

WT	a-value	Zn
22:35:24	5.9 A	089.7
22:37:08	5.7 A	089.9
22:38:19	7.9 A	090.0
22:40:06*	6.7 A	090.2

▶**Problem 26.** 2240 FIX using C217, S5.7
 22° 48.9'N, 154° 05.7'W

Look at the bearing trend (Zn) for Vega above compared to the other bodies, here and on other sights. Does this make sense? Look at other Vega sights as well. Hint: "Star path" section of the book *Emergency Navigation*.

Problem 19. Precise DR Plotting Practice*									
Date		WT	Log	dT	Run	C	S	Exact log	Exact S and WT
16	P18 FIX	2213	1981	—	—	243	7.8	27° 58.0', 144° 32.0'	27° 58.0', 144° 32.0'
17		0000	1995	1.783	14	243	7.5	27° 51.6', 144° 46.0'	27° 51.7', 144° 46.0'
17		1128	2081	11.467	86	243	6.8	27° 12.6', 146° 12.0'	27° 12.7', 146° 12.0'
17		1450	2104	3.366	23	240	7.4	27° 02.2', 146° 34.9'	27° 02.3', 146° 34.8'
17		1611	2114	1.350	10	240	8.6	26° 57.2', 146° 44.6'	26° 57.2', 146° 44.6'
17	P19 DR	2000	2147	3.816	33	240	8.5	26° 40.7', 147° 16.5'	26° 40.9', 147° 16.2'
18		0000	2181	4.000	34	240	7.4	26° 23.7', 147° 49.2'	26° 23.9', 147° 48.9'
18		0740	2238	7.667	57	242	7.3	25° 55.2', 148° 43.9'	25° 55.5', 148° 43.3'
18	P20 DR	1121	2265	3.683	27			25° 42.5', 149° 10.2'	25° 42.9', 149° 09.5'

* The answers differ slightly because the Logbook has log readings only precise to the nearest mile.

Log 2689	Problem 27	July 21

Sights #38

Polaris (58)—July 21, 1982

DR 22° 05' N, 155° 12' W (0831)

WT	a-value	Zn
07:51:02*	4.0 T	000.4
07:53:38	2.7 T	000.4
08:09:14	4.8 T	000.3
08:11:00	2.2 T	000.3

Capella (12)—July 21, 1982

WT	a-value	Zn	
07:55:12*	12.2 T	048.5	
07:56:34	11.0 T	048.5	
08:01:40	10.2 T	048.5	
08:15:25	13.8 A	048.6	X

Vega (49)—July 21, 1982

WT	a-value	Zn
08:04:41	8.3 A	306.9
08:06:50	12.2 A	307.0
08:15:25*	8.4 A	307.6

Venus—July 21, 1982

WT	a-value	Zn
07:58:24	12.9 T	071.1
08:29:44	9.5 T	073.3
08:30:48	10.0 T	073.4
08:31:37*	9.6 T	073.4
08:33:38	8.7 T	073.5

▶**Problem 27.** 0831 FIX using C232, S7.6

22° 05.2'N, 155° 01.3'W (omitting 0815 Capella)

HP 41C Navigation Computer

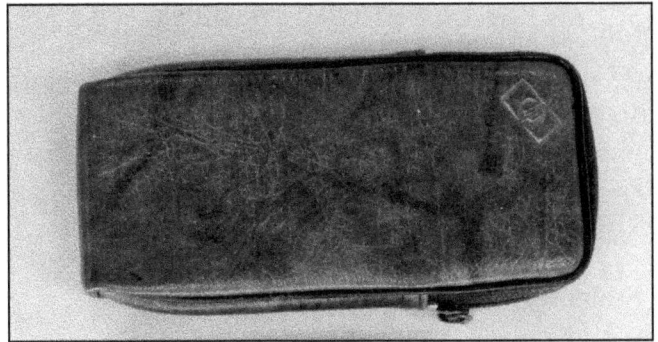

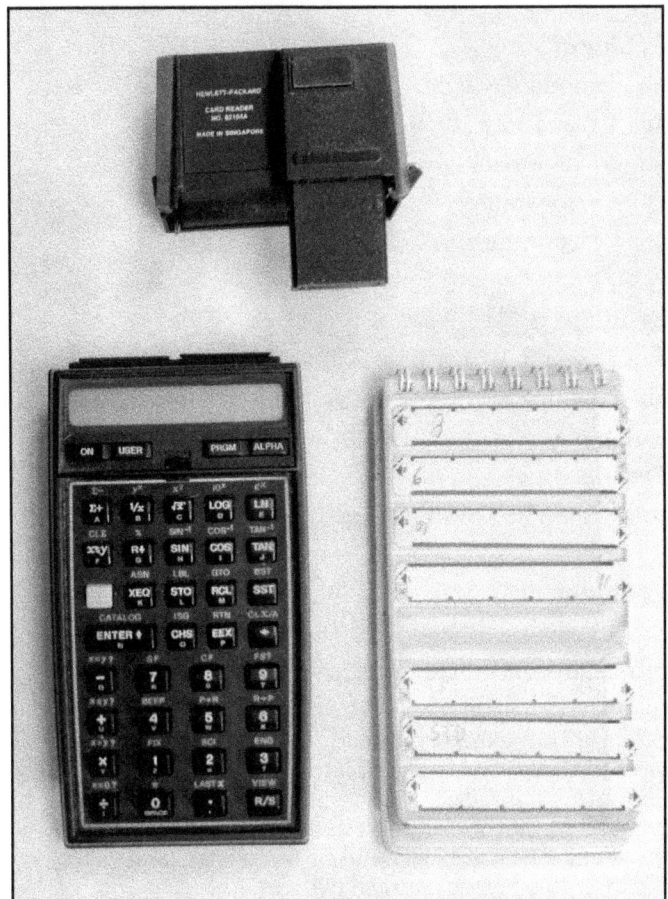

The HP 41C we used for computer navigation during this voyage and many others. Starpath had developed a set of navigation programs for the calculator that were read into it with magnetic cards. This handheld device was one of the first such instruments devoted to marine navigation. There was also a commercial Navigation module available from Hewlett Packard, and we used some of their subroutines for our computations. Though long forgotten, we found this going through old boxes looking for the original plotting sheets!

Using a computer for navigation, it is best to do sight reductions from a DR position, find an approximate fix, then redo the computations again using that fix as the new DR, with all sights advanced to a common time relative to that new position. This guarantees small a-values that can be conveniently plotted on an expanded scale to get the final position. Samples are shown on pages 63 and 71.

Answers to Special Problems

Problem 1

1b - Nautical twilight = 04:15:44 = 0416.

Civil twilight = 05:05:22 = 0505.

Sunrise = 05:43:35 = 0544.

So Venus sight taken at about civil twilight, and the sun sight was about 3h after sunrise.

Problem 2

2a - 1522 sunline is bad.

Problem 3

3b - Evening Twilight - 2213

3c - DR at Twilight - 40° 44.4', 131° 48.7'

3d -   1 - Vega   54° 27'   077

          2 - Jupiter   34° 20'   208

          3 - Alioth   60° 30'   314

Problem 6

6a - 37° 44' LAN Latitude

6b - No hope here. Data not good enough for a narrow fix.

Problem 10

10a - Phase 88% waning, Age 17.26 days , Setting

Problem 12

12a - Kochab

12b - nautical twilight 0603, civil 0637, sunrise 0706

12c - The star sights were not consistent with the moon and venus within expected uncertainties. Normally we would have to accept that and just have a large uncertainty in the fix, but in this case we very specifically had a warning to ourselves that the horizon was bad, so we can safely throw these out. The sights were taken when it was too dark, several minutes before nautical twilight.

Problem 14

14a - Zn at 1415 is 179.0° and at 1418 is 183.9°.

See Azimuth Interpolation example.

Problem 23

23a - Altair

Problem 25

25a - 23° 10.5' LAN Latitude

25c - Eve Twilight - 2241

25d - DR at Twilight - 22° 39.5', 153° 59'

25e -   1 - Deneb   22° 32'   048

           2 - Antares   38° 13'   160

           3 - Regulus   15° 28'   277

Problem 27

27a. The last Capella sight is clearly a blunder, and must be discarded. Most likely the dial was read incorrectly.

27b -   Approximate values are

Polaris about 23.0°

Capella about 30.4°

Vega   about 12.5°

Venus   about 16.5°

Read more accurate values from the individual plots.

27d - Range 107.5 nmi & Bearing 237° to Pailolo

27e - Log 2824.3 - 75.0 = logged Dist. 2749.3 nmi.   Great Circle = 2238.4 nmi. Difference = 510.9 nmi = extra miles sailed.

Sample Workform Solutions*

Problem 1. July 5

Sights #1   5-Jul-1982

1	WT	5 h 3 m 58 s	date	5-Jul-1982	body	Venus	Hs	12° 06.5'
	WE +S-F	m 0 s	DR Lat	46° 30' N	log	250	index corr. + off, - on	0
	ZD +W-E	7	DR Lon	127° 49' W	HE ft	9	DIP -	-2.9
	GMT	12 h 3 m 58 s	GMT date / LOP label		C-	197 T	Ha	12° 03.6'
				Sights #1 5-Jul-1982	S-	6.0 Kt		

| 2 | GHA hr. | 32° 37.1' | v moon planets | -0.7 | DEC hr | N20° 48.7' | d + − | +0.5 | HP moon | |

3	GHA + m.s.	59.5'			d corr.	+ −	0	additional altitude corr. moon, mars, venus	+	+0.1'
	SHA + or v corr.	360°		stars or moon, planets	DEC deg	N20°	DEC min	48.7	altitude corr. all sights	+ −	-4.4'
	GHA	393° 36.6'						upper limb moon subtract 30'		
			tens d		32.5	d upper		Ho	11° 59.3'	T
	a-Lon -W+E	127° 36.6'	units d		1.9	d lower				
	LHA	266° 00' W/60' E	dsd corr.	+		dsd		Hc	12° 08.4'	A
			d corr.	Pub. 229	34.4			a =	9.1 A	

4	LHA	266			5	tab Hc	11° 34.0'	d + −	+42.3	Z 73.1	Zn =	073.1
	Dec deg	20	N S	N		d corr.	Pub.249 & 229	34.4	Dec min.	48.7	a - Lat =	46 N
	a-Lat	46	N S	N		Hc	12° 08.4'			6	a - Lon =	127° 36.6' W

N Lat   L.H.A. greater than 180 .... Zn = Z
L.H.A. less than 180 .... Zn = 360 - Z

S Lat   L.H.A. greater than 180 .... Zn = 180 - Z
L.H.A. less than 180 .... Zn = 180 + Z

Sights #2   5-Jul-1982

1	WT	8 h 43 m 55 s	date	5-Jul-1982	body	Sun L/L	Hs	27° 24.0'
	WE +S-F	m 0 s	DR Lat	46° 09' N	log	272	index corr. + off, - on	0
	ZD +W-E	7	DR Lon	127° 58' W	HE ft	9	DIP -	-2.9
	GMT	15 h 43 m 55 s	GMT date / LOP label		C-	197 T	Ha	27° 21.1'
				Sights #2 5-Jul-1982	S-	6.0 Kt		

| 2 | GHA hr. | 43° 52.6' | v moon planets | | DEC hr | N22° 46.8' | d + − | -0.2 | HP moon | |

3	GHA + m.s.	10° 58.8'			d corr.	+ −	-0.1	additional altitude corr.		
	SHA + or v corr.	360°		stars or moon, planets	DEC deg	N22°	DEC min	46.7	moon, mars, venus altitude corr. all sights	+ + −	+14.2'
	GHA	414° 51.4'						upper limb moon subtract 30'		
			tens d		23.4	d upper		Ho	27° 35.3'	T
	a-Lon -W+E	127° 51.4'	units d		7.6	d lower				
	LHA	287° 00' W/60' E	dsd corr.	+		dsd		Hc	27° 45.6'	A
			d corr.	Pub. 229	31.0			a =	10.3 A	

4	LHA	287			5	tab Hc	27° 14.6'	d + −	39.8	Z 85.8	Zn =	085.8
	Dec deg	22	N S	N		d corr.	Pub.249 & 229	31.0	Dec min.	46.7	a - Lat =	46 N
	a-Lat	46	N S	N		Hc	27° 45.6'			6	a - Lon =	127°51.4' W

* See notes on the workform solutions in the Instructions to this Solutions section.

Problem 2. July 6

Sights #3

	WT	10 h 45 m 56 s	date	6-Jul-1982	body	Sun L/L	Hs	46° 42.3'
1	WE +S-F	m 0 s	DR Lat	44° 18' N	log	447	index corr. + off, - on	0
	ZD +W-E	+ 7	DR Lon	131° 00' W	HE ft 9		DIP -	-2.9
	GMT	17 h 45 m 56 s	GMT date / LOP label	Sights #3 6-Jul-1982	C- 200 T		Ha	46° 39.4'
					S- 7.3 Kt			

	GHA hr.	73° 49.8'	v moon planets		DEC hr	N22° 40.5'	d +-	-0.3	HP moon

	GHA + m.s.	11° 29.0'			d corr. +-		-0.2	additional altitude corr. moon, mars, venus +	
3	SHA + or v corr.	360°	stars or moon, planets		DEC deg	N22°	DEC min	40.3	altitude corr. all sights +-	+15.1
	GHA	445° 18.8'							upper limb moon subtract 30'	

tens d 20.1 | d upper
units d 6.3 | d lower
dsd corr. + | dsd

	a-Lon -W+E	131° 18.8'				Ho	**T**	46° 54.5'
	LHA	314°	00' W/60' E	d corr. Pub. 229 26.4		Hc	**A**	46° 47.2'

	LHA	314						a = 7.3 T
4	Dec deg	22	N S	N	**5** tab Hc 46° 20.8'	d +- +39.4	Z 104.9	Zn = 104.9
	a-Lat	44	N S	N	d corr. Pub.249 & 229 26.4	Dec min. 40.3		a - Lat = 44 N
					Hc 46° 47.2'		**6**	a - Lon = 131° 18.8' W

N Lat   L.H.A. greater than 180 .... Zn = Z
         L.H.A. less than 180 .... Zn = 360 - Z

S Lat   L.H.A. greater than 180 .... Zn = 180 - Z
         L.H.A. less than 180 .... Zn = 180 + Z

Sights #4

	WT	15 h 26 m 57 s	date	6-Jul-1982	body	Sun L/L	Hs	60° 31.0'
1	WE +S-F	m 0 s	DR Lat	43° 47' N	log	480	index corr. + off, - on	0
	ZD +W-E	7	DR Lon	131° 15' W	HE ft 9		DIP -	-2.9
	GMT	22 h 26 m 57 s	GMT date / LOP label	Sights #4 6-Jul-1982	C- 200 T		Ha	60° 28.1'
					S- 7.3 Kt			

	GHA hr.	148° 49.3'	v moon planets		DEC hr	N22° 39.2'	d +-	-0.3	HP moon

	GHA + m.s.	6° 44.3'			d corr. +-		-0.1	additional altitude corr. moon, mars, venus +	
3	SHA + or v corr.	360°	stars or moon, planets		DEC deg	N22°	DEC min	39.1	altitude corr. all sights +-	+15.4
	GHA	155° 33.6'							upper limb moon subtract 30'	

tens d 26.0 | d upper
units d 5.3 | d lower
dsd corr. + | dsd

	a-Lon -W+E	131° 33.6'				Ho	**T**	60° 43.5'
	LHA	24°	00' W/60' E	d corr. Pub. 229 31.3		Hc	**A**	60° 55.5'

	LHA	24						a = 12.0 A
4	Dec deg	22	N S	N	**5** tab Hc 60° 24.2'	d +- 48.0	Z 130.2	Zn = 229.8
	a-Lat	44	N S	N	d corr. Pub.249 & 229 31.3	Dec min. 39.1		a - Lat = 44 N
					Hc 60° 55.5'		**6**	a - Lon = 131° 33.6' W

Problem 3. July 7

1	WT	8 ʰ	32 ᵐ	28 ˢ	date	7-Jul-1982	body	Sun L/L	Hs	22°	0.6
	WE +S-F		ᵐ	00 ˢ	DR Lat	42° 12' N	log	599	index corr. + off, - on		00
	ZD +W-E	+7			DR Lon	131° 33' W	HE ft	9	DIP -	-	-2.9
	GMT	15 ʰ	32 ᵐ	28 ˢ	GMT date / LOP label		C-	180 T	Ha	21°	57.7
						Sights #5 7-Jul-82	S-	6.5 Kt			

2	GHA hr.	43°	47.6	v moon planets		DEC hr	N22°	34.7	d +−	-0.3	HP moon	

3	GHA + m.s.	8°	07.0 '			d corr.	+-		-0.2	additional altitude corr. moon, mars, venus	+	
	SHA + or v corr.	360°		stars or moon, planets	DEC deg	N22°	DEC min	34.5	altitude corr. all sights	+-	+13.6
	GHA	411°	54.6						upper limb moon subtract 30'		
				tens d	17.3	d upper		Ho	T	22°	11.3
	a-Lon -W+E	131°	54.6	units d	3.9	d lower					
	LHA	280°	00' W/60' E	dsd corr.	+	dsd		Hc	A	22°	05.3
				d corr.	Pub. 229	21.2			a =	6.0 T	

4	LHA	280		5	tab Hc	21°	44.1	d +-	36.8	Z	79.4	Zn =	079.4
	Dec deg	22	N / S	N		d corr.	Pub.249 & 229	21.2	Dec min.	34.5		a - Lat =	42 N
	a-Lat	42	N / S	N		Hc	22°	05.3					
											6	a - Lon =	131° 54.6'W

N Lat
L.H.A. greater than 180 .... Zn = Z
L.H.A. less than 180 .... Zn = 360 - Z

S Lat
L.H.A. greater than 180 .... Zn = 180 - Z
L.H.A. less than 180 .... Zn = 180 + Z

1	WT	14 ʰ	00 ᵐ	05 ˢ	date	7-Jul-1982	body	Sun L/L	Hs	70°	38.5
	WE +S-F		ᵐ	00 ˢ	DR Lat	41° 36' N	log	634	index corr. + off, - on		0
	ZD +W-E	+7			DR Lon	131° 33' W	HE ft	9	DIP -	-	-2.9
	GMT	21 ʰ	00 ᵐ	05 ˢ	GMT date / LOP label		C-	180 T	Ha	70°	35.6
						Sights #6 7-Jul-82	S-	6.5 Kt			

2	GHA hr.	133°	47.0	v moon planets		DEC hr	N 22°	33.1	d +−	- 0.3	HP moon	

3	GHA + m.s.	0°	1.3 '			d corr.	+-		-00.0	additional altitude corr. moon, mars, venus	+	
	SHA + or v corr.	0°		stars or moon, planets	DEC deg	N 22°	DEC min	33.1	altitude corr. all sights	+-	15.6
	GHA	133°	48.3						upper limb moon subtract 30'		
				tens d	27.6	d upper		Ho	T	70°	51.2
	a-Lon -W+E	131°	48.3	units d	5.5	d lower					
	LHA	2°	00' W/60' E	dsd corr.	+	dsd		Hc	A	70°	28.9
				d corr.	Pub. 229	33.1			a =	22.3 T	

4	LHA	2		5	tab Hc	69°	55.8	d +-	59.8	Z	174.6	Zn =	185.4
	Dec deg	22	N / S	N		d corr.	Pub.249 & 229	33.1	Dec min.	33.1		a - Lat =	42 N
	a-Lat	42	N / S	N		Hc	70°	28.9					
											6	a - Lon =	131° 48.3' W

Problem 4. July 8

Sight #7

1 WT	10 h 09 m 35 s	date	8-Jul-1982	body	Sun L/L	Hs	40° 35.5'
WE +S-F	m 00 s	DR Lat	39° 24' N	log	769	index corr. + off, - on	00
ZD +W-E	+7	DR Lon	131° 40' W	HE ft	9	DIP -	-2.9
GMT	17 h 09 m 35 s	GMT date / LOP label		C-	169 T	Ha	40° 32.6
		Sights #7 8-Jul-1982		S-	6.7 Kt		

2 GHA hr.	73° 45.1	v moon planets	DEC hr	N22° 27.5	d +-	-0.3	HP moon

3

					additional altitude corr.
GHA + m.s.	2° 23.8'	d corr. +-		0	moon, mars, venus +
SHA + or v corr.	360°	stars or moon, planets	DEC N22°	DEC 27.5	altitude corr. all sights +- +14.9
GHA	436° 08.9'				upper limb moon subtract 30'

tens d	13.8	d upper
units d	1.1	d lower
dsd corr.	+	dsd
d corr. Pub. 229	14.9	

Ho **T**	40°	47.5
Hc **A**	39°	56.5
a =	51.0 T	

| a-Lon -W+E | 132° 08.9' |
| LHA | 304° 00' W/60' E |

4

LHA	304	**5** tab Hc	39° 41.6	d +- 32.5	Z 92.6	Zn = 092.6
Dec deg	22 N/S N	d corr. Pub.249 & 229	14.9	Dec min. 27.5		a - Lat = 39 N
a-Lat	39 N/S N	Hc	39° 56.5		**6**	a - Lon = 132° 08.9'W

N Lat   L.H.A. greater than 180 .... Zn = Z
L.H.A. less than 180 .... Zn = 360 - Z

S Lat   L.H.A. greater than 180 .... Zn = 180 - Z
L.H.A. less than 180 .... Zn = 180 + Z

Sight #8

1 WT	13 h 07 m 23 s	date	8-Jul-1982	body	Sun L/L	Hs	70° 54.0
WE +S-F	m 00 s	DR Lat	39° 05'N	log	789	index corr. + off, - on	0
ZD +W-E	+7	DR Lon	131° 33' W	HE ft	9	DIP -	-2.9
GMT	20 h 07 m 23 s	GMT date / LOP label		C-	169 T	Ha	70° 51.1
		Sights #8 8-Jul-1982		S-	6.7 Kt		

2 GHA hr.	118° 44.8	v moon planets	DEC hr	N 22° 26.7	d +-	-0.3	HP moon

3

					additional altitude corr.
GHA + m.s.	1° 50.8	d corr. +-		-00.0	moon, mars, venus +
SHA + or v corr.	360°	stars or moon, planets	DEC N 22°	DEC 26.7	altitude corr. all sights +- +15.6
GHA	480° 35.6				upper limb moon subtract 30'

tens d	22.3	d upper
units d	1.5	d lower
dsd corr.	+	dsd
d corr. Pub. 229	23.4	

Ho **T**	71°	06.7
Hc **A**	70°	58.2
a =	8.5 T	

| a-Lon -W+E | 131° 35.6 |
| LHA | 349° 00' W/60' E |

4

LHA	349	**5** tab Hc	70° 34.4	d +- 52.5	Z 145.4	Zn = 147.9
Dec deg	22 N/S N	d corr. Pub.249 & 229	23.4	Dec min. 26.7		a - Lat = 39 N
a-Lat	39 N/S N	Hc	70° 58.2		**6**	a - Lon = 131°35.6' W

Notice in the 1009 sight, we have an a-value of near due East of 51'. This has to be a warning that the DR longitude was wrong, or we chose the wrong a-Lon. When this happens we have to carry on with the analysis to figure out what is going on, which we might not learn for a while. But the flag is up and waving.

Problem 5. July 9

Sights #9 — 9-Jul-1982

1	WT	10 h 37 m 33 s	date	9-Jul-1982	body	Sun L/L	Hs	45°	15.5 '
	WE +S-F	m 00 s	DR Lat	37° 57' N	log	923	index corr. + off, - on		00
	ZD +W-E	+7	DR Lon	132° 14' W	HE ft	9	DIP -		-2.9
	GMT	17 h 37 m 33 s	GMT date / LOP label		C-	222 T	Ha	45°	12.6

| **2** | GHA hr. | 73° 42.8 | v moon planets | | DEC hr | N22° 20.5 | d +- | -0.3 | HP moon | |

3	GHA + m.s.	9° 23.3 '			d corr. +-		-0.2 '	additional altitude corr. moon, mars, venus	+
	SHA + or v corr.	360°	stars or moon, planets	DEC deg	N22°	DEC min	20.3	altitude corr. all sights	+- 15
	GHA	443° 06.1 '					upper limb moon subtract 30'		
			tens d	30	10.1	d upper		Ho	T 45° 27.6 '
	a-Lon -W+E	132° 06.1	units d	1.8	0.6	d lower			
	LHA	311° 00' W/60' E	dsd corr.	+		dsd		Hc	A 45° 24.6 '
				d corr.	Pub. 229	10.7		a =	3.0 T

4	LHA	311			5 tab Hc	45° 13.9 '	d +-	31.8 Z 96.5	Zn =	096.5
	Dec deg	22	N S	N	d corr.	Pub.249 & 229	10.7	Dec min.	20.3	a - Lat =	38 N
	a-Lat	38	N S	N	Hc	45° 24.6 '		**6** a - Lon =	132° 06.1'W

N Lat L.H.A. greater than 180 .... Zn = Z
L.H.A. less than 180 .... Zn = 360 - Z

S Lat L.H.A. greater than 180 .... Zn = 180 - Z
L.H.A. less than 180 .... Zn = 180 + Z

Sights #10 — 9-Jul-1982

1	WT	13 h 24 m 55 s	date	9-Jul-1982	body	Sun L/L	Hs	73°	8.4 '
	WE +S-F	m 00 s	DR Lat	37° 44' N	log	942	index corr. + off, - on		0
	ZD +W-E	+7	DR Lon	132° 30'W	HE ft	9	DIP -		-2.9
	GMT	20 h 24 m 55 s	GMT date / LOP label		C-	222 T	Ha	73°	5.5

| **2** | GHA hr. | 118° 42.6 | v moon planets | | DEC hr | N 22° 19.6 | d +- | - 0.3 | HP moon | |

3	GHA + m.s.	6° 13.8 '			d corr. +-		-0.1 '	additional altitude corr. moon, mars, venus	+
	SHA + or v corr.	360°	stars or moon, planets	DEC deg	N 22°	DEC min	19.5	altitude corr. all sights	+- 15.6
	GHA	484° 56.4 '					upper limb moon subtract 30'		
			tens d	50	16.3	d upper		Ho	T 73° 21.1 '
	a-Lon -W+E	132° 56.4	units d	5.6	1.8	d lower			
	LHA	352° 00' W/60' E	dsd corr.	+		dsd		Hc	A 72° 53.1 '
				d corr.	Pub. 229	18.1		a =	28.0 T

4	LHA	352			5 tab Hc	72° 35.0 '	d +-	55.6 Z 154.5	Zn =	154.5
	Dec deg	22	N S	N	d corr.	Pub.249 & 229	18.1	Dec min.	19.5	a - Lat =	38 N
	a-Lat	38	N S	N	Hc	72° 53.1 '		**6** a - Lon =	132°56.4 W

Problem 6. July 9

LAN Workform Example

(See also Problem 25.)

Step 1 Correct Hs to get Ho		Sights #11		
1-1 Record Maximum Sextant Height (Hs = peak height of the Sun at Noon), and mark limb	Lower Upper Hs	**74** °	**23.3** '
1-2 Record Index Correction (mark sign + if off, - if on)	IC	Off **+** On **-**	**0** '
1-3 Record eye height (HE) and look up Dip Correction on the right-hand side of Table A2, front of Almanac (T-8 in notes) HE (ft) 9	Dip	**-**	**2.9** '
1-4 Record Maximum Sextant Height (Hs = peak height of the Sun at Noon), and mark limb	Ha	**74** °	**20.4** '
1-5 Look up the altitude correction on the left-hand side of Table A2, front of the Almanac (T-8 in notes) (correction depends on Ha, Limb, and month) (mark sign + for lower limb, - for upper limb)	Alt corr.	**+** **-**	**+15.7** '
1-6 Sum the above two numbers to get Observed Height	Ho	**74** °	**36.1** '

Starpath Form 107 for Local Apparent Noon Sights

Step 1 Determine the Zenith Distance		**89** °	**60.0** '
2-1 Record Ho from Step 1, above, and then subtract it from 90° to get the zenith distance.	Ho	**74** °	**36.1** '
2-2 Zenith Distance	**z**	**15** °	**23.9** '

Step 3 Use the Almanac to Find Sun's Declination	GMT date =	**9-Jul-82**	
3-1 Record the date and GMT of the sight (the time the Sun reached its peak height)	GMT (hr) = **20**	GMT (min)= **55**	
3-2 Turn to the daily page of the Almanac for the date of the sight, and find the Sun's declination (dec) for the hour of the sight (line 3-1) and record it here	Dec (hr)	N **N 22** ° S	**19.6** '
3-3 Record the d-value from the bottom of the dec column in the Almanac. Mark the signs of the d-value and the d-corr + if the dec for the next hour is larger, or - if it is smaller.	d-value **+** **-** **-0.3**	d-corr = **+** **-** **-0.3**	
3-4 Turn to the Increments and Corrections pages at the back of the Almanac (T-9 to 12, in the notes) and find the minutes table for thr GMT minutes (line 3-1). On the right-hand side of the double line in the table, find the d-corr corresponding to the d-value of line 3-3	Declination =	N **N 22** ° S	**19.3** '
	3-5 Apply the d-corr to the dec (hr) and record it above		

Step 4 Find Latitude from Zenith Distance and Declination			
Record DR Latitide to use as a guide, and then take the sum or difference of zenith distance and declination to find your true Latitude at LAN DR Lat = **37° 42'**	Declination or Zenith Distance	**N 22** °	**19.3** '
	Zenith Distance or Declination	**15** °	**23.9** '
	Latitude =	**37** °	**43.2** '

This LAN sight is discussed in the Analysis Section

Problem 7. July 9

Sight #12a (Jupiter)

1 WT	21 h 44 m 32 s	date **9-Jul-1982**	body **Jupiter**	Hs	39° 37.9'
WE +S-F	m 00 s	DR Lat **36° 55' N**	log **991**	index corr. + off, - on	00
ZD +W-E	**+7**	DR Lon **132° 36' W**	HE ft **9**	DIP -	-2.9
GMT	04 h 44 m 32 s	GMT date / LOP label Sights #12a 10-Jul-1982	C- **197** T S- **6.0** Kt	Ha	39° 35.0

2 GHA hr.	138° 47.1	v moon planets **2.4**	DEC hr **S10°** 35.4	d +- **0**	HP moon		

3 GHA + m.s.	11° 08.0		d corr. +- **0**		additional altitude corr. moon, mars, venus **+**		
SHA + or v corr.	° 1.8	stars or moon, planets	DEC deg **S10°**	DEC min 35.4	altitude corr. all sights +- **-1.2**		
GHA	149° 56.9		tens d **29.5**	d upper	upper limb moon subtract 30'		
			units d **4.3**	d lower	Ho **T** 39° 33.8		
a-Lon -W+E	132° 56.9		dsd corr. **+**	dsd			
LHA	17° 00' W/60' E		d corr. Pub. 229 **33.8**		Hc **A** 39° 48.0		
					a = **14.2 A**		

4 LHA	17		**5** tab Hc **40°** 21.8	d +- **-57.2**	Z **157.8**	Zn = **202.2**		
Dec deg	10	N S **S**	d corr. Pub.249 & 229 **-33.8**	Dec min. 35.4		a - Lat = **37 N**		
a-Lat	37	N S **N**	Hc **39°** 48.0		**6**	a - Lon = **132° 56.9'W**		

N Lat L.H.A. greater than 180 .... Zn = Z
L.H.A. less than 180 .... Zn = 360 - Z

S Lat L.H.A. greater than 180 .... Zn = 180 - Z
L.H.A. less than 180 .... Zn = 180 + Z

Sight #12b (Vega)

1 WT	21 h 59 m 07 s	date **9-Jul-1982**	body **Vega (49)**	Hs	51° 46.6'
WE +S-F	m 00 s	DR Lat **36° 55' N**	log **992**	index corr. + off, - on	0
ZD +W-E	**+7**	DR Lon **132° 36'W**	HE ft **9**	DIP -	-2.9
GMT	04 h 59 m 07 s	GMT date / LOP label Sights #12b 10-Jul-1982	C- **197** T S- **6.0** Kt	Ha	51° 43.7

2 GHA γ hr.	347° 45.3	v moon planets	DEC hr °	d +-	HP moon		

3 GHA + m.s.	14° 49.2		d corr. +-		additional altitude corr. moon, mars, venus **+**		
SHA + or v corr.	80° 54.5	stars or moon, planets	DEC deg **N 38°**	DEC min 46.1	altitude corr. all sights +- **-0.8**		
GHA γ	443° 29.0		tens d **7.7**	d upper	upper limb moon subtract 30'		
			units d **3.2**	d lower	Ho **T** 51° 42.9		
a-Lon -W+E	132° 29.0		dsd corr. **+**	dsd			
LHA	311° 00' W/60' E		d corr. Pub. 229 **10.9**		Hc **A** 51° 45.2		
					a = **2.3 A**		

4 LHA	311		**5** tab Hc **51°** 34.3	d +- **14.1**	Z **73.1**	Zn = **073.1**		
Dec deg	38	N S **N**	d corr. Pub.249 & 229 **10.9**	Dec min. 46.1		a - Lat = **37 N**		
a-Lat	37	N S **N**	Hc **51°** 45.2		**6**	a - Lon = **132°29.0'W**		

Problem 8. July 10

	WT	11 h	02 m	2 s	date	10-Jul-1982	body	Sun L/L	Hs	49°	24.5'
1	WE +S-F		m	00 s	DR Lat	36° 31' N	log	1066	index corr. + off, - on		00'
	ZD +W-E	+7			DR Lon	133° 28' W	HE ft	9	DIP -		-2.9'
	GMT	18 h	02 m	2 s	GMT date / LOP label		C-	276 T	Ha	49°	21.6'
						Sights #13 10-Jul-1982	S-	5.7 Kt			

	GHA hr.	88°	40.6'	v moon planets		DEC hr	N22°	12.7'	d +–	-0.3	HP moon

	GHA + m.s.	0°	30.5'		d corr. +-		0		additional altitude corr. moon, mars, venus	+	
3	SHA + or v corr.	360°		stars or moon, planets	DEC or deg	N22°	DEC min	12.7'	altitude corr. all sights	+-	15.2'
	GHA	449°	11.1'						upper limb moon subtract 30'		

tens d	4.3	d upper		Ho	T	49°	36.8'
units d	2.0	d lower					
dsd corr.	+	dsd		Hc	A	49°	32.9'

	a-Lon -W+E	133°	11.1'	d corr. Pub. 229	6.3				a =	3.9 T
	LHA	316°	00' W/60' E						Zn =	097.9

	LHA	316		**5**	tab Hc	49°	26.6'	d +-	29.7	Z	97.9		a - Lat =	36° N
4	Dec deg	22	N S N		d corr.	Pub.249 & 229	6.3	Dec min.	12.7					
	a-Lat	36	N S N		Hc	49°	32.9'					**6**	a - Lon =	133° 11.1'W

N Lat   L.H.A. greater than 180 .... Zn = Z
         L.H.A. less than 180 .... Zn = 360 - Z

S Lat   L.H.A. greater than 180 .... Zn = 180 - Z
         L.H.A. less than 180 .... Zn = 180 + Z

	WT	13 h	34 m	46 s	date	10-Jul-1982	body	Sun L/L	Hs	74°	42.0'
1	WE +S-F		m	00 s	DR Lat	36° 32' N	log	1082	index corr. + off, - on		0'
	ZD +W-E	+7			DR Lon	133° 46'W	HE ft	9	DIP -		-2.9'
	GMT	20 h	34 m	46 s	GMT date / LOP label		C-	276 T	Ha	74°	39.1'
						Sights #14 10-Jul-1982	S-	5.7 Kt			

	GHA hr.	118°	40.4'	v moon planets		DEC hr	N 22°	12.1'	d +–	- 0.3	HP moon

	GHA + m.s.	8°	41.5'		d corr. +-		-0.2		additional altitude corr. moon, mars, venus	+	
3	SHA + or v corr.	360°		stars or moon, planets	DEC or deg	N 22°	DEC min	11.9'	altitude corr. all sights	+-	+15.7'
	GHA	487°	21.9'						upper limb moon subtract 30'		

tens d	10.0	d upper		Ho	T	74°	54.8'
units d	1.0	d lower					
dsd corr.	+	dsd		Hc	A	74°	54.9'

	a-Lon -W+E	134°	21.9'	d corr. Pub. 229	11.0				a =	0.1' A
	LHA	353°	00' W/60' E						Zn =	154.6

	LHA	353		**5**	tab Hc	74°	43.9'	d +-	55.4	Z	154.6		a - Lat =	36° N
4	Dec deg	22	N S N		d corr.	Pub.249 & 229	11.0	Dec min.	11.9					
	a-Lat	36	N S N		Hc	74°	54.9'					**6**	a - Lon =	134°21.9' W

The a-Lat was not rounded properly in these two reductions, but the a-values are still small. However, this is not a proper check. See the plot to appreciate the implication of choosing the wrong a-Lat. It definitely jeopardizes the accuracy of the fix. We do not want any line on the plot to be over 30 miles long.

Problem 9. July 11

Sight 1 (Vega)

1					date	11-Jul-1982	body	Vega (49)	Hs	37°	47.3
	WT	05 h	42 m	36 s							
	WE +S-F			m 00 s	DR Lat	35° 16' N	log	1161	index corr. + off, - on		00
	ZD +W-E	+7			DR Lon	134° 11' W	HE ft	9	DIP -		-2.9
	GMT	12 h	42 m	36 s	GMT date / LOP label		C-	210 T	Ha	37°	44.4
					Sights #15 11-Jul-1982		S-	4.8 Kt			

2	GHA ♈ hr.	109°	4.1	v moon planets		DEC hr	°		d +-	HP moon	

3	GHA + m.s.	10°	40.7			d corr. +-			additional altitude corr. moon, mars, venus	+	
	SHA + or v corr.	80°	54.5	stars or moon, planets	DEC deg	N38	°DEC min	46.1	altitude corr. all sights	+-	-1.3
	GHA	200°	39.3		tens d	7.7	d upper		upper limb moon subtract 30'		
	a-Lon -W+E	133°	39.3		units d	6.9	d lower		Ho T	37°	43.1
	LHA	67°	00' W/60' E		dsd corr.	+	dsd		Hc A	37°	29.8
					d corr.	Pub. 229 14.6			a =	13.3 T	

4	LHA	67		5	tab Hc	37°	15.2	d +-	18.9	Z	65.7	Zn =	294.3
	Dec deg	38	N S N		d corr.	Pub.249 & 229	14.6	Dec min.	46.1			a - Lat =	35° N
	a-Lat	35	N S N		Hc	37°	29.8					6 a - Lon =	133° 39.3'W

N Lat L.H.A. greater than 180 .... Zn = Z
L.H.A. less than 180 .... Zn = 360 - Z

S Lat L.H.A. greater than 180 .... Zn = 180 - Z
L.H.A. less than 180 .... Zn = 180 + Z

Sight 2 (Venus)

1					date	11-Jul-1982	body	VENUS	Hs	15°	10.5
	WT	06 h	05 m	19 s							
	WE +S-F			m 00 s	DR Lat	35° 16' N	log	1161	index corr. + off, - on		00
	ZD +W-E	+7			DR Lon	134° 11' W	HE ft	9	DIP -		-2.9
	GMT	13 h	05 m	19 s	GMT date / LOP label		C-	210 T	Ha	15°	07.6
					Sights #15 11-Jul-1982		S-	4.8 Kt			

2	GHA hr.	45°	54.9	v moon planets	-0.7	DEC hr	N 21°	49.2	d +-	0.4	HP moon	

3	GHA + m.s.	1°	19.8			d corr. +-		0	additional altitude corr. moon, mars, venus	+	+0.1
	SHA + or v corr.	360°	-0.1	stars or moon, planets	DEC deg	N 21	°DEC min	49.2	altitude corr. all sights	+-	-3.5
	GHA	407°	14.6		tens d	24.6	d upper		upper limb moon subtract 30'		
	a-Lon -W+E	134°	14.6		units d	1.7	d lower		Ho T	15°	04.2
	LHA	273°	00' W/60' E		dsd corr.	+	dsd		Hc A	14°	39.2
					d corr.	Pub. 229 26.3			a =	25.0 T	

4	LHA	273		5	tab Hc	14°	12.9	d +-	32.1	Z	74.1	Zn =	074.1
	Dec deg	21	N S N		d corr.	Pub.249 & 229	26.3	Dec min.	49.2			a - Lat =	35° N
	a-Lat	35	N S N		Hc	14°	39.2					6 a - Lon =	134° 14.6' W

The a-Lon choice in the top sight is not strictly optimum, as it can always be chosen to be within 30' of the DR Lon, but this one is very close and it would not likely change the results.

Problem 9. July 11

Polaris Workform Example

(See also Problems 22 and 27.)

Step 1 Correct Hs to get Ho		Sights #15		
1-1 Record Maximum Sextant Height		Hs	35°	57.5'
1-2 Record Index Correction (mark sign + if off, - if on)		IC	**Off** + **On** -	0
1-3 Record eye height (HE) and look up Dip Correction on the right-hand side of Table A2, front of Almanac	HE (ft) 9	Dip	-	2.9'
1-4 Record Maximum Sextant Height		Ha	35°	54.6'
1-5 Look up the altitude correction in the center of Table A2, front of the Almanac		Alt corr.	+ -	-1.3
1-6 Sum the above two numbers to get Observed Height		Ho	35°	53.3'

Starpath Form 110 for Polaris Sights

Step 2 Find LHA Aries	GMT date =	11-Jul-82
2-1 GMT Time in Hours, Minutes and Seconds	GMT time =	12:45:03
2-2 Find GHA Aries on Left Hand Daily Page of the Nautical Almanac (far left column) for GMT Day and Hour	GHA Aries (Hr) =	109° 04.1'
2-3 Find GHA Aries minutes correction from Increments and Corrections pages	GHA Aries (Min) =	11° 17.6'
2-4 GHA Aries - Sum the above two numbers	GHA Aries =	120° 21.7'
2-5 DR Longitude (-W, +E)	DR Lon =	134° 11.0'
2-6 LHA Aries (Combine previous numbers)	LHA Aries =	346° 08.9'
Step 3 Latitude Determination		
3-1 HO	HO =	35° 53.3'
3-2 a0 from Polaris Table (using LHA Aries)	a0 =	25.9'
3-3 a1 from Polaris Table (using DR Latitude)	a1 =	0.5'
3-4 a2 from Polaris Table (using Month)	a2 =	0.3'
3-5 Subtract 1 Degree	- 1 =	-1°
3-6 Sum the above five numbers to get LATITUDE	LATITUDE =	35° 20.0'
3.7 Check the value for the Azimuth	Zn =	000.8

Note this reduction uses an actual sight taken (35° 57.5') and gets Lat 35° 20.1'. But we had only two sights and they differed quite a bit (35° 53.3'). So a better Lat is obtained from the average of the two: 35° 55.4'. This lowers the above lat by 2.1' to 35° 18.0'. This average was at about 0543, and we are advancing to 0605 along C210, S4.8. This moves the lat down another 1.5' [(22/60) x 4.8 x cos(30)... or just plot it!] to Lat at 0605 of 35° 16.5', which is what we have plotted.

Problem 10. July 11

Sight 1 — MOON U/L

WT	11 h 08 m 06 s	date	11-Jul-1982	body	MOON U/L	Hs 7° 01.0'
WE +S-F	m 00 s	DR Lat	35° 01' N	log 1181	index corr. + off, - on	00'
ZD +W-E	+7	DR Lon	133° 56' W	HE ft 9	DIP -	-2.9'
GMT	18 h 08 m 06 s	GMT date / LOP label		C- 197 T	Ha 6° 58.1'

Sights #16   11-Jul-1982   S- 4.0 Kt

GHA hr.	206° 36.2'	v moon planets 13.7	DEC hr S 8° 26.3'	d +– -11.5	HP moon 56.0	

GHA + m.s.	1° 56.0'		d corr. +– -1.6'	additional altitude corr. moon, mars, venus + 2.5'
SHA + or v corr.	1.9'	stars or moon, planets	DEC S 8° DEC deg min 24.7'	altitude corr. all sights +- 60.5'
GHA	208° 34.1'			upper limb moon subtract 30' -30'
		tens d 12.4	d upper	Ho T 7° 31.1'
a-Lon -W+E	133° 34.1'	units d 2.5	d lower	
LHA	75° 00' W/60' E	dsd corr. +	dsd	Hc A 7 13.7
		d corr. Pub. 229 14.9		a = 17.4 T

LHA	75	5	tab Hc 7° 28.6'	d +- -36.2	Z 105.3	Zn = 254.7
Dec deg	8	N S S	d corr. Pub.249 & 229 -14.9	Dec min. 24.7		a - Lat = 35° N
a-Lat	35	N S N	Hc 7° 13.7'		6	a - Lon = 133° 34.1'W

N Lat
L.H.A. greater than 180 .... Zn = Z
L.H.A. less than 180 .... Zn = 360 - Z

S Lat
L.H.A. greater than 180 .... Zn = 180 - Z
L.H.A. less than 180 .... Zn = 180 + Z

Sight 2 — SUN L/L

WT	11 h 10 m 23 s	date	11-Jul-1982	body	SUN L/L	Hs 50° 28.0'
WE +S-F	m 00 s	DR Lat	35° 01' N	log 1181	index corr. + off, - on	00'
ZD +W-E	+7	DR Lon	133° 56' W	HE ft 9	DIP -	-2.9'
GMT	18 h 10 m 23 s	GMT date / LOP label		C- 197 T	Ha 50° 25.1'

Sights #16   11-Jul-1982   S- 4.0 Kt

GHA hr.	88° 38.6'	v moon planets -0.7	DEC hr N 22° 04.9'	d +– -0.3	HP moon	

GHA + m.s.	2° 35.8'		d corr. +- -0.1'	additional altitude corr. moon, mars, venus +
SHA + or v corr.	360°	stars or moon, planets	DEC N 22° DEC deg min 04.8'	altitude corr. all sights +- +15.2'
GHA	451° 14.4'			upper limb moon subtract 30'
		tens d 1.6	d upper	Ho T 50° 40.3'
a-Lon -W+E	134° 14.4'	units d 0.6	d lower	
LHA	317° 00' W/60' E	dsd corr. +	dsd	Hc A 50° 25.2'
		d corr. Pub. 229 2.2		a = 15.1 T

LHA	317	5	tab Hc 50° 23.0'	d +- 28.5	Z 97.4	Zn = 097.4
Dec deg	22	N S N	d corr. Pub.249 & 229 02.2	Dec min. 04.8		a - Lat = 35° N
a-Lat	35	N S N	Hc 50° 25.2'		6	a - Lon = 134°14.4' W

Problem 11. July 12

Sight #17

					date	body		Hs		
1	WT	14 h	45 m	57 s	12-Jul-1982	SUN L/L			74 °	44.4 '
	WE +S-F		m	00 s	DR Lat 34° 00' N	log 1271	index corr. + off, - on			00
	ZD +W-E	+7			DR Lon 135° 20' W	HE ft 9	DIP -		-	-2.9
	GMT	21 h	45 m	57 s	GMT date / LOP label	C- 230 T	Ha		74 °	41.5
					Sights #17 12-Jul-1982	S- 7.0 Kt				

					v moon planets	DEC		d	HP moon	
2	GHA hr.	133 °	36.4			N 21 °	55.6 '	-0.4		

						d corr. +-		-0.3	additional altitude corr. moon, mars, venus	+	
3	GHA + m.s.	11 °	29.3 '						altitude corr. all sights	+-	15.7
	SHA + or v corr.	°		stars or moon, planets	DEC N 21	° DEC deg	55.3 min		upper limb moon subtract 30'		
	GHA	145 °	05.7	tens d	46.1	d upper			Ho T	74 °	57.2
				units d	0.3	d lower					
	a-Lon -W+E	135 °	05.7	dsd corr. +		dsd			Hc A	75	03.4
	LHA	10 °	00' W/60' E	d corr. Pub. 229	46.4				a =		6.2 A

					tab Hc	d +-	Z			
4	LHA	10		**5**	74 ° 17.0	50.3	143.2	Zn =	216.8	
	Dec deg	21	N S N		d corr. Pub.249 & 229 46.4	Dec min. 55.3		a - Lat =	34° N	
	a-Lat	34	N S N		Hc 75 ° 03.4			**6** a - Lon =	135° 05.7'W	

N Lat L.H.A. greater than 180 .... Zn = Z
L.H.A. less than 180 .... Zn = 360 - Z

S Lat L.H.A. greater than 180 .... Zn = 180 - Z
L.H.A. less than 180 .... Zn = 180 + Z

Sight #18

					date	body		Hs		
1	WT	16 h	45 m	20 s	12-Jul-1982	SUN L/L			52 °	55.4 '
	WE +S-F		m	00 s	DR Lat 33° 51' N	log 1285	index corr. + off, - on			00
	ZD +W-E	+7			DR Lon 135° 32' W	HE ft 9	DIP -		-	-2.9
	GMT	23 h	45 m	20 s	GMT date / LOP label	C- 230 T	Ha		52 °	52.5
					Sights #18 12-Jul-1982	S- 7.0 Kt				

					v moon planets	DEC		d	HP moon	
2	GHA hr.	163 °	36.3			N 21 °	54.9 '	-0.4		

						d corr. +-		-0.3	additional altitude corr. moon, mars, venus	+	
3	GHA + m.s.	11 °	20 '						altitude corr. all sights	+-	+15.3
	SHA + or v corr.	°		stars or moon, planets	DEC N 21	° DEC deg	54.6 min		upper limb moon subtract 30'		
	GHA	174 °	56.3	tens d	18.2	d upper			Ho T	53 °	07.8
				units d	7.9	d lower					
	a-Lon -W+E	135 °	56.3	dsd corr. +		dsd			Hc A	53 °	44.7
	LHA	39 °	00' W/60' E	d corr. Pub. 229	26.1				a =		36.9 A

					tab Hc	d +-	Z			
4	LHA	39		**5**	53 ° 18.6	28.7	100.5	Zn =	259.5	
	Dec deg	21	N S N		d corr. Pub.249 & 229 26.1	Dec min. 54.6		a - Lat =	34° N	
	a-Lat	34	N S N		Hc 53 ° 44.7			**6** a - Lon =	135°56.3' W	

Problem 12. July 13

Form 1 — KOCHAB

1					
WT	06 h 00 m 18 s	date 13-Jul-1982	body KOCHAB (40)	Hs	23° 00.7'
WE +S-F	m 00 s	DR Lat 33° 10' N	log 1360	index corr. + off, - on	00
ZD +W-E	+7	DR Lon 136° 30' W	HE ft 9	DIP -	-2.9
GMT	13 h 00 m 18 s	GMT date / LOP label	C- 235 T	Ha	22° 57.8'
		Sights #19 13-Jul-1982	S- 5.7 Kt		

2					
GHA ♈ hr.	126° 04.9'	v moon planets	DEC hr N 74° 14.0'	d + −	HP moon

3				
GHA + m.s.	0° 04.5'	d corr. + -		additional altitude corr. moon, mars, venus +
SHA + or v corr.	137° 18.5'	stars or moon, planets	DEC deg N 74° DEC min N 74° 14.0	altitude corr. all sights +- -2.3
GHA	263° 27.9'			upper limb moon subtract 30'
		tens d 09.3	d upper	Ho T 22° 55.5'
a-Lon -W+E	136° 27.9'	units d 0.3	d lower	
LHA	127° 00' W/60' E	dsd corr. +	dsd	Hc A 22 46.1
		d corr. Pub. 229 09.6		a = 9.4 T

4					
LHA	127	5 tab Hc 22° 36.5'	d +- 41.1 Z 13.8	Zn =	346.2
Dec deg	74 N/S N	d corr. Pub.249 & 229 09.6	Dec min 14.0	a - Lat =	33° N
a-Lat	33 N/S N	Hc 22° 46.1'		6 a - Lon =	136° 27.9'W

N Lat   L.H.A. greater than 180 .... Zn = Z
L.H.A. less than 180 .... Zn = 360 - Z

S Lat   L.H.A. greater than 180 .... Zn = 180 - Z
L.H.A. less than 180 .... Zn = 180 + Z

Form 2 — VENUS

1					
WT	06 h 19 m 57 s	date 13-Jul-1982	body VENUS	Hs	15° 14.4'
WE +S-F	m 00 s	DR Lat 33° 10' N	log 1362	index corr. + off, - on	00
ZD +W-E	+7	DR Lon 136° 30' W	HE ft 9	DIP -	-2.9
GMT	13 h 19 m 57 s	GMT date / LOP label	C- 235 T	Ha	15° 11.5'
		Sights #19 13-Jul-1982	S- 5.7 Kt		

2					
GHA hr.	45° 19.4'	v moon planets -0.7	DEC hr N 22° 04.7'	d + − +0.3	HP moon

3				
GHA + m.s.	4° 59.3'	d corr. + - 0.1		additional altitude corr. moon, mars, venus + 0.1
SHA + or v corr.	360° -0.2'	stars or moon, planets	DEC deg N 22° DEC min 04.8	altitude corr. all sights +- -3.5
GHA	410° 18.5'			upper limb moon subtract 30'
		tens d 20 1.6	d upper	Ho T 15° 08.1'
a-Lon -W+E	136° 18.5'	units d 9.9 0.7	d lower	
LHA	274° 00' W/60' E	dsd corr. +	dsd	Hc A 15° 00.3'
		d corr. Pub. 229 2.3		a = 7.8 T

4					
LHA	274	tab Hc 14° 58.0'	d +- 29.9 Z 73.2	Zn =	073.2
Dec deg	22 N/S N	d corr. Pub.249 & 229 02.3	Dec min 04.8	a - Lat =	33° N
a-Lat	33 N/S N	Hc 15° 00.3'		a - Lon =	136°18.5' W

Note: The Kochab form is just an example of star sight reduction. We chose to not use the Kochab sights because the horizon was poor (taken before nautical twilight; it was just too dark) and this did indeed reflect in the results. So this fix is from Moon and Venus only.

Problem 12. July 13 - Cont.

1	WT	06 h	42 m	22 s	date	13-Jul-1982	body	**MOON L/L**		Hs	53 °	52.8 '
	WE +S-F		m	00 s	DR Lat	33° 10' N	log	1364		index corr. + off, - on		00 '
	ZD +W-E	+7			DR Lon	136° 30' W	HE ft	9		DIP -	−	-2.9 '
	GMT	13 h	42 m	22 s	GMT date / LOP label		C-	235 T		Ha	53 °	49.9 '
					Sights #19 13-Jul-1982		S-	5.7 Kt				

2	GHA hr.	111 °	54.6 '	v moon planets	13.1	DEC hr	N 0 °	19.4 '	d +−	12.8	HP moon	57.2	

3	GHA + m.s.	10 °	06.5 '			d corr. +−		9.1	additional altitude corr. moon, mars, venus	+	4.5
	SHA + or v corr.	360 °	9.3 '	stars or moon, planets	DEC deg	N 0 °	DEC min	28.5	altitude corr. all sights	+-	44.0
	GHA	482 °	10.4 '						upper limb moon subtract 30'		'
				tens d	23.8	d upper			Ho **T**	54 °	38.4 '
	a-Lon -W+E	136 °	10.4 '	units d	2.9	d lower					
	LHA	346 °	00' W/60' E	dsd corr.	+	dsd			Hc **A**	54	54.6
				d corr.	Pub. 229	26.7			a =		16.2 A

4	LHA	346		**5**	tab Hc	54 °	27.9 '	d +−	56.1	Z	155.4		Zn =		155.4
	Dec deg	0	N S	N	d corr.	Pub.249 & 229	26.7	Dec min.	28.5	a - Lat =	33° N
	a-Lat	33	N S	N	Hc	54 °	54.6 '			**6** a - Lon =	**136° 10.4'W**

N Lat   L.H.A. greater than 180 .... Zn = Z
         L.H.A. less than 180 .... Zn = 360 - Z

S Lat   L.H.A. greater than 180 .... Zn = 180 - Z
         L.H.A. less than 180 .... Zn = 180 + Z

Problem 13. July 13

Sight #1

1					
WT	15ʰ 03ᵐ 34ˢ	date	13-Jul-1982	body	SUN L/L
WE +S-F	ᵐ 00ˢ	DR Lat	32° 29' N	log	1412
ZD +W-E	+7	DR Lon	136° 20' W	HE ft 9	
GMT	22ʰ 03ᵐ 34ˢ	GMT date / LOP label	Sights #20 13-Jul-1982	C- 170 T S- 6.3 Kt	

Hs	73° 48.4'
index corr. + off, - on	00
DIP -	-2.9
Ha	73° 45.5

| 2 | GHA hr. | 148° 34.5 | v moon planets | | DEC hr | N 21° 46.6' | d +- | -0.4 | HP moon | |

3	GHA + m.s.	0° 53.5'		d corr. +-	0	additional altitude corr. moon, mars, venus	+
	SHA + or v corr.	°	stars or moon, planets	DEC deg	N 21° DEC 46.6' min	altitude corr. all sights	+- 15.7
	GHA	149° 28.0	Must use 229 due to 74° Dec	tens d	31.1	d upper	upper limb moon subtract 30'
				units d	1.9	d lower	Ho T 74° 1.2
	a-Lon -W+E	136° 28.0		dsd corr. +		dsd	
	LHA	13° 00' W/60' E		d corr. Pub. 229	33.0		Hc A 74 33.9

4	LHA	13				a = 32.7 A
	Dec deg	21 N/S N	5	tab Hc	74° 00.9	d +- 42.4	Z 130.3	Zn = 229.7
	a-Lat	32 N/S N		d corr. Pub.249 & 229	33.0	Dec min. 46.6	a - Lat = 32° N
				Hc	74° 33.9	6	a - Lon = 136° 28.0'W

N Lat L.H.A. greater than 180 .... Zn = Z
L.H.A. less than 180 .... Zn = 360 - Z

S Lat L.H.A. greater than 180 .... Zn = 180 - Z
L.H.A. less than 180 .... Zn = 180 + Z

Sight #2

1					
WT	17ʰ 41ᵐ 37ˢ	date	13-Jul-1982	body	SUN L/L
WE +S-F	ᵐ 00ˢ	DR Lat	32° 13' N	log	1429
ZD +W-E	+7	DR Lon	136° 17' W	HE ft 9	
GMT	0ʰ 41ᵐ 37ˢ	GMT date / LOP label	Sights #21 14-Jul-1982	C- 170 T S- 6.3 Kt	

Hs	42° 6.1'
index corr. + off, - on	00
DIP -	-2.9
Ha	42° 03.2

| 2 | GHA hr. | 178° 34.4 | v moon planets | | DEC hr | N 21° 45.8' | d +- | -0.4 | HP moon | |

3	GHA + m.s.	10° 24.3'		d corr. +-	-0.3	additional altitude corr. moon, mars, venus	+
	SHA + or v corr.	°	stars or moon, planets	DEC deg	N 21° DEC 45.5' min	altitude corr. all sights	+- 14.9
	GHA	188° 58.7		tens d	20 15.2	d upper	upper limb moon subtract 30'
				units d	4.7 3.6	d lower	Ho T 42° 18.1
	a-Lon -W+E	135° 58.7		dsd corr. +		dsd	
	LHA	53° 00' W/60' E		d corr. Pub. 229	18.8		Hc A 42° 06.1

4	LHA	53				a = 12.0 T
	Dec deg	21 N/S N	5	tab Hc	41° 47.3	d +- 24.7	Z 89.5	Zn = 270.5
	a-Lat	32 N/S N		d corr. Pub.249 & 229	18.8	Dec min. 45.5	a - Lat = 32° N
				Hc	42° 06.1	6	a - Lon = 135°58.7' W

Problem 14. July 14

Sight 1

1 WT	14 h 15 m 06 s	date	14-Jul-1982	body	SUN L/L	Hs 80° 57.7'
WE +S-F	m 00 s	DR Lat	30° 31' N	log	1554	index corr. + off, - on 00
ZD +W-E	+7	DR Lon	137° 15' W	HE ft 9	DIP - -2.9
GMT	21 h 15 m 06 s	GMT date / LOP label		C- 205 T	Ha 80° 54.8
		Sights #22 14-Jul-1982		S- 6.1 Kt	

2							
GHA hr.	133° 32.9	v moon planets		DEC hr	N 21° 37.9	d +- -0.4	HP moon

3					
GHA + m.s.	3° 46.5	d corr. +-	-0.1	additional altitude corr. moon, mars, venus	+
SHA + or v corr.	°	stars or moon, planets	DEC deg N 21° / DEC min 37.8	altitude corr. all sights	+- 15.8
GHA	137° 19.4	tens d * / units d *	d upper / d lower	upper limb moon subtract 30'	
		dsd corr. +	dsd	Ho **T**	81° 10.6
a-Lon -W+E	137° 19.4	d corr. Pub. 229	37.8	Hc **A**	80° 37.8
LHA	0° 00' W/60' E			a =	32.8 T

4 / 5					
LHA	0	**5** tab Hc 80° 00.0	d +- 60.0 Z 180	Zn =	180.0
Dec deg	21 N/S N	d corr. Pub.249 & 229 37.8	Dec min. 37.8	a - Lat =	31° N
a-Lat	31 N/S N	Hc 80° 37.8		**6** a - Lon =	137°19.4'W

N Lat   L.H.A. greater than 180 .... Zn = Z
L.H.A. less than 180 .... Zn = 360 - Z

S Lat   L.H.A. greater than 180 .... Zn = 180 - Z
L.H.A. less than 180 .... Zn = 180 + Z

Sight 2

1 WT	14 h 18 m 32 s	date	14-Jul-1982	body	SUN L/L	Hs 80° 55.4'
WE +S-F	m 00 s	DR Lat	30° 31' N	log	1554	index corr. + off, - on 00
ZD +W-E	+7	DR Lon	137° 15' W	HE ft 9	DIP - -2.9
GMT	21 h 18 m 32 s	GMT date / LOP label		C- 205 T	Ha 80° 52.5
		Sights #22 14-Jul-1982		S- 6.1 Kt	

2							
GHA hr.	133° 32.9	v moon planets		DEC hr	N 21° 37.9	d +- -0.4	HP moon

3					
GHA + m.s.	4° 38.0	d corr. +-	-0.1	additional altitude corr. moon, mars, venus	+
SHA + or v corr.	°	stars or moon, planets	DEC deg N 21° / DEC min 37.8	altitude corr. all sights	+- 15.8
GHA	138° 10.9	tens d 31.5 / units d 6.1	d upper / d lower	upper limb moon subtract 30'	
		dsd corr. +	dsd	Ho **T**	81° 08.3
a-Lon -W+E	137° 10.9	d corr. Pub. 229	37.6	Hc **A**	80° 35.2
LHA	1° 00' W/60' E			a =	33.1 T

4 / 5					
LHA	1	**5** tab Hc 79° 57.6	d +- 59.7 Z 174.6	Zn =	** 185.7
Dec deg	21 N/S N	d corr. Pub.249 & 229 37.6	Dec min. 37.8 ** -0.3	a - Lat =	31° N
a-Lat	31 N/S N	Hc 80° 35.2		**6** a - Lon =	137°10.9' W

* With d=60, there is no need for the interpolation tables, as the Hc then scales directly with the minutes part of the declination.
** Interpolating for dec, the Z goes from 174.6 to 174.3, with a corresponding Zn = 185.7.

This fix is plotted in the Plotted Workforms section, but it is also plotted on the next page using the interpolated Z values and an expanded scale. Also shown is another approach of plotting computed solutions from the DR position on an even more expanded scale.

Azimuth Interpolation Example

Problem 14, Expanded Solution

This problem has two sunlines, just 3 minutes apart, but the sun is high and crossing the meridian at the time, so we can hope for some modest separation in azimuth, and with that at least an approximate fix from the intersection of two LOPS, separated by just 5° or so.

This type of narrow-angle fix has enhanced uncertainty because a small error in a-values or Zn creates a scissors effect of a large shift in the intersection location.

Thus this type of fix is best done by computation, including a computation of the intersection. We provided that answer in the Solutions by Computation section. The goal now is to see how well we can reproduce that using tables alone, which is how these problems are solved by many navigators routinely, and by anyone if their computer fails. All USCG exams require this as well.

The main issue is the azimuth angle Z, because we round things off to get access to the table data. We round off the DR-Lat to get a-Lat, but that is not a problem, since we are plotting from the a-Lat position.

We also round off declination, and then proceed to make a correction to Hc for the declination increments (dec'), but we do not often need to adjust the Z, although it is always a good idea to check it. In narrow fixes like this example, it is crucial to interpolate to get the most accurate Z. Figure best Z = Z(dec°) + [Z(dec°+1) - Z(dec°)] x (dec'/60). In our example Z = 174.6 + [174.1 - 174.6] x (37.8/60) = 174.6 - 0.3 = 174.3. Then find Zn = 360 - Z.

An alternative shortcut when not crucial, is just look at dec'. If they are much larger than 30' take the Z from dec° + 1, but remember we must always use Hc at dec°.

The main message is to keep an eye on Z if the plotting is crucial. High altitude sights can call for a large correction.

We also round off the LHA by judicious choice of a-Lon, but this does not affect Hc or Z in this case because we are plotting from the assumed position.

On the other hand, if your task is to find an accurate Z for a compass check using Pub 229 from a known or DR position, then you must do a *triple* interpolation of the Pub 229 result: for lat, dec, and LHA. Do that just a few times, and you will shortly be looking for a computer solution to the job. USCG exams require doing this by hand–it is their way of supporting navigation schools.

Compute and Plot from DR

On the next page, we show another approach to accurate position plotting that is best done by computation. Namely we compute the Hc and Zn for each sight from the DR position, and then plot from this DR position on an expanded scale. In this example, we have for the 1415 sight: a-Lat = DR-Lat = 30° 31'N, dec = N21° 37.8', and LHA = GHA - DR-Lon = 137° 19.4'-137° 15' =000° 04.4'. Then compute Hc = 81° 06.8' and Zn = 180.4, and for 1418: a-Lat = 30° 31'N, dec = N21° 37.8', LHA = 138° 10.9' - 137° 15' =000° 55.9'. This then will give you Hc = 81° 04.4' and Zn = 185.6°. You can compute online at starpath.com/calc. There are numerous free and commercial programs available for computers and mobile devices.

Combine these Hc with the measured Ho to get

$$1415: a = 3.8T\ 180.4$$

$$1418: a = 3.9T\ 185.6$$

These are the values plotted on the next page from the DR position of 30° 31'N, 137° 15' W.

Sometimes if the DR is off, we do a standard analysis to get a fix, then call this fix the new DR, and then do the above computations. This guarantees small a-values that will fit nicely onto an expanded plot sheet, usually 6' per parallel on standard universal plotting sheets. All sights of the original voyage were done that way at the time of the passage, after a fit-slope analysis to check their consistency (see Analysis section.). We have not, however, followed that procedure in this book.

Pub 229	
Lat 31° & LHA 359°, 1°	
Dec.	Z
21°	174.6
21° 37.8'	174.3
22°	174.1

Pub 229	
Lat 31° & LHA 360°, 0°	
Dec.	Z
21°	180
21° 37.8'	180
22°	180

Above. *The values in the gray boxes are interpolations for Z (azimuth angle) from the tabulated data in Pub 229.*

Right. *Sample selection from Pub. 229.*

When we plot, we need the azimuth (Zn) which is determined by Z and the LHA by rules repeated on each of the workforms.

1°, 359° L.H.A.			LATITUDE SAME NAME											
	30°			31°			32°			33°				
Dec.	Hc	d	Z	Hc	d	Z	Hc	d	Z	Hc	d	Z	Hc	
°	° '	'	°	° '	'	°	° '	'	°	° '	'	°	° '	
0	59 59.1	+60.0	178.0	58 59.1	+60.0	178.1	57 59.2	+59.9	178.1	56 59.2	+60.0	178.2	55 59.	
1	60 59.1	+59.9	177.9	59 59.1	+60.0	178.0	73 58.1	+89.9	178.1	72 58.3	+59.9	178.1	71 58.	
17	76 58.1	+59.8	175.8	75 58.2	+59.9	176.1	74 58.4	+59.9	176.3	73 58.5	+59.9	176.5	72 58.	
18	77 57.9	+59.9	175.4	76 58.1	+59.9	175.8	75 58.3	+59.8	176.1	74 58.4	+59.9	176.3	73 58.	
19	78 57.8	+59.8	175.1	77 58.0	+59.8	175.5	76 58.1	+59.9	175.8	75 58.3	+59.9	176.1	74 58.	
20	79 57.6	+59.7	174.6	78 57.8	+59.8	175.1	77 58.0	+59.8	175.5	76 58.2	+59.8	175.8	75 58.	
21	80 57.3	+59.7	174.1	79 57.6	+59.7	174.6	78 57.8	+59.8	175.1	77 58.0	+59.9	175.5	76 58.	
22	81 57.0	+59.6	173.4	80 57.3	+59.7	174.1	79 57.6	+59.8	174.7	78 57.9	+59.8	175.2	77 58.	
23	82 56.6	+59.5	172.5	81 57.0	+59.6	173.4	80 57.4	+59.7	174.1	79 57.7	+59.7	174.7	78 57.	
24	83 56.1	+59.2	171.3	82 56.6	+59.5	172.5	81 57.1	+59.6	173.5	80 57.4	+59.7	174.2	79 57.	

Expanded Plot Example

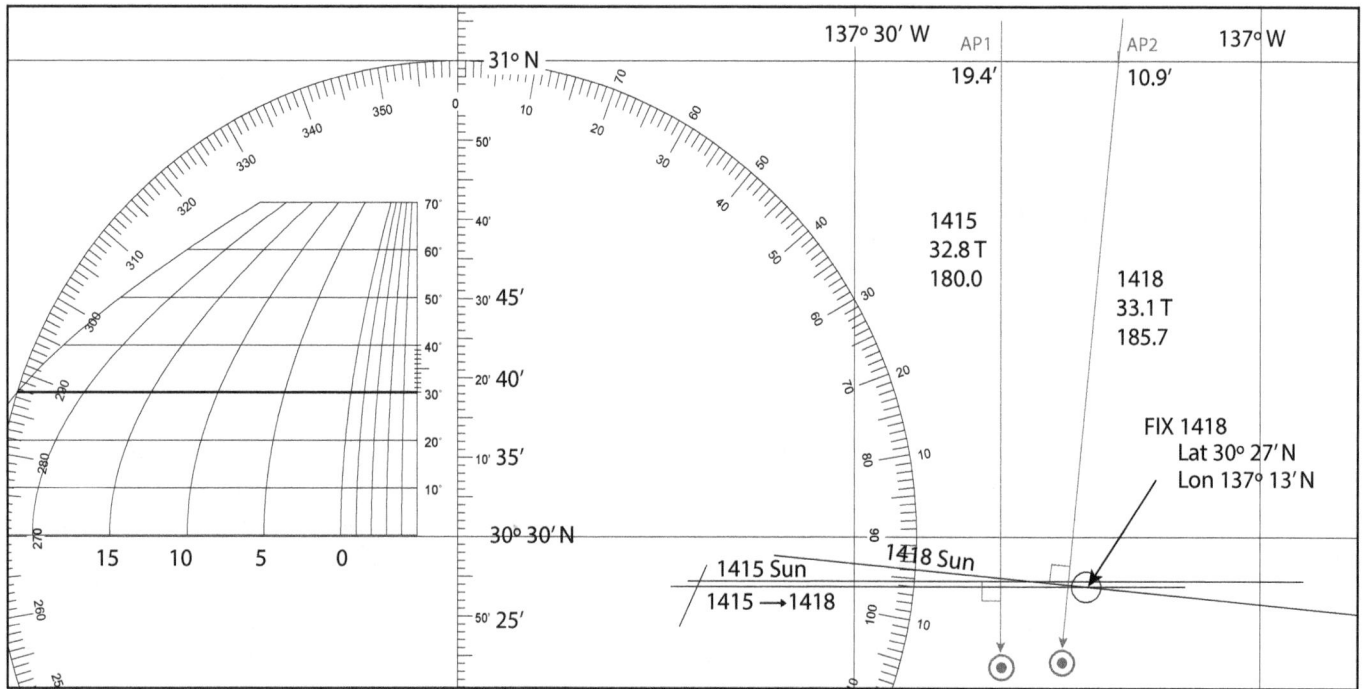

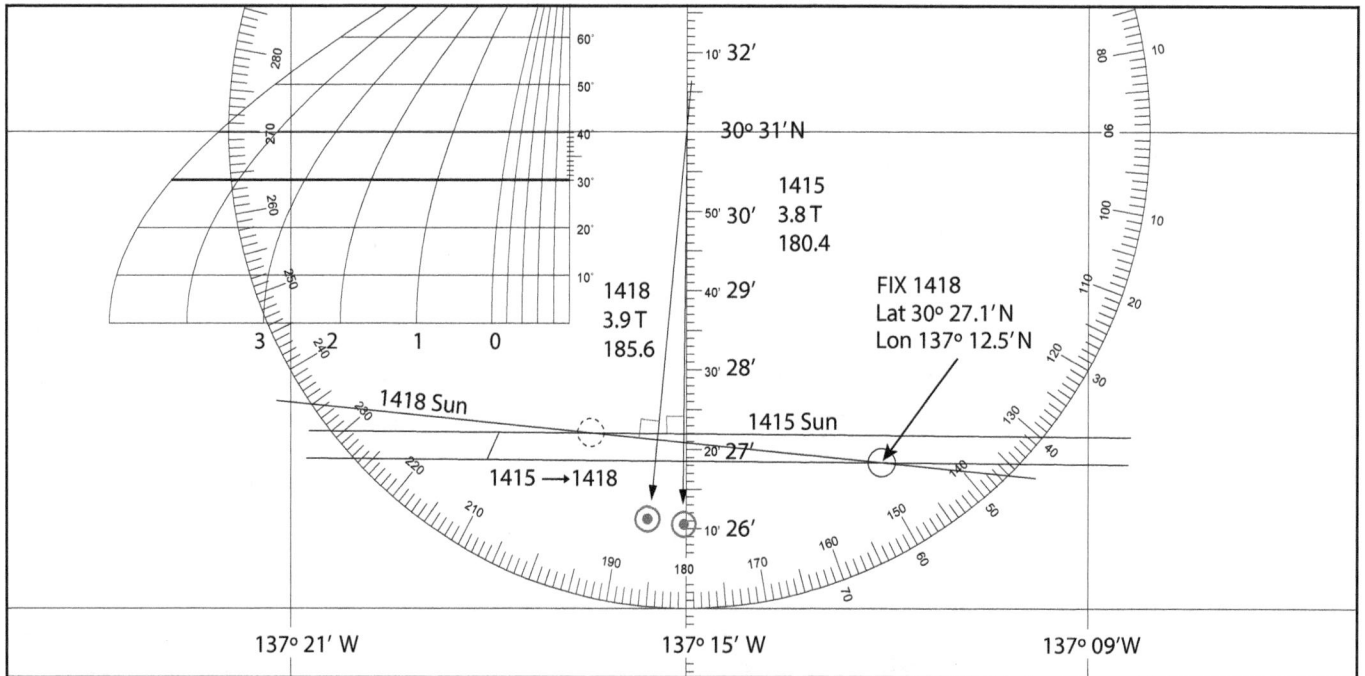

A narrow-intersection fix. *An expanded plot of Sights #22 using interpolated Z values. We gained about 13' of longitude accuracy with a careful plot including correction for the 3-min run between sights (S6.1, C205). We get more confidence and improved accuracy with a still bigger expansion, which we can achieve by plotting from the DR position, as shown in the lower plot. We used a similar procedure for all sights in the actual voyage. Namely, find a fix from standard methods, then call that fix the new DR position, then analyze the sights from that DR and plot on an expanded scale (6' per parallel) centered on that DR position. Other examples of this type of plot are shown on pages 63 and 71.*

The improved position has been transferred to the ongoing series of plotting sheets in the Plotted Workform Solutions.

Sights #22 Solutions compared	
Standard scale plot	30° 27' N, 137° 26' W
Expanded	30° 27.0' N, 137° 13' W
Much expanded	30° 27.0' N, 137° 12.5' W
Computed (17:41:00)	30° 27.1' N, 137° 12.0' W

Problem 15. July 15

Sight #1 — MOON L/L

1	WT	07 h 28 m 04 s	date 15-Jul-1982	body **MOON L/L**
	WE +S-F	m 00 s	DR Lat 30° 05' N	log 1682
	ZD +W-E	+7	DR Lon 139° 40' W	HE ft 9
	GMT	14 h 28 m 04 s	GMT date / LOP label	C- 260 T
			Sights #23 15-Jul-1982	S- 7.5 Kt

Hs 55° 33.7'
index corr. + off, - on 00
DIP - -2.9
Ha 55° 30.8'

2	GHA hr.	103° 04.1'	v moon planets 10.1	DEC hr N 10° 39.5'	d +- 12.0	HP moon 58.9

3	GHA + m.s.	6° 41.8'	d corr. +- 5.7	additional altitude corr. moon, mars, venus + 6.0
	SHA + or v corr.	360° 4.8'	stars or moon, planets / DEC deg N 10° DEC min 45.2'	altitude corr. all sights +- 42.7
	GHA	469° 50.7'		upper limb moon subtract 30'
			tens d 22.6 / d upper	Ho T 56° 19.5'
			units d 6.1 / d lower	
	a-Lon -W+E	139° 50.7'	dsd corr. + / dsd	Hc A 56 06.6
	LHA	330° 00' W/60' E	d corr. Pub. 229 28.7	a = 12.9 T

4	LHA	330			tab Hc 55° 37.9'	d +- 38.1	Z 119.3	Zn = 119.3
	Dec deg	10	N S	N	d corr. Pub.249 & 229 28.7	Dec min. 45.2		a - Lat = 30° N
	a-Lat	30	N S	N	Hc 56° 06.6'		**6**	a - Lon = 139°50.7'W

N Lat   L.H.A. greater than 180 .... Zn = Z
L.H.A. less than 180 .... Zn = 360 - Z

S Lat   L.H.A. greater than 180 .... Zn = 180 - Z
L.H.A. less than 180 .... Zn = 180 + Z

Sight #2 — SUN L/L

1	WT	09 h 17 m 01 s	date 15-Jul-1982	body **SUN L/L**
	WE +S-F	m 00 s	DR Lat 30° 00' N	log 1696
	ZD +W-E	+7	DR Lon 139° 54' W	HE ft 9
	GMT	16 h 17 m 01 s	GMT date / LOP label	C- 240 T
			Sights #24 15-Jul-1982	S- 7.5 Kt

Hs 21° 5.1'
index corr. + off, - on 00
DIP - -2.9
Ha 21° 02.2'

2	GHA hr.	58° 31.7'	v moon planets	DEC hr N 21° 30.5'	d +- -0.4	HP moon

3	GHA + m.s.	4° 15.3'	d corr. +- -0.1	additional altitude corr. moon, mars, venus +
	SHA + or v corr.	360°	stars or moon, planets / DEC deg N 21° DEC min 30.4'	altitude corr. all sights +- 13.5
	GHA	422° 47.0'		upper limb moon subtract 30'
			tens d 10.1 / d upper	Ho T 21° 15.7'
			units d 2.7 / d lower	
	a-Lon -W+E	139° 47.0'	dsd corr. + / dsd	Hc A 21° 22.7'
	LHA	283° 00' W/60' E	d corr. Pub. 229 12.8	a = 7.0 A

4	LHA	283			tab Hc 21° 09.9'	d +- 25.4	Z 77.3	Zn = 077.3
	Dec deg	21	N S	N	d corr. Pub.249 & 229 12.8	Dec min. 30.4		a - Lat = 30° N
	a-Lat	30	N S	N	Hc 21° 22.7'		**6**	a - Lon = 139°47.0' W

Note when plotting this fix, there is a small course change between the two sights.

Problem 16. July 15

Sights #25

1	WT	10ʰ 52ᵐ 26ˢ	date 15-Jul-1982	body Sun L/L	Hs	41° 20.4
	WE +S-F	ᵐ 0 ˢ	DR Lat 29° 42' N	log 1710	index corr. + off, - on	0
	ZD +W-E	7	DR Lon 140° 03' W	HE ft 9	DIP -	-2.9
	GMT	17ʰ 52ᵐ 26ˢ	GMT date / LOP label	C- 233 T	Ha	41° 17.5
			Sights #25 15-Jul-1982	S- 7.4 Kt		

2	GHA hr.	73° 31.6	v moon planet	DEC hr N 21° 30.1	d +- -0.4	HP moor

3	GHA + m.s.	13° 6.5	d corr +- -0.4	additional altitude corr. moon, mars, venus +	
	SHA + or v corr.	360°	stars or moon, planets / DEC deg N 21° / DEC min 29.7	altitude corr. all sights +- +14.9	
	GHA	446° 38.1	upper limb moon subtract 30'		
			tens d 9.9 / d upper	Ho T	41° 32.4
	a-Lon -W+E	140° 38.1	units d 1.1 / d lower		
	LHA	306° 00' W/60' E	dsd corr + / dsd	Hc A	41° 03.5
			d corr Pub. 229 11.0	a =	28.9 T

4	LHA	306	5 tab Hc 40° 52.5	d +- 22.2	Z 87.3	Zn = 087.3
	Dec deg	21 N/S N	d corr Pub.249 & 229 11.0	Dec min 29.7		a - Lat = 30° N
	a-Lat	30 N/S N	Hc 41° 03.5		6	a - Lon = 140° 38.1W

N Lat   L.H.A. greater than 180 .... Zn = Z
L.H.A. less than 180 .... Zn = 360 - Z

S Lat   L.H.A. greater than 180 .... Zn = 180 - Z
L.H.A. less than 180 .... Zn = 180 + Z

Sights #26

1	WT	13ʰ 38ᵐ 05ˢ	date 15-Jul-1982	body Sun L/L	Hs	76° 5.4
	WE +S-F	ᵐ 0 ˢ	DR Lat 29° 29' N	log 1730	index corr. + off, - on	0
	ZD +W-E	7	DR Lon 140° 24' W	HE ft 9	DIP -	-2.9
	GMT	20ʰ 38ᵐ 05ˢ	GMT date / LOP label	C- 233 T	Ha	76° 2.5
			Sights #26 15-Jul-1982	S- 7.4 Kt		

2	GHA hr.	118° 31.4	v moon planet	DEC hr N 21° 28.9	d +- -0.4	HP moor

3	GHA + m.s.	9° 31.3	d corr +- -0.3	additional altitude corr. moon, mars, venus +	
	SHA + or v corr.	360°	stars or moon, planets / DEC deg N 21° / DEC min 28.6	altitude corr. all sights +- 15.7	
	GHA	488° 02.7	upper limb moon subtract 30'		
			tens d 14.3 / d upper 41.4	Ho T	76° 18.2
	a-Lon -W+E	140° 02.7	units d 4.3 / d lower 36.4		
	LHA	348° 00' W/60' E	dsd corr + 0.3 / dsd 5.0	Hc A	76° 15.0
			d corr Pub. 229 18.9	a =	3.2 T

4	LHA	348	5 tab Hc 75° 56.1	d +- 39.1	Z 127.0	Zn = 127.0
	Dec deg	21 N/S N	d corr Pub.249 & 229 18.9	Dec min 28.6		a - Lat = 30° N
	a-Lat	30 N/S N	Hc 76° 15.0		6	a - Lon = 140° 02.7' W

Problem 17. July 16

Sight 1 — Deneb (53)

1	WT	06 h	55 m	50 s	date	16-Jul-1982	body	Deneb (53)	Hs	47°	23.0'
	WE +S-F		m	0 s	DR Lat	28° 33' N	log	1863	index corr. + off, - on		0
	ZD +W-E	7			DR Lon	142° 41' W	HE ft	9	DIP -	-	-2.9
	GMT	13 h	55 m	50 s	GMT date / LOP label		C-	245 T	Ha	47°	20.1
					Sights #27	16-Jul-1982	S-	7.7 Kt			

2	GHA ᵧ hr.	129°	02.3'	v moon planets		DEC hr		d +–		HP moon	

3	GHA + m.s.	13°	59.8'			d corr. + -			additional altitude corr. moon, mars, venus	+	
	SHA + or v corr.	49°	47.2'	stars or moon, planets		DEC deg	N 45	DEC min 13.0	altitude corr. all sights	+-	-0.9
	GHA	192°	49.3'						upper limb moon subtract 30'		
				tens d	0	d upper			Ho T	47°	19.2
	a-Lon -W+E	142°	49.3'	units d	1.5	d lower					
	LHA	50°	00' W/60' E	dsd corr.	+	dsd			Hc A	47°	08.2
				d corr. Pub. 229	1.5				a =	11 T	

4	LHA	50			5	tab Hc	47°	9.7'	d +-	-6.6	Z 52.8	Zn =	307.2
	Dec deg	45	N S	N		d corr. Pub.249 & 229		-1.5	Dec min.	13.0		a - Lat =	28° N
	a-Lat	28	N S	N		Hc	47°	08.2'				6	a - Lon = 142° 49.3' W

N Lat — L.H.A. greater than 180 .... Zn = Z
L.H.A. less than 180 .... Zn = 360 - Z

S Lat — L.H.A. greater than 180 .... Zn = 180 - Z
L.H.A. less than 180 .... Zn = 180 + Z

Sight 2 — Venus

1	WT	06 h	58 m	30 s	date	16-Jul-1982	body	Venus	Hs	15°	56.0'
	WE +S-F		m	0 s	DR Lat	28° 33' N	log	1863	index corr. + off, - on		0
	ZD +W-E	7			DR Lon	142° 41' W	HE ft	9	DIP -	-	-2.9
	GMT	13 h	58 m	30 s	GMT date / LOP label		C-	245 T	Ha	15°	53.1
					Sights #27	16-Jul-1982	S-	7.7 Kt			

2	GHA hr.	44°	24.7'	v moon planets	-0.8	DEC hr	N 22°	23.3	d +–	+0.2	HP moon	

3	GHA + m.s.	14°	37.5'			d corr. + -		0.2	additional altitude corr. moon, mars, venus	+	+0.1
	SHA + or v corr.	360°	-0.8	stars or moon, planets		DEC deg	N 22	DEC min 23.5	altitude corr. all sights	+-	-3.4
	GHA	419°	01.4'						upper limb moon subtract 30'		
				tens d	7.8	d upper			Ho T	15°	49.8
	a-Lon -W+E	143°	01.4'	units d	1.9	d lower					
	LHA	276°	00' W/60' E	dsd corr.	+	dsd			Hc A	15°	19.0
				d corr. Pub. 229	9.7				a = 30.8 T		

4	LHA	276			5	tab Hc	15°	9.3'	d +-	24.8	Z 72.8	Zn =	072.8
	Dec deg	22	N S	N		d corr. Pub.249 & 229		9.7	Dec min.	23.5		a - Lat =	28° N
	a-Lat	28	N S	N		Hc	15°	19.0'				6	a - Lon = 143° 01.4' W

Problem 17. July 16 - Cont.

1	WT	07 h	14 m	25 s	date	16-Jul-1982	body	MOON L/L	Hs	42 °	6.8 '
	WE +S-F		m	0 s	DR Lat	28° 33' N	log	1865	index corr. + off, - on		0 '
	ZD +W-E	7			DR Lon	142° 41' W	HE ft	9	DIP -	-	-2.9 '
	GMT	14 h	14 m	25 s	GMT date / LOP label		C-	245 T	Ha	42 °	3.9 '
						Sights #27 16-Jul-1982	S-	7.7 Kt			

2	GHA hr.	90 °	17.1	v moon planets	7.9	DEC hr	N 15 °	13.4	d +−	10.5	HP moon	59.7

3	GHA + m.s.	3 °	26.4 '			d corr. +−		2.5	additional altitude corr. moon, mars, venus	+	7.0
	SHA + or v corr.	360 °	1.9	stars or moon, planets		DEC deg	N 15 °	DEC min 15.9	altitude corr. all sights	+−	52.4 '
	GHA	453 °	45.4						upper limb moon subtract 30'		
				tens d	5.3	d upper		Ho **T**		43 °	03.3
	a-Lon -W+E	142 °	45.4 '	units d	1.1	d lower					
	LHA	311 °	00' W/60' E	dsd corr.	+	dsd		Hc **A**		43 °	01.9
				d corr.	Pub. 229 6.4			a =			1.4 T

4	LHA	311			**5**	tab Hc	42 °	55.5	d +− 24.4	Z 95.4	Zn =	095.4
	Dec deg	15	N S	N		d corr.	Pub.249 & 229	6.4	Dec min 15.9	a - Lat =	28° N
	a-Lat	28	N S	N		Hc	43 °	01.9 '	**6**	a - Lon = 142° 45.4' W

N Lat   L.H.A. greater than 180 .... Zn = Z
        L.H.A. less than 180 .... Zn = 360 - Z

S Lat   L.H.A. greater than 180 .... Zn = 180 - Z
        L.H.A. less than 180 .... Zn = 180 + Z

Problem 18. July 16

Form 1 — Jupiter

1	WT	21ʰ 58ᵐ 17ˢ	date	16-Jul-1982	body	Jupiter	Hs	48° 32.7
	WE +S-F	ᵐ 0ˢ	DR Lat	27° 47' N	log	1979	index corr. + off, - on	0
	ZD +W-E	7	DR Lon	144° 40' W	HE ft	9	DIP -	-2.9
	GMT	4ʰ 58ᵐ 17ˢ	GMT date / LOP label	17 July '82	C- 247 T S- 7.7 Kt		Ha	48° 29.8

2	GHA hr.	145° 23.0	v moon planets	2.3	DEC hr	S 10° 43.9	d +-	0.1	HP moon	

3	GHA + m.s.	14° 34.3			d corr. +-		0.1	additional altitude corr. moon, mars, venus	+
	SHA + or v corr.	2.2	stars or moon, planets		DEC deg	S 10	DEC min 44.0	altitude corr. all sights +-	-0.9
	GHA	159° 59.5						upper limb moon subtract 30'	
			tens d	50	36.6	d upper		Ho **T**	48° 28.9
			units d	6.3	4.7	d lower			
	a-Lon -W+E	144° 59.5	dsd corr.	+		dsd		Hc **A**	48° 38.0
	LHA	15° 00' W/60' E	d corr.	Pub. 229	41.3			a =	9.1 A

4	LHA	15			**5** tab Hc	49° 19.3	d +- -56.3	Z 157.0	Zn =	203.0
	Dec deg	10	N S	S	d corr. Pub.249 & 229	-41.3	Dec min 44.0	dZ 0.37 Zn 157.4	a - Lat =	28° N
	a-Lat	28	N S	N	Hc	48° 38.0		**6**	a - Lon =	144° 59.5' W

N Lat L.H.A. greater than 180 .... Zn = Z
L.H.A. less than 180 .... Zn = 360 - Z

S Lat L.H.A. greater than 180 .... Zn = 180 - Z
L.H.A. less than 180 .... Zn = 180 + Z

Form 2 — Vega (49)

1	WT	22ʰ 13ᵐ 00ˢ	date	16-Jul-1982	body	Vega (49)	Hs	46° 57.6
	WE +S-F	ᵐ 0ˢ	DR Lat	27° 46' N	log	1981	index corr. + off, - on	0
	ZD +W-E	7	DR Lon	144° 42' W	HE ft	9	DIP -	-2.9
	GMT	5ʰ 13ᵐ 00ˢ	GMT date / LOP label	17 July '82	C- 247 T S- 7.7 Kt		Ha	46° 54.7

2	GHA γ hr.	9° 41.7	v moon planets		DEC hr		d +-		HP moon	

3	GHA + m.s.	363° 15.5			d corr. +-			additional altitude corr. moon, mars, venus	+
	SHA + or v corr.	80° 54.5	stars or moon, planets		DEC deg	N 38	DEC min 46.1	altitude corr. all sights +-	-0.9
	GHA	453° 51.7						upper limb moon subtract 30'	
			tens d		0	d upper		Ho **T**	46° 53.8
			units d	1.9	1.5	d lower			
	a-Lon -W+E	144° 51.7	dsd corr.	+		dsd		Hc **A**	46° 39.1
	LHA	309° 00' W/60' E	d corr.	Pub. 229	1.5			a =	14.7 T

4	LHA	309			**5** tab Hc	46° 37.6	d +- 1.9	Z 63.1	Int Zn =	061.9
	Dec deg	38	N S	N	d corr. Pub.249 & 229	1.5	Dec min 46.1	dZ 1.15 Zn 61.9	a - Lat =	28 N
	a-Lat	28	N S	N	Hc	46° 39.1		**6**	a - Lon =	144° 51.7W

* The azimuth angles Z have been interpolated for declination minutes. This was not done on most forms, though it should be for best results.

Problem 20. July 18

Form 1 (Sights #29)

1	WT	07 h	43 m	18 s	date	18-Jul-1982	body	Venus	Hs	19°	3.8 '
	WE +S-F		m	0 s	DR Lat	25° 56' N	log	2238	index corr. + off, - on		0
	ZD +W-E	7			DR Lon	148° 48' W	HE ft	9	DIP -	-	-2.9
	GMT	14 h	43 m	18 s	GMT date / LOP label		C-	242 T	Ha	19°	0.9
					Sights #29 18-Jul-1982		S-	7.3 Kt			

2	GHA hr.	58°	46.7	v moon planets	-0.8	DEC hr	N 22°	32.9	d +-	0.1	HP moon

3	GHA + m.s.	370°	49.5 '			d corr. +-		0.1	additional altitude corr. moon, mars, venus +	0.1
	SHA + or v corr.	+1°	-0.6	stars or moon, planets		DEC deg	N 22°	DEC min 33.0	altitude corr. all sights +-	-2.8
	GHA	429°	35.6						upper limb moon subtract 30'	
				tens d	11.0	d upper		Ho T	18°	58.2
				units d	0.8	d lower				
	a-Lon -W+E	148°	35.6	dsd corr. +		dsd		Hc A	19°	03.3
	LHA	281°	00' W/60' E	d corr. Pub. 229	11.8			a =	5.1 A	

4	LHA	281			5	tab Hc	18°	51.5	d +-	21.5	Z	74.1	Zn =	074.1
	Dec deg	22	N S	N		d corr. Pub.249 & 229	11.8	Dec min.	33.0			a - Lat =	26° N
	a-Lat	26	N S	N		Hc	19°	03.3		6	a - Lon = 148° 35.6' W

N Lat   L.H.A. greater than 180 .... Zn = Z
L.H.A. less than 180 .... Zn = 360 - Z

S Lat   L.H.A. greater than 180 .... Zn = 180 - Z
L.H.A. less than 180 .... Zn = 180 + Z

Form 2 (Sights #30)

1	WT	11 h	21 m	11 s	date	18-Jul-1982	body	SUN L/L	Hs	39°	6.0 '
	WE +S-F		m	0 s	DR Lat	25° 43' N	log	2265	index corr. + off, - on		0
	ZD +W-E	7			DR Lon	149° 13.7' W	HE ft	9	DIP -	-	-2.9
	GMT	18 h	21 m	11 s	GMT date / LOP label		C-	242 T	Ha	39°	3.1
					Sights #30 18-Jul-1982		S-	7.3 Kt			

2	GHA hr.	88°	27.5	v moon planets		DEC hr	N 20°	59.5	d +-	-0.5	HP moon

3	GHA + m.s.	5°	17.8			d corr. +-		-0.2	additional altitude corr. moon, mars, venus +	
	SHA + or v corr.	360°		stars or moon, planets		DEC deg	N 20°	DEC min 59.3	altitude corr. all sights +-	+14.8
	GHA	453°	45.3						upper limb moon subtract 30'	
				tens d	9.9	d upper		Ho T	39°	17.9
				units d	7.8	d lower				
	a-Lon -W+E	148°	45.3	dsd corr. +		dsd		Hc A	39°	40.1
	LHA	305°	00' W/60' E	d corr. Pub. 229	17.7			a =	22.2 A	

4	LHA	305			5	tab Hc	39°	22.4	d +-	17.9	Z	84.7	Zn =	084.7
	Dec deg	20	N S	N		d corr. Pub.249 & 229	17.7	Dec min.	59.3			a - Lat =	26 N
	a-Lat	26	N S	N		Hc	39°	40.1		6	a - Lon = 148° 45.3'W

Problem 21. July 18

Sight 1 — Vega

1	WT	22 h 37 m 30 s	date 18-Jul-1982	body **Vega (49)**	Hs 47° 22.5'
	WE +S-F	m 0 s	DR Lat 25° 29' N	log 2343	index corr. + off, - on 0'
	ZD +W-E	7	DR Lon 150° 25' W	HE ft 9	DIP − -2.9'
	GMT	5 h 37 m 30 s	GMT date / LOP label Sights #31 19-Jul-1982	C- 242 T S- 6.9 Kt	Ha 47° 19.6'

2	GHA ϒ hr.	11° 40.0'	v moon planets	DEC hr	d + −	HP moon

3	GHA + m.s.	369° 24.0'		d corr. + -		additional altitude corr. moon, mars, venus +	
	SHA + or v corr.	80° 54.5'	stars or moon, planets	DEC deg N38	DEC min 46.1	altitude corr. all sights +- -0.9'	
	GHA	461° 58.5'				upper limb moon subtract 30'	
			tens d	0	d upper	Ho T 47° 18.7'	
			units d	-3.2	d lower		
	a-Lon -W+E	149° 58.5'	dsd corr. +		dsd	Hc A 47° 30.8'	
	LHA	312° 00' W/60' E	d corr. Pub. 229	-3.2		a = 12.1 A	

4	LHA	312	**5**	tab Hc 47° 34.0'	d + - -4.1 Z 60.2	Zn = 060.2	
	Dec deg	38 N/S N		d corr. Pub.249 & 229 -3.2	Dec min. 46.1	a - Lat = 25° N	
	a-Lat	25 N/S N		Hc 47° 30.8'		**6** a - Lon = 149° 58.5' W	

N Lat   L.H.A. greater than 180 .... Zn = Z   S Lat   L.H.A. greater than 180 .... Zn = 180 - Z
        L.H.A. less than 180 .... Zn = 360 - Z   L.H.A. less than 180 .... Zn = 180 + Z

Sight 2 — Alkaid

1	WT	22 h 40 m 14 s	date 18-Jul-1982	body **Alkaid (34)**	Hs 59° 14.0'
	WE +S-F	m 0 s	DR Lat 25° 19' N	log 2343	index corr. + off, - on 0'
	ZD +W-E	7	DR Lon 150° 25' W	HE ft 9	DIP − -2.9'
	GMT	5 h 40 m 14 s	GMT date / LOP label Sights #31 19-Jul-1982	C- 242 T S- 6.9 Kt	Ha 59° 11.1'

2	GHA ϒ hr.	11° 40'	v moon planets	DEC hr	d + −	HP moon

3	GHA + m.s.	10° 5.2'		d corr. + -		additional altitude corr. moon, mars, venus +	
	SHA + or v corr.	153° 17.4'	stars or moon, planets	DEC deg N 49	DEC min 24.4	altitude corr. all sights +- -0.6'	
	GHA	175° 02.6'				upper limb moon subtract 30'	
			tens d	16.3	d upper	Ho T 59° 10.5'	
			units d	0.2	d lower		
	a-Lon -W+E	150° 02.6'	dsd corr. +		dsd	Hc A 58° 48.0'	
	LHA	25° 00' W/60' E	d corr. Pub. 229	-16.5		a = 22.5 T	

4	LHA	25	**5**	tab Hc 59° 4.5'	d + - -40.5 Z 32.6	Zn = 327.4	
	Dec deg	49 N/S N		d corr. Pub.249 & 229 -16.5	Dec min. 24.4	a - Lat = 25 N	
	a-Lat	25 N/S N		Hc 58° 48.0'		**6** a - Lon = 150° 02.6' W	

Problem 22. July 19

1										
WT	7 h	41 m	16 s	date	19-Jul-1982	body	**Vega (49)**	Hs	17°	24.8'
WE +S-F		m	0 s	DR Lat	24° 38' N	log	2401	index corr. + off, - on		0
ZD +W-E	7			DR Lon	151° 12' W	HE ft	9	DIP -	**-**	-2.9
GMT	14 h	41 m	16 s	GMT date / LOP label		C-	232 T	Ha	17°	21.9
					Sights #32 19-Jul-1982	S-	6.3 Kt			

2										
GHA ϒ hr.	147°	2.2	v moon planets		DEC hr	°	'	d + –	HP moon	

3										
GHA + m.s.	10°	20.7'	d corr.	+ –			additional altitude corr. moon, mars, venus		+	
SHA + or v corr.	80°	54.5	stars or moon, planets	DEC deg	N38	DEC min	46.1	altitude corr. all sights	+–	-3.1
GHA	238°	17.4						upper limb moon subtract 30'		
			tens d	7.7	d upper		Ho T	17°	18.8
a-Lon -W+E	151°	17.4	units d	6.9	d lower				
LHA	87°	00' W/60' E	dsd corr.	+	dsd		Hc A	17°	33.3
			d corr.	Pub. 229	14.6			a = **14.5 A**	

4										
LHA	87		tab Hc	17°	18.7	d + –	18.9	Z	55.5	
								Zn =	304.5	
Dec deg	38	N S **N**	d corr.	Pub.249 & 229	14.6	Dec min.	46.1	a - Lat =	25 N	
a-Lat	25	N S **N**	Hc	17°	33.3			a - Lon =	151° 17.4' W	

N Lat   L.H.A. greater than 180 .... Zn = Z   S Lat   L.H.A. greater than 180 .... Zn = 180 - Z
        L.H.A. less than 180 .... Zn = 360 - Z   L.H.A. less than 180 .... Zn = 180 + Z

1										
WT	7 h	46 m	58 s	date	19-Jul-1982	body	**Capella (12)**	Hs	30°	20.8'
WE +S-F		m	0 s	DR Lat	24° 38' N	log	2401	index corr. + off, - on		0
ZD +W-E	7			DR Lon	151° 12' W	HE ft	9	DIP -	**-**	-2.9
GMT	14 h	46 m	58 s	GMT date / LOP label		C-	232 T	Ha	30°	17.9
					Sights #32 19-Jul-1982	S-	6.3 Kt			

2										
GHA ϒ hr.	147°	2.2	v moon planets		DEC hr	°	'	d + –	HP moon	

3										
GHA + m.s.	11°	46.4'	d corr.	+ –			additional altitude corr. moon, mars, venus		+	
SHA + or v corr.	281°	9.8	stars or moon, planets	DEC deg	N45	DEC min	58.7	altitude corr. all sights	+–	-1.7
GHA	439°	58.4						upper limb moon subtract 30'		
			tens d	0	d upper		Ho T	30°	16.2
a-Lon -W+E	150°	58.4	units d	5.8	d lower				
LHA	289°	00' W/60' E	dsd corr.	+	dsd		Hc A	30°	35.6
			d corr.	Pub. 229	5.8			a = **19.4 A**	

4										
LHA	289		tab Hc	30°	29.8	d + –	5.9	Z	50.9	
								Zn =	050.9	
Dec deg	45	N S **N**	d corr.	Pub.249 & 229	5.8	Dec min.	58.7	a - Lat =	25 N	
a-Lat	25	N S **N**	Hc	30°	35.6			a - Lon =	150° 58.4'W	

Problem 22. July 19 - Cont.

	WT	7 h	53 m	18 s	date	19-Jul-1982	body	**Venus**		Hs	18 °	28.4 '
1	WE +S-F		m	0 s	DR Lat	24° 38' N	log	2401		index corr. + off, - on		0 '
	ZD +W-E	7			DR Lon	151° 12' W	HE ft	9		DIP -	**-**	-2.9 '
	GMT	14 h	53 m	18 s	GMT date / LOP label		C-	232	T	Ha	18 °	25.5 '
						Sights #32 19-Jul-1982	S-	6.3	Kt			

	GHA hr.	58 °	27.9 '	v moon planets	-0.8	DEC hr	N 22 °	36.6 '	d +–	+0.1 '	HP moon	
2												

	GHA + m.s.	373 °	19.5 '			d corr.	+–		0.1 '	additional altitude corr. moon, mars, venus	**+**	0.1
3	SHA + or v corr.	°	-0.7	stars or moon, planets		DEC deg	N 22 °	DEC min	36.7 '	altitude corr. all sights	**+–**	-2.9
	GHA	431 °	46.7 '							upper limb moon subtract 30'		
			'	tens d		12.3	d upper		Ho **T**	18 °	22.7 '	
	a-Lon -W+E	151 °	46.7 '	units d		0.5	d lower		Hc **A**	17 °	55.5 '	
	LHA	280 °	00' W/60' E	dsd corr.	**+**		dsd		a = **27.2 T**			
				d corr.	Pub. 229	12.8						

	LHA	280				tab Hc	17 °	42.7 '	d +–	20.8	Z 73.4	Zn =	073.4
4	Dec deg	22	N S	**N**	**5**	d corr.	Pub.249 & 229	12.8	Dec min.	36.7		a - Lat =	**25 N**
	a-Lat	25	N S	**N**		Hc	17 °	55.5 '				**6** a - Lon	**151° 46.7' W**

N Lat	L.H.A. greater than 180 .... Zn = Z		S Lat	L.H.A. greater than 180 .... Zn = 180 - Z
	L.H.A. less than 180 .... Zn = 360 - Z			L.H.A. less than 180 .... Zn = 180 + Z

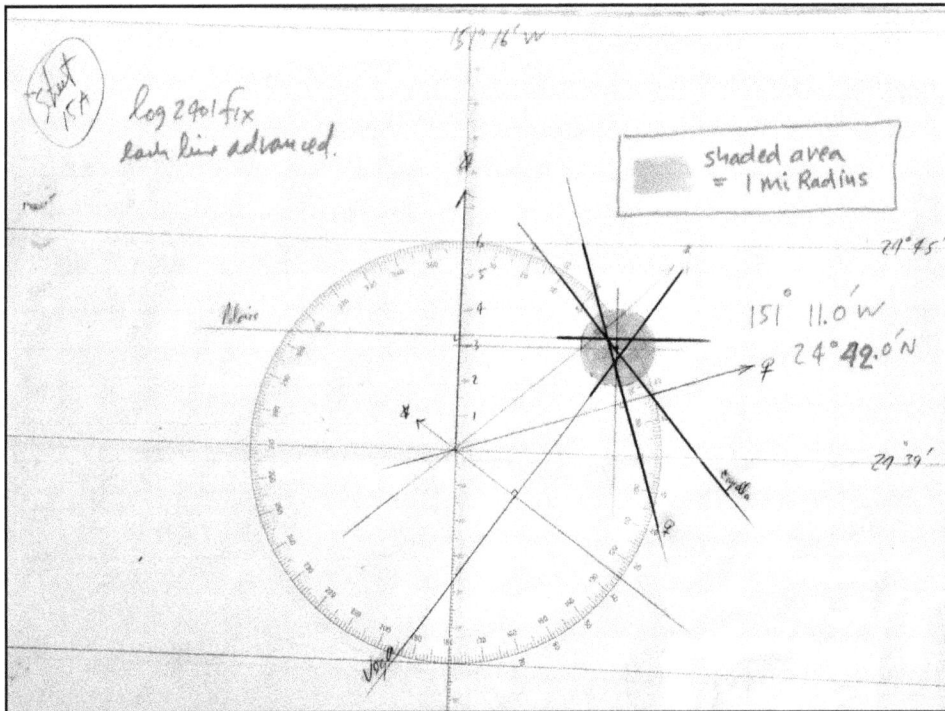

A plot of Problem 22 from the original plotting sheets in 1982. This is Sheet 15a. We also found Sheet 17 (page 71), but the rest of the sheets are missing. This was a computed solution with auto advancement (Analysis section) plotted on an expanded scale.

Problem 22. July 19

Step 1 Correct Hs to get Ho		Sights #32		
1-1 Record Maximum Sextant Height	Hs	25 °		28.8 '
1-2 Record Index Correction (mark sign + if off, - if on)	IC	**Off** **+** **On** **-**		0 '
1-3 Record eye height (HE) and look up Dip Correction on the right-hand side of Table A2, front of Almanac (T-8 in notes) HE (ft) 9	Dip		-	2.9 '
1-4 Record Maximum Sextant Height	Ha	25 °		25.9 '
1-5 Look up the altitude correction in the center of Table A2, front of the Almanac (T-8 in notes)	Alt corr.		+ -	-2.0 '
1-6 Sum the above two numbers to get Observed Height	Ho	25 °		23.9 '

Starpath Form 110 for Polaris Sights

Step 2 Find LHA Aries	GMT date =	19-Jul-82
2-1 GMT Time in Hours, Minutes and Seconds	GMT time =	14:28:04
2-2 Find GHA Aries on Left Hand Daily Page of the Nautical Almanac (far left column) for GMT Day and Hour	GHA Aries (Hr) =	147° 02.2'
2-3 Find GHA Aries minutes correction from Increments and Corrections pages	GHA Aries (Min) =	7° 02.2'
2-4 GHA Aries - Sum the above two numbers	GHA Aries =	154° 04.4'
2-5 DR Longitude (-W, +E)	DR Lon =	151° 12.0'
2-6 LHA Aries (Combine previous numbers)	LHA Aries =	2° 52.4'

Step 3 Latitude Determination		
3-1 HO	HO =	25° 23.9'
3-2 a0 from Polaris Table (using LHA Aries)	a0 =	16.9'
3-3 a1 from Polaris Table (using DR Latitude)	a1 =	0.5'
3-4 a2 from Polaris Table (using Month)	a2 =	0.2'
3-5 Subtract 1 Degree	- 1 =	-1°
3-6 Sum the above five numbers to get LATITUDE	LATITUDE =	24° 41.5'
3.7 Check the value for the Azimuth	Zn =	000.4

Problem 23. July 19

Sight 1 — Jupiter

1	WT	22 h 18 m 54 s	date	19-Jul-1982	body	**Jupiter**	Hs	51° 57.0'
	WE +S-F	m 0 s	DR Lat	23° 56' N	log	2485	index corr. + off, - on	0
	ZD +W-E	7	DR Lon	152° 29' W	HE ft	9	DIP -	-2.9
	GMT	5 h 18 m 54 s	GMT date / LOP label	Sights #33 20-Jul-1982	C-	238 T	Ha	51° 54.1'
					S-	5.8 Kt		

2	GHA hr.	163° 12.6'	v moon planets 2.3	DEC hr	S 10° 48.5'	d +− +0.1	HP moon

3	GHA + m.s.	4° 43.5'		d corr. +− 0		additional altitude corr. moon, mars, venus +	
	SHA + or v corr.	0.7'	stars or moon, planets	DEC deg S 10°	DEC min 48.5'	altitude corr. all sights +- -0.8	
	GHA	167° 56.8'		tens d 40.4	d upper	upper limb moon subtract 30'	
				units d 3.8	d lower	Ho T 51° 53.3'	
	a-Lon -W+E	151° 56.8'		dsd corr. +	dsd		
	LHA	16° 00' W/60' E		d corr. Pub. 229 44.2		Hc A 51° 50.5'	
						a = 2.8 T	

4	LHA	16		**5**	tab Hc 52° 34.7'	d +- -54.7	Z 153.5	Zn = 206.5
	Dec deg	10	N/S S		d corr. Pub.249 & 229 -44.2	Dec min 48.5		a - Lat = 24 N
	a-Lat	24	N/S N		Hc 51° 50.5'		**6**	a - Lon = 151° 56.8' W

N Lat L.H.A. greater than 180 .... Zn = Z
L.H.A. less than 180 .... Zn = 360 - Z

S Lat L.H.A. greater than 180 .... Zn = 180 - Z
L.H.A. less than 180 .... Zn = 180 + Z

Sight 2 — Altair (51)

1	WT	22 h 41 m 10 s	date	19-Jul-1982	body	**Altair (51)**	Hs	24° 36.2'
	WE +S-F	m 0 s	DR Lat	23° 56' N	log	2487	index corr. + off, - on	0
	ZD +W-E	7	DR Lon	152° 29' W	HE ft	9	DIP -	-2.9
	GMT	5 h 41 m 10 s	GMT date / LOP label	Sights #33 20-Jul-1982	C-	238 T	Ha	24° 33.3'
					S-	5.8 Kt		

2	GHA Υ hr.	12° 39.1'	v moon planets	DEC hr	°	d +−	HP moon

3	GHA + m.s.	370° 19.2'		d corr. +−		additional altitude corr. moon, mars, venus +	
	SHA + or v corr.	62° 30.9'	stars or moon, planets	DEC deg N 8°	DEC min 49.3'	altitude corr. all sights +- -2.1	
	GHA	445° 29.2'		tens d 16.4	d upper	upper limb moon subtract 30'	
				units d 2.5	d lower	Ho T 24° 31.2'	
	a-Lon -W+E	152° 29.2'		dsd corr. +	dsd		
	LHA	293° 00' W/60' E		d corr. Pub. 229 18.9		Hc A 24° 31.5'	
						a = 0.3 A	

4	LHA	293		**5**	tab Hc 24° 12.6'	d +- 23.0	Z 91.9	Zn = 091.9
	Dec deg	8	N/S N		d corr. Pub.249 & 229 18.9	Dec min 49.3		a - Lat = 24 N
	a-Lat	24	N/S N		Hc 24° 31.5'		**6**	a - Lon = 152° 29.2' W

Problem 24. July 20

Form 1 — Sights #34

WT	9 h 42 m 47 s	date	20-Jul-1982	body	Sun L/L
WE +S-F	m 0 s	DR Lat	23° 32' N	log	2546
ZD +W-E	7	DR Lon	153° 21.3' W	HE ft	9
GMT	16 h 42 m 47 s	GMT date / LOP label	Sights #34 20-Jul-1982	C-	228 T
				S-	5.0 Kt

Hs	13°	6.9'				
index corr. + off, - on		0				
DIP -	-	-2.9				
Ha	13°	4.0				

2

GHA hr.	58°	25.6'	v moon planets		DEC hr	N 20°	38.5'	d +-	-0.5	HP moon	

3

GHA + m.s.	10°	41.8'		d corr. + -			-0.4
SHA + or v corr.	360°		stars or moon, planets	DEC deg	N 20°	DEC min	38.1
GHA	429°	7.4'					
a-Lon -W+E	153°	7.4'					
LHA	276°	00' W/60' E					

tens d	12.7	d upper		
units d	0.3	d lower		
dsd corr.	+	dsd		
d corr.	Pub. 229	13.0		

additional altitude corr. moon, mars, venus	+	
altitude corr. all sights	+-	11.9
upper limb moon subtract 30'		
Ho **T**	13°	15.9
Hc **A**	13°	9.8
a =	6.1 T	

4

LHA	276		
Dec deg	20	N/S	N
a-Lat	23	N/S	N

5

tab Hc	12°	56.8	d +-	20.5	Z	73.5
d corr.	Pub.249 & 229	13.0	Dec min.	38.1		
Hc	13°	9.8				

Zn =	073.5
a - Lat =	23 N

6 a - Lon = 153° 07.4' W

N Lat L.H.A. greater than 180 .... Zn = Z
L.H.A. less than 180 .... Zn = 360 - Z

S Lat L.H.A. greater than 180 .... Zn = 180 - Z
L.H.A. less than 180 .... Zn = 180 + Z

Form 2 — Sights #35

WT	12 h 27 m 45 s	date	20-Jul-1982	body	Sun L/L
WE +S-F	m 0 s	DR Lat	23° 22' N	log	2560
ZD +W-E	7	DR Lon	153° 30' W	HE ft	9
GMT	19 h 27 m 45 s	GMT date / LOP label	Sights #35 20-Jul-1982	C-	228 T
				S-	5.0 Kt

Hs	49°	59.6'
index corr. + off, - on		0
DIP -	-	-2.9
Ha	49°	56.7

2

GHA hr.	103°	25.5'	v moon planets		DEC hr	N 20°	37.1'	d +-	-0.5	HP moon	

3

GHA + m.s.	6°	56.3'		d corr. + -			-0.2
SHA + or v corr.	360°		stars or moon, planets	DEC deg	N 20°	DEC min	36.9
GHA	470°	21.8'					
a-Lon -W+E	153°	21.8'					
LHA	317°	00' W/60' E					

tens d	6.2	d upper		
units d	1.3	d lower		
dsd corr.	+	dsd		
d corr.	Pub. 229	7.5		

additional altitude corr. moon, mars, venus	+	
altitude corr. all sights	+-	15.2
upper limb moon subtract 30'		
Ho **T**	50°	11.9
Hc **A**	50°	8.6
a =	3.3 T	

4

LHA	317		
Dec deg	20	N/S	N
a-Lat	23	N/S	N

5

tab Hc	50°	1.1	d +-	12.2	Z	85.9
d corr.	Pub.249 & 229	7.5	Dec min.	36.9		
Hc	50°	8.6				

Zn =	085.9
a - Lat =	23 N

6 a - Lon = 153° 21.8' W

The a-Lat was not rounded properly in the top form, but the a-value ended up small because the DR was wrong!

Problem 25. July 20

1	WT	15 h 11 m 40 s	date	20-Jul-1982	body	Sun L/L	Hs 86° 25.6'
	WE +S-F	m 0 s	DR Lat	23° 02' N	log	2572	index corr. + off, - on 0
	ZD +W-E	7	DR Lon	153° 28' W	HE ft 9	DIP - -2.9
	GMT	22 h 11 m 40 s	GMT date / LOP label	Sights #36 20-Jul-1982	C- 228 T S- 4.3 Kt	Ha 86° 22.7

2	GHA hr.	148° 25.4'	v moon planets	DEC hr	N 20° 35.7	d +- -0.5	HP moon

3	GHA + m.s.	2° 55.0'		d corr. +-	-0.1	additional altitude corr. moon, mars, venus +	
	SHA + or v corr.	360°	stars or moon, planets	DEC deg N 20	DEC min 35.6	altitude corr. all sights +- 15.8	
	GHA	510° 80.4'	tens d 23.7	d upper 53.0	upper limb moon subtract 30'	
		511° 20.4'	units d 4.9	d lower 37.5	Ho **T** 86° 38.5	
	a-Lon -W+E	153° 20.4'	dsd corr. + 0.9	dsd 15.5		
	LHA	358° 00' W/60' E	d corr. Pub.229 29.5	Hc **A** 86° 57.7		
				a = 19.2 A	

4	LHA	358				
	Dec deg	20	N/S **N**		
	a-Lat	23	N/S **N**		

5	tab Hc	86° 28.2	d +- 48.2*	Z 147.8
	d corr. Pub.249 & 229	29.5	Dec min 35.6	-6.5 / 141.3
	Hc	86° 57.7		

| Zn = 141.3 |
| a - Lat = 23 N |
| **6** a - Lon = 153° 20.4' W |

N Lat   L.H.A. greater than 180 .... Zn = Z
        L.H.A. less than 180 .... Zn = 360 - Z

S Lat   L.H.A. greater than 180 .... Zn = 180 - Z
        L.H.A. less than 180 .... Zn = 180 + Z

1	WT	15 h 18 m 30 s	date	20-Jul-1982	body	Sun L/L	Hs 87° 2.6'
	WE +S-F	m 0 s	DR Lat	23° 01.5' N	log	2572	index corr. + off, - on 0
	ZD +W-E	7	DR Lon	153°28' W	HE ft 9	DIP - -2.9
	GMT	22 h 18 m 30 s	GMT date / LOP label	Sights #36 20-Jul-1982	C- 228 T S- 4.3 Kt	Ha 86° 59.7

2	GHA hr.	148° 25.4'	v moon planets	DEC hr	N 20° 35.7	d +- -0.5	HP moon

3	GHA + m.s.	4° 37.5'		d corr. +-	-0.2	additional altitude corr. moon, mars, venus +	
	SHA + or v corr.		stars or moon, planets	DEC deg N 20	DEC min 35.5	altitude corr. all sights +- 15.9	
	GHA	152° 62.9'	tens d	d upper	upper limb moon subtract 30'	
		153° 2.9'	units d	d lower	Ho **T** 87° 15.6	
	a-Lon -W+E	153° 2.9'	dsd corr. +	dsd	Hc **A** 87° 35.5	
	LHA	0° 00' W/60' E	d corr. Pub. 229		a = 19.9 A	

4	LHA	0				
	Dec deg	20	N/S **N**		
	a-Lat	23	N/S **N**		

5	tab Hc	87° 0.0	d +- 60.0	Z 180.0
	d corr. Pub.249 & 229	35.5	Dec min 35.5	
	Hc	87° 35.5		

| Zn = 180.0 |
| a - Lat = 23 N |
| **6** a - Lon = 153° 2.9' W |

These are just sample sight reductions, pulling out two sights from the list of 15 taken. We use the LAN Lat and LAN Lon for the plot. Note that with LHA = 0, we get Zn = 180, but we know this was not the time of LAN. Special care is required with these high sights, which is discussed in the Analysis section.

Problem 25. July 20

Step 1	Correct Hs to get Ho		Sights #36		
1-1	Record Maximum Sextant Height (Hs = peak height of the Sun at Noon), and mark limb	Lower Upper Hs	87 °		5.2 '
1-2	Record Index Correction (mark sign + if off, - if on)	IC	Off + On -		0
1-3	Record eye height (HE) and look up Dip Correction on the right-hand side of Table A2, front of Almanac (T-8 in notes) HE (ft) 9	Dip	-		2.9 '
1-4	Record Maximum Sextant Height (Hs = peak height of the Sun at Noon), and mark limb	Ha	87 °		2.3 '
1-5	Look up the altitude correction on the left-hand side of Table A2, front of the Almanac (T-8 in notes) (correction depends on Ha, Limb, and month) (mark sign + for lower limb, - for upper limb)	Alt corr.	+ -		+15.9 '
1-6	Sum the above two numbers to get Observed Height	Ho	87 °		18.2 '

Starpath Form 107 for Local Apparent Noon Sights

Step 1	Determine the Zenith Distance		89 °	60.0 '
2-1	Record Ho from Step 1, above, and then subtract it from 90° to get the zenith distance.	Ho	87 °	18.2 '
2-2	Zenith Distance	z	2 °	41.8 '

Step 3	Use the Almanac to Find Sun's Declination	GMT date =		20-Jul-82	
3-1	Record the date and GMT of the sight (the time the Sun reached its peak height)	GMT (hr) = 22	GMT (min)= 20		
3-2	Turn to the daily page of the Almanac for the date of the sight, and find the Sun's declination (dec) for the hour of the sight (line 3-1) and record it here	Dec (hr)	N S N 20 °		35.7 '
3-3	Record the d-value from the botom of the dec column in the Almanac. Mark the signs of the d-value and the d-corr + if the dec for the next hour is larger, or - if it is smaller.	d-value + - -0.5	d-corr = + - -0.2		
3-4	Turn to the Increments and Corrections pages at the back of the Almanac (T-9 to 12, in the notes) and find the minutes table for thr GMT minutes (line 3-1). On the right-hand side of the double line in the table, find the d-corr corresponding to the d-value of line 3-3	Declination =	N S N 20 °		35.5 '
		3-5	Apply the d-corr to the dec (hr) and record it above		

Step 4 Find Latitude
from Zenith Distance and Declination
Record DR Latitide to use as a guide, and then take the sum or difference of zenith distance and declination to find your true Latitude at LAN

DR Lat =   23° 00'

Declination or Zenith Distance	N 20 °	35.5 '
Zenith Distance or Declination	2 °	41.8 '
Latitude =	23 °	17.3 '

Hawaii Winds

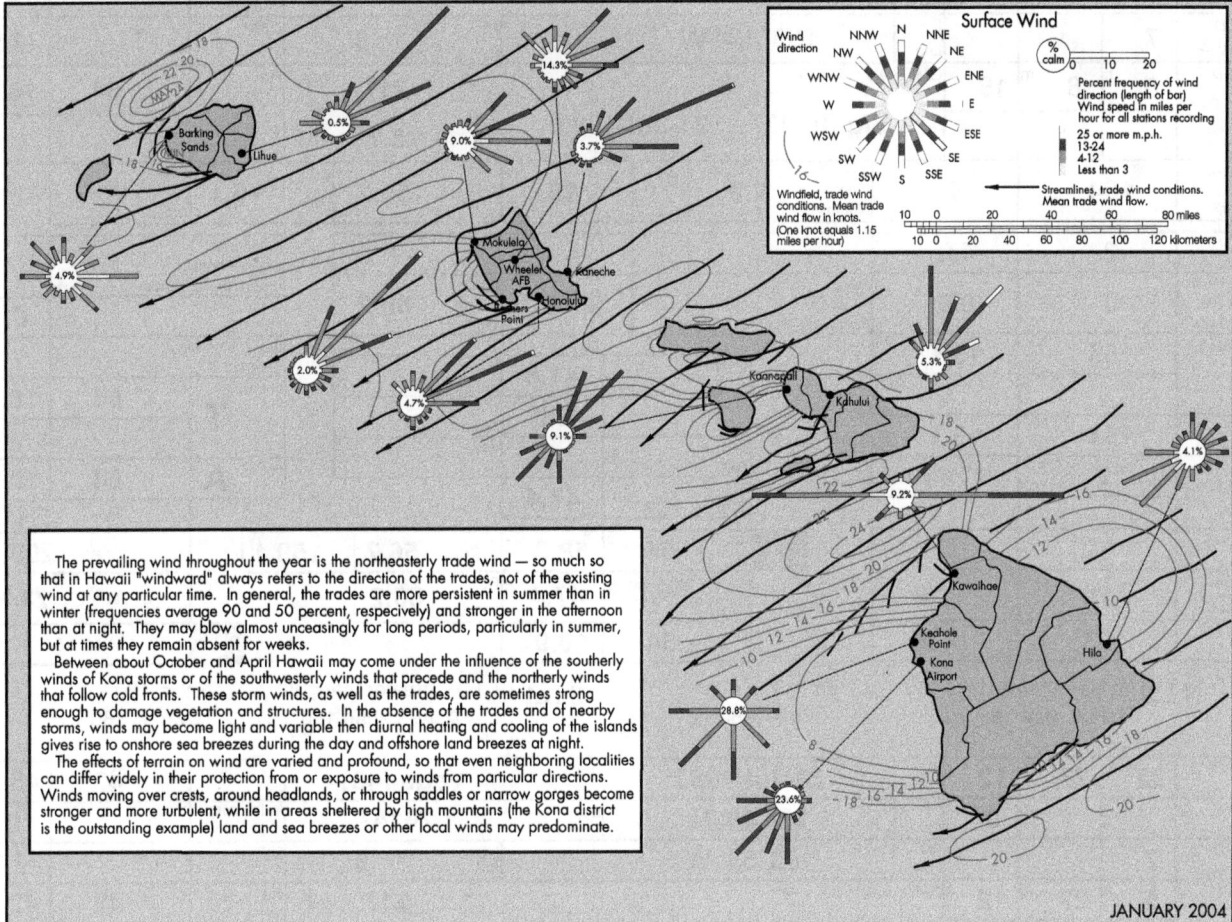

The prevailing wind throughout the year is the northeasterly trade wind — so much so that in Hawaii "windward" always refers to the direction of the trades, not of the existing wind at any particular time. In general, the trades are more persistent in summer than in winter (frequencies average 90 and 50 percent, respecively) and stronger in the afternoon than at night. They may blow almost unceasingly for long periods, particularly in summer, but at times they remain absent for weeks.

Between about October and April Hawaii may come under the influence of the southerly winds of Kona storms or of the southwesterly winds that precede and the northerly winds that follow cold fronts. These storm winds, as well as the trades, are sometimes strong enough to damage vegetation and structures. In the absence of the trades and of nearby storms, winds may become light and variable then diurnal heating and cooling of the islands gives rise to onshore sea breezes during the day and offshore land breezes at night.

The effects of terrain on wind are varied and profound, so that even neighboring localities can differ widely in their protection from or exposure to winds from particular directions. Winds moving over crests, around headlands, or through saddles or narrow gorges become stronger and more turbulent, while in areas sheltered by high mountains (the Kona district is the outstanding example) land and sea breezes or other local winds may predominate.

JANUARY 2004

This diagram is from the Marine Weather Services Chart No. 13, now discontinued by NOAA, though this data remains valid. The wind roses shown are for land based stations identified by the thin blue lines. The one at Kahului is misleading. The trades just offshore there are more like the one shown for north shore of Oahu (Kaneche) and represented by the stream lines above all the islands. The red line bulging out of the Pailolo Channel is a real marker of where the typically 10 to 15 kt trade winds become 20 to 30 kt channel winds.

Problem 26. July 20

Workform 1

1	WT	22ʰ 8ᵐ 19ˢ	date	20-Jul-1982	body	Jupiter	Hs	54°	19.6	
	WE +S-F	ᵐ 0ˢ	DR Lat	22° 46' N	log	2614	index corr. + off, - on		0	
	ZD +W-E	7	DR Lon	153° 54' W	HE ft	9	DIP -	-	-2.9	
	GMT	5ʰ 8ᵐ 19ˢ	GMT date / LOP label		C-	217 T	Ha	54°	16.7	
				Sights #37 21-Jul-1982	S-	5.7 Kt				
2	GHA hr.	164° 8	v moon planets	2.3	DEC hr	S 10°	50.2	d +−	+0.1	HP moon
3	GHA + m.s.	2° 4.8			d corr. +-		0	additional altitude corr. moon, mars, venus	+	
	SHA + or v corr.	0° 0.3	stars or moon, planets		DEC deg	S 10°	DEC min 50.2	altitude corr. all sights +-	-0.7	
	GHA	166° 13.1						upper limb moon subtract 30'		
				tens d	41.8	d upper		Ho T	54°	16.0
	a-Lon -W+E	154° 13.1		units d	5.6	d lower				
	LHA	12° 00' W/60' E		dsd corr. +		dsd		Hc A	54°	10.9
4	LHA	12		d corr. Pub. 229	47.4			a =	5.1 T	
			5	tab Hc	54° 58.3	d +- -56.7	Z 159.1	Zn =	200.9	
	Dec deg	10 N/S S		d corr. Pub.249 & 229	-47.4	Dec min 50.2		a - Lat =	23 N	
	a-Lat	23 N/S N		Hc	54° 10.9		**6**	a - Lon	154° 13.1' W	

N Lat   L.H.A. greater than 180 .... Zn = Z
        L.H.A. less than 180 .... Zn = 360 - Z

S Lat   L.H.A. greater than 180 .... Zn = 180 - Z
        L.H.A. less than 180 .... Zn = 180 + Z

Workform 2

1	WT	22ʰ 27ᵐ 12ˢ	date	20-Jul-1982	body	Vega (49)	Hs	42°	45.2	
	WE +S-F	ᵐ 0ˢ	DR Lat	22° 46' N	log	2614	index corr. + off, - on		0	
	ZD +W-E	7	DR Lon	153°54' W	HE ft	9	DIP -	-	-2.9	
	GMT	5ʰ 27ᵐ 12ˢ	GMT date / LOP label		C-	217 T	Ha	42°	42.3	
				Sights #37 21-Jul-1982	S-	5.7 Kt				
2	GHA Υ hr.	13° 38.3	v moon planets		DEC hr	°		d +−		HP moon
3	GHA + m.s.	366° 49.1			d corr. +-			additional altitude corr. moon, mars, venus	+	
	SHA + or v corr.	80° 54.5	stars or moon, planets		DEC deg	N 38°	DEC min 46.1	altitude corr. all sights +-	-1.1	
	GHA	461° 21.9						upper limb moon subtract 30'		
				tens d	0	d upper		Ho T	42°	41.2
	a-Lon -W+E	154° 21.9		units d	2.5	d lower				
	LHA	307° 00' W/60' E		dsd corr. +		dsd		Hc A	42°	34.5
4	LHA	307		d corr. Pub. 229	2.5			a =	6.7 T	
			5	tab Hc	42° 37.0	d +- -3.2	Z 58.8	Zn =	058.8	
	Dec deg	38 N/S N		d corr. Pub.249 & 229	-2.5	Dec min 46.1		a - Lat =	23 N	
	a-Lat	23 N/S N		Hc	42° 34.5		**6**	a - Lon	154° 21.9' W	

Problem 26. July 20 - Cont.

	WT	22 ʰ	40 ᵐ	6 ˢ	date	20-Jul-1982	body	**Altair (51)**		Hs	23 °	49.0 '
1	WE +S-F		ᵐ	0 ˢ	DR Lat	22° 46' N	log	2614		index corr. + off, - on		0
	ZD +W-E	7			DR Lon	153° 54' W	HE ft	9		DIP -	-	-2.9
	GMT	5 ʰ	40 ᵐ	6 ˢ	GMT date / LOP label		C-	217	T	Ha	23 °	46.1
					Sights #37 21-Jul-1982		S-	5.7	Kt			

2	GHA ɣ hr.	13 °	38.3	v moon planets		DEC hr	°	d + –	HP moon		
3	GHA + m.s.	370 °	3.1 '	d corr.	+ -			additional altitude corr. moon, mars, venus	**+**		
	SHA + or v corr.	62 °	30.9	stars or moon, planets	DEC deg	**N 8**	°DEC min	**49.3**	altitude corr. all sights	**+- -2.2**	
	GHA	446 °	12.3					upper limb moon subtract 30'			
				tens d		16.4	d upper	Ho **T**	23 °	43.9	
				units d		1.6	d lower				
	a-Lon -W+E	154 °	12.3	dsd corr.	**+**		dsd	Hc **A**	23 °	37.1	
	LHA	292 °	00' W/60' E	d corr.	Pub. 229	18.0		a =	6.8 T		

	LHA	292		**5**	tab Hc	23 ° 19.1	d + - 22.0	Z 91.1	Zn =	091.1
4	Dec deg	8	N S **N**		d corr.	Pub.249 & 229 18.0	Dec min. 49.3		a - Lat =	**23 N**
	a-Lat	23	N S **N**		Hc	23 ° 37.1		**6**	a - Lon	154° 12.3' W

N Lat L.H.A. greater than 180 .... Zn = Z
L.H.A. less than 180 .... Zn = 360 - Z

S Lat L.H.A. greater than 180 .... Zn = 180 - Z
L.H.A. less than 180 .... Zn = 180 + Z

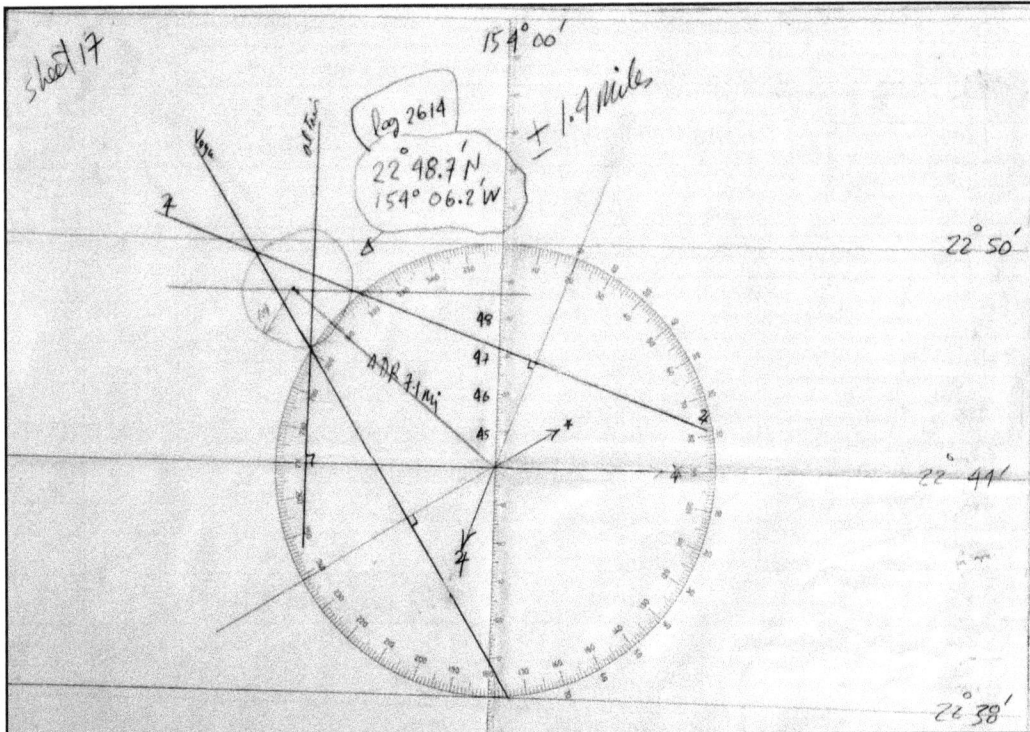

A plot of Problem 26 from the original plotting sheets in 1982. See page 35 for procedure used. A similar plot is shown on page 63. These samples were saved to illustrate in the classroom the level of accuracy possible from a small boat at sea with careful procedures.

Problem 27. July 21

					date		body			Hs		
1	WT	7 h	55 m	12 s		21-Jul-1982			Capella (12)		28 °		50.2 '
	WE +S-F		m	0 s	DR Lat	22° 09' N		log	2685	index corr. + off, - on			0
	ZD +W-E	7			DR Lon	155° 08' W		HE ft	9	DIP -	**-**		-2.9 '
	GMT	14 h	55 m	12 s	GMT date / LOP label			C-	232 T	Ha	28 °		47.3 '
					Sights #38　21-Jul-1982			S-	7.6 Kt				

					v		DEC	°		d	HP	
2	GHA γ hr.	149 °	0.4 '		moon planets		hr			+ –	moon	

						d corr.	+ -			additional altitude corr. moon, mars, venus	**+**	
3	GHA + m.s.	13 °	50.3 '									
	SHA + or v corr.	281 °	9.7	stars or moon, planets	DEC deg	N 45		°DEC min	58.7	altitude corr. all sights	**+-** -1.8	
	GHA	444 °	0.4							upper limb moon subtract 30'		
				tens d		0	d upper		Ho		28 °	45.5 '
	a-Lon -W+E	155 °	0.4	units d		3.0	d lower		**T**			
	LHA	289 °	00' W/60' E	dsd corr.	**+**		dsd		Hc **A**		28 °	37.7 '
				d corr.	Pub. 229	3.0				a =		7.8 T

					tab Hc	28 °	34.6 '	d + -	3.2	Z	49.6		Zn =	049.6*
4	LHA	289		**5**	d corr.	Pub.249 & 229	3.0	Dec min.	58.7				a - Lat =	22 N
	Dec deg	45	N S N		Hc	28 °	37.7					**6**	a - Lon =	155° 00.4' W
	a-Lat	22	N S N											

　　N Lat　L.H.A. greater than 180 .... Zn = Z　　　　　　S Lat　L.H.A. greater than 180 .... Zn = 180 - Z
　　　　　　L.H.A. less than 180 .... Zn = 360 - Z　　　　　　　　L.H.A. less than 180 .... Zn = 180 + Z

						date		body			Hs		
1	WT	8 h	15 m	22 s		21-Jul-1982			Vega (49)		10 °		56.1 '
	WE +S-F		m	0 s	DR Lat	22° 05' N		log	2688	index corr. + off, - on			0
	ZD +W-E	7			DR Lon	155° 12' W		HE ft	9	DIP -	**-**		-2.9 '
	GMT	15 h	15 m	22 s	GMT date / LOP label			C-	232 T	Ha	10 °		53.2 '
					Sights #38　21-Jul-1982			S-	7.6 Kt				

					v		DEC	°		d	HP	
2	GHA γ hr.	164 °	2.9		moon planets		hr			+ –	moon	

						d corr.	+ -			additional altitude corr. moon, mars, venus	**+**	
3	GHA + m.s.	3 °	51.1 '									
	SHA + or v corr.	80 °	54.5	stars or moon, planets	DEC deg	N 38		°DEC min	46.1	altitude corr. all sights	**+-** -4.9	
	GHA	248 °	48.5							upper limb moon subtract 30'		
				tens d		15.3	d upper		Ho		10 °	48.3 '
	a-Lon -W+E	154 °	48.5	units d		0.3	d lower		**T**			
	LHA	94 °	00' W/60' E	dsd corr.	**+**		dsd		Hc **A**		10 °	36.6 '
				d corr.	Pub. 229	15.6				a =		11.7 T

					tab Hc	10 °	21.0 '	d + -	20.4	Z	53.0		Zn =	307.0
4	LHA	94		**5**	d corr.	Pub.249 & 229	15.6	Dec min.	46.1				a - Lat =	22 N
	Dec deg	38	N S N		Hc	°	36.6 '					**6**	a - Lon =	154° 48.5' W
	a-Lat	22	N S N											

✱ *Use declination 46° to get Zn = 048.5, which is more accurate.*

Problem 27. July 21 - Cont.

1	WT	8 ʰ 31 ᵐ 37 ˢ	date	**21-Jul-1982**	body	**Venus**		Hs	**22** °	**11.8** '
	WE +S-F	ᵐ 0 ˢ	DR Lat	**22° 05' N**	log	**2689**		index corr. + off, - on		**0** '
	ZD +W-E	**7**	DR Lon	**155° 12' W**	HE ft	**9**		DIP -	**-**	**-2.9** '
	GMT	15 ʰ 31 ᵐ 37 ˢ	GMT date / LOP label **Sights #38 21-Jul-1982**		C- **232** T		S- **7.6** Kt	Ha	**22** °	**8.9** '

2	GHA hr.	**72** ° **49.1** '	v moon planets	**-0.8**	DEC hr	**N 22** ° **42.2** '	d +-	**+0.1**	HP moon	

3	GHA + m.s.	**367** ° **54.3** '		d corr. +-	**0.1**	additional altitude corr. moon, mars, venus	**+**	**0.1** '
	SHA + or v corr.	° **-0.4** '	stars or moon, planets	DEC deg	**N 22** ° DEC min **42.3** '	altitude corr. all sights	**+-**	**-2.4** '
	GHA	**440** ° **43.0** '				upper limb moon subtract 30'		
			tens d	**7.0**	d upper	Ho **T**	**22** °	**6.6** '
	a-Lon -W+E	**154** ° **43.0** '	units d	**4.3**	d lower			
	LHA	**286** ° **00' W/60' E**	dsd corr. **+**		dsd	Hc **A**	**22** °	**21.2** '
			d corr. Pub. 229	**11.3**			a =	**14.6 A**

4	LHA	**286**			**5**	tab Hc	**22** ° **9.9** '	d +- **16.1**	Z **74.2**	Zn = **074.2**
	Dec deg	**22**	N S	**N**		d corr. Pub.249 & 229	**11.3**	Dec min. **42.3**		a - Lat = **22 N**
	a-Lat	**22**	N S	**N**		Hc	**22** ° **21.2** '		**6**	a - Lon **154° 43.0' W**

N Lat L.H.A. greater than 180 .... Zn = Z
L.H.A. less than 180 .... Zn = 360 - Z

S Lat L.H.A. greater than 180 .... Zn = 180 - Z
L.H.A. less than 180 .... Zn = 180 + Z

Problem 27. July 21

Step 1 Correct Hs to get Ho		Sights #38		
1-1	Record Maximum Sextant Height	Hs	**22** °	**58.2** '
1-2	Record Index Correction (mark sign + if off, - if on)	IC	Off + On -	**0**
1-3	Record eye height (HE) and look up Dip Correction on the right-hand side of Table A2, front of Almanac (T-8 in notes) HE (ft) 9	Dip	-	**2.9** '
1-4	Record Maximum Sextant Height	Ha	**22** °	**55.3** '
1-5	Look up the altitude correction in the center of Table A2, front of the Almanac (T-8 in notes)	Alt corr.	+ -	**2.3** '
1-6	Sum the above two numbers to get Observed Height	Ho	**22** °	**53.0** '

Starpath Form 110 for Polaris Sights

Step 2 Find LHA Aries		GMT date =	**21-Jul-82**
2-1	GMT Time in Hours, Minutes and Seconds	GMT time =	**14:51:02**
2-2	Find GHA Aries on Left Hand Daily Page of the Nautical Almanac (far left column) for GMT Day and Hour	GHA Aries (Hr) =	**149° 00.4'**
2-3	Find GHA Aries minutes correction from Increments and Corrections pages	GHA Aries (Min) =	**12° 47.6'**
2-4	GHA Aries - Sum the above two numbers	GHA Aries =	**161° 48.0'**
2-5	DR Longitude (-W, +E)	DR Lon =	**155° 12.5'**
2-6	LHA Aries (Combine previous numbers)	LHA Aries =	**6° 35.5'**

Step 3 Latitude Determination			
3-1	HO	HO =	**22°53.0'**
3-2	a0 from Polaris Table (using LHA Aries)	a0 =	**15.3'**
3-3	a1 from Polaris Table (using DR Latitude)	a1 =	**0.5'**
3-4	a2 from Polaris Table (using Month)	a2 =	**0.2'**
3-5	Subtract 1 Degree	- 1 =	**-1°**
3-6	Sum the above five numbers to get LATITUDE	LATITUDE =	**22° 09.0'**
3.7	Check the value for the Azimuth	Zn =	**000.4**

Plotted Workform Solutions

We start by showing below a section of the last nautical chart that was used before switching to universal plotting sheets for the ocean voyage. There is no fixed rule on how or when to make this transition. It depends on your own convenience and the charts you have available. At the end of the voyage, we again transition back onto a nautical chart.

For the plotting we use standard notation. A fix is a full circle; a DR position is a half circle. In this voyage we consider the DR position to be our best estimate of our position taking into account all we might know about the boat. That is, if we are sailing to weather on course 200 and we believe we have a leeway of 6°, then the course we record would be 206. With GPS values of COG, SOG, etc, you might choose to do this another way, but with only cel

nav to go by this is the most direct and simplest approach to logbook records.

Each course line is labeled with the course recorded in the logbook (ie C206), which had to be an average estimated by the navigator during that leg, as well as the SMG for that leg (ie S6.5), which was determined by subtracting log readings at course changes, and dividing by the time between them. The speed is more accurate than the course in this form of record keeping.

The assumed positions of each sight are marked as AP. The line between DR and fix is shown dotted.

Keep in mind that the universal plotting sheets require some compromise in accuracy when using one longitude scale to cover several degrees of latitude.

Last Chart before Plotting Sheets

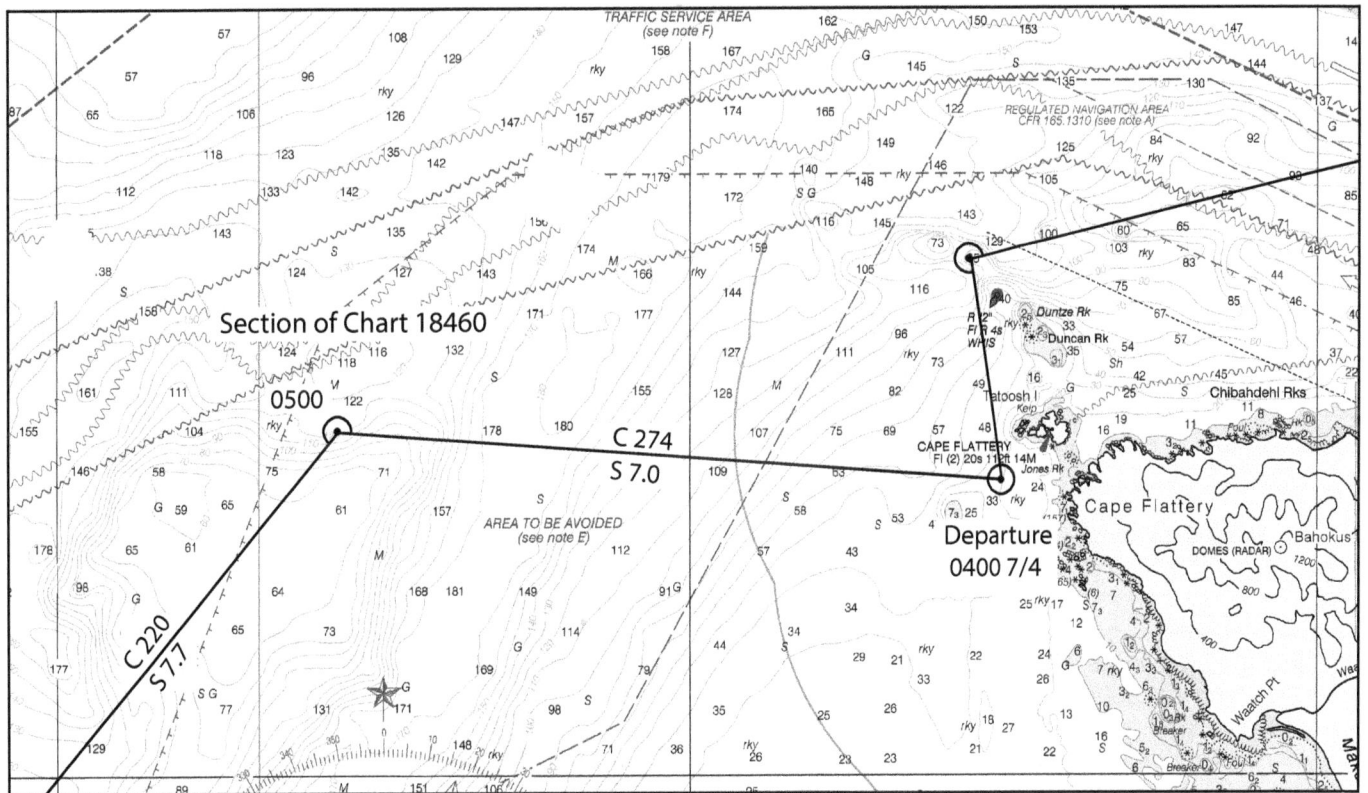

July 4th - Last Chart Before Plotting Sheets

Departure. *We took our departure as a bearing and estimated distance off of Cape Flattery Light at 0400 on July 4. Question: what could we guess (looking back) about the state of daylight at 0400 PDT? Answer: At this latitude civil twilight was at about 0350 WT and sunrise was at about 0430 WT. (Use the data from the Almanac and the position given to confirm that this is true). So this was just before sunrise, but if the day had been clear there was some twilight.*

Daily Plotting Sheets

0400 July 4th → 0000 July 5th

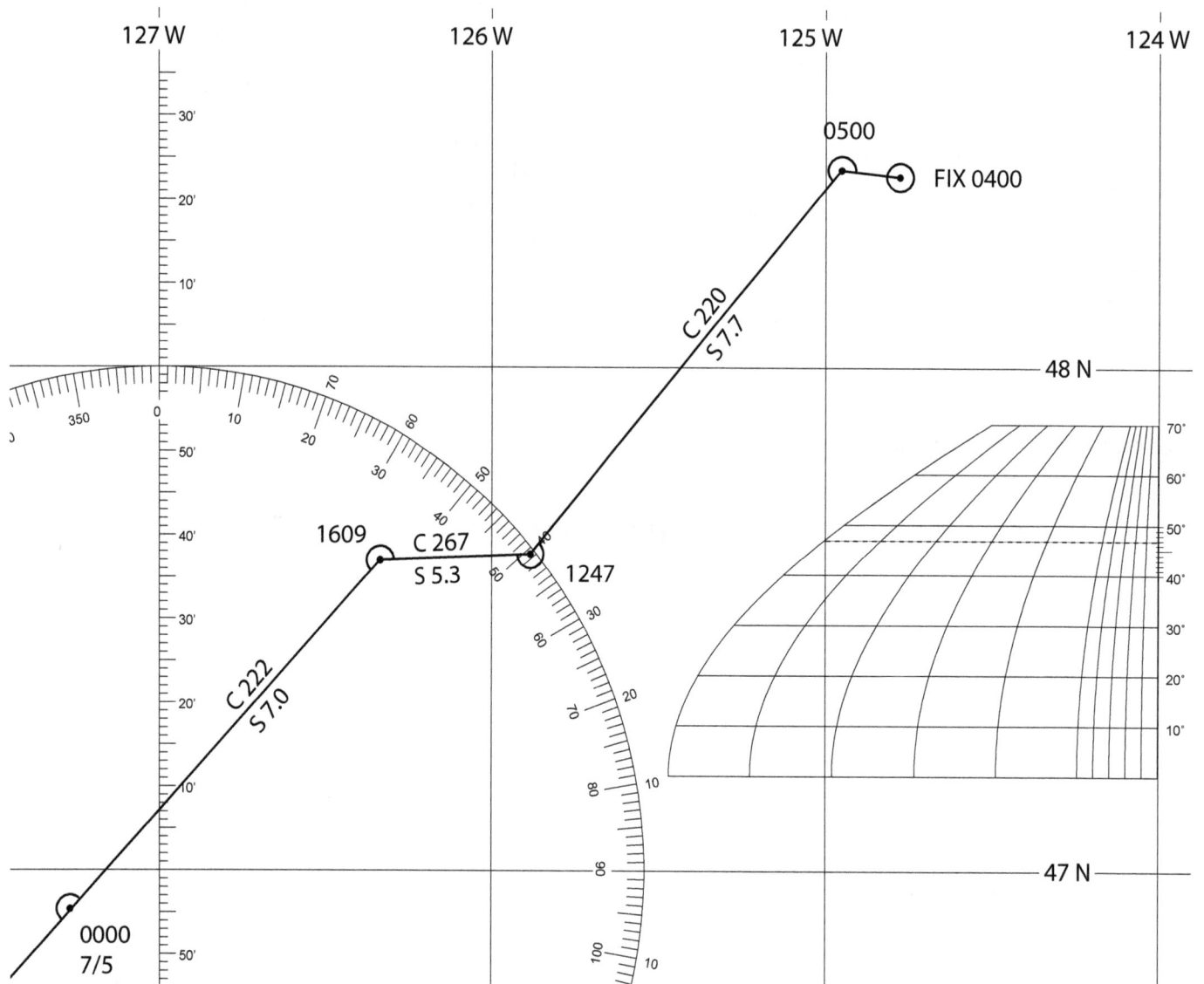

The fix at 0400 is from piloting, our departure 0.75 miles SW of Cape Flattery Light. DR track lines are labeled with course (C) and speed (S). For short legs without labels, refer to the logbook. From 0400 to 0500 the average course was 274 T, at an average speed of 7.0 kts. At 0500 we turned to course 220 T. Courses were recorded as compass headings underway, but all have been transferred to true headings in this book. The time system used on all plots was Watch Time, which was ZD=+7, PDT. We use standard notation. A fix is a full circle; a DR position is an arc along the track line. Trip log readings at various DR positions are given in the logbook. There were no position fixes for the first day of the voyage; it was all DR. DR positions were computed and recorded to a precision of about ±1 nmi, but it will be clear as your proceed here that they were not that accurate. In several cases in the logbook, we skipped several intermediate course changes and just listed course made good (CMG) between a series of changes. There could well be half a dozen intermediate changes between the recorded course change, but the CMG and log readings listed should be an accurate reflection of the DR between sights.

0000 July 5th → 0000 July 6th

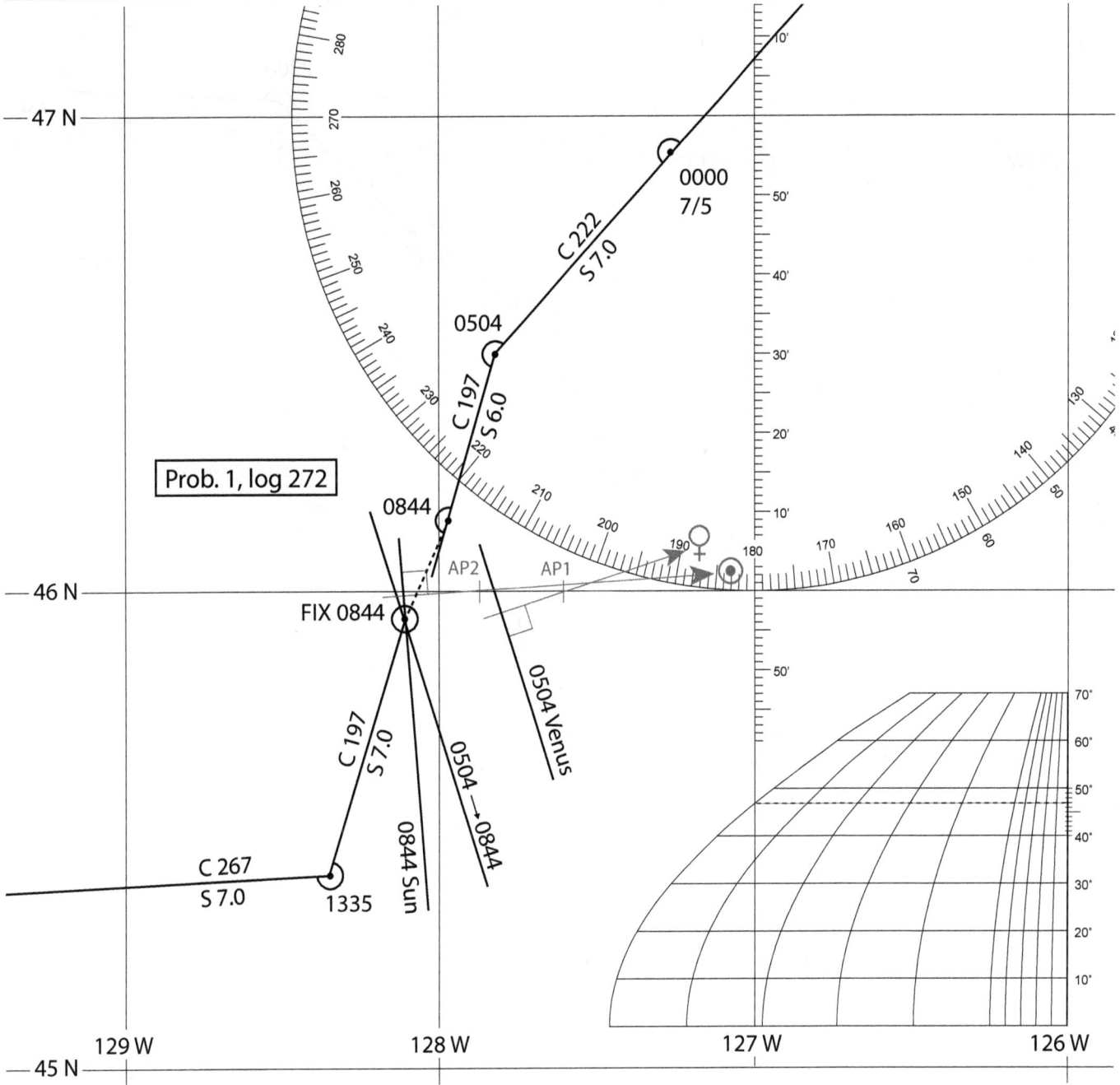

Prob. 1, log 272

The first position fix of the voyage was a running fix between the morning star Venus (at 0504), showing briefly in a patch of clear sky about 45m before sunrise, and the sun (at 0844), which peeked out of the clouds briefly some 3 hours after rising. I recall standing with sextant waiting as the sun kept teasing us with an appearance. The line labeled 0504 → 0844 is the Venus sight advanced to the sun sight time. The sights plotted are the selected ones shown in the Workform Solutions. The single line is intended to represent several sights, but you need to analyze each set to confirm which is the best to use. We may not have selected the optimum sights for all fixes of the voyage (in this book), but this first example is one covered in the Analysis section. Filled out workforms for the plotted sights are shown in the Workform Solutions section. The sights selected are marked in the Computed Solutions section.

Normally we would not do a fix with two bodies this close together in azimuth. But when cel nav is all you have to go by, you take what you can get! The range and bearing from DR to fix (dotted line) was 13 nmi at 205. This is one of the most important pieces of data we get from the fix, which we must watch from day to day to learn about our navigation.

0000 July 6th ➝ 0000 July 7th

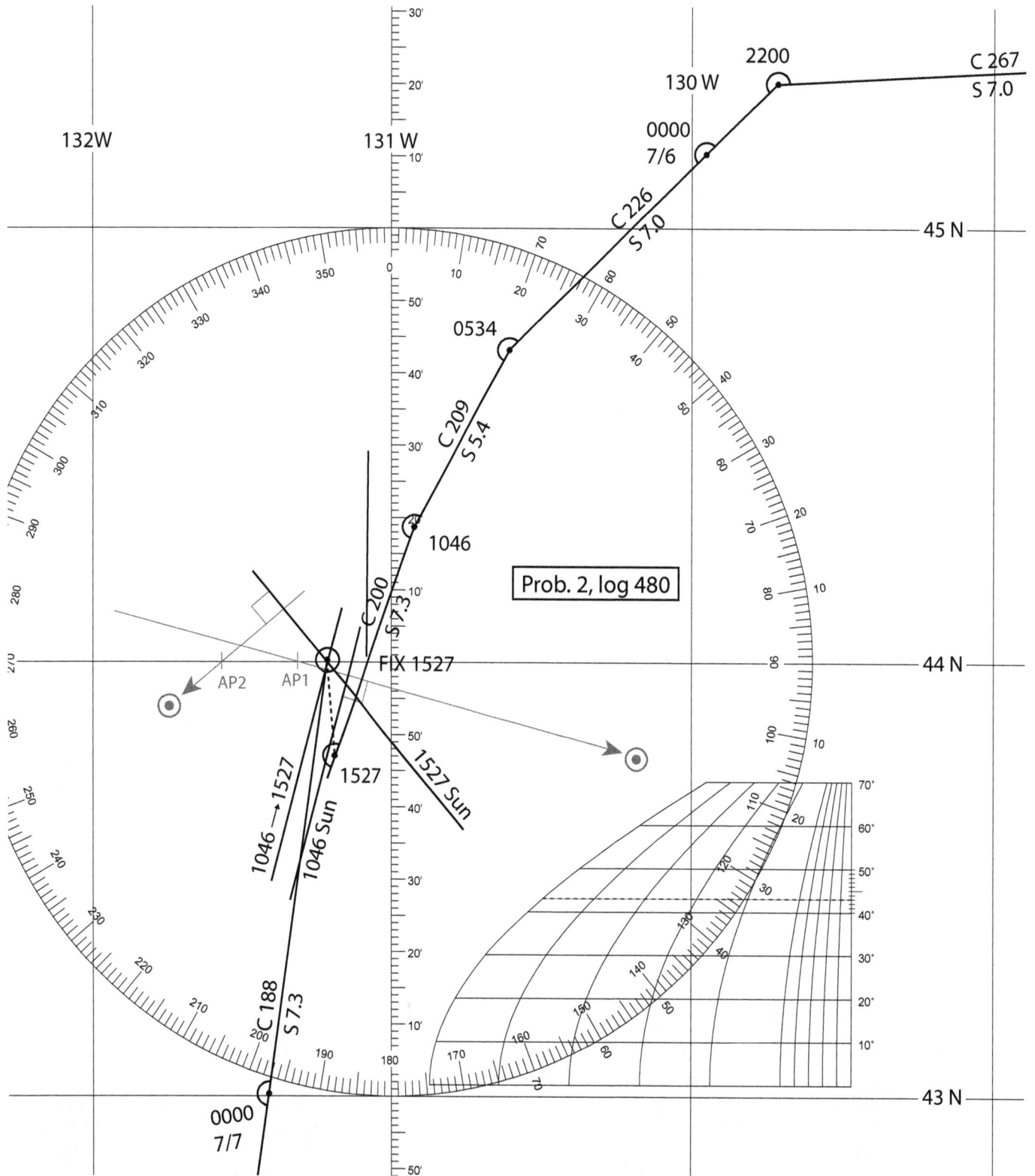

132W

131 W

130 W

2200

C 267
S 7.0

0000
7/6

45 N

C 226
S 7.0

0534

C 209
S 5.4

1046

Prob. 2, log 480

C 200
S 17.3

FIX 1527

44 N

AP2   AP1

1046 → 1527

1046 Sun

1527

1527 Sun

C 188
S 7.3

0000
7/7

43 N

In the afternoon of the 6th we did two sun sights and obtained another running fix and found that we were NNE of where our 6 hrs of DR had us located. This is a large shift so we have to think on what might have caused this.

0000 July 7th → 0000 July 8th

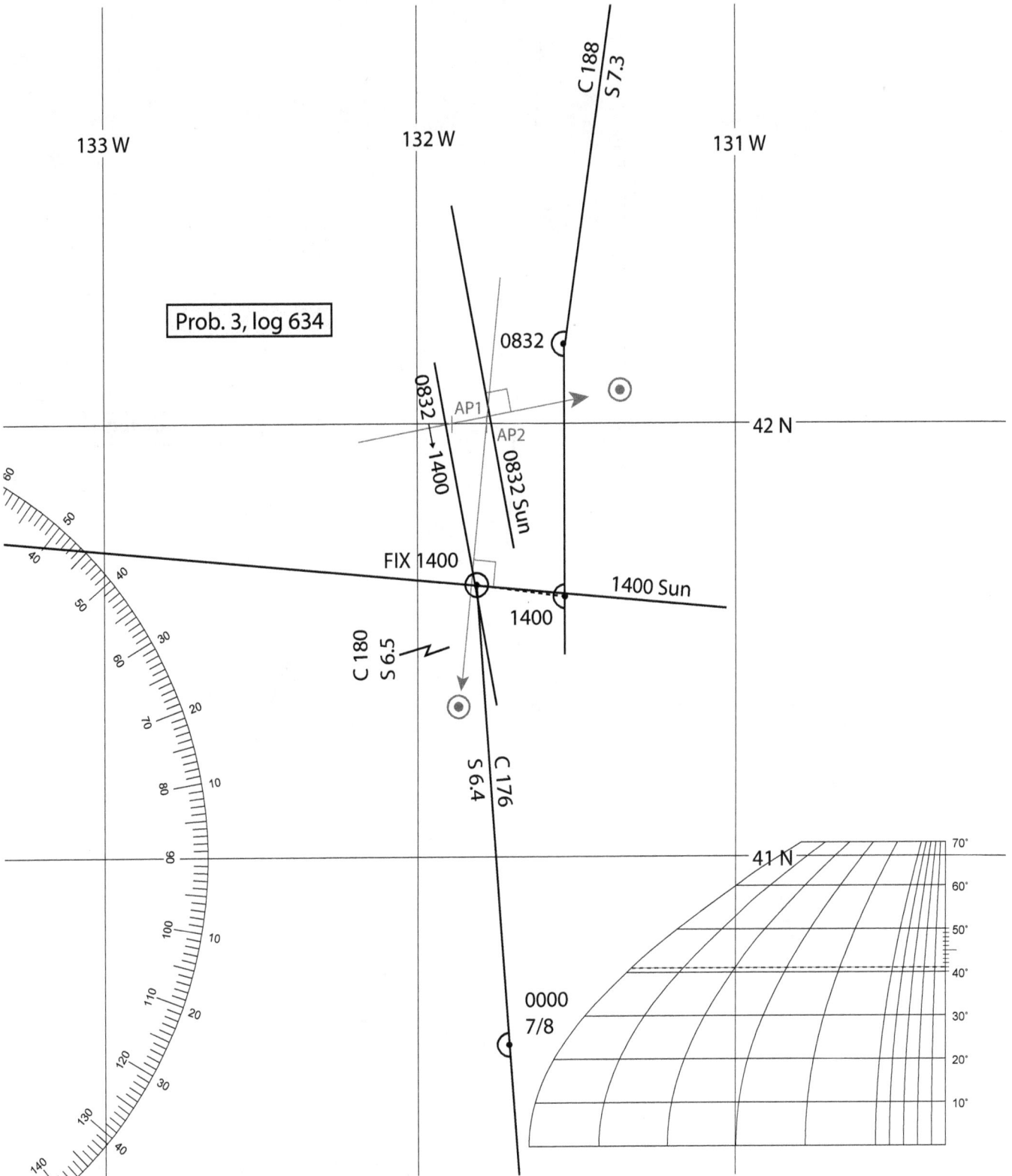

133 W

132 W

131 W

C 188
S 7.3

Prob. 3, log 634

0832

0832

AP1

0832
1400

AP2

0832 Sun

42 N

FIX 1400

1400 Sun

1400

C 180
S 6.5

C 176
S 6.4

41 N

0000
7/8

After a morning sun sight at 0832, we did another sun sight and used the two to obtain an afternoon running fix at 1400, and make a course change at the time. The DR has moved to the west.

0000 July 8th → 0000 July 9th

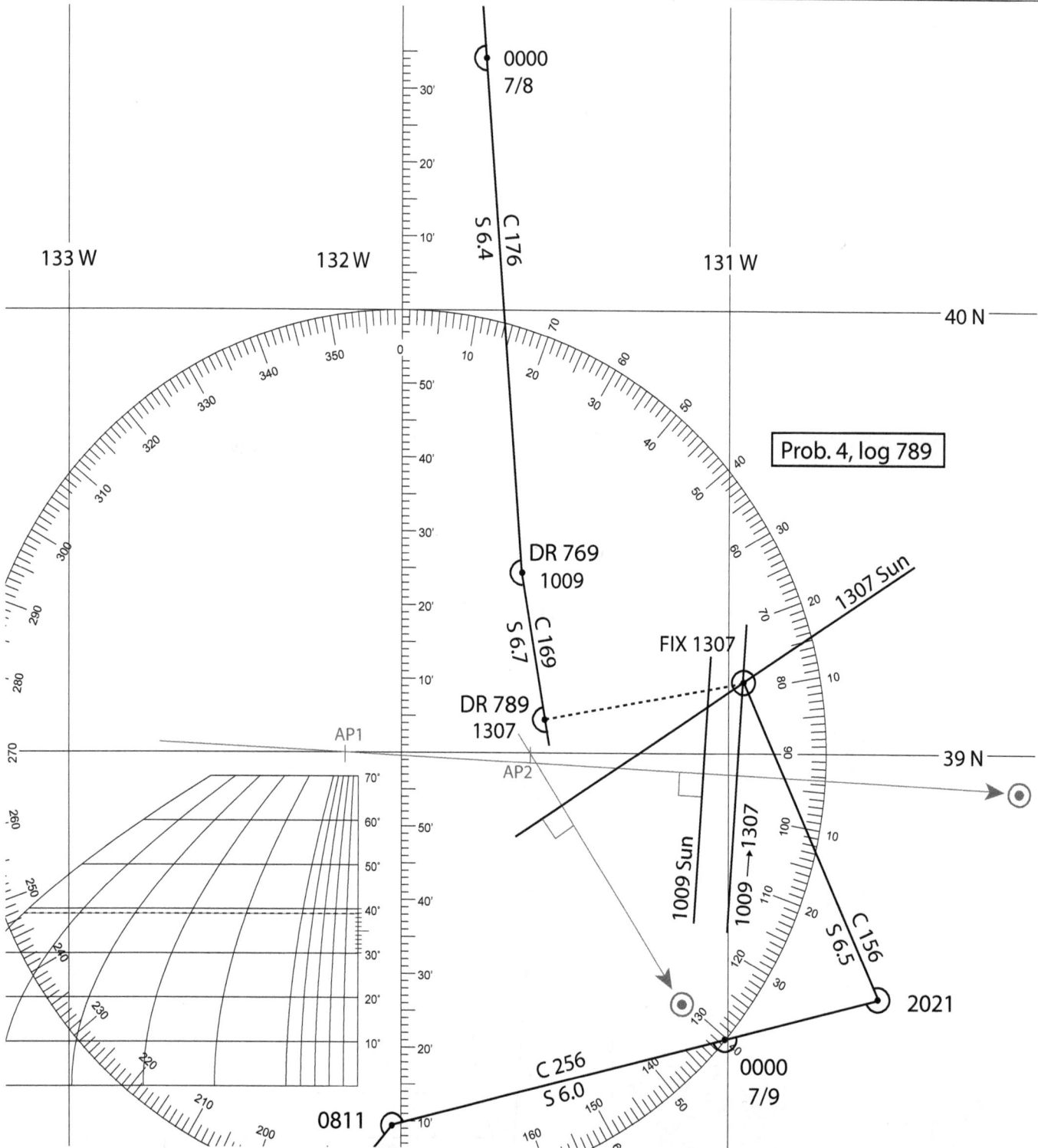

0000
7/8

C 176
S 6.4

133 W   132 W   131 W

40 N

350   340   330   320   310   300   290   280

DR 769
1009

C 169
S 6.7

DR 789
1307

FIX 1307

1307 Sun

AP1

AP2

39 N

270   260   250   240   230   220   210   200

1009 Sun

1009 → 1307

C 156
S 6.5

2021

C 256
S 6.0

0000
7/9

0811

Prob. 4, log 789

Another running fix; this one over a three hour period. We see a huge shift of DR to the east. There may be some helm bias here (11° over the 155 nmi would account for it), or we are getting set east by unexpected currents—the climatic ocean flow is not east at this location. See Ocean Currents note in the Analysis section. When something like this happens, we must keep an eye on the DR-fix comparison to try to learn what is going on. An aside: "helm bias" can also be "logbook bias." When thinking over the average course steered to enter the logbook, a helmsman might bias toward the direction you wanted to go and not admit what was actually steered.

0000 July 9th ➞ 0000 July 10th

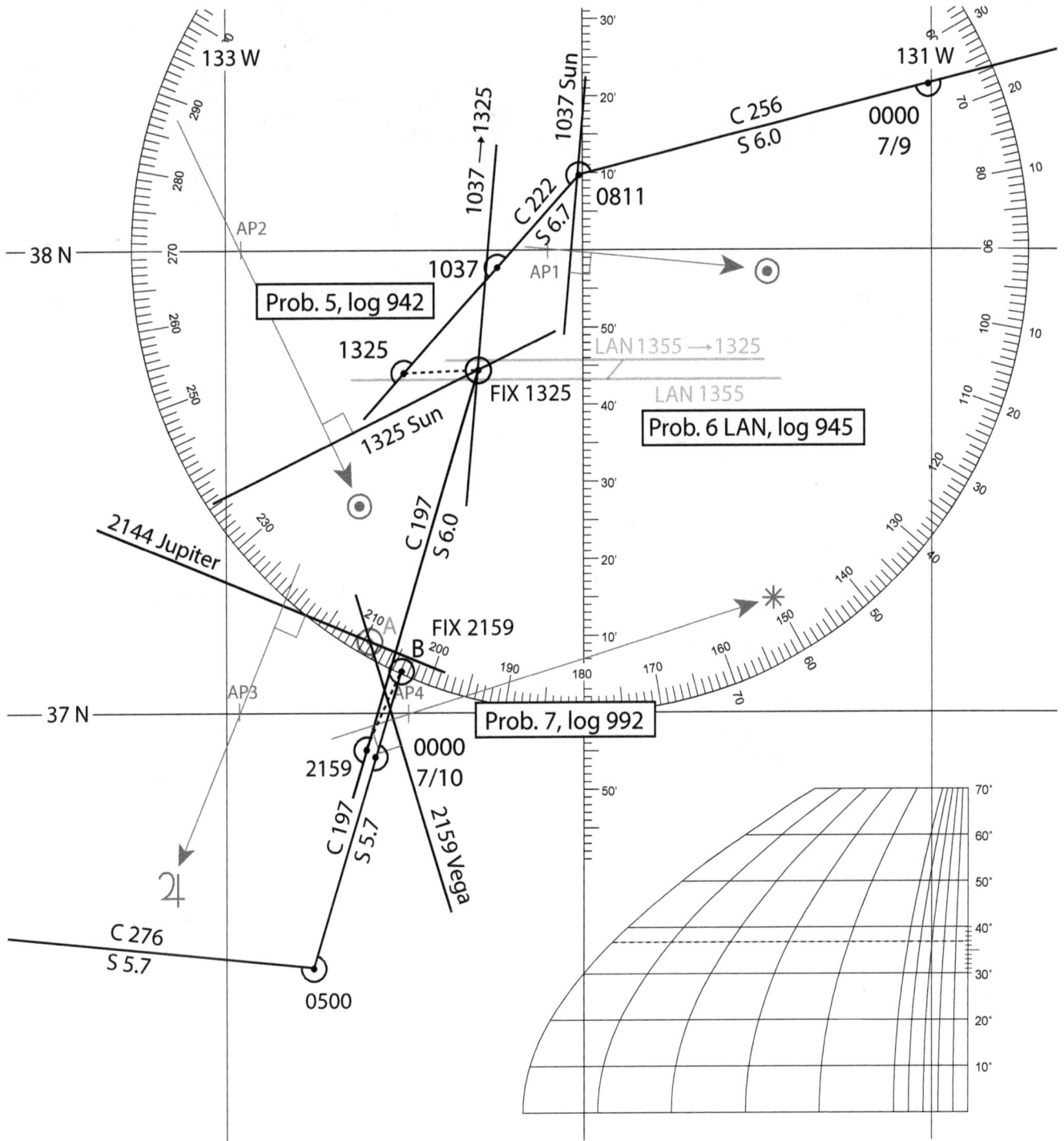

More cel nav on this day. A DR track from 0811 to 1325, then shifted to the fix at 1325, then DR to 2159, and another shift of the track to the Jupiter-Vega fix at 2159. The DR is still pushed east. This is current or helm bias; a compass error is unlikely the source, and if that were suspect, we could easily check it with a compass bearing to the sun and a sight reduction. The LAN lat of Problem 6 is discussed in the Analysis section.

Special exercise. *The Problem 7 fix marked A is from the two LOPs selected to reduce in workforms and plot. You have the full set of sights taken at this time. Analyze these to show that the two plotted are not a good representation of all the data and that the position marked B would be a better choice for the fix. This should illustrate the importance of taking many sights and averaging them in some manner, as discussed in the Analysis section.*

1055 July 10th ➝ 0000 July 12th

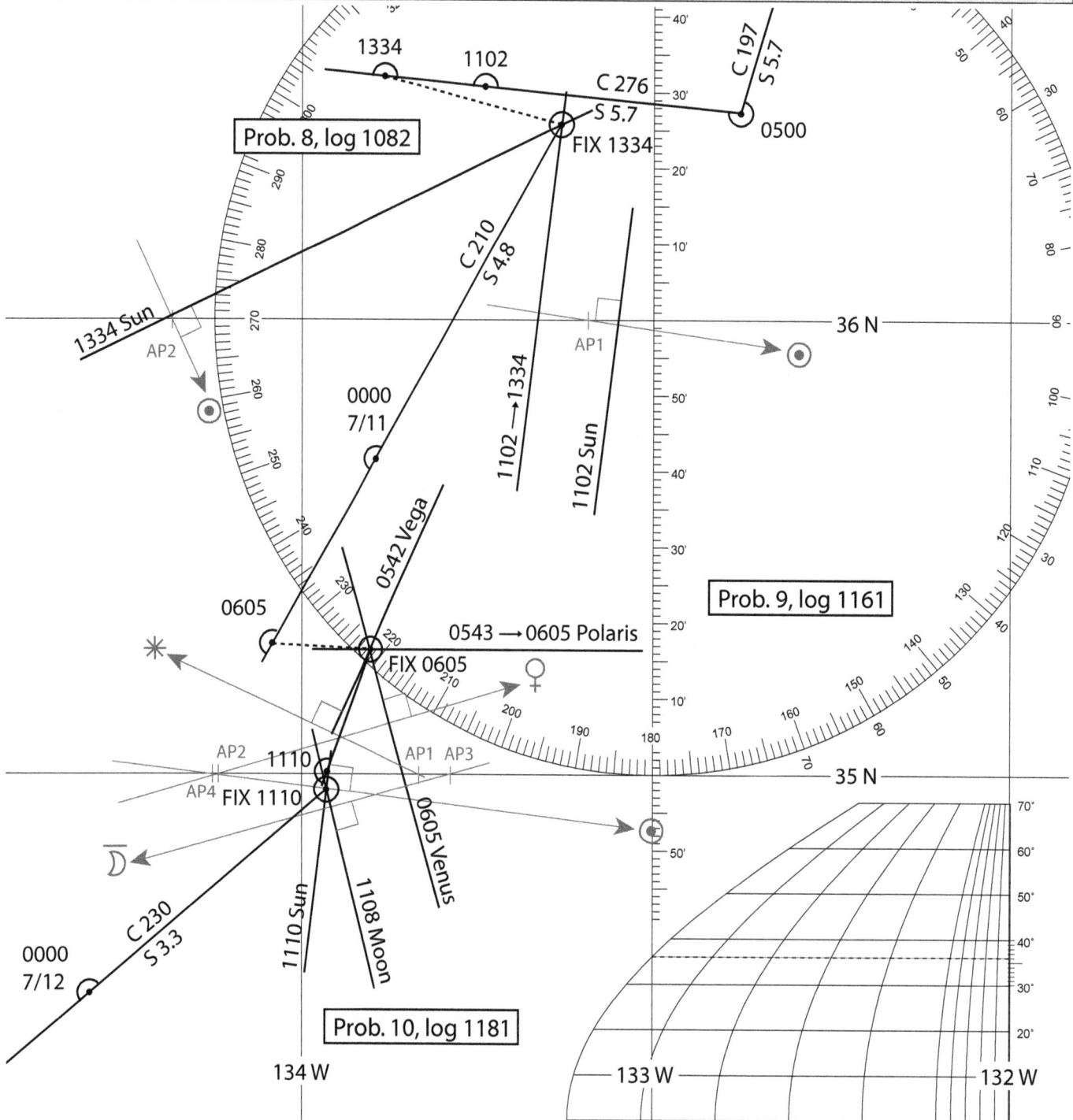

The 1334 rfix moved our DR quite a bit more to the east, then the next morning a star fix moved it again to the east. The Polaris sight used is discussed in the Workforms section. The Vega sight was essentially on the beam, which means there is no advancing required., ie the LOP is your actual course line. Note the long line on the 1334 sun line. This is due to the wrong choice of a-Lat for the sight reduction. Using a-Lat = 37 would give a more accurate fix.

From 0605 to 1110 we sailed C197 at S4.0 and now we are much closer with a fix just a couple miles S-SE of the DR at 1110. On the actual voyage we used a hybrid approach of computing a correction to each LOP to account for the motion and then plotted the LOPs using the corrected a-values. This procedure is discussed in the Analysis.

1445 July 12th ⟶ 0000 July 14th

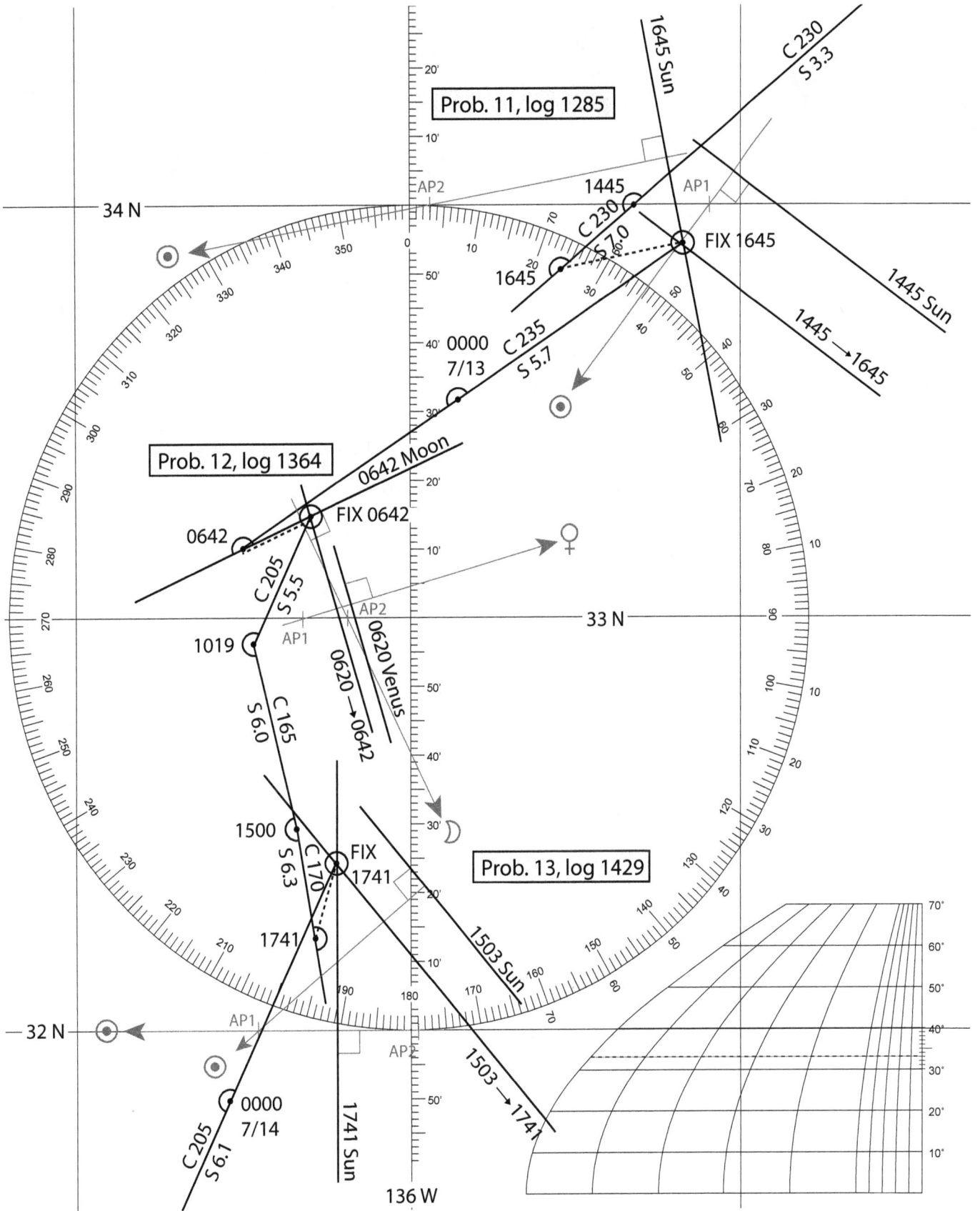

Prob. 11, log 1285

34 N

1645 Sun

C 230
S 3.3

AP2

1445

AP1

C 230

S 7.0

1645

FIX 1645

1445 Sun

1445 ⟶ 1645

0000
7/13

C 235
S 5.7

0642 Moon

Prob. 12, log 1364

0642

FIX 0642

C 205
S 5.5

AP2

1019

AP1

♀

0620 Venus

0620 ⟶ 0642

C 165
S 6.0

1500

S 6.3

C 170

FIX
1741

Prob. 13, log 1429

1741

1503 Sun

1503 ⟶ 1741

32 N

AP1

AP2

0000
7/14

C 205
S 6.1

1741 Sun

136 W

33 N

0514 July 14th ➞ 0000 July 15th

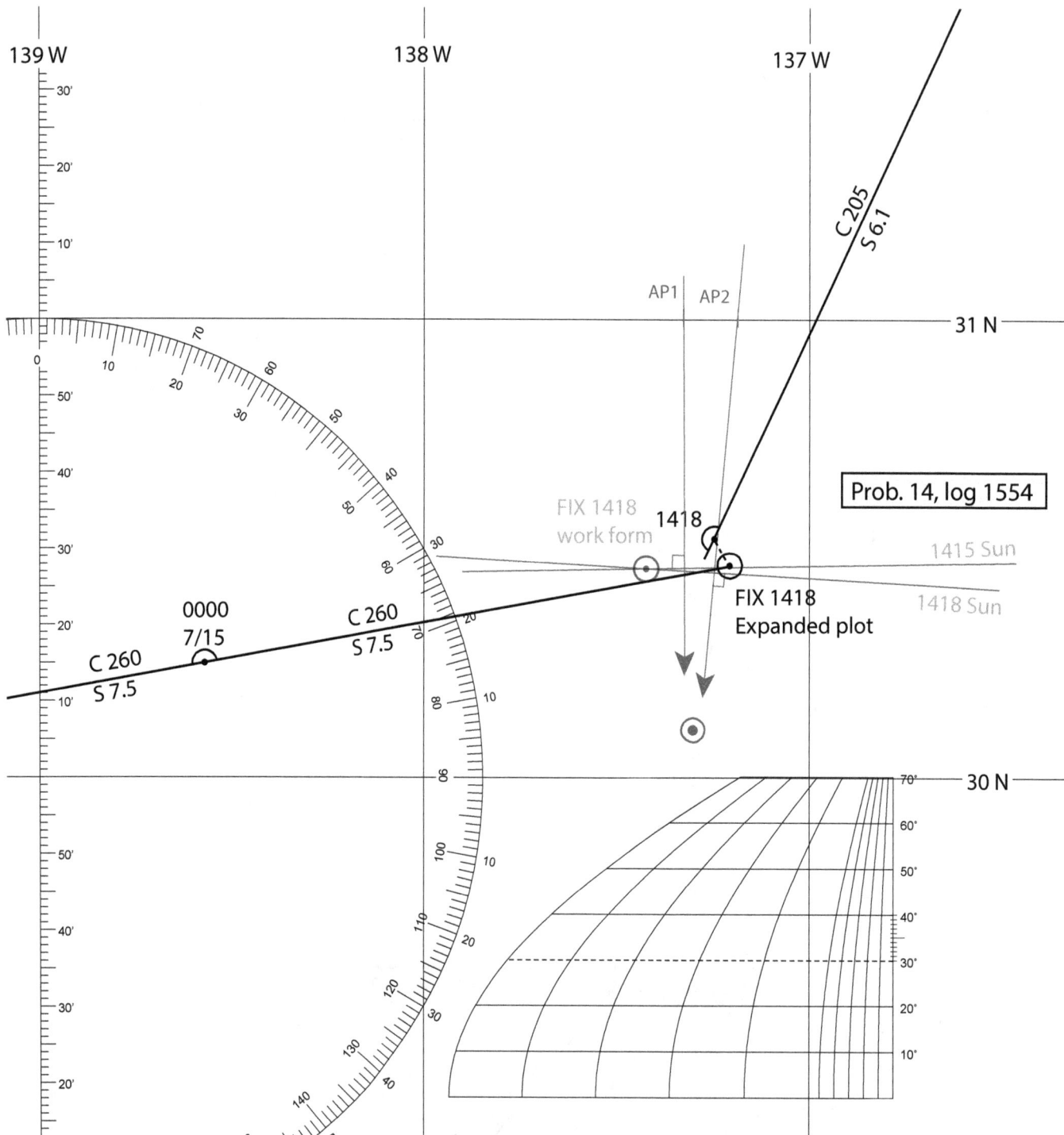

139 W

138 W

137 W

31 N

AP1 AP2

C 205
S 6.1

FIX 1418
work form

1418

Prob. 14, log 1554

1415 Sun

FIX 1418
Expanded plot

1418 Sun

0000
7/15

C 260
S 7.5

C 260
S 7.5

30 N

This was the attempt to get a fix from two sunlines just 3 min apart. The gray position and LOPs above are from the standard sight reduction from the workform on this standard scale. The 1418 position used is from the expanded scale plotted from the DR position. The extra work paid off. We are closer to the DR on this sight, confirmed also on the next fix. This process is easier and more accurate by computation, but we must admit to a large uncertainty here. The big shift in position came from a more accurate account of the motion between sights, which is difficult to plot on this standard scale. Notice that this shift of the DR undid part of the shift north of the last sight. We like to see these DR errors being small and random!

0000 July 15th → 1343 July 15th

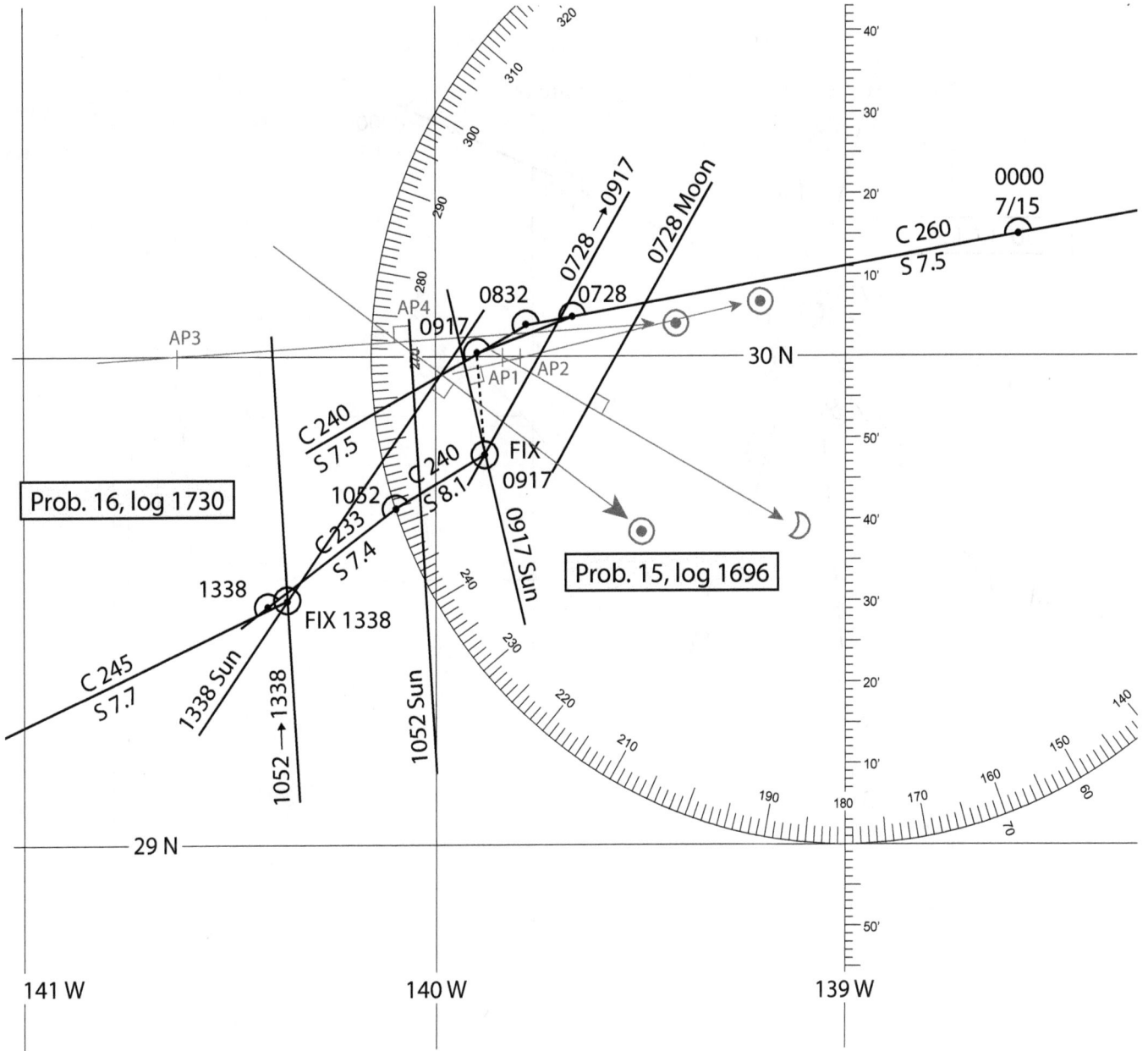

A long running fix has not taken us much off of the DR. Most errors have been to push us forward and to the east. The last fix was an exception. Note the 0917 fix (Log 1696) includes a course change between sights. The SMG and CMG between 0728 and 0917 is S7.1, C250.

0000 July 16th → 0717 July 16th

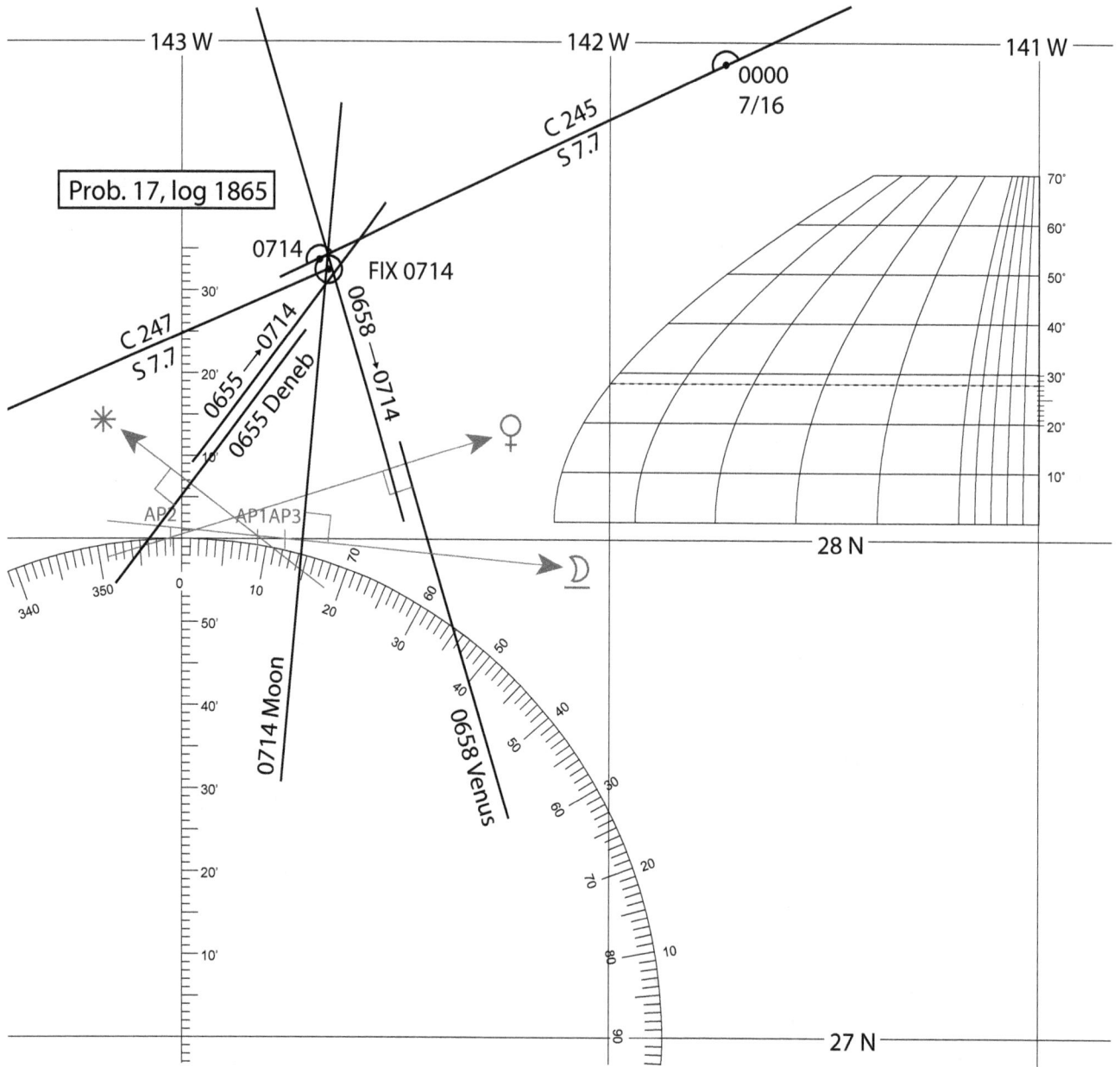

Again, pushed a bit to southeast. The fix is in the center of a triangle of 3 sights, one each representing sets of several. This could likely be analyzed more carefully for a more accurate position, as done in the Analysis section. All the data are given. In any event, the DR has been pretty good the last day or so.

1325 July 16th → 0000 July 17th

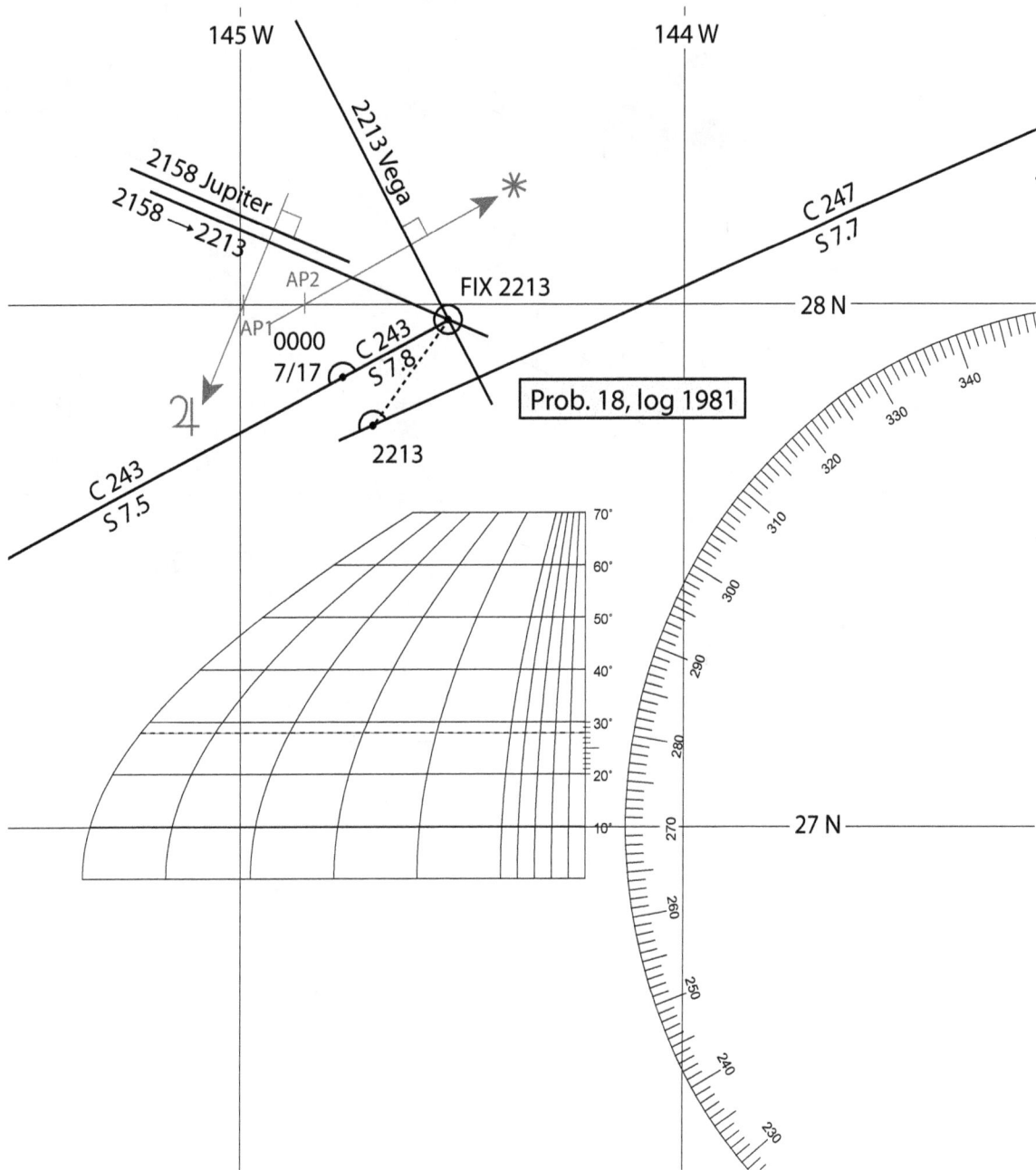

A good fix pushes us back to the north, but still to the east. Note too this was a long run of 116 miles, shown here as one straight course, but it was not actually sailed that way. We had many course changes during this leg and many speed changes. What is shown here is the CMG and SMG from fix to DR. The logbook had us actually listed as S9.0 during parts of this leg, so obviously slower at times.

The next exercise is a long practice at DR plotting, so to compare answers, assume this Problem 18 fix is 27° 58.0'N, 144° 32.0' W at time 2213 on 7/16, log reading 1981. Then we ask for the DR position at 2000 on 7/17.

0000 July 17th ➜ 0740 July 18th

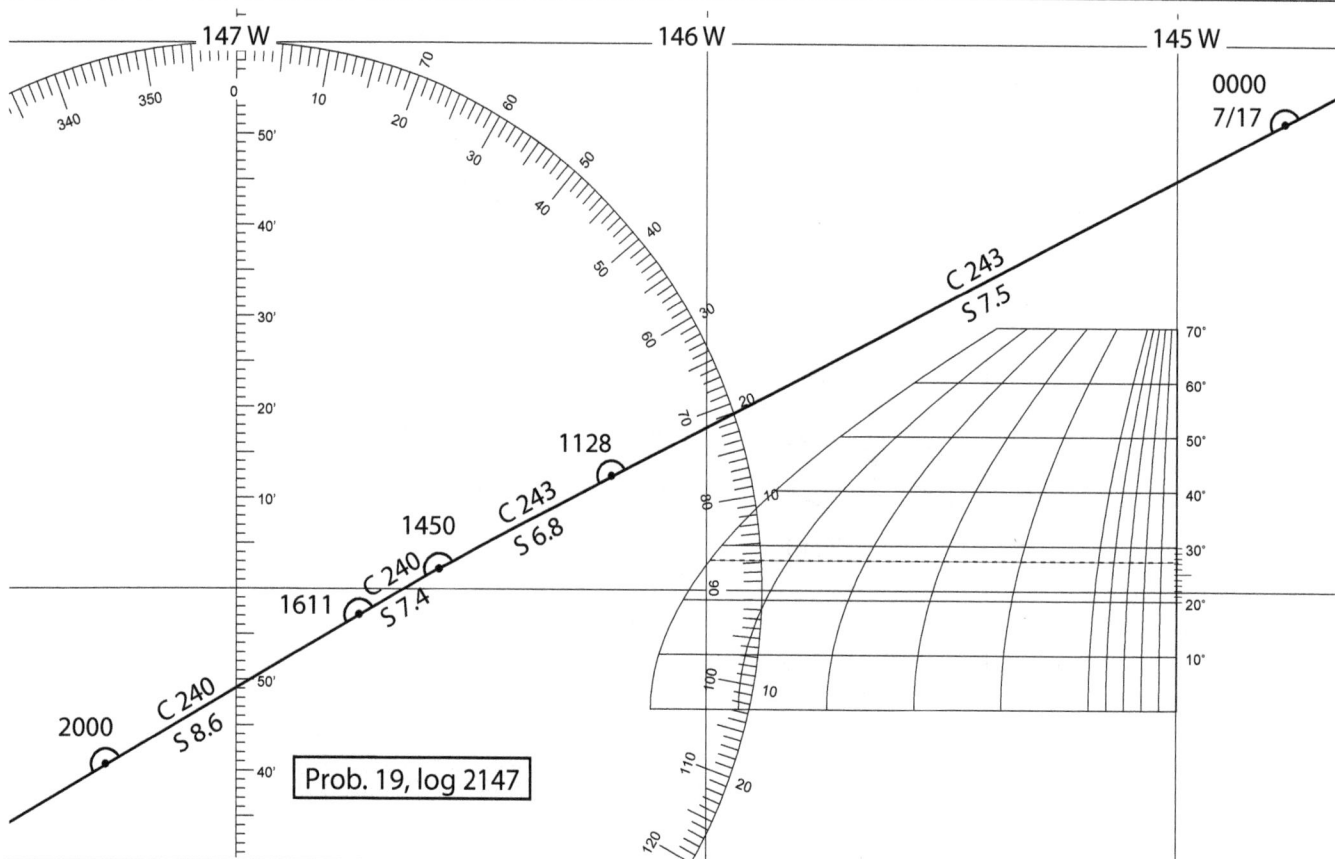

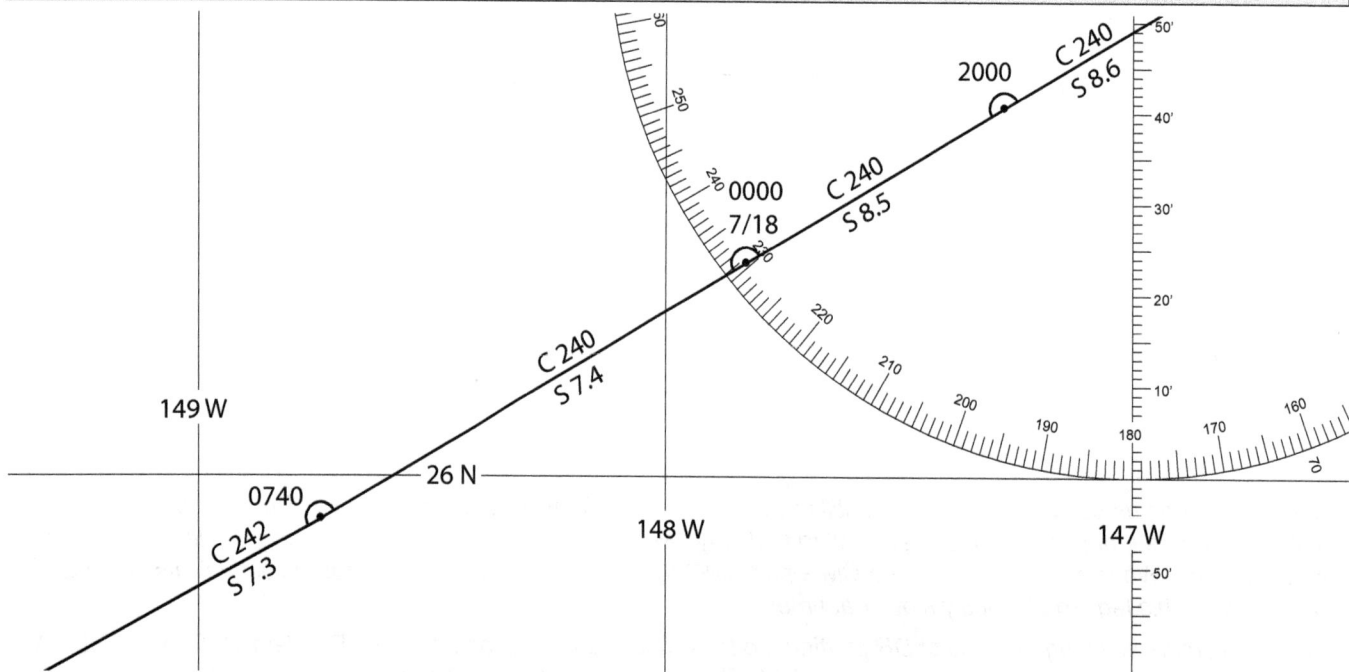

147 W   146 W   145 W

0000
7/17

C 243
S 7.5

1128

C 243
S 6.8

1450

C 240
S 7.4

1611

C 240
S 8.6

2000

Prob. 19, log 2147

2000   C 240
S 8.6

C 240
S 8.5

0000
7/18

C 240
S 7.4

149 W

26 N

0740

C 242
S 7.3

148 W   147 W

No celestial at this time. Only one question on finding DR at 2000. We have a very long run with DR only, so the next fix will tell us if we are learning any more about the DR.

* Note this page has a slightly compressed scale compared to other pages in the book.

0740 July 18th → 0000 July 19th

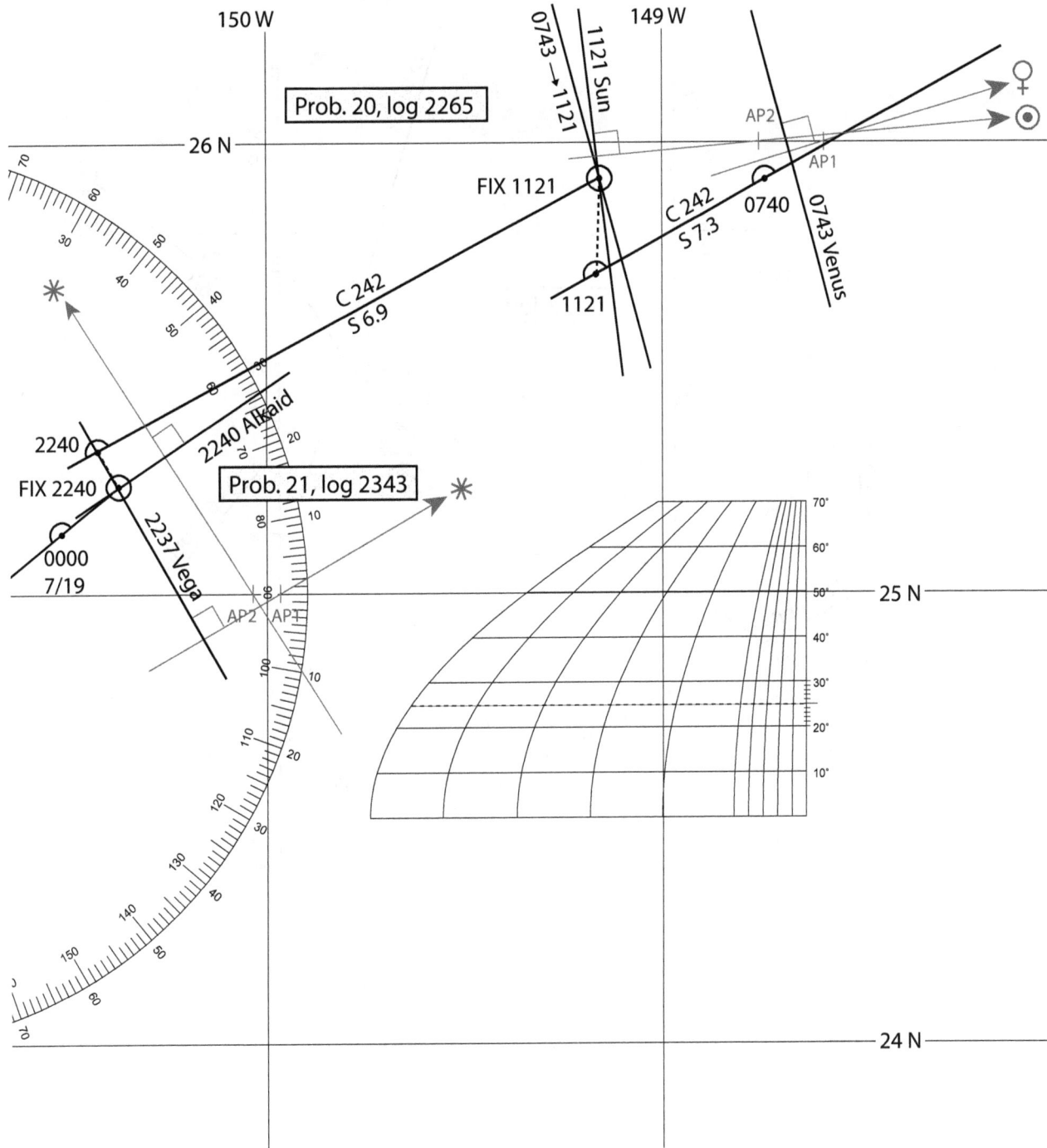

150 W

149 W

Prob. 20, log 2265

0743 → 1121

1121 Sun

26 N

AP2

♀

☉

AP1

FIX 1121

C 242
S 7.3

0740

0743 Venus

C 242
S 6.9

1121

2240 Alkaid

2240

FIX 2240

Prob. 21, log 2343

*

2237 Vega

0000
7/19

AP2 AP1

70°
60°
50°
40°
30°
20°
10°

25 N

24 N

DR not too bad at all for such a long run, especially considering how narrow the fix was. This is a good example of taking a lot of careful sights and then averaging them. The fix uncertainty (primarily latitude) remains large, but the centroid is likely a good contribution to the navigation when that is all you have to go by. The navigation is getting better, as it must as we get closer to land.

0000 July 19th → 0000 July 20th

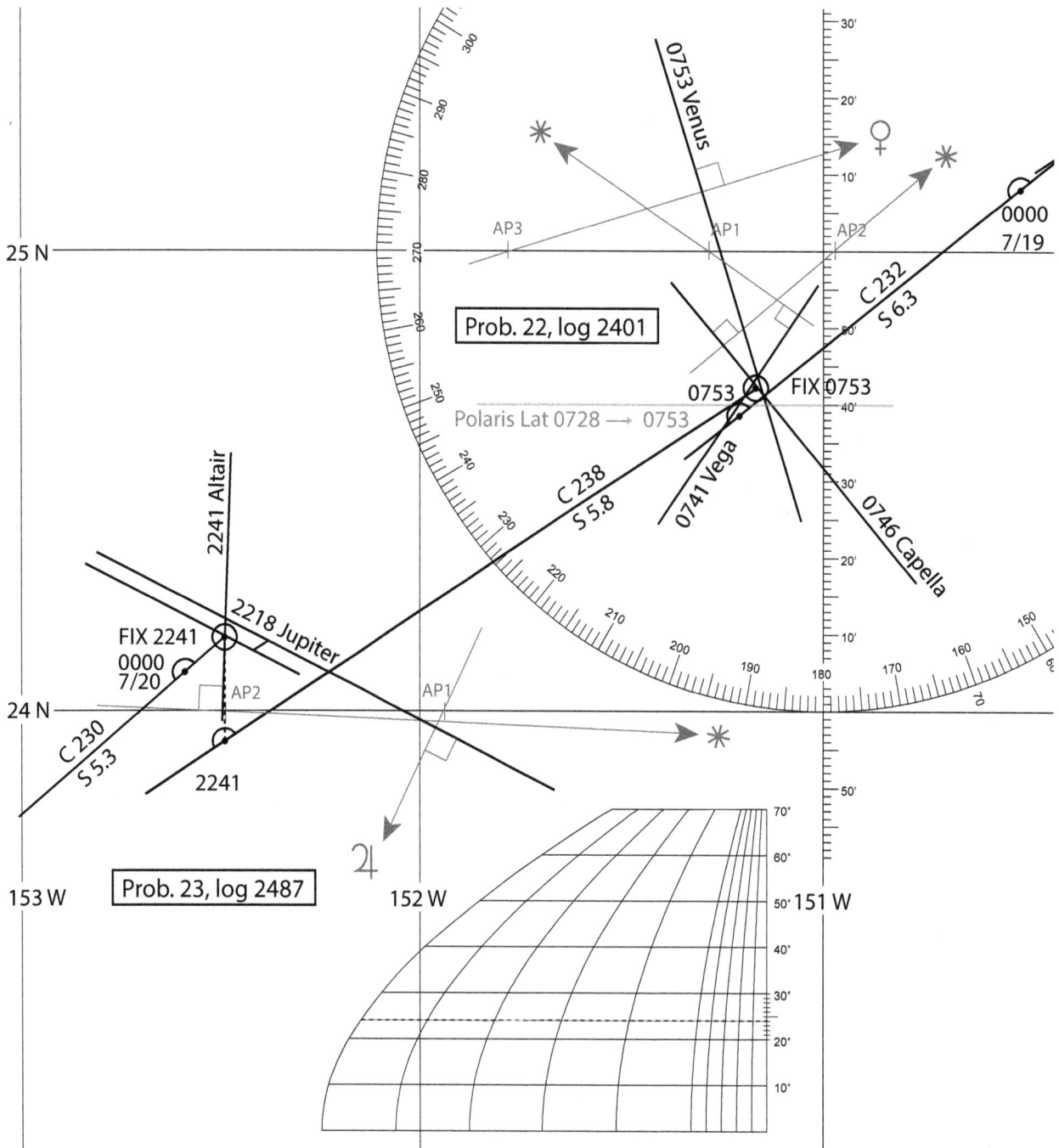

Prob. 22, log 2401

Polaris Lat 0728 → 0753

Prob. 23, log 2487

Navigation looks good at 0753. So whatever was causing the persistent shift to the east seems past. Now we can look more into what we might expect as random uncertainties, which we propose is about 7% of distance run plus an error current of 0.7 kts. Here we run 86 miles from 0753 to 2241. The error current would lead to 0.7 x 14.8 = 10.4 miles and the 7% of 86 = 6.0 miles, so we might expect random errors of about 12 miles [sqrt (10.4^2 + 6.0^2)], which is about what we see at 2241. Note the single Polaris sight shown is not as good as the average of all of them.

0000 July 20th → 0000 July 21st

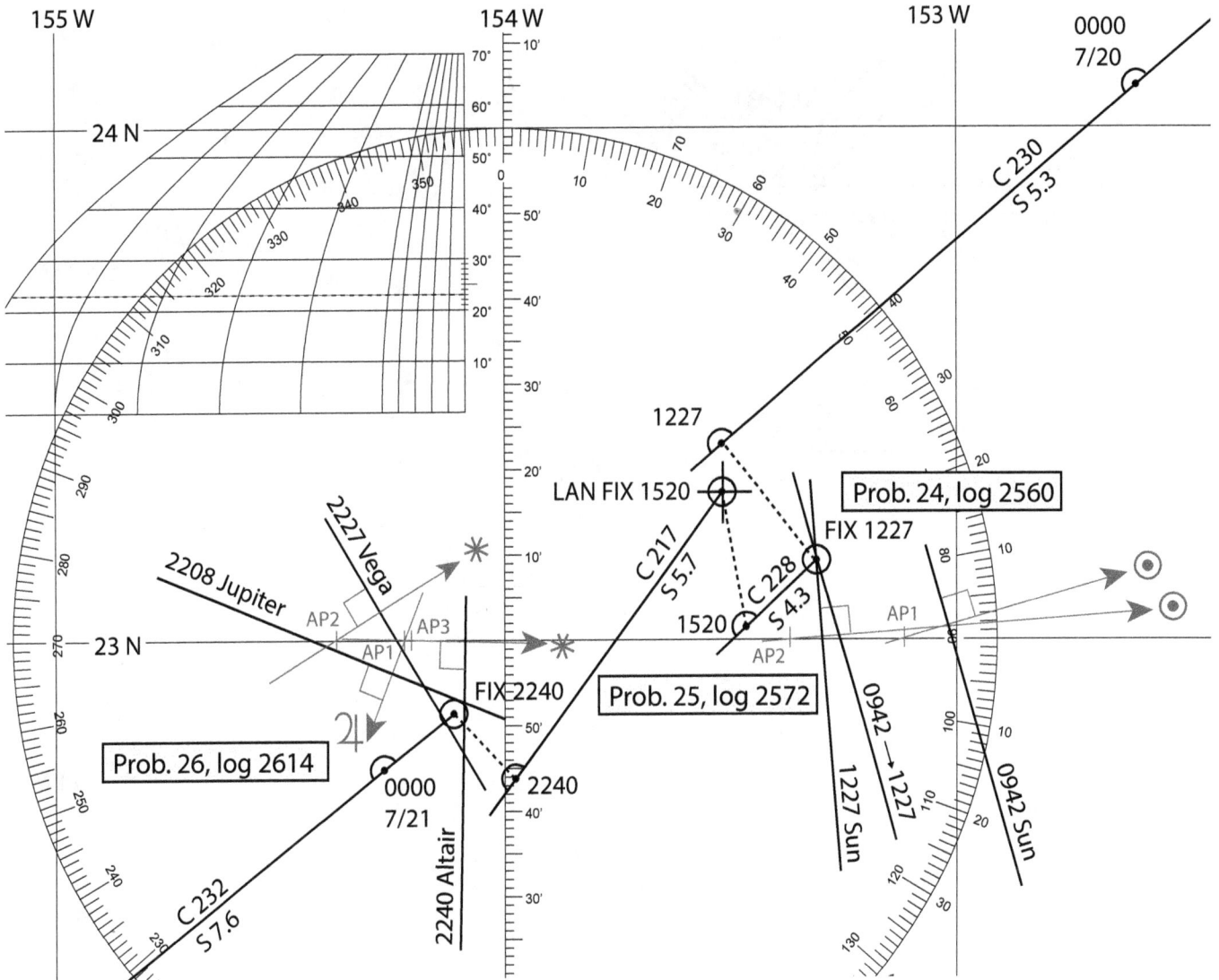

The narrow rfix at 1227 (Prob 24) pushed the DR south, but 3 hours later with a better fix it was pushed back north, but still leaving easterly component. Then after just 42 miles it is pushed back west. There is clearly some DR uncertainties here. The net SMG was relatively low, here, but I recall long runs off course in severe squalls. Surviving records are only the DR positions at sight times, based on several legs. There is clearly some uncertainty here. In difficult conditions, the boat gets more attention than the logbook, though clearly that policy should be avoided whenever possible. The net DR error over this full plotting sheet, however, is well within expected uncertainties. A sketch of these errors are shown below.

In retrospect, another interpretation is the 1227 rfix is just wrong. Throw it out and the navigation looks more normal. But when all you have is cel nav, you take what you can get and try to sort things out as you proceed. Chances are it was just poor DR records during this period.

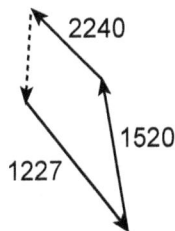

Vector sum of the DR errors from Log 2487 to Log 2614. A net error of 10 nmi to the south after a run of 127 miles over a period of 24 hours.

0000 July 21th ➝ 0831 July 21st

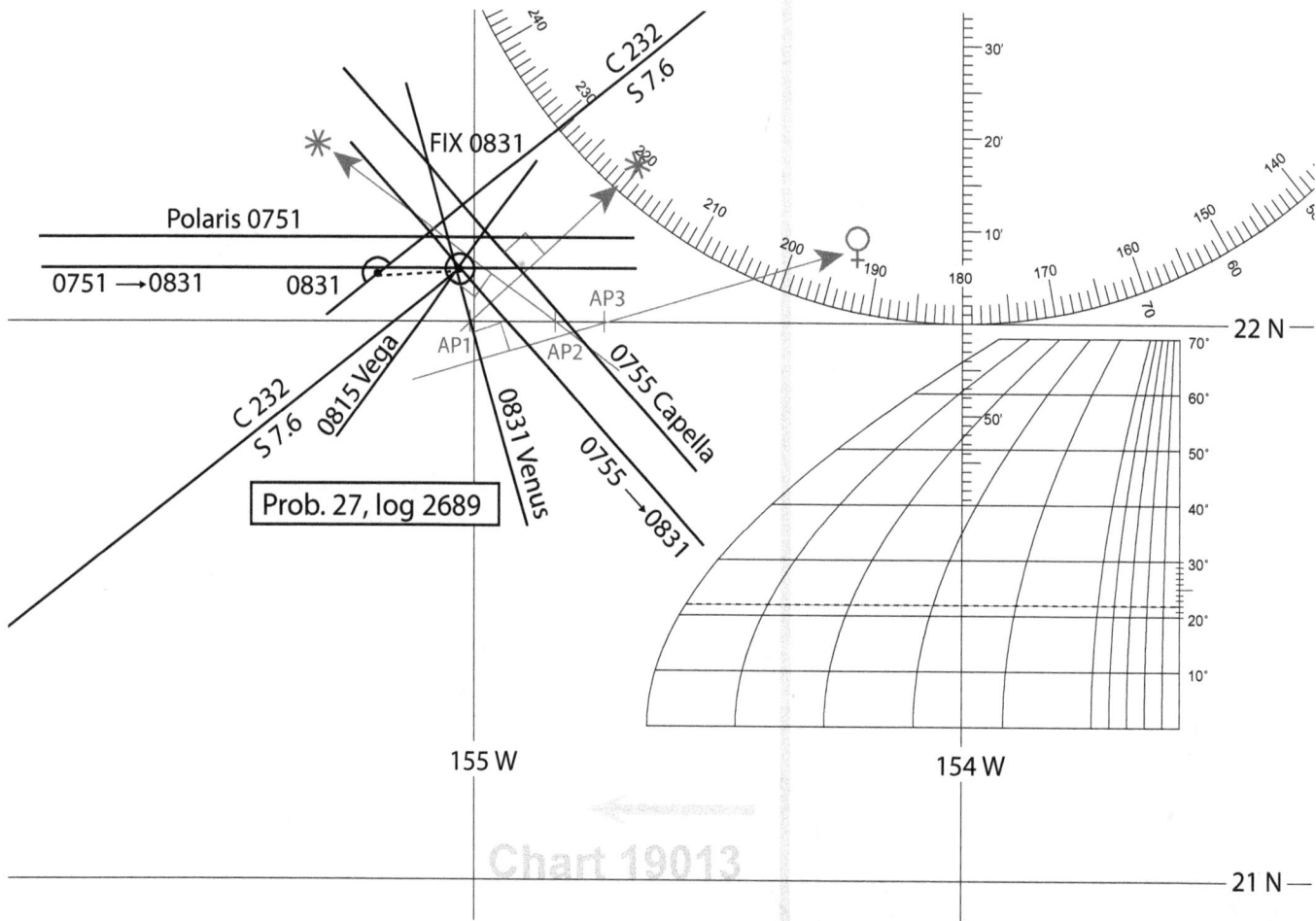

This is the last celestial navigation fix of the passage. The sextant gets put away now, and we start thinking about how to enter the channel. Channels in Hawaii are famous for having very sharp wind boundaries that bulge out of the channel where the wind changes from some 15 kts of trades to 20 to 25 kts of channel winds. The seas are generally big, so one has to be prepared for that sudden transition in sailing and the jibe into the channel.

On the right are the two approach charts to Pailolo Channel, with the approximate visible ranges of the lights shown. It is good practice to plot these for a nighttime approach. For a nighttime approach in dying trades, a close-in route along the north shore (rather than straight into the channel) is a good hope for a land breeze. Visible range is the smaller of the geographic and nominal ranges. The approximate first sight of land in clear weather is shown in the top chart. Often stationary cumulus clouds will indicate the bearing to land before it is sighted. On our approach we passed through a squall with rain so heavy (called violent rain) that we could not see the bow of this 40-ft boat!

Lights on the Approach to Pailolo			
Name	Elevation (ft)	Geographic Range (nmi)	Nominal Range (nmi)
Molokai	213	16	21
Cape Halawa	321	23	6
Nakalene Pt	142	13	6
Hawea Pt	75	10	9
Pauwela Pt	161	14	12
Mt. Puu Kukui	5,788	76	
Mt. Haleakala	10,000	100	

Back onto Nautical Charts

July 21st - Back onto Charts

chart 19340

FIX 0831
7/21

C 232
S 7.6

Pailolo

Hawaiian Islands, Northern Part
SOUNDINGS IN FATHOMS · SCALE 1:675,000

19013

Section of chart 19340

PAILOLO CHANNEL

Logbook with Answers *

#	July	ID	WT	Log	C	S	Computed			Plotted	Range	Bearing
1	4		0400	075	274	7.0				48.23 , 124.45		
2	4		0500	082	220	7.7						
3	4		1247	142	267	5.3						
4	4		1609	160	222	7.0						
5	5		0000	215	222	7.0						
6	5		0504	250	197	6.0						
7	5	P1 DR	0844	272						46.09 , 127.58		
8	5	P1 FIX	0844	272	197	7.0	45.515 , 128.064			45.56 , 128.06	13	205
9	5		1335	306	267	7.0						
10	5		2200	365	226	7.0						
11	6		0000	379	226	7.0						
12	6		0534	418	209	5.4						
13	6		1046	446	200	7.3						
14	6	P2 DR	1527	480						43.47 , 131.12		
15	6	P2 FIX	1527	480	188	7.3	44.050 ,131.119			44.00 , 131.13	13	355
16	7		0000	539	188	7.3						
17	7		0832	599	180	6.5						
18	7	P3 DR	1400	634						41.36, 131.33		
19	7	P3 FIX	1400	634	176	6.4	41.379 ,131.487			41.38, 131.50	12	277
20	8		0000	698	176	6.4				40.35 , 131.48		
21	8		1009	769	169	6.7				39.25 , 131.41		
22	8	P4 DR	1307	789						39.05 , 131.33		
23	8	P4 FIX	1307	789	156	6.5	39.046 ,130.567			39.10 , 130.56	30	082
24	8		2021	836	256	6.0						
25	9		0000	858	256	6.0						
26	9		0811	907	222	6.7						
27	9	P5 DR	1325	942						37.44 , 132.30		
28	9	P5 FIX	1325	942	197	6.0	37.427 ,132.186			37.45 , 132.17	10	090
29	9	P6 LAN	1355	945	197	6.0	from 1355 LAN			37.45	--	--
30	9	P7 DR	2159	992						36.55 , 132.36		
31	9	P7 FIX	2159	992	197	5.7	37.065 ,132.321			37.06 , 132.31	11	025

* Notes. (1) First column just numbers the entries this sheet; no nav significance. Column 2 is the date. (2) In these "computer units" 43.268 = 43° 26.8', and 128.095 = 128° 09.5'. (3) DR used for computed solutions are not crucial to the computed fixes. (4) Range and Bearing is DR to Fix. (5) All course and bearings are True. (6) "Px" labels Problem X. (7) Another reminder that logbooks should be kept to the nearest tenth of a mile, although we do not have that data for this passage. (8) The blank columns can be used to mark progress or sights checked.

#	July	ID	WT	Log	C	S	Computed			Plotted	Range	Bearing
32	10		0000	1003	197	5.7						
33	10		0500	1032	276	5.7						
34	10	P8 DR	1334	1082						36.32 , 133.46		
35	10	P8 FIX	1334	1082	210	4.8	36.229 , 133.178			36.26 , 133.15	25	104
36	11		0000	1132	210	4.8						
37	11	P9 DR	0605	1161						35.17 , 134.05		
38	11	P9 FIX	0605	1161	197	4.0	35.153 , 133.479			35.18 , 133.48	13	093
39	11	P10 DR	1110	1181						35.01 , 133.56		
40	11	P10 FIX	1110	1181	230	3.3	35.024 , 133.554			34.58 , 133.55	3	166
41	12		0000	1222	230	3.3						
42	12		1445	1271	230	7.0						
43	12	P11 DR	1645	1285						33.51 , 135.32		
44	12	P11 FIX	1645	1285	235	5.7	33.554 , 135.101			33.54 , 135.11	19	078
45	13		0000	1326	235	5.7						
46	13	P12 DR	0642	1364						33.10 , 136.30		
47	13	P12 FIX	0642	1364	205	5.5	33.150 , 136.175			33.15 , 136.18	11	065
48	13		1019	1384	165	6.0						
49	13		1500	1412	170	6.3						
50	13	P13 DR	1741	1429						32.13 , 136.17		
51	13	P13 FIX	1741	1429	205	6.1	32.254 , 136.129			32.24 , 136.13	11	016
52	14		0000	1467	205	6.1						
53	14	P14 DR	1418	1554						30.31 , 137.15		
54	14	P14 FIX	1418	1554	260	7.5	30.271 , 137.120			30.278 , 137.13	4	150
55	15		0000	1627	260	7.5						
56	15		0728	1682	260	7.5						
57	15		0832	1690	240	7.5						
58	15	P15 DR	0917	1696						30.00 , 139.54		
59	15	P15 FIX	0917	1696	240	8.1	29.484 , 139.519			29.48 , 139.53	13	175
60	15		1052	1709	233	7.4						
61	15	P16 DR	1338	1730						29.29 , 140.24		
62	15	P16 FIX	1338	1730	245	7.7	29.324 , 140.230			29.30 , 140.22	2	074
63	16		0000	1809	245	7.7						
64	16	P17 DR	0714	1865						28.33 , 142.41		
65	16	P17 FIX	0714	1865	247	7.7	28.320 , 142.396			28.33 , 142.40	2	147
66	16	P18 DR	2213	1981						27.46, 144.42		
67	16	P18 FIX	2213	1981	243	7.8	27.578 , 144.318			27.58 , 144.32	15	037

#	July	ID	WT	Log	C	S	Computed			Plotted	Range	Bearing
68	17		0000	1995	243	7.5						
69	17		1128	2081	243	6.8						
70	17		1450	2104	240	7.4						
71	17		1611	2114	240	8.6						
72	17	P19 DR	2000	2147						26.41 , 147.16		
73	17	P19 FIX	2000	2147	240	8.5				No Fix Problem 19	--	--
74	18		0000	2181	240	7.4						
75	18		0740	2238	242	7.3						
76	18	P20 DR	1121	2265						25.43 , 149.10		
77	18	P20 FIX	1121	2265	242	6.9	25.517 , 149.089			25.55 , 149.09	12	002
78	18	P21 DR	2240	2343						25.19 , 150.25		
79	18	P21 FIX	2240	2343	232	6.3	25.150 , 150.259			25.14 , 150.22	6	151
80	19		0000	2351	232	6.3						
81	19	P22 DR	0753	2401						24.38 , 151.12		
82	19	P22 FIX	0753	2401	238	5.8	24.414 , 151.105			24.42 , 151.10	6	034
83	19	P23 DR	2241	2487						23.56 , 152.29		
84	19	P23 FIX	2241	2487	230	5.3	24.097, 152.294			24.12 , 152.29	13	359
85	20		0000	2494	230	5.3						
86	20	P24 DR	1227	2560						23.23 , 153.31		
87	20	P24 FIX	1227	2560	228	4.3	23.067 , 153.187			23.10 , 153.19	17	141
88	20	P25 DR	1520	2572						23.02 , 153.28		
89	20	P25 FIX	1520	2572	217	5.7	23.176,153.312			23.17 , 153.31	16	350
90	20	P26 DR	2240	2614						22.44 , 153.58		
91	20	P26 FIX	2240	2614	232	7.6	22.489 , 154.057			22.52 , 154.07	11	315
92	21		0000	2624	232	7.6						
93	21	P27 DR	0831	2689						22.05 , 155.12		
94	21	P27 FIX	0831	2689	232	7.6	22.052 , 155.013			22.06 , 155.02	10	088

On the next page we show that the overall DR accuracy was consistent with our guidelines of 7% of distance run and 0.7 kts of error current. This supports our proposal that when you observe local variations of your DR by more than these values you have reason to be on the alert for some special circumstances hindering your DR.

Likewise, if you are left to go by DR alone, it would be a good starting point to consider that you can proceed within these limits. This can then be taken into account for the planning of any voyage that must rely on DR alone. With careful measurements and record keeping, one might do better, but we would not want to count on it without definite evidence to support it.

DR to FIX Summary

Prob	WT	dT	dT(h)	Log	dLog	Error	%	Drift	Set	
	7/4 0400			075		—	—	—	—	—
P1	7/5 0844	28:44	28.73	272	197	13	7%	0.5	205	S-SW
P2	7/6 1527	30:43	30.72	480	208	13	6 %	0.4	355	N
P3	7/7 1400	22:33	22.55	634	154	12	8 %	0.5	277	W
P4	7/8 1307	23:07	23.12	789	155	30	19 %	1.3	082	E
P5	7/9 1325	24:18	24.30	942	153	10	7 %	0.4	090	E
P6	7/9 1356	00:30	00.50	945	3	—	—	—	—	—
P7	7/9 2159	07:58	07.97	992	50	11	22 %	1.4	025	N-NE
P8	7/10 1334	15:35	15.58	1082	90	25	28 %	1.6	104	E-SE
P9	7/11 0605	16:31	16.52	1161	79	13	16 %	0.8	093	E
P10	7/11 1110	05:05	05.08	1181	20	3	15 %	0.6	166	E-SE
P11	7/12 1645	29:35	29.58	1285	104	19	18 %	0.6	078	E-NE
P12	7/13 0642	13:57	13.95	1364	79	11	14 %	0.8	065	E-NE
P13	7/13 1741	11:01	11.02	1429	65	11	17 %	1.0	016	N
P14	7/14 1418	20:35	20.58	1554	125	4	3 %	0.2	150	S-SE
P15	7/15 0917	18:59	18.98	1696	142	13	9 %	0.7	175	S
P16	7/15 1338	04:21	04.35	1730	34	2	6 %	0.5	074	E-NE
P17	7/16 0714	17:36	17.60	1865	135	2	1 %	0.1	147	S-SE
P18	7/16 2213	14:59	14.98	1981	116	15	13 %	1.0	037	NE
P19	7/17 2000	21:44	21.73	2147	166	—	—	—	—	—
P20	7/18 1121	15:21	15.35	2265	118	12	10 %	0.8	002	N
P21	7/18 2240	11:19	11.32	2343	78	6	8 %	0.5	151	S-SE
P22	7/19 0753	09:13	09.22	2401	58	6	10 %	0.7	034	N-NE
P23	7/19 2241	14:48	14.80	2487	86	13	15 %	0.9	000	N
P24	7/20 1227	13:46	13.77	2560	73	17	23 %	1.2	141	SE
P25	7/20 1520	02:53	02.88	2572	12	16	133 %	5.6	350	N
P26	7/20 2240	07:20	07.33	2614	42	11	26 %	1.5	315	NW
P27	7/21 0831	09:51	09.85	2689	75	10	13 %	1.0	088	E

Notes. (1) P is problem number. (2) WT is watch time and date. (3) dT is time difference between fixes in hh:mm:ss. (4) dT(h) is same time interval in decimal hours. (5) dLog is log difference, or distance run between fixes. (6) Error is the range from DR to Fix. (7) % is (Error/dLog)*100. (8) Drift is Error/dT(h), which is the speed of the error current. (9) Set is bearing from DR to Fix, which is the direction of the error current.

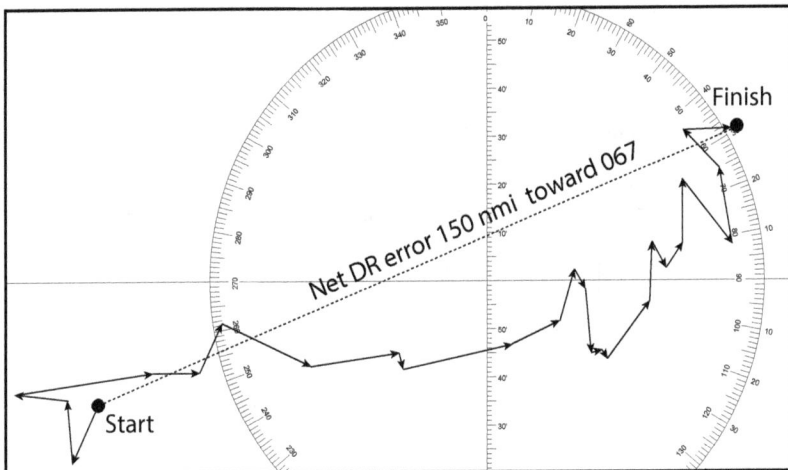

Net vector sum of DR errors. *Had we gone by DR alone, we would have been off by 150 nmi after logging 2,614, which is a net error of 5.7% of distance run, or an equivalent error current over the 17 days of 9 nmi per day or 0.4 kts. The errors were clearly not random, but biased to the E for about one week, then to the NE for the last week.*

For 5 days (7/7 to 7/13) while crossing latitudes 39N to 33N, we were pushed 135 miles to the east. This is consistent with a mesoscale eddy circulation with a drift of 1.1 kts.

The large excursion to the N just after that, immediately corrected back to the S, was likely due to inaccurate DR records. A similar short-term digression occurred toward the end of the voyage.

Analysis

We review first two procedures that we use routinely for cel nav analysis today, as well as during this passage from 1982. Following that are sample applications to sight sessions from this book to illustrate the methods, but the conclusions achieved were not all applied to the sample solutions given earlier in the book.

Automatic Advancement of LOPs

We know that running fixes must be advanced as they are typically taken over a period of several hours, but it is equally important for the best fix to advance *all* LOPs, even those from the same session. Over a 30-minute sight session when moving at 8 kts, you have a 4-mile uncertainly on the sights if this is not accounted for.

The typical plotting scale we use, however, makes it difficult to precisely make corrections that are just a mile or two long. Thus we can use a trick to compute the shift in the a-value that will account for the advancement to a common time. The preparation of this book was a reminder that we were using this back in 1982, but have not discussed it much in our recent courses. It is a good technique, and should be considered for general use.

The origin of the formula is shown in Figure A1, followed by a photocopy of a page from the 1982 logbook that shows it in use in Figure A2.

This is the analysis of Problem 26 done underway at the time. The actual IC was 0.8' On the Scale, and the watch error on this date was 3 seconds fast, but in this book we have removed these corrections from the data. PM means *evening*, in this case. Before the sight session, we recorded the log as 2611 at a time of 2200 WT.

Looking at the bottom of the page, the log reading at the end of the sight session was 2616 at 2241. The leading 2 was not recorded. Then from these two log readings (a run of 5 nmi), we computed the SMG during the 41 minute sight session, which was 7.32 kts.

We then did the sight reductions of all of the sights by computer. In those days we computed with an HP 41 calculator using a set of navigation routines that we had developed at Starpath and distributed on magnetic cards! One of the programs computed the almanac data (dec and GHA) and another did the sight reductions, then we had a third routine that did this "automatic advancement," but we still had to compute the runs for each sight by hand.

When doing sight reduction by computation, we must choose a DR to use, and we chose a midpoint at 2614 for all of the computations. That value is recorded at the top right of the page.

We chose here to advance them all to the time of the last sight, so that one at 0540 had a zero run. The first sight was done 4.4 miles earlier on course 227 T. Note the magnetic variation was applied to a compass course from the logbook in the bottom right corner. That variation of 12° E for that location in 1982 has since changed to 10°E in 2014.

Comparing the initial values to the corrected values, we see as expected that the early sights have larger corrections than the later ones. The Jupiter a-value average changed from 6.7 to 3.0, but the Altair average changed only from

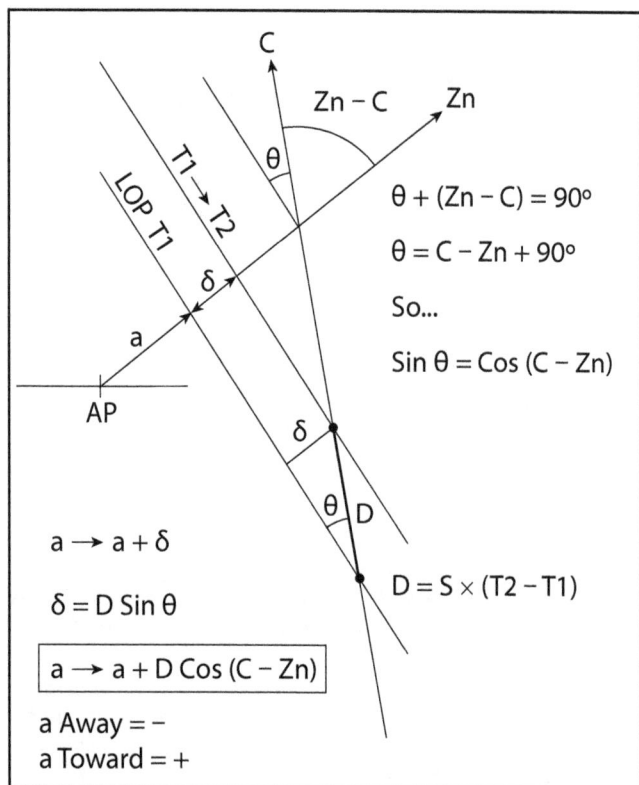

In the figure:

C

Zn – C   Zn

θ

$\theta + (Zn - C) = 90°$

$\theta = C - Zn + 90°$

So...

$Sin\ \theta = Cos\ (C - Zn)$

LOP T1

T1 → T2

δ

a

AP

δ

θ D

$D = S \times (T2 - T1)$

$a \rightarrow a + \delta$

$\delta = D\ Sin\ \theta$

$\boxed{a \rightarrow a + D\ Cos\ (C - Zn)}$

a Away = –
a Toward = +

Figure A1. *To advance or retard an LOP that has an a-value and azimuth Zn for a distance D run in true direction C, add algebraically to the a-value a correction given by D x Cos (Zn - C). D is figured from the speed made good between sights, times the time difference between the two sights. This correction can be positive or negative. Initial and corrected a-values Toward Zn are positive; those Away from Zn are negative. Then plot from the same assumed position and Zn, but use the corrected a-value in place of the original.*

Thus a = 5T, with correction +2, the new a is 7T. A correction of -8 would give a new a = 3A. An initial a=5A with a correction of +6, yields a new a = 1T.

Problem 26

Distance Run, $\boxed{D}$

Corrected a-values

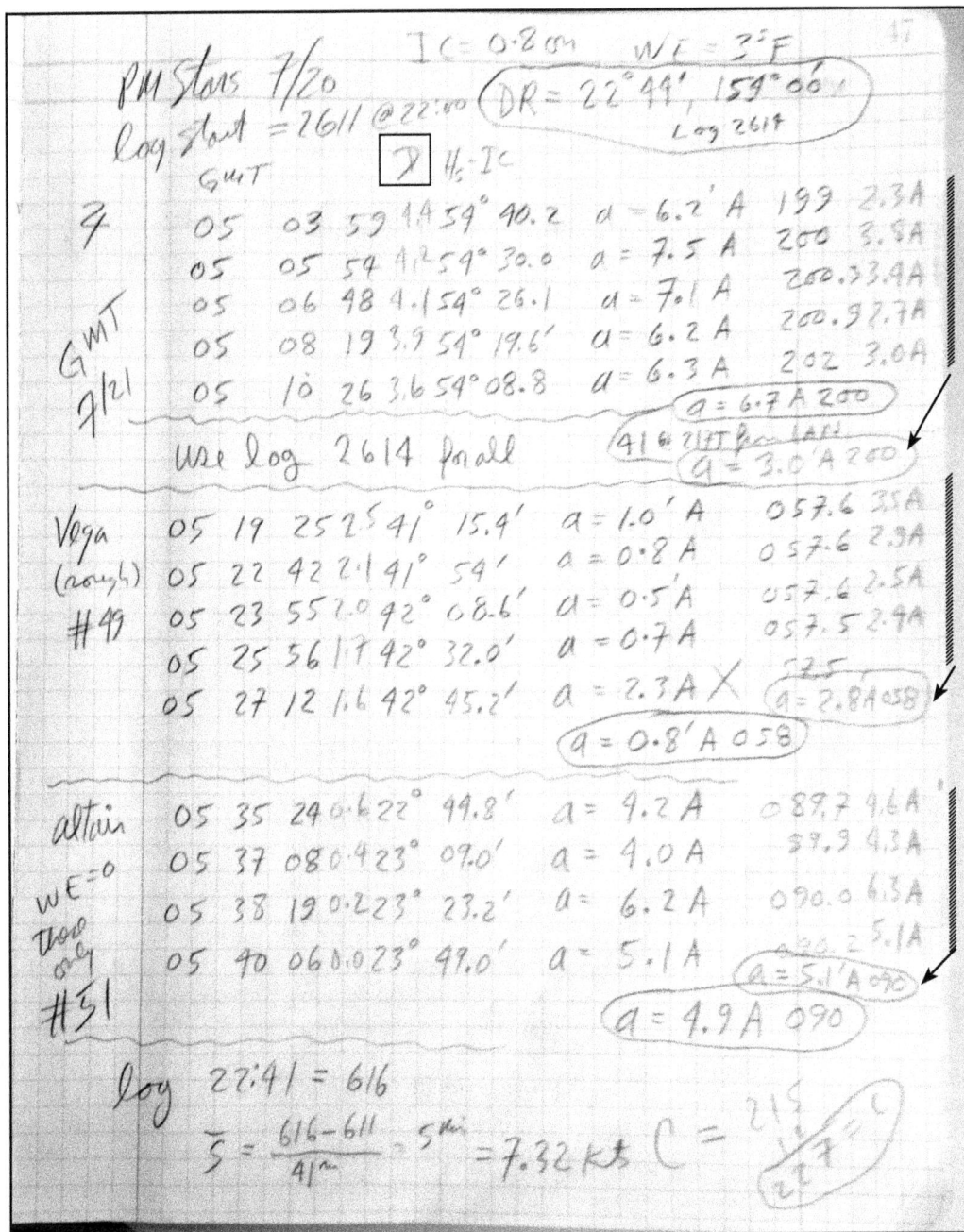

Figure A2. *Page from original logbook showing analysis done underway of a set of star sights, called Problem 26 in this book. Viewed in color, the red additions are the automatic advancement computations. In our present analysis we came up with slightly different DR, and resulting SMG and CMG. Our procedure underway was to record log before and after each sight session and compute SMG from that data. In the present analysis, we found SMG and CMG from successive logbook entries. The former approach is more accurate, but we did not have enough surviving data to do that for all sights, so we adopted the method used. In most cases the difference is not significant.*

4.9 to 5.1. In the Vega sights we could tell from the first level analysis that the 0527 sight was too low (a Away too big), and it can be discarded before further analysis.

It did not show up in this example, but in some cases a sight that looks out of the average in the uncorrected sights does not stand out at all in the corrected ones. The fit-slope method discussed next is the best way to identify outlying sights.

In this example, a fix plotted with and without advancing LOPs differs by about 2 nmi, and clearly the one without the advancement is wrong.

The next step is to see how to choose the best average sight from each set to be representative of the full set, so that we do not have to plot every one of them–though often we learn most by both analyzing and plotting.

Fit-Slope Method

This is good procedure for routine work, but crucial for times when we must rely on sights taken in poor conditions. For convenience, we use computer solutions here to demonstrate the process, but we want to stress that a great virtue of this method is it does not take a computer to solve underway. The only requirement is plotting a few points on graph paper and adding two extra standard sight reductions.

Since any one sight can be off somewhat, it is standard procedure to take multiple sights of any body and then average them in some manner, or figure which one of the set might be the best representative of all of them.

A simple numerical average of the Hs values will not work: first they are changing with time as the body rises or sets, and second we are moving as well during the time we take the sights. So it is not a trivial task to figure the best way to average a set of sights, and we must be prepared to spend some time on the project when it is called for.

The analysis is easier when doing sight reduction by computation, because then you can simply find the a-values for all of them, correct each one for the vessel motion, and then average these a-values. That is not a bad approach, but it is still not taking advantage of all we know about the sights.

Instead, we can do this fairly quickly by just analyzing the Hs and WT values, with just two special sight reductions required. We will use Problem 1 to explain the method, then give more examples from this passage.

Figure A3 shows the issue at hand in Problem 1. It is a plot of all of the sights taken, each corrected to a common time. This is three Venus sights, then four sun sights taken 3h 40m later, all in poor conditions, which means they are not the best sights, so we need to study them carefully to get the best results. Furthermore, they have nearly the same azimuth, which makes things even worse. Such a challenge is not uncommon in any real voyage that relies solely on cel nav.

This case, as poor as it looks, is not as bad as some. We have 4 sunlines that even without analysis looks like include two reasonable ones and two outliers; and with the Venus sights, maybe two good ones and one outlier. In other sight sessions, there might not be this type of guess to be made from just looking at the plotted LOPs corrected for course and speed.

To see if this interpretation makes sense, we plot the lines as Hs vs. WT and compare their trend to the predicted slope of the line as would be viewed from our changing position. Lines that are equally good should all have the same slope–that is, the same rate of change of Hs with WT.

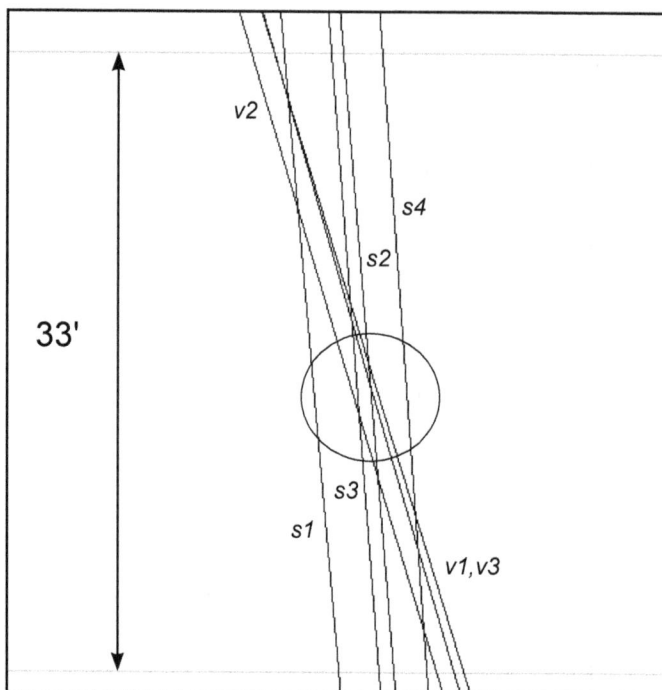

Figure A3. *Problem 1 all sights corrected to 0847 using S5.7, C197. These were all sights in poor conditions of rough seas and broken clouds and only intermittent views of the bodies being sighted. Three Venus sights, then 3 hr later four sun sights (the more vertical set). Without some analysis here, the fix is fairly uncertain. If all sights were equal, we might consider the fix as roughly at the center of the circle shown, with the radius as an estimate of the uncertainty. With some analysis we can do better.*

In other words, we do not know where we are, so we do not know what the heights will be, but we do know the computed height for any time and place on earth, so we just compute the heights from our DR positions and compare, not the values, but the rate of change. We call this process the fit-slope method.

Figure A4 shows the sunlines plotted this way, and then in Figure A5 we add the computed slope. The top figure is raw sextant data and no DR position is called for, but for the predicted sights we do need a DR. In fact, we need the DR at the start of the sights and at the end of the sights. Then we look up the GHA and dec for these two times and compute Hc in each case. We do not care about Zn. It is best at this point to compute the Hc rather than try to use tables. (This can be done with Pub 229, but for the precision we want from given DR positions it is a lot of work). The formula for Hc computation is given in textbooks (Appendix A5) and it can be programmed into calculators, or use starpath.com/calc to get the answers, among other sources.

Then plot the two Hc values on the same page as the Hs data, and draw a line between them. Note we assume here that the sights are not too far apart in time, because if too far apart the line joining the sights is a curve, not a straight line. If in doubt about this, compute also an Hc for the midpoint between the two.

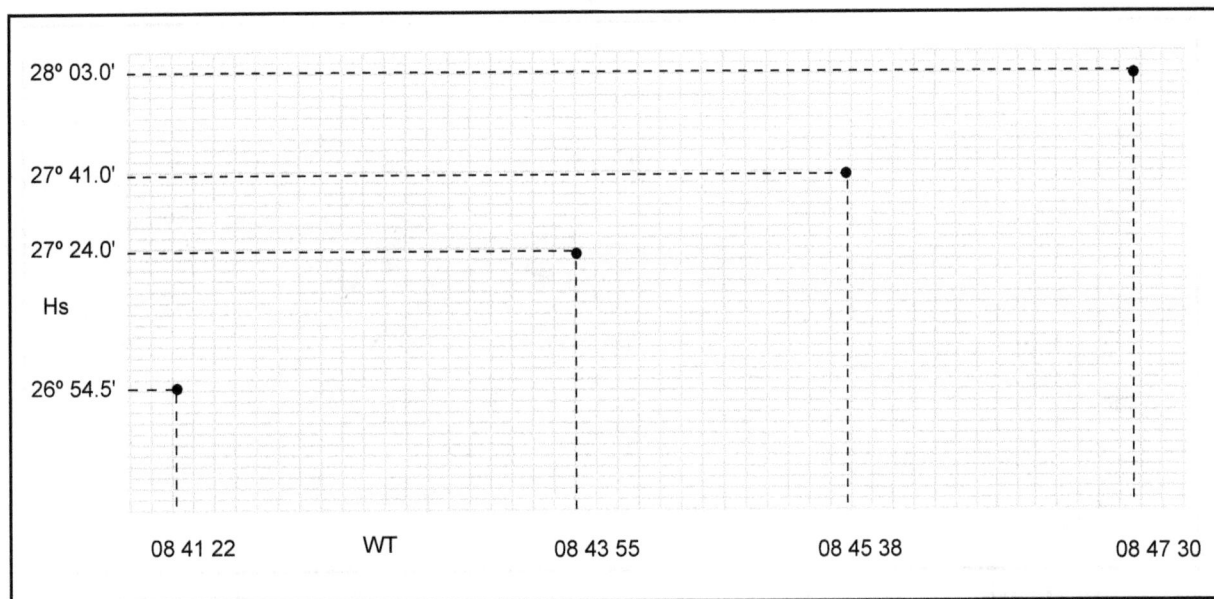

Figure A4. *Plot of Hs vs WT on cross hatch paper for the sun sights of Problem 1. Choose a scale to show the most detail with the paper you have. Or type the data into a spread sheet and convert dd.mmm to dd.dd and hh.mm.ss to hh.hh and then let the spread sheet do the plot.*

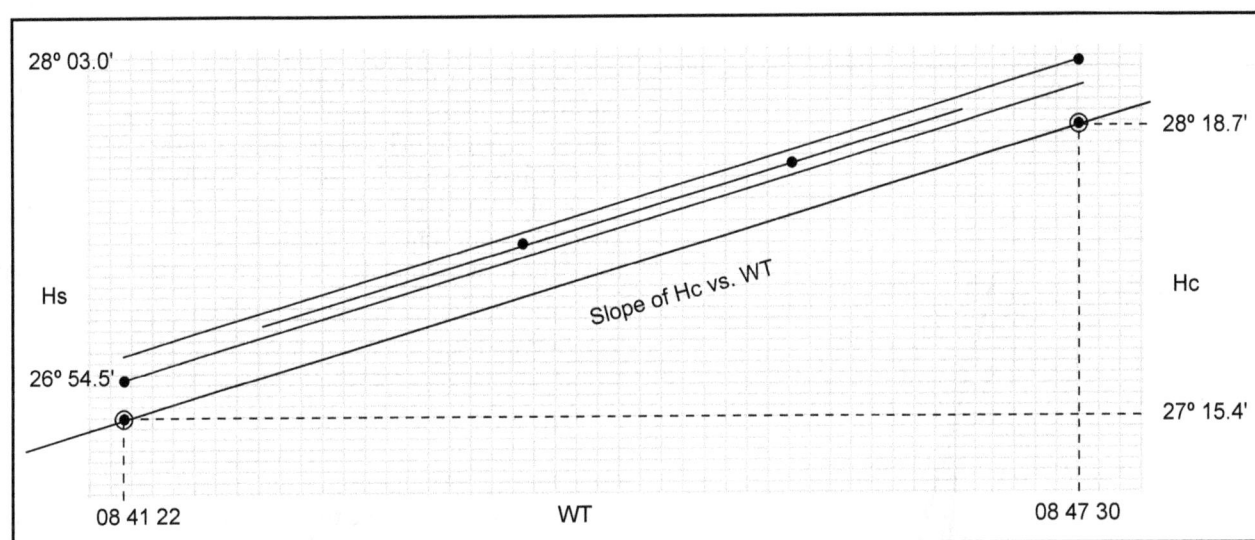

Figure A5. *Next we add to the plot above the motion-corrected slope of Hc vs WT, which we compute from two sight reductions. We need Hc at the time of the first sight and at the time of the last sight. These two times will have different DR positions (46° 09.3' N, 127° 57.9' W and 46° 8.7' N, 127° 58.1' W). When plotting, the vertical scales for Hc and Hs must be the same (2.4 per line in this case), but they will be notably shifted because the values differ by the altitude corrections, semi-diameter, and so on. The DR positions for Hc shown were computed using S6.0, C197.*

Once the line is plotted, you can use parallel rulers or roller plotter to move the slope line into the region of the actual data, as shown in Figure A5. In this case we see that all of the sights do not fall on the same line, so they are definitely not equally good.

At this stage we must make some assumptions. First we assume that in good conditions all of our sights would be equally good, spread over some statistical variation of uncertainty. In poor conditions we expect that spread to increase. Then we will judge the validity of individual sights based on their trend relative to the theoretically correct trend.

There is a certain faith that goes into this: if three sights are right on the theoretical trend line (slope), and one is notably off, we will believe it is that one that is wrong. It could be that the three were wrong and the one was right. But if our assumption about sights in good conditions is true, then we will be right more often than wrong when we use this guideline in poor conditions.

In Figure A5 we see the predicted slope line moved up to compare to the actual sights. The four sights do not all fit on the line, in fact, 1 and 3 are inconsistent with each other and with the middle 2. The middle two, on the other hand, do follow the right slope, so we can make a reason-

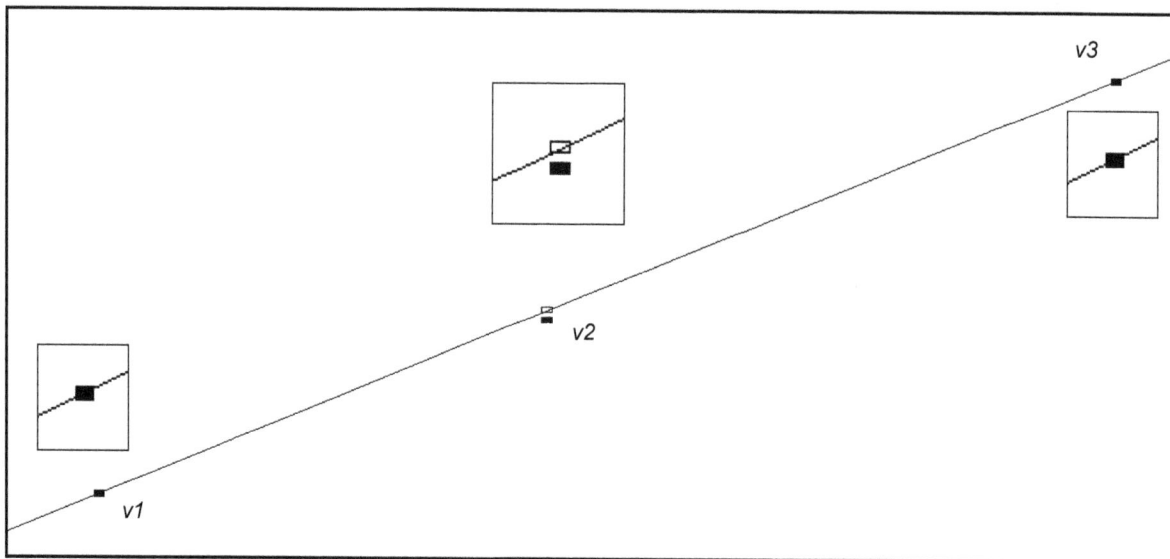

Figure A6. *Venus sights of Problem 1 compared to the theoretical slope from two computed Hc values using C197, S5.7. The second sight is below the prediction by about 1.5 miles, so we are safe using the average of v1 and v3 for the fix. In this presentation the solid rectangles are the Hs; the open rectangles are the Hc.*

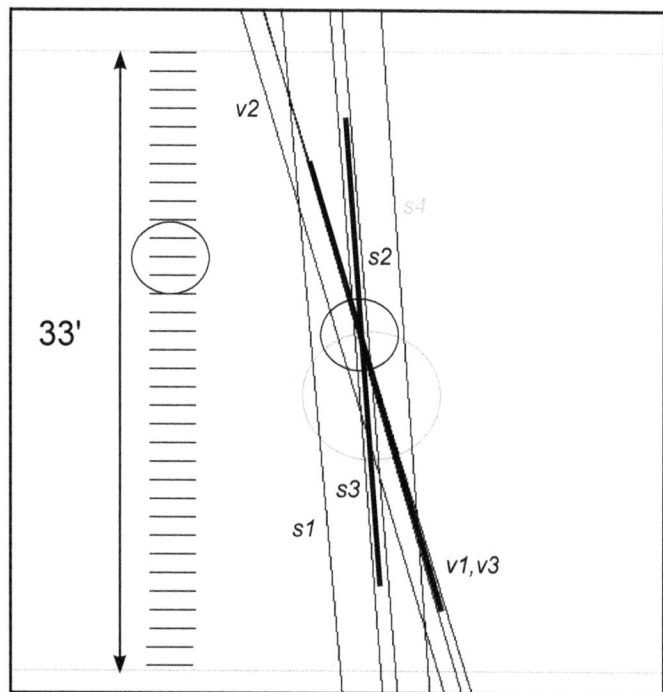

Figure A7. *All sights from Problem 1, with the selected LOPs marked in bold. We chose average of s2 and s3, and v1 and v3. We have reduced our longitude uncertainty a lot, and our lat uncertainty by a factor of two or so. We might now think of this fix as accurate to within about ± 2 nmi, which is very good considering what we had to start with. The fix also shifted north 2 or 3 miles from the un-analyzed set of lines. This means that if you used a computer that found a fix from all LOPs using least squares, it would be off by about that much. We improve the computations by choosing the best sights ahead of time.*

able guess that these are the best two sunlines, and that the average of the these two is a good representative of the full set of 4 sights. This is not the most satisfying situation, but it is best we can do with what we have. We can also be encouraged that 1 is below and 4 is above the 2-3 line by about the same amount. These two would average to about the right value, which is also clear from the plotted LOPs.

Figure A6 shows a similar plot for the 3 Venus sights. The first and last are consistent; the middle one is low, so we can choose an average of v1 and v3 for the fix.

Figure A7 is a reproduction of A3 showing our improvement in the fix by this analysis. Still not what we can hope for in good conditions, but a reasonable approach to improving what we have to work with. Clearly, though, our uncertainly in latitude on the fix is larger than it is for the longitude.

The job then in such a situation is to carry on with the DR to see how this pans out on the next cel nav fix.

To carry on with this Analysis section, we will bounce back and do the slope analysis to Prob 26 that we started with, then carry on with a couple other examples.

Problem 26 Fit Slope

Now we return to the sights that we used as an example of auto advancing–Altair, Vega, and Jupiter sights. The analyses of all three sets are shown in Figure A8, along with comments on the choices made, then the final fix is shown in Figure A9.

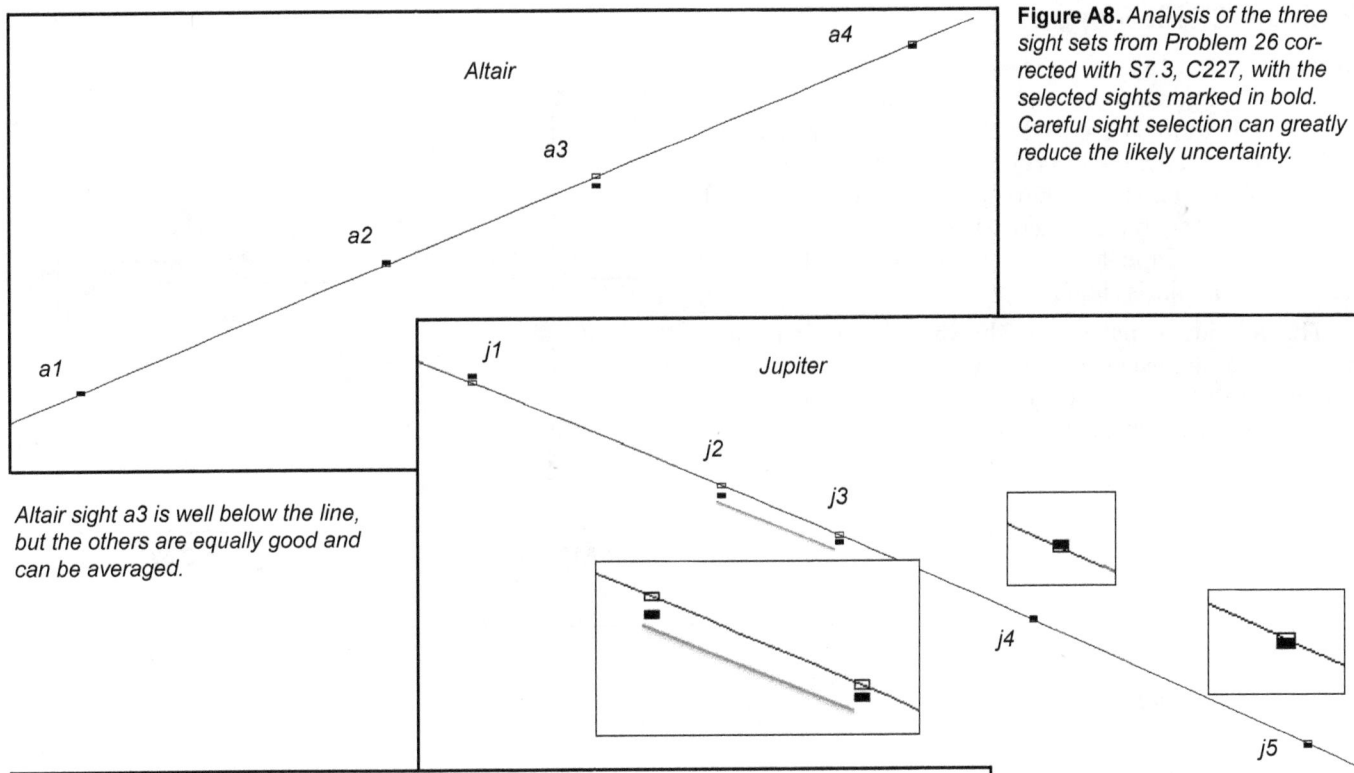

Figure A8. *Analysis of the three sight sets from Problem 26 corrected with S7.3, C227, with the selected sights marked in bold. Careful sight selection can greatly reduce the likely uncertainty.*

Altair sight a3 is well below the line, but the others are equally good and can be averaged.

Jupiter sight j5 is low and j1 is high, relative to j4. Since that is the best line between all, an average of these 3 seems best. We abandon j2 (1.2' below the line) and j3. This also brings LOP closer to the Altair-Vega fix, which might support this interpretation.

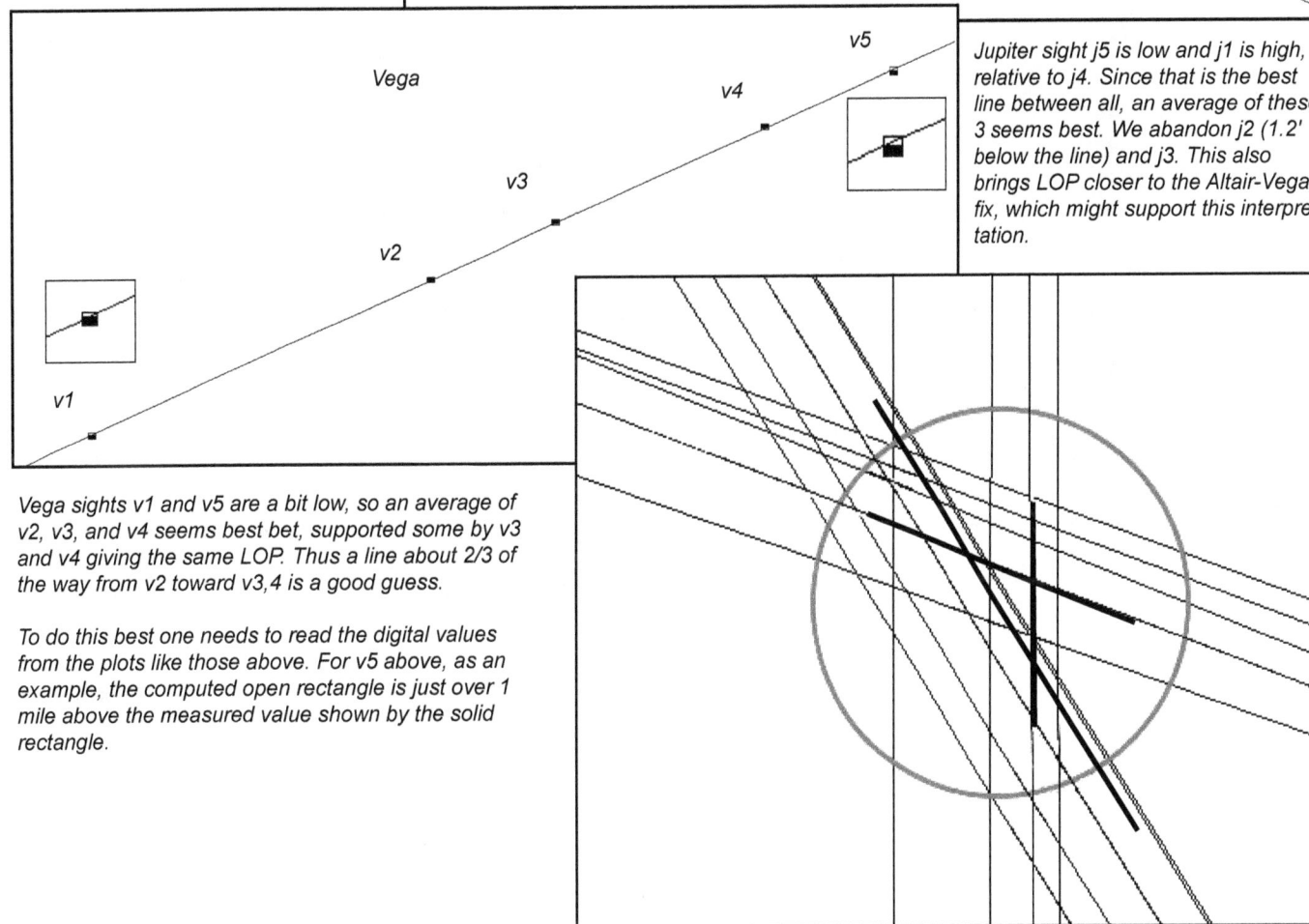

Vega sights v1 and v5 are a bit low, so an average of v2, v3, and v4 seems best bet, supported some by v3 and v4 giving the same LOP. Thus a line about 2/3 of the way from v2 toward v3,4 is a good guess.

To do this best one needs to read the digital values from the plots like those above. For v5 above, as an example, the computed open rectangle is just over 1 mile above the measured value shown by the solid rectangle.

Figure A9. *All sights of Problem 26 corrected with S7.3, C227, with the selected sights marked in bold. Careful sight selection can greatly reduce the probable error size. Compare the choices made here with what might be made based on the corrected a-values alone in Figure A2.*

Problem 27 Fit Slope

As we get closer to land we want to do the best we can to pin down our position, so when there is time this calls for a close evaluation. We looked at Problem 26, now a quick look at Problem 27, the last cel nav fix of the passage. Figure A10 shows all sights plotted, which gives us without further work a good idea where we are, but we can do better. Clearly one Capella sight is off, and we have to look at the Vega and Polaris sights.

The individual analyses are shown, then the fix is plotted again using the chosen sights in Figure A14, which is a notable improvement. We are ready then to proceed on in and find our destination where we expect it.

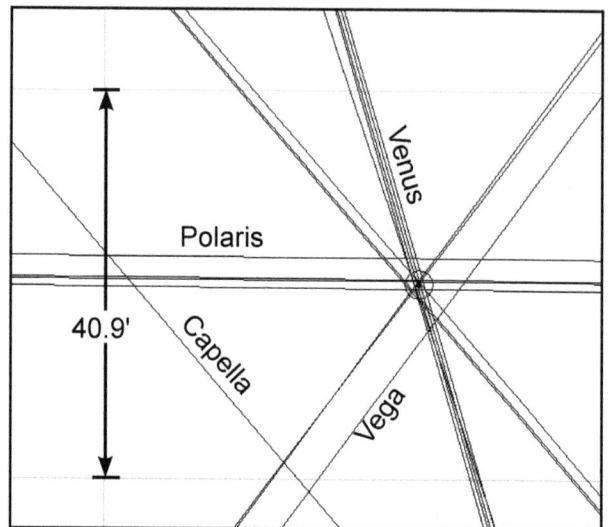

Figure A10. *Problem 27 all LOPs at 0831 using C 232, S 7.6.*

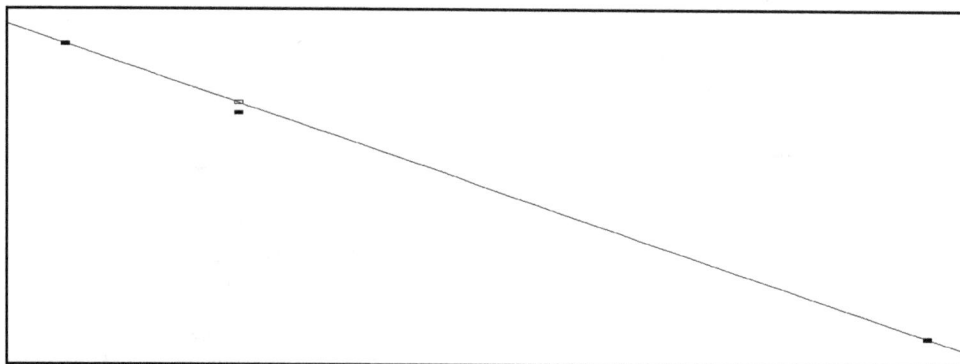

Figure A11. *Vega sights. The second is definitely off the slope of the other two, which matches the prediction. Without the prediction, you would not know if 2 and 3 were right, leaving 1 high, or if 1 and 2 were right, leaving 3 very high.*

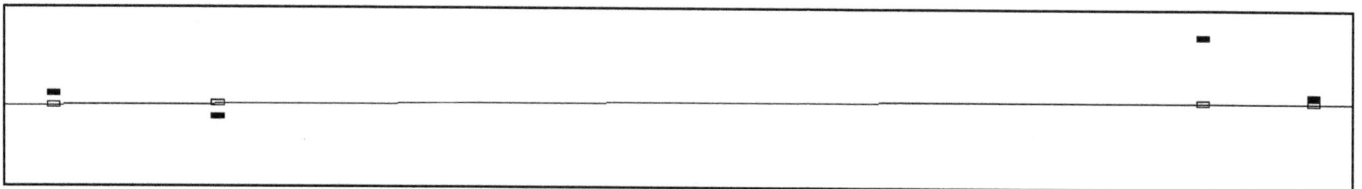

Figure A12. *Polaris sights. The third is high, but we must average the others.*

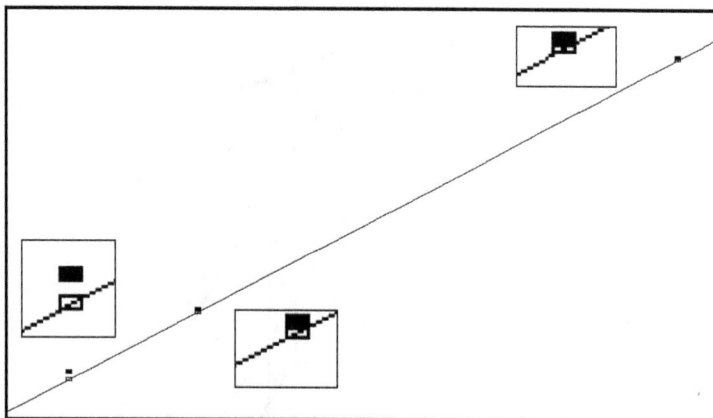

Figure A13. *Capella sights. After discarding the bad sight, the last 3 have more information. Relative to the second two, one above and one below the line, the first is clearly too high. So we are safe here with taking the average of these last two.*

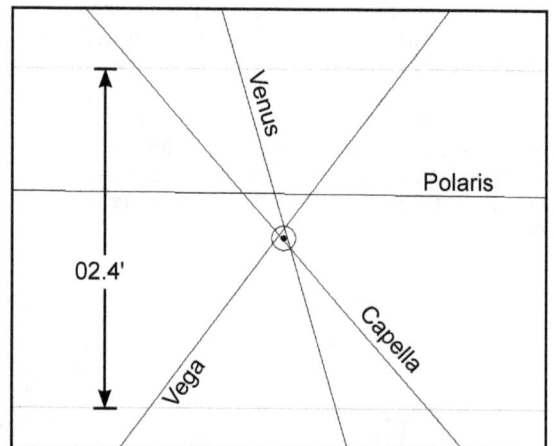

Figure A14. *Problem 27 all LOPs at 0831 using C 232, S 7.6 after selecting out the best value for each set.*

Problem 17 Fit Slope... And Hope

This is a tough one. The original logbook says "sky very obscured and seas rough," and warns that the time of the one Venus sight may be wrong. Then there is a logbook note that says "Rough DR at log 865 is 28° 34'N, 142° 36'W."

This DR note must mean we did not have good records recently, or that there was not time to plot out each course change. I have since learned the great value of frequent logbook entries, but either knowledge, available time, or circumstances kept this from happening then.

But with that said, the a-values shown in the original logbook all came out fairly small relative to that DR position, namely: Deneb 0.1' A from 307; Venus 1.1' A from 073, and the moon sights 5.3'A, 3.9'A, and 5.0'A from 096. This would be relatively encouraging underway, and there was not much to do about it anyway. Now, in retrospect, we can note that a good Jupiter-Vega fix 15h later was off the DR by 36 miles, based on this fix using an equal average of all sights taken. So despite encouraging numerical results, something was wrong with the navigation at this point—or during the next leg of DR.

Since two bodies had only one sight each, our only hope is to have a look at the moon lines to see if we can lean toward any specific value. The fit-slope plot of these moon sights is shown in Figure A15.

Here we learn, however, that there is no magic to be called upon for these sights. This is just a weak fix, and all we have for the moment. The results are shown in Figure A16.

Problem 9 Fit Slope

These sights are shown in Figure A17, and from this plot it looks like we might gain precision with analysis, but we do not know for sure until we plot the slopes. Polaris must be just averaged; we have only two sights. The Polaris sights are 4.2' apart, so that shows the scale.

We have 3 of Venus, two being very close to each other, and 5 of Vega, in groups of 2 and 3. The fit slope-plots (Figure A18 and A19) show we could favor Venus 2,3 and Vega 4,5,6 but in this case that choice only shifts the fix longitude to the east by a mile or so. The averages of all sights shown in Figure A17 is likely the safest choice, with an uncertainty of about ± 2 nmi.

In this case the fit slope did not improve the fix itself, but it did improve the uncertainty, as we are confident now that the sights are all within statistical errors and there are no outliers throwing off the location.

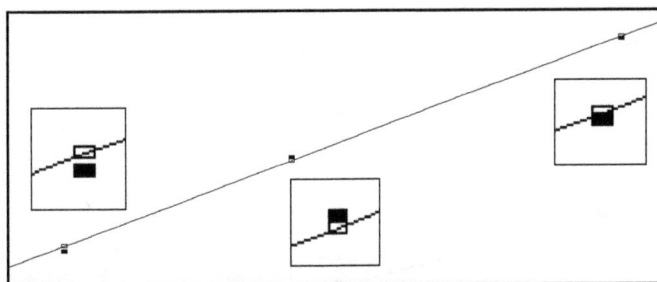

Figure A15. *Moon sights from Problem 17. There does not seem any reasonable way to favor one over the others, so we have to average all, which is shown in Figure A16 as a bold moon line.*

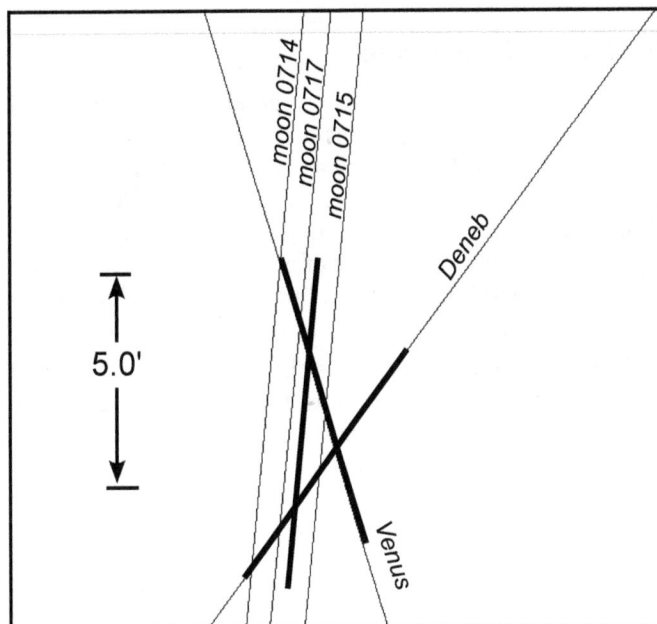

Figure A16. *Problem 17 fix using two single sights and the average of 3 moon sights. Fit slope did not help us on this one.*

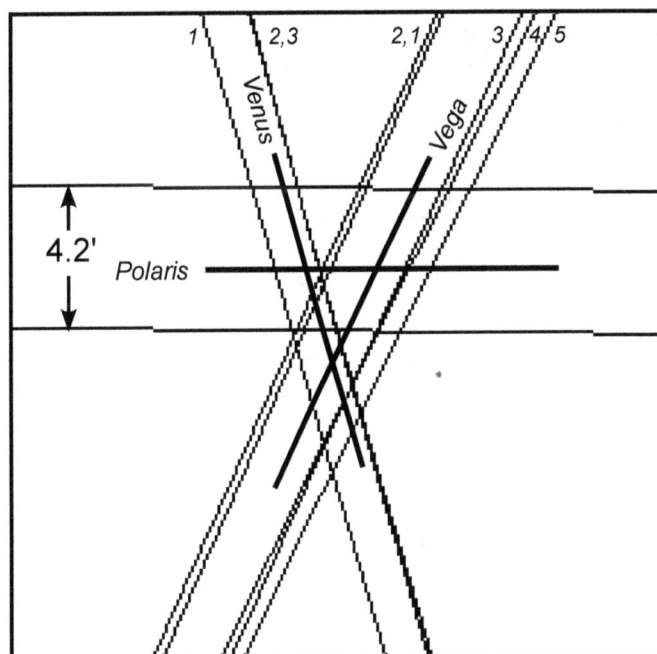

Figure A17. *Problem 17 all LOPs at 0610 using C210, S4.8. Bold lines are the average of all LOPs.*

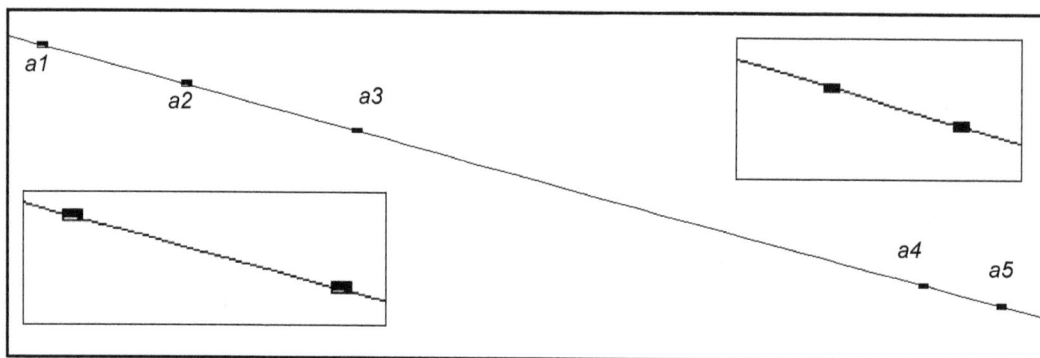

Figure A18. *Problem 9 Vega sights corrected with C210, S4.8. The first two are slightly high, but the last 3 are right on the line. This is a close call, but favors using an average of the last 3, even though taken at different times. That is, the first three were taken in a row, then a pause for other sights, then back to take the last 2.*

Problem 22 Fit Slope

In this example we have pretty good sights, and could maybe come to the right conclusion by just looking at all the plotted LOPs, but we will see what we gain by a more careful analysis. All the LOPs are shown in Figure A19, along with a computer's choice of a fix based on the least squares method of averaging of all sights. Unfortunately, we got only one Capella sight, but did get multiple sights of the other bodies.

The solid lines are the ones chosen for best fix. Notice that they move the choice more than a mile south of the computer choice based on least squares fit of all sights.

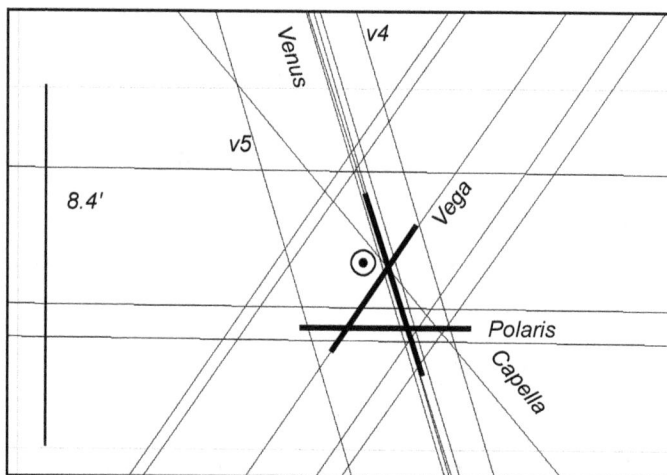

Figure A19. *Problem 22 all LOPs at 0756 using C232, S6.3. The fix position shown is based on least squares using all sights, considered otherwise of equal value. The solid lines are our choices.*

Figure A20. Right. *Problem 22 Vega sights. The best fit slope line leaves the first two and the last two above and below, all about the same amount, with the third sight being the best average of all of them, which in this case was consistent with conclusions from the plotted LOPs.*

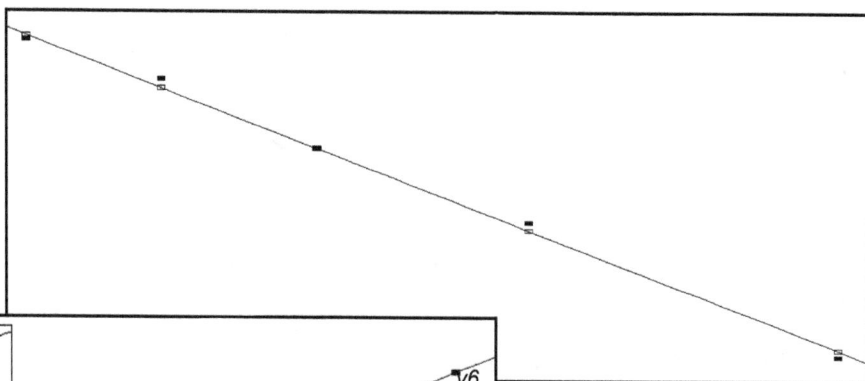

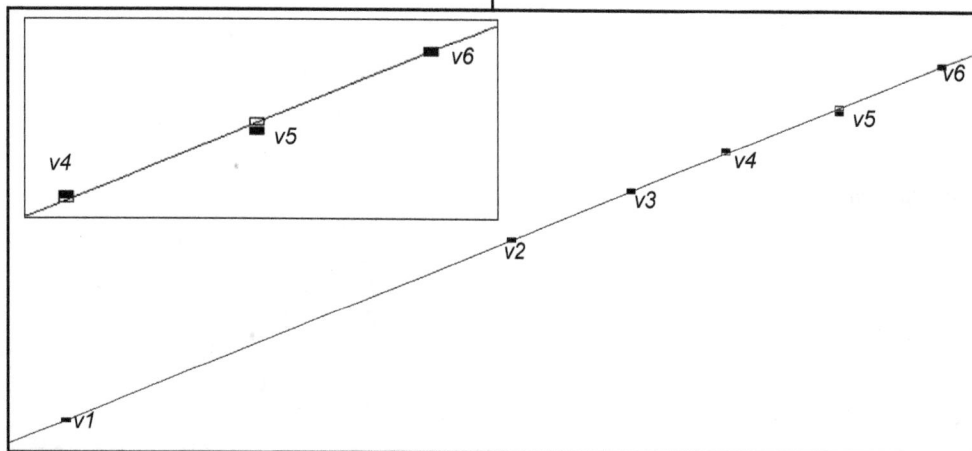

Figure A21. Left. *Problem 22 Venus sights. The best fit slope line goes through the first 3 and the last, leaving 5 far off and 4 just off, so we can not use these when attempting to get the best fix. Again, in this case we are confirming by an Hs vs WT plot of which ones we could call off if we did the full sight reductions and plotting of all 6 lines.*

Problem 25 Fit LAN Curve

The fit slope method can be applied to sights whose path is curved such as an LAN series, but the process is more easily executed with computed Hc values. We illustrate this with the LAN series from Problem 25. We can fairly easily find inconsistent sights in the same manner as straight slopes, but fitting the curve is not just a matter of sliding a straight line up and down to fit the slope. We must essentially fit the shape of the curve by adjusting the DR position, while still correcting each sight for the course and speed of the vessel.

Thus a good starting DR is valuable, which we can get by just using a few of the lines to make a fix, as shown in Figure A22. We see the third sight is off, as well as getting a first pass fix. You could also do this with sights on the descent as well, we just need a range of azimuths to get an intersection.

Then using that fix as a DR we can look at the full curve as shown in Figure A22a, where several DR Lon are used in an attempt to fit the curve. All three lead to the same Lat (23° 17.3') as would be expected. The best Lon would be about 153° 31', but this is not a very tidy procedure. The Lon value from Hs vs. WT alone without any analysis at all as we did at the time of the voyage was 153° 32', as shown in the later section called "Longitude from LAN." So we have not gained much from this, but it could be very much more help for lower noon sights, where the peak is much broader in time.

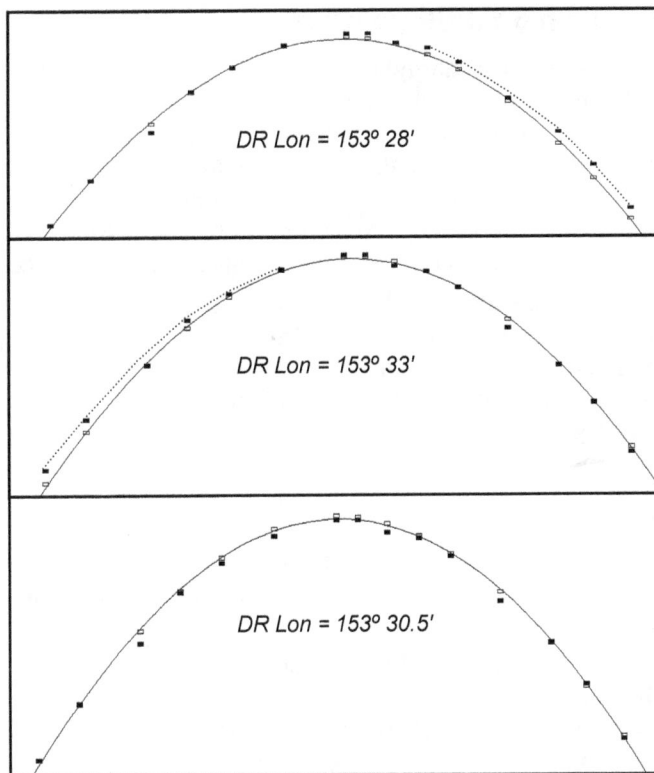

Figure A22a. *Problem 25, computed Hs vs WT for S4.3, C228 (open symbols and line) compared to measurements (solid symbols) using 3 different DR-Lon.*

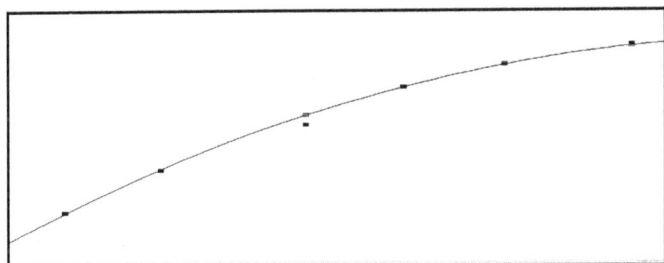

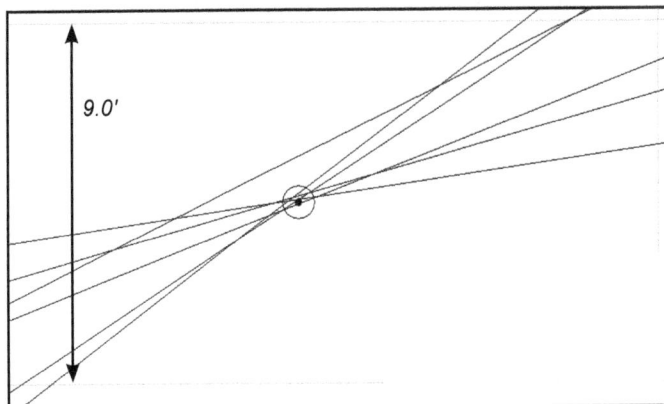

This analysis is a reminder that the fit-slope method requires a good DR position, even for the straight-line applications. It is just more crucial when fitting a curve. We can always find a good DR by finding a first estimate fix, then use it as the DR to fine tune the final fix.

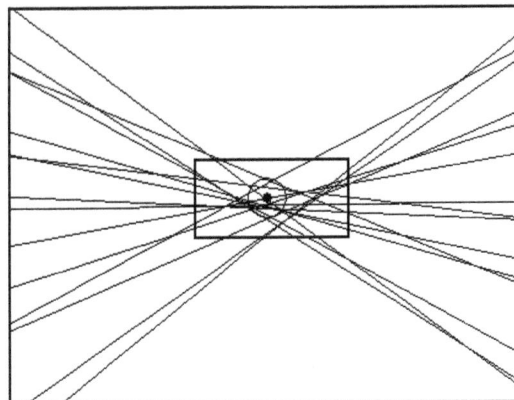

Figure A22. Top left. *First 6 sights of Prob 25 analyzed.* **Bottom left.** *Same sights as plotted LOPs for fix time 1518, with C228, S4.3. The third sight stands out as bad in both of them, otherwise, these sights provide a reasonable fix. In the later section Longitude by LAN we learn that this third sight may have had the wrong time, not height.* **Bottom right.** *All the sights plotted as LOPs, corrected to WT 1528. The rectangle shown is 3 nmi tall and 6 nmi wide. The least squares intersection is consistent with other analysis, but this approach alone does not lend much confidence to the conclusion.*

Problem 6 Fit Slope (Curve)

Here is another example of trying to fit a series of noon sights to the proper shape. Figure A23 is the plot from the Logbook, where we assumed we had seen the peak and went on to choose a peak height at about 1356. Just below that is the fit slope analysis based on computed DR positions using S6.0, C197. We can now change our minds a bit, and take the computed value at 1355 as a better choice.

These are not very good sights, and we do not know the history of them at this point. If they were student sights, they might not have been optimized. We teach that all sights should be made independently, that is, between each sight give the micrometer drum a random turn or so, and then align each sequential sight from the beginning. In other words, do not just follow the sun by turning the dial, which in this case would be slowly turning it up and then at the peak we start turning it down. In hindsight, we do not know if these sights were taken properly, with each one independent.

Several factors could have contributed to the laxness. One, I do not have proper respect for the noon sight! Normally I do not take them at all because it calls for doing something at a specific time, which is often not convenient. Furthermore, it generally takes a long time to do right. It is usually faster and more accurate to just take a quick series of sunlines–it takes just five or six minutes to get four or five sights–then in a couple hours, do it again for a running fix.

When such noon sights are taken, it is usually just to demo the process or to experiment with finding the midpoint, which is useful in emergency navigation solutions for longitude. Also, in this case we clearly missed getting started early enough (implying some laxness), and we were not counting on this data for a fix. We had clear skies and a lot of navigation that day.

Bear in mind as well that when the sun is high like this it is often very hot under a very bright sun. This does not lend itself to careful work without extra effort.

In any event, we got an LAN latitude at 1355 (log 945) shown on page 42, which we can retard to the time of the last fix at 1326 for a check. Notice we used here an Hs value we did not actually measure, but interpolated from the Hc computations. As it turns out, the LAN did not agree very well with the earlier fix, so it is not clear which one was right.

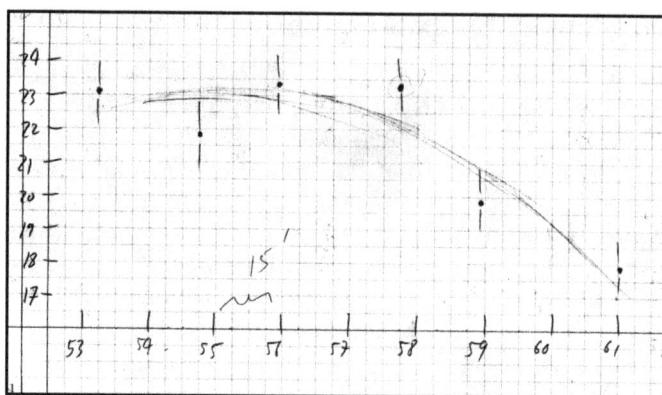

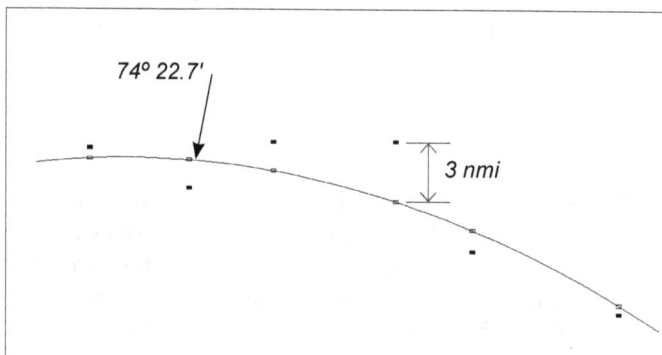

Figure A23. Top. *The sun sights of Prob 6 plotted in the original logbook with the assumption of the curve shape. It lists the log reading at 1355 = 945. Bottom is a fit slope computation of the actual expected shape using S6.0, C197. We can confirm that the 4th sight was off, but we still get a reasonable latitude, though we do not have a good measure of the full shape. We can also choose a better max Hs for the LAN Lat than we actually measured. Solid symbols are Hs; hollow are Hc.*

Problem 3 Fit Slope – A Basic Example

We finish this discussion of the fit-slope method with a basic example of the value of the procedure in that the sights appear of near-equal value when plotted, but after analysis they are clearly not equal. Figure A24 shows all sights of Problem 3 plotted for C180, S6.5. Also shown is the fix a computer (or good human eye) would choose based on least squares fit of all sights–that is, each line of each set gets weighted by its location relative to the average of the set.

Also shown is the LOPs we would choose after applying the fit-slope method, with a note on what we gain.

In the afternoon sights (PM) there is a slight curvature to the slope line, but not enough to cause problems when approximating it as a straight line between first and last sight, which were less than 4 minutes apart. When the sun

Figure A24. *All sights of Problem 3 at 1400 correcting at S6.5, C180. At the right side of the plot, the 3 PM (p) sights seem about equal, but on the left it looks like p3 is off, but still the separation from this view alone could not favor one over the other. For the AM (a) sights, we might think of a2 as off, but again, the overall spacing from this plot alone does not justify throwing any out. For example, if a4, a6 were off, then the a1, a3 location is a good average of all. The analysis below, however, shows very clearly which is off.*

The position marked by a circle (41° 37.4'N, 131° 50.0'W) is the mathematical mean value from a least squares fit of all sights. The two bold lines are the LOPs we choose based on the analysis below. It provides a fix of 41° 37.9'N, 131° 48.7'W. We gain about half a mile accuracy in lat and about 1 mile in longitude. We still have an overall uncertainty in the fix of about ± 1 mile, but the location is now more precise, and if we did not do the analysis, we would have to accept a larger position uncertainty, probably about twice as large.

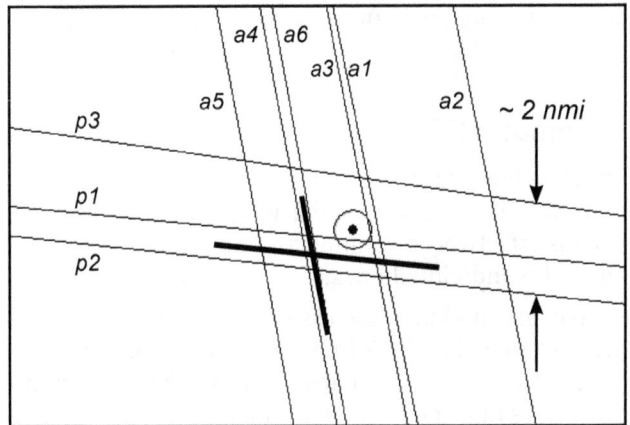

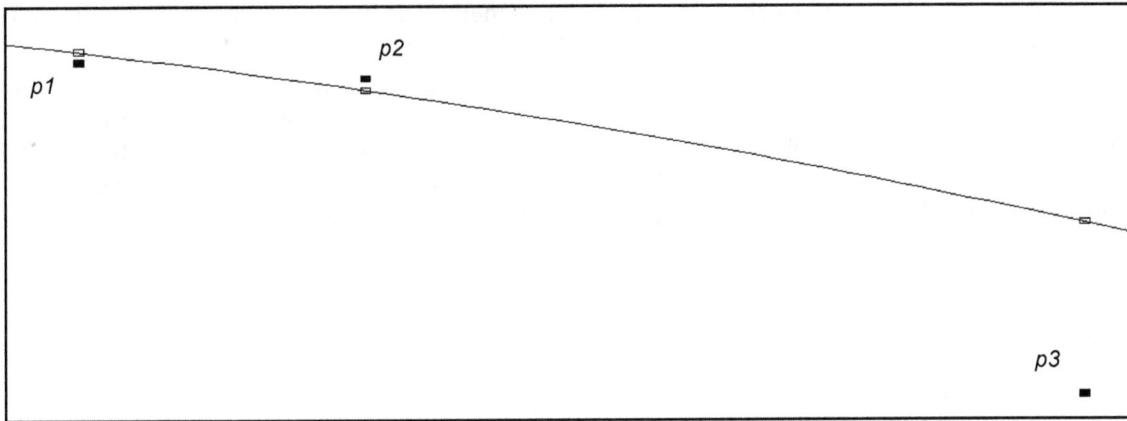

Figure A25. *Problem 3 PM sun sights, with S6.5,C180. Solid symbols are the Hs; open symbols the computed Hc, connected by their slope line, which we then move up and down without rotation to get the best fit to the data. The last sight p3 is clearly not consistent with either of the first two and can be discarded, which we can determine from the first two even though they differ in Hs by only 0.3'. We must conclude that the first was 1' low, and the second about 1' high, but the third was 11' low, leaving an average of the first two as the best representative of the full set. By computing the slope, we know which one is off. The average of 1 and 2 is shown in Figure A24.*

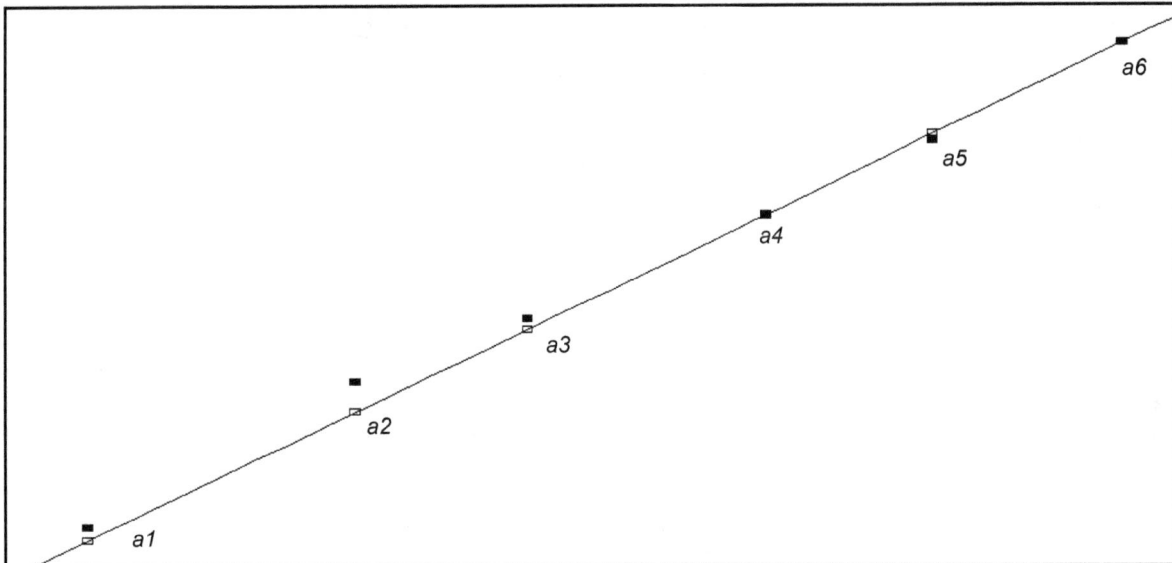

Figure A26. *Problem 3 AM sun sights, with S6.5,C180. The second one is clearly inconsistent with the others, but we cannot judge any of the others as special. Sights 4, 5, and 6 are pretty consistent, but other than 2 being off, it is difficult to choose the best fit to the remaining five. You could also draw the line with the last three low by about the same amount as the first and third were high. So we can only remove 2 and average the rest, which is shown in Figure A24.*

is high like this, we cannot use a straight-line approximation for very long.

Automatic Rfix

Once we have practice with the Fit-Slope Method, we can apply it to the full set of sights within a sight session to get what is effectively a running fix without having to advance any of the individual lines.

We are making the assumption with the Fit-Slope Method that the slope line we choose is an effective average of the sights we chose it from. Thus any point on this line is in principle better than any one sight of the set. Thus we can just choose any time we like and read the Hs from the line that would correspond to that time.

If we think of this option before the sights, we can alternate the sights so that each body has several sights over the same time period. This is in principle a more accurate way to do the sights in the first place as it makes each sight more independent of the others of the same body.

That is, if our goal is to get 4 sights each of 3 different stars, then the best approach is to take star 1, then star 2,

then star 3, and then go back to star 1 again, as opposed to the rather easier method of taking four sights in a row of star 1 and the moving on to star 2.

Alternating the sights is definitely a slower process, and may not work well when trying to combine star and planet sights. We have conflicting virtues to balance. With Venus sights, for example, it is usually best to take a series of them when the twilight is very bright with a sharp horizon, but then when it comes time to do the stars, the time interval is large, which means the slope line might have some curve to it, or something else might have changed.

Figure A27 shows the sights from Problem 27, all plotted on the same sheet, with the slope lines plotted as well. This was a session taken with good intentions (the sights were alternated) but still not the best representation of this method. It does a better job of pointing out the limits and things to think on.

The first Venus sight is over 30 minutes from the others to be used in this method,, which is not an ideal distribution of sights. As it turned out, these sights were all equally good according to a fit slope, so we just averaged them—which in practice means you just draw the best fit

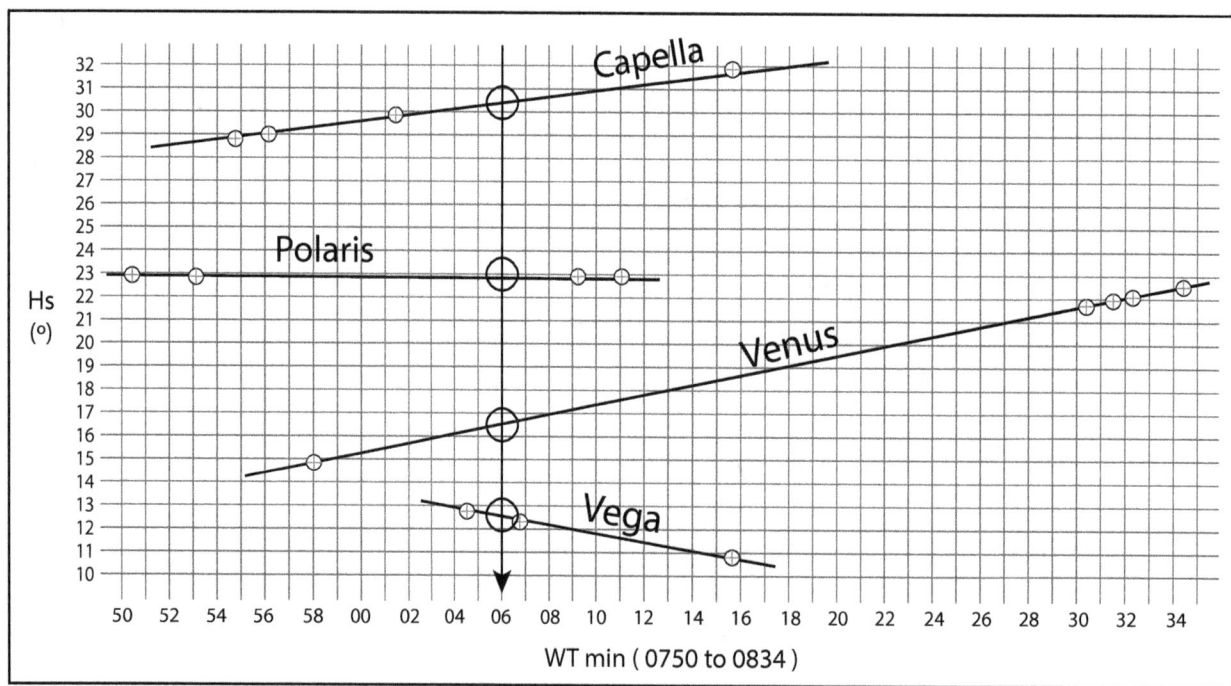

Figure A27. *Using fit-slope to find sight values that correspond to a common time, thus eliminating the need for advancing lines. Procedure: make a rough plot like this to see what might be a good common time. Here we choose 0806. Then go back to the expanded plots of each body to choose the corresponding value from the fitted-slope line. The scale here is crude, so we cannot read final values from this. For Capella, we threw out the last sight (see Fit-Slope Prob 27 discussion) so we have to project the line forward to 0806 to get the Hs. For Polaris, we threw out the 3rd and use the fit of the others to get the 0806 value. (The Polaris line can have a slope if we change latitude during the sight session, in addition to its own slight motion around the Pole.) The Venus sights are equally good, but with most of the sights so much later, we must be careful in plotting the line that will cover the 0806 time. It is best to have the sights all spread over a common time interval to avoid that plotting sensitivity. With Vega, we dropped the second sight, so we will pull the 0806 value off of the line between first and third.*

line and choose a sight that happens to be on the line. If they are equally good, usually at least one will be on the line. Other points are mentioned in the caption.

To follow through with this example, we went back to our higher-resolution slope plots for the individual bodies and read off these Hs values for the time 0806.

Venus	16° 34.9'
Vega	12° 39.0'
Capella	30° 40.4'
Polaris	22° 58.0'

According to this reasoning, these would be the values we would have measured if we could have taken them all simultaneously at 0806.

The fix we get from these data at 0806 using S =0 is 22° 06.8' N, 154° 59.5'W. From this you can DR to compare with a position found at another time by advancing all of the LOPs.

This method will not always save time. The Auto Advancement of LOPs described earlier is very fast. Also the sights must be alternated to have this work well. To some level it removes uncertainty in your DR needed to advance the lines individually, but it does not remove it entirely because we must use two DR positions to compute the slope properly that we use to evaluate the data.

Ocean Dead Reckoning

We have taught for many years that learning to do accurate dead reckoning (DR) is the key to ocean navigation, for the simple reason that we might end up with nothing but our own log and compass to go by. This means that a main goal of our daily cel nav sights is to test how well we are doing DR in the present conditions. The log tells us how far we went, and the compass tells us which way we went. From our last position fix, we can plot out the records of our travel from the logbook (log and course) and get our first estimate of where we are at the present log reading.

But this simple approach to finding a DR position is usually not adequate. In the ocean we can expect some ocean or coastal current that will take us off that position, and if the wind is blowing and we are sailing upwind, we expect to slip to leeward by some amount. Thus our best DR estimate must usually be corrected for some estimate of the current and leeway.

Leeway is only important going upwind and it increases as the wind speed increases up to some practical limit in a normal sailboat of some 15°, because when the wind gets too strong in a normal sailboat, we fall off and that dramatically reduces the leeway.

What is less well known is that leeway is also large in very light air. The voyage covered in this book does not itemize wind data nor actual boat speeds, instead the logbook is giving only course and speed made good. Some of

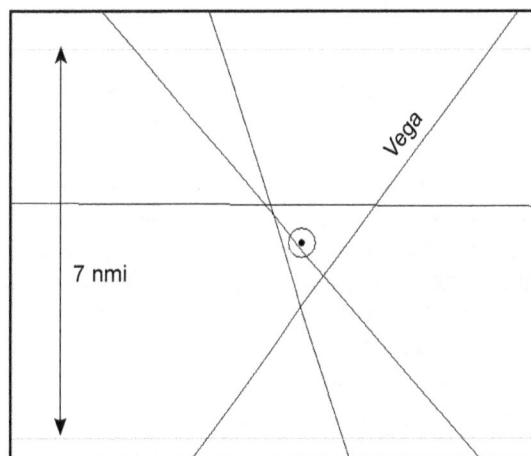

Figure A28. *New plot of Problem 27 sights chosen at 0806, with S=0. Now it appears that the Vega sight is a mile or so off, whereas in the earlier analysis (Figure A14), it appeared the Polaris sight differed from the others. These differences have to be accepted as within the uncertainties of the analysis. There is no realistic way to re-interpret the Vega sights that would move this 0806 value onto the triangle. We are simply looking at the limits of our navigation.*

the low speed legs of the voyage were very slow at times, and in some cases the boat was dead in the water and the crew were swimming in the ocean.

But there are more nuanced factors to account for. In large waves, or in strong or very light winds, our course will tend to be biased over what we intended it to be. Going to weather we might tend to fall off on each wave to keep from pounding. Going downwind we might bias upwind to go fast, or bias downwind in big waves for long surfs. It is the navigator's task to carefully watch the helm and the compass to spot these biases and record them. This important influence of helm bias on accurate DR was known to mariners in the 1500s, and discussed in navigation texts over the centuries.

The key question that arises is how do we learn to do good DR? We obviously compare our DR position to our fix positions each day, but we then need to know how close they must be to be called good–or how far off to be called poor. This is the crucial criteria to know, and we have studied this for many years. The basis of our conclusions are presented in our textbooks. As it turns out, the voyage of this book (one of only three we have done by pure cel nav) was part of the original study.

We state in summary what we might expect as the statistical uncertainty in our DR position in various conditions in the ocean. There are two parts.

The first is due to errors in log and course. It is 7% of the distance run. In other words if your run 100 miles, you might expect to be off by 7 miles; sometimes less, sometimes more, but the 7% of distance run is a baseline to keep in mind.

The second is due to uncertainties in ocean currents. We must assume we are sailing (or sitting dead in the water) in a current of unknown direction with a speed of 0.7 kts. In other words, if you are not moving at all, you still have to assume your position is growing uncertain by about 0.7 nmi every hour. In 14 hours your position grows uncertain by about 10 miles, regardless of how fast you are moving or in what direction. We discuss this in the Ocean Currents section below.

These may seem large uncertainties, but they are not. They are typical in a typical ocean voyage. This magnitude of uncertainty was also known and analyzed in the mid 1800s, though our values come from our own research. We only recently learned of the late 1800s work of Kelvin and others on this topic. A historical study will show that mariners proceeded to gain rather more confidence in their DR than was justified as time went by, which is reflected in some early 20th century training manuals.

One might argue that our instruments are much better now than they were in the 1800s, but our practice at DR is way down. Mariners were expert at DR back when it mattered everyday. We remind navigators that it is still crucial to safe, efficient, versatile ocean navigation. Once we are on our own with a log and compass (sky overcast and no GPS), it does not matter what century we are in, nor what kind of boat we are in.

For more information on this topic is covered in the books of Appendix A5.

Ocean Currents

Mariner's gained much information about ocean currents in the mid and late 1800s, in large part from compilations of ship's records by M. F. Maury in the US and H.W. Dove in Europe. Rather strangely, this information from that era is still pretty much what we read on modern Pilot Charts and in classic references like *Bowditch* and the *British Admiralty Navigation Manuals*.

The scientific community, on the other hand, have learned very much more about the flow of the ocean over the intervening 150 years, with a huge burst in knowledge coming with the advent of environmental satellites. Now we know that the surface of the ocean is a dynamic, boiling cauldron of current patterns that include—in some places more frequently than others—meandering rivers and swirling eddies of flow that can reach several knots in speed and remain in place for weeks, or drift across the ocean at a rate of up to several knots.

There might well be specific areas of the ocean with a climatic average current speed and direction that is about what we read on the Pilot Charts, but we will also learn

from the same data that the actual probability of experiencing that climatic average value at any one time is very small. The Pilot Charts could call for a drift of 10 miles a day to the SW, and you could be there when it is 30 miles a day to the NE.

This does not mean that we cannot rely at all on Pilot Chart data, but we must be careful about how and where we use it. The average value at a specific point in the Gulf Stream, for example, could be fairly close, but you might still be at that point at a specific time and have the current running the wrong direction.

Areas of the ocean with strong currents like the Gulf Stream are monitored closely and well forecasted with ocean current prediction models. So we can today cross the Gulf Stream and know exactly what to expect from resources we download from NOAA by sat phone, but it will unlikely be what the Pilot Chart says it should be for that spot on that day.

Away from such prominent rivers of global current, the prediction process is far less reliable, and in 1982, the time of this voyage, no such model data were available to even attempt such predictions. Now in retrospect, we do have some evidence from our DR to Fix errors that some mesoscale current flow might have affected our DR accuracy.

A list of ocean current resources and related notes are posted at starpath.com/currents and covered in the text *Modern Marine Weather, 2nd edition*. Even in modern times, this knowledge evolves. Our evaluation of ocean current predictions changed notably between the first and second editions.

To get a feeling for these matters, we show in Figure A29 a comparison of the Pilot Chart predictions over this route at the time of writing this section with recent numerical model predictions. If we had a boat in these waters with GPS, we could measure the current, and we do not hesitate to say that it would be different from either one of these!

In short, even though the average speed of ocean currents away from places like the Gulf Stream is only about 0.5 kts or so, we still have to accept that our position can go uncertain by as much as 0.7 kts, even if we do apply what Pilot Charts report as the climatic average.

This is important to know about for modern ocean sailors with GPS, which lets them measure the currents. Do not be surprised to run across large currents in the middle of the ocean. Then if so, look at model predictions for any signs of predicted rivers or eddies in the region to try to guess where the good and bad water is located in order to take advantage of the windfall or to get out of a bad luck situation.

"Mesoscale" as a current pattern dimension in oceanography means something in a range of 10 to 600 nmi in extent with a lifetime of a few days to several months. (In meteorology, the term covers a larger range in size, with no time factor involved.)

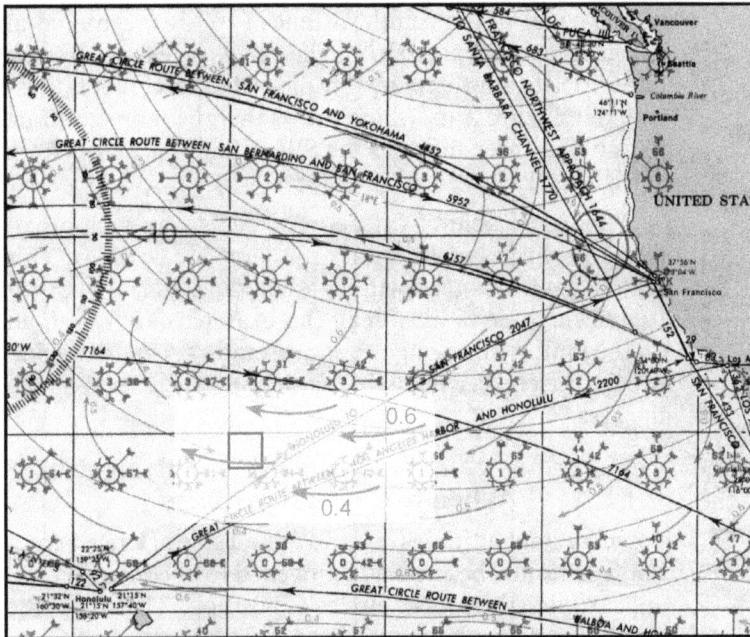

Figure A29. Top. *Section of a July Pilot Chart covering the route of this voyage. Currents in this example are shown as green arrows, labeled with the speed in kts. We have highlighted a few. Some charts show currents in miles drifted per day. We see a large gyre circulating the climatic location of the Pacific High, since these average mid-ocean currents are in large part wind-driven. The current flow closer to the equator is stronger and more persistent as are the trade winds driving them.*

In this note we are discussing common and usually random variations from this pattern, but as a rule one must also interpret the Pilot Chart data themselves with some uncertainty, typically about ± 50%. That is, a current shown as 0.6 kts, could be 0.3 or 0.9, with the larger value occurring when the wind has been moderate to strong in the same direction as the current for at least a day, and the weaker value occurring when the wind has been lighter than average for a few days.

The indicated area at 30N, 150W shows a prediction of 0.5 kts flowing west, but more generally, the ocean route of this voyage follows the large gyre, with an expected 0.5 kts or so pushing the boat all along the route. That is almost certainly not what took place, and in light of modern knowledge, not what we would expect.

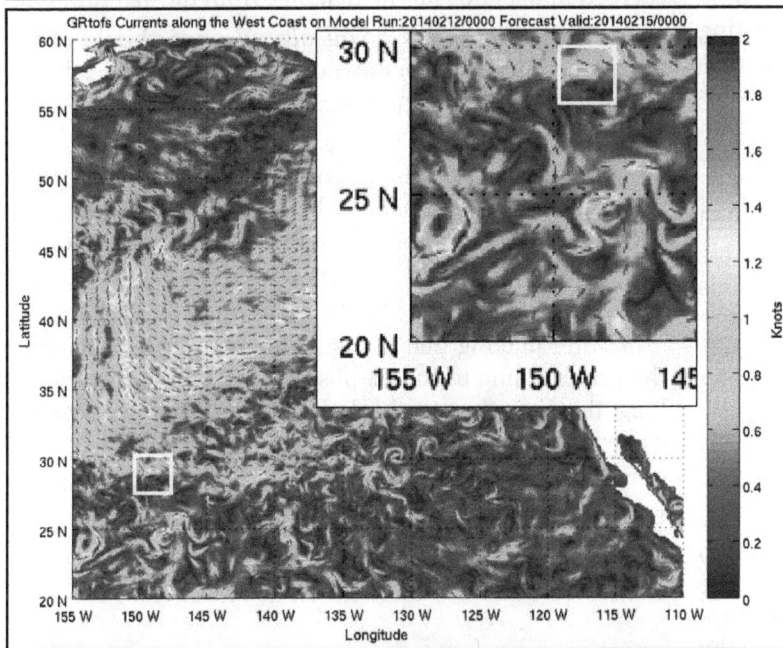

Figure A29. Middle. *Sample of live current predictions from the Ocean Prediction Center at the time of writing (mid Feb, 2014). The strong currents at 35 to 40 N are due to a large storm north of there, but this is not the area of interest. The goal is to show the mesoscale structure to the flow, seen in the eddies and rivers across the ocean. The nature of these patterns does not depend much on the time of year in this region. The value marked above for July is 0.4 kts flowing SW in February, even more in contrast to live predictions. These real currents are responses to variable conditions in the ocean. The inset marks the same area shown above. Orange to red marks currents of 1.4 to 1.8 kts. The eddy in the box is not even the biggest one seen in this sample.*

The data are from the GRTOFS model presented at opc.ncep.noaa.gov. For more resources see starpath.com/currents.

Figure A29. Bottom. *A closer look at the Global RTOFS prediction for the same time, over the highlighted area. We see better detail of the predicted eddy, which shows that instead of the February prediction of 0.4 to the SW, we see up to 1.1 kts to the NE. These data were obtained in GRIB format from the commercial product Ocens WeatherNet. Other sources in GRIB format are listed at starpath.com/currents.*

We have learned from careful study of many current prediction models that these data are just guidelines, and must not be trusted in fine detail. In other words, we learn there is a predicted eddy in this region, its approximate size and intensity. Its actual location and specific details may be different in the real world.

Our main point is this: ocean currents can be much larger and more random than we might guess, and we must keep this in mind when evaluating DR results.

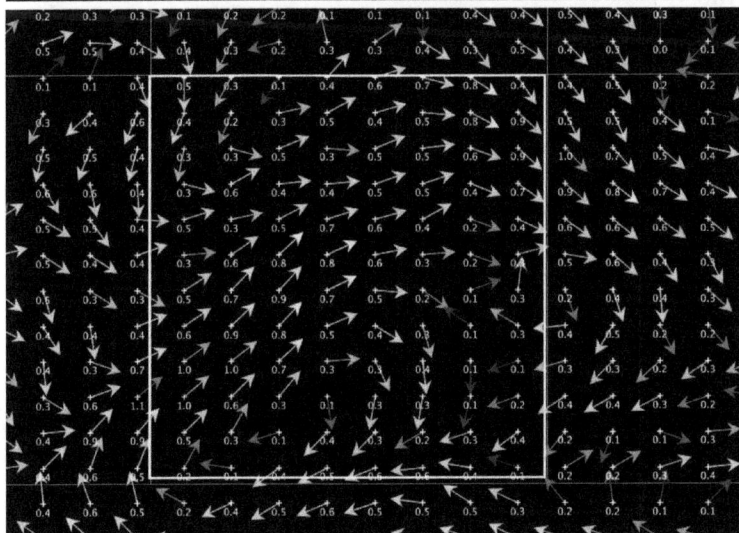

High Altitude Sights

Sights above 86° or so take special care because the approximations we make using *lines* of position grow less dependable as we get closer to the geographical position of the body we are sighting.

Problem 25 is an example. It was originally intended as a noon sight for LAN latitude along with an attempt to get a midpoint for an estimate of the longitude, as described in the Analysis section (Longitude by LAN?). It was also an exercise it taking high sights, which are difficult to take because with the sun nearly overhead, it is difficult to tell which direction to face as you rock the sextant.

In the Analysis section (Problem 25 Fit Slope Curve section) we learned, however, that the data do not make a good noon sight curve, so we decided to do a fix from the rising sights, throwing out sight 3. The workform and plotted examples were sights 1 and 6 shown in these respective sections.

High sights are best done by computation, and some programs even solve for the fix properly (intersecting circles of position), but most programs just treat them as intersecting lines of position, regardless of the altitudes involved. If you are forced to reduce sights by tables, then we need Pub 229 for best results, because these tables offer small corrections that are important for high sights. High sights usually call for an additional correction called the Double Second Difference (dsd) Correction. When this extra correction is required, the altitude difference (d) is listed in italics with a small dot beside it. They also require a careful interpolation of the Zn value. Following standard procedures used for lower sights could lead to large errors on high sights.

In the 1511 example from Sights 36, the extra corrections and interpolations contributed about 0.6' to the Hc and about 6.5° to the Zn value, and even after applying all the tabulated extra corrections the answer from Pub 229 is off the correct value by 0.2' in Hc and 0.7° in Zn. The bearing Zn to the very high sun in this example is changing at a rate of about 4° per minute, so it is easy to see the challenge to a set of tables to get this right to the tenth for each second.

But that is not the end of the story for very high sights. The job of sight reduction tables is to simply solve an equation to get Hc and Zn. That is how we know the answer they gave was not quite right—we compare the table results with the computation. We have to read deeper into the Pub 229 Table Instructions, however, to learn that this is not the right approach to an actual position fix from high altitude sights, even if the values came out precisely correct.

We come back then to the point first raised. When we are almost under the body we sight, the circle of position we are on cannot be approximated by a straight-line segment. We need to either plot the circles directly, with a radius equal to the zenith distance (90°-Ho) centered at the geographical position of the body, or we need some other trick to approximate this plot. The direct plot is illustrated in Figure A30, which shows that the more accurate fix is about three miles to the SW of the best we get from straight LOPs.

Pub. 229 Table of Offsets provides a way to approximate the circles of position on a larger scale chart. This is valuable for better accuracy when the sights are not extremely high (ie radii larger). Our example of 87° is about on the limit for drawing the circles, and as seen in the Figure the offsets do a fine job in reshaping the lines to match the arcs.

When to Check for Offsets

For all sextant altitudes over 80°, the Table of Offsets from Pub 229 should be checked for needed corrections that will approximate the proper circles of position. The size of the correction depends on the distance from the azimuth line.

However for *sights of all altitudes* we should check for corrections whenever any of the important lines in the plotting get to be over 30 miles long.

If we chose the proper assumed position, altitude intercepts (a-values) over 30' long usually mean the DR is notably off. This can usually be solved by making a new DR equal to the location of the first estimate fix, and then doing the sight reduction again from this new DR. That will make the a-values smaller.

If after making that adjustment, any line lengths from the azimuth line to the fix position are still over 30 miles long, then it is time to check the Offsets Table for possible corrections.

Table of Offsets is a feature of the Pub 229 tables. There is not any similar adjustment table in Pub 249.

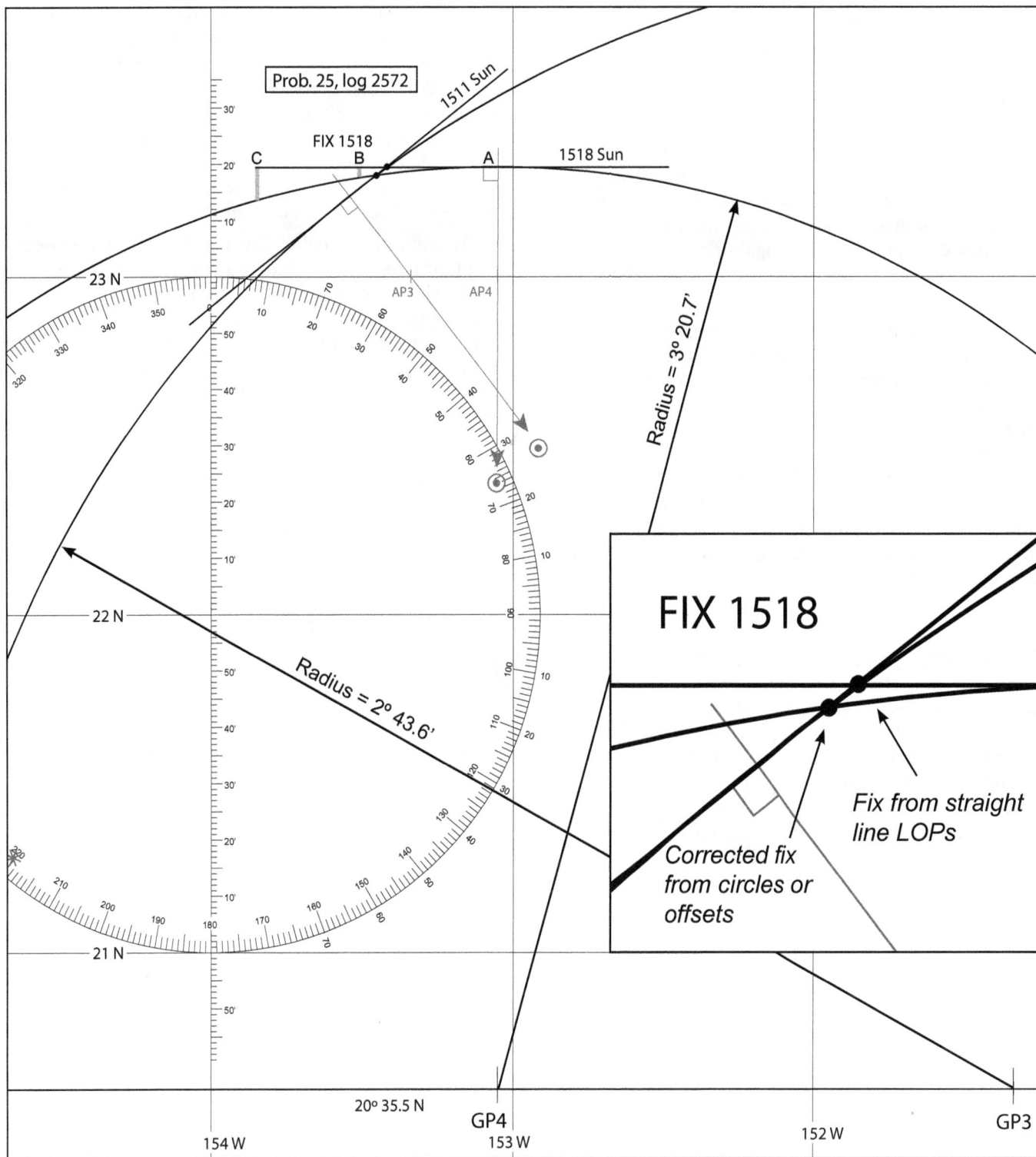

Figure A30. *Plot of the high altitude sights 1 and 6 of Sights #36. The straight LOPs are plotted form the assumed positions shown in the workforms. The circles of position are plotted from the geographic positions of the bodies at the time of the sight. The radii are equal to the zenith distance, 90° - Ho. The intersection of the two circles is a more accurate fix than that of the straight lines.*

Points A, B, C are the locations along the original LOP of offset points given from Pub 229 Table of Offsets, which tells us how to adjust the straight line LOPs to better approximate the circles of position. In this example the offsets reproduce the arc of the circle near the fixes very well, in that the line between them essentially coincides with the true arc.

The inset shows the corrected fix, which shifts the position about 3 nmi to the SW.

Longitude by LAN

At LAN the sun is crossing our meridian. If we had a way to accurately determine the midpoint of the distribution corresponding to the peak height of the sun we could look up the GHA of the sun at that peak time and that would be our longitude. Problem 25 included such a set of sights that were taken to test that process underway–although we stress in all of our teaching materials that this method is typically not very accurate and should be reserved for emergency navigation when no other options are available. This one was even more challenging because the sights were so high.

At the time of the voyage we simply made the plot shown in Figure A30. These sights were simply taken sequentially and recorded. A better approach to getting longitude from LAN would be to measure several sights when rising, then after the peak, set the sextant back to exactly what was observed earlier and just record the times the sun dropped back to these heights as it starts down. Then figure the midpoints between these equal altitude times, and average those results. This gets a better midpoint, but does not remove other inherent uncertainties in this method.

The midpoint in this example was determined by finding the average midpoints from the plot of Hs vs. WT at seven points along the curve. One interesting historical observation is the 3rd sight was it appears the 3rd sight was plotted originally 30s to the left, then erases and replotted as shown. The earlier Fit-slope Analysis of this data showed that as plotted this sight is wrong, but in the original location it would have been consistent.

The results we used at the time are shown in the figure. The fit slope analysis done earlier in this section showed that a Lon of 30 or 31' was likely a better fit taking into account the vessel motion, which was not much in this case at S4.3, C228. Traveling much faster to the east or west would have a larger effect. For our ongoing plot we will use what we find now: 23° 17.5 N, 153° 31'W, and just remain aware that this longitude is uncertain–though not likely as much as indicated in the figure.

We maintain our belief that Lon by LAN should be reserved for emergencies when no other methods are available, in which case we might even get an estimate from the halfway point between sunrise and sunset. And we also maintain our belief that noon sights for Lat are not worth the extra trouble called for. A simple running fix from AM to PM is a better approach to mid day navigation with the sun.

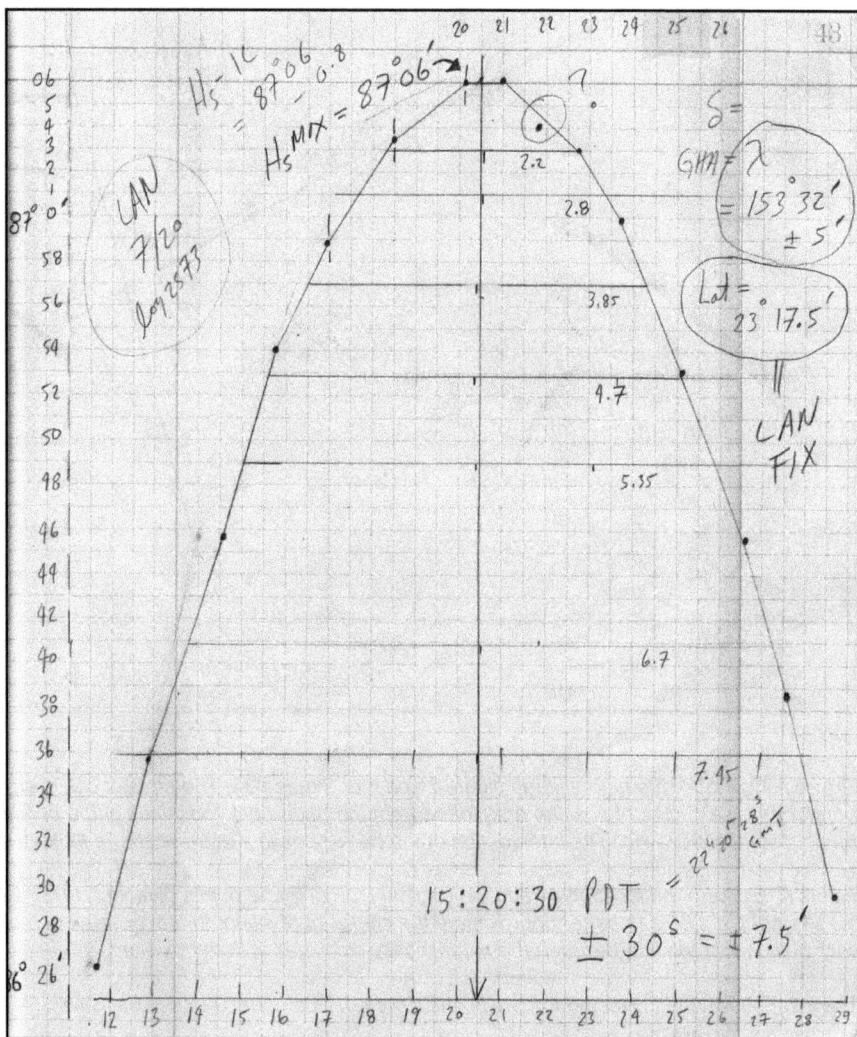

Figure A30. *A page from the original logbook showing an attempt to analyze LAN sights for longitude, a method we do not recommend. Hs is plotted vs. WT (15h + minutes shown.) A couple values in the fix on this page seem to be off a bit. The third sight rising and the first going back down can be seen to be in error from this type of plot, but only a fit slope curve analysis shown earlier shows more convincingly which sights are likely off. Even folding the paper and noting a different shape is not enough, as the motion of the boat can cause that asymmetry.*

Table Selections

List of Tables

Increments and Corrections
    Use from any *Nautical Almanac*, or download from starpath.com/HBS

Altitude Corrections

ALTITUDE CORRECTION TABLES 0°–10°—SUN, STARS, PLANETS A3

App. Alt.	OCT.–MAR. SUN Lower Limb	OCT.–MAR. SUN Upper Limb	APR.–SEPT. SUN Lower Limb	APR.–SEPT. SUN Upper Limb	STARS PLANETS
0 00	−18·2	50·5	−18·4	50·2	−34·5
03	17·5	49·8	17·8	49·6	33·8
06	16·9	49·2	17·1	48·9	33·2
09	16·3	48·6	16·5	48·3	32·6
12	15·7	48·0	15·9	47·7	32·0
15	15·1	47·4	15·3	47·1	31·4
0 18	−14·5	46·8	−14·8	46·6	−30·8
21	14·0	46·3	14·2	46·0	30·3
24	13·5	45·8	13·7	45·5	29·8
27	12·9	45·2	13·2	45·0	29·2
30	12·4	44·7	12·7	44·5	28·7
33	11·9	44·2	12·2	44·0	28·2
0 36	−11·5	43·8	−11·7	43·5	−27·8
39	11·0	43·3	11·2	43·0	27·3
42	10·5	42·8	10·8	42·6	26·8
45	10·1	42·4	10·3	42·1	26·4
48	9·6	41·9	9·9	41·7	25·9
51	9·2	41·5	9·5	41·3	25·5
0 54	−8·8	−41·1	−9·1	−40·9	−25·1
0 57	8·4	40·7	8·7	40·5	24·7
1 00	8·0	40·3	8·3	40·1	24·3
03	7·7	40·0	7·9	39·7	24·0
06	7·3	39·6	7·5	39·3	23·6
09	6·9	39·2	7·2	39·0	23·2
1 12	−6·6	−38·9	−6·8	−38·6	−22·9
15	6·2	38·5	6·5	38·3	22·5
18	5·9	38·2	6·2	38·0	22·2
21	5·6	37·9	5·8	37·6	21·9
24	5·3	37·6	5·5	37·3	21·6
27	4·9	37·2	5·2	37·0	21·2
1 30	−4·6	−36·9	−4·9	−36·7	−20·9
35	4·2	36·5	4·4	36·2	20·5
40	3·7	36·0	4·0	35·8	20·0
45	3·2	35·5	3·5	35·3	19·5
50	2·8	35·1	3·1	34·9	19·1
1 55	2·4	34·7	2·6	34·4	18·7
2 00	−2·0	−34·3	−2·2	−34·0	−18·3
05	1·6	33·9	1·8	33·6	17·9
10	1·2	33·5	1·5	33·3	17·5
15	0·9	33·2	1·1	32·9	17·2
20	0·5	32·8	0·8	32·6	16·8
25	−0·2	32·5	0·4	32·2	16·5
2 30	+0·2	−32·1	−0·1	−31·9	−16·1
35	0·5	31·8	+0·2	31·6	15·8
40	0·8	31·5	0·5	31·3	15·5
45	1·1	31·2	0·8	31·0	15·2
50	1·4	30·9	1·1	30·7	14·9
2 55	1·6	30·7	1·4	30·4	14·7
3 00	+1·9	−30·4	+1·7	−30·1	−14·4
05	2·2	30·1	1·9	29·9	14·1
10	2·4	29·9	2·1	29·7	13·9
15	2·6	29·7	2·4	29·4	13·7
20	2·9	29·4	2·6	29·2	13·4
25	3·1	29·2	2·9	28·9	13·2
3 30	+3·3	−29·0	+3·1	−28·7	−13·0
3 30	+3·3	−29·0	+3·1	−28·7	−13·0
35	3·6	28·7	3·3	28·5	12·7
40	3·8	28·5	3·5	28·3	12·5
45	4·0	28·3	3·7	28·1	12·3
50	4·2	28·1	3·9	27·9	12·1
3 55	4·4	27·9	4·1	27·7	11·9
4 00	+4·5	−27·8	+4·3	−27·5	−11·8
05	4·7	27·6	4·5	27·3	11·6
10	4·9	27·4	4·6	27·2	11·4
15	5·1	27·2	4·8	27·0	11·2
20	5·2	27·1	5·0	26·8	11·1
25	5·4	26·9	5·1	26·7	10·9
4 30	+5·6	−26·7	+5·3	−26·5	−10·7
35	5·7	26·6	5·5	26·3	10·6
40	5·9	26·4	5·6	26·2	10·4
45	6·0	26·3	5·8	26·0	10·3
50	6·2	26·1	5·9	25·9	10·1
4 55	6·3	26·0	6·0	25·8	10·0
5 00	+6·4	−25·9	+6·2	−25·6	−9·9
05	6·6	25·7	6·3	25·5	9·7
10	6·7	25·6	6·4	25·4	9·6
15	6·8	25·5	6·6	25·2	9·5
20	6·9	25·4	6·7	25·1	9·4
25	7·1	25·2	6·8	25·0	9·2
5 30	+7·2	−25·1	+6·9	−24·9	−9·1
35	7·3	25·0	7·0	24·8	9·0
40	7·4	24·9	7·2	24·6	8·9
45	7·5	24·8	7·3	24·5	8·8
50	7·6	24·7	7·4	24·4	8·7
5 55	7·7	24·6	7·5	24·3	8·6
6 00	+7·8	−24·5	+7·6	−24·2	−8·5
10	8·0	24·3	7·8	24·0	8·3
20	8·2	24·1	8·0	23·8	8·1
30	8·4	23·9	8·1	23·7	7·9
40	8·6	23·7	8·3	23·5	7·7
6 50	8·7	23·6	8·5	23·3	7·6
7 00	+8·9	−23·4	+8·6	−23·2	−7·4
10	9·1	23·2	8·8	23·0	7·2
20	9·2	23·1	9·0	22·8	7·1
30	9·3	23·0	9·1	22·7	7·0
40	9·5	22·8	9·2	22·6	6·8
7 50	9·6	22·7	9·4	22·4	6·7
8 00	+9·7	−22·6	+9·5	−22·3	−6·6
10	9·9	22·4	9·6	22·2	6·4
20	10·0	22·3	9·7	22·1	6·3
30	10·1	22·2	9·8	22·0	6·2
40	10·2	22·1	10·0	21·8	6·1
8 50	10·3	22·0	10·1	21·7	6·0
9 00	+10·4	−21·9	+10·2	−21·6	−5·9
10	10·5	21·8	10·3	21·5	5·8
20	10·6	21·7	10·4	21·4	5·7
30	10·7	21·6	10·5	21·3	5·6
40	10·8	21·5	10·6	21·2	5·5
9 50	10·9	21·4	10·6	21·2	5·4
10 00	+11·0	−21·3	+10·7	−21·1	−5·3

A2 ALTITUDE CORRECTION TABLES 10°–90°—SUN, STARS, PLANETS

OCT.–MAR.	SUN	APR.–SEPT.		STARS AND PLANETS			DIP			
App. Alt.	Lower Limb	Upper Limb	App. Alt. Lower Limb Upper Limb	App. Alt.	Corrⁿ	App. Alt. Additional Corrⁿ	Ht. of Eye	Corrⁿ	Ht. of Eye	Ht. of Eye Corrⁿ

OCT.–MAR. SUN App. Alt. / Lower Limb / Upper Limb	APR.–SEPT. App. Alt. / Lower Limb / Upper Limb	STARS AND PLANETS App. Alt. / Corrⁿ	Additional Corrⁿ	DIP (m) Corrⁿ	(ft)	(m) Corrⁿ
9 34 +10·8 −21·5	9 39 +10·6 −21·2	9 56 −5·3	**1982** **VENUS** Jan. 1–Jan. 3	2·4 −2·8	8·0	1·0 — 1·8
9 45 +10·9 −21·4	9 51 +10·7 −21·1	10 08 −5·2		2·6 −2·9	8·6	1·5 — 2·2
9 56 +11·0 −21·3	10 03 +10·8 −21·0	10 20 −5·1		2·8 −3·0	9·2	2·0 — 2·5
10 08 +11·1 −21·2	10 15 +10·9 −20·9	10 33 −5·0	°	3·0 −3·1	9·8	2·5 — 2·8
10 21 +11·2 −21·1	10 27 +11·0 −20·8	10 46 −4·9	6 + 0·5	3·2 −3·2	10·5	3·0 — 3·0
10 34 +11·3 −21·0	10 40 +11·1 −20·7	11 00 −4·8	20 + 0·6	3·4 −3·3	11·2	See table ←
10 47 +11·4 −20·9	10 54 +11·2 −20·6	11 14 −4·7	31 + 0·7	3·6 −3·4	11·9	
11 01 +11·5 −20·8	11 08 +11·3 −20·5	11 29 −4·6		3·8 −3·5	12·6	m
11 15 +11·6 −20·7	11 23 +11·4 −20·4	11 45 −4·5	Jan. 4–Feb. 7	4·0 −3·6	13·3	20 — 7·9
11 30 +11·7 −20·6	11 38 +11·5 −20·3	12 01 −4·4	°	4·3 −3·7	14·1	22 — 8·3
11 46 +11·8 −20·5	11 54 +11·6 −20·2	12 18 −4·3	4 + 0·6	4·5 −3·8	14·9	24 — 8·6
12 02 +11·9 −20·4	12 10 +11·7 −20·1	12 35 −4·2	12 + 0·7	4·7 −3·9	15·7	26 — 9·0
12 19 +12·0 −20·3	12 28 +11·8 −20·0	12 54 −4·1	22 + 0·8	5·0 −4·0	16·5	28 — 9·3
12 37 +12·1 −20·2	12 46 +11·9 −19·9	13 13 −4·0	Feb. 8–Feb. 14	5·2 −4·1	17·4	
12 55 +12·2 −20·1	13 05 +12·0 −19·8	13 33 −3·9		5·5 −4·2	18·3	30 — 9·6
13 14 +12·3 −20·0	13 24 +12·1 −19·7	13 54 −3·8	°	5·8 −4·3	19·1	32 — 10·0
13 35 +12·4 −19·9	13 45 +12·2 −19·6	14 16 −3·7	6 + 0·5	6·1 −4·4	20·1	34 — 10·3
13 56 +12·5 −19·8	14 07 +12·3 −19·5	14 40 −3·6	20 + 0·6	6·3 −4·5	21·0	36 — 10·6
14 18 +12·6 −19·7	14 30 +12·4 −19·4	15 04 −3·5	31 + 0·7	6·6 −4·6	22·0	38 — 10·8
14 42 +12·7 −19·6	14 54 +12·5 −19·3	15 30 −3·4	Feb. 15–Mar. 2	6·9 −4·7	22·9	
15 06 +12·8 −19·5	15 19 +12·6 −19·2	15 57 −3·3		7·2 −4·8	23·9	40 — 11·1
15 32 +12·9 −19·4	15 46 +12·7 −19·1	16 26 −3·2	°	7·5 −4·9	24·9	42 — 11·4
15 59 +13·0 −19·3	16 14 +12·8 −19·0	16 56 −3·1	11 + 0·4	7·9 −5·0	26·0	44 — 11·7
16 28 +13·1 −19·2	16 44 +12·9 −18·9	17 28 −3·0	41 + 0·5	8·2 −5·1	27·1	46 — 11·9
16 59 +13·2 −19·1	17 15 +13·0 −18·8	18 02 −2·9	Mar. 3–Mar. 28	8·5 −5·2	28·1	48 — 12·2
17 32 +13·3 −19·0	17 48 +13·1 −18·7	18 38 −2·8		8·8 −5·3	29·2	ft.
18 06 +13·4 −18·9	18 24 +13·2 −18·6	19 17 −2·7	°	9·2 −5·4	30·4	2 — 1·4
18 42 +13·5 −18·8	19 01 +13·3 −18·5	19 58 −2·6	46 + 0·3	9·5 −5·5	31·5	4 — 1·9
19 21 +13·6 −18·7	19 42 +13·4 −18·4	20 42 −2·5	Mar. 29–May 12	9·9 −5·6	32·7	6 — 2·4
20 03 +13·7 −18·6	20 25 +13·5 −18·3	21 28 −2·4		10·3 −5·7	33·9	8 — 2·7
20 48 +13·8 −18·5	21 11 +13·6 −18·2	22 19 −2·3	°	10·6 −5·8	35·1	10 — 3·1
21 35 +13·9 −18·4	22 00 +13·7 −18·1	23 13 −2·2	47 + 0·2	11·0 −5·9	36·3	
22 26 +14·0 −18·3	22 54 +13·8 −18·0	24 11 −2·1	May 13–Dec. 31	11·4 −6·0	37·6	See table ←
23 22 +14·1 −18·2	23 51 +13·9 −17·9	25 14 −2·0		11·8 −6·1	38·9	
24 21 +14·2 −18·1	24 53 +14·0 −17·8	26 22 −1·9	°	12·2 −6·2	40·1	ft.
25 26 +14·3 −18·0	26 00 +14·1 −17·7	27 36 −1·8	42 + 0·1	12·6 −6·3	41·5	70 — 8·1
26 36 +14·4 −17·9	27 13 +14·2 −17·6	28 56 −1·7		13·0 −6·4	42·8	75 — 8·4
27 52 +14·5 −17·8	28 33 +14·3 −17·5	30 24 −1·6	**MARS**	13·4 −6·5	44·2	80 — 8·7
29 15 +14·6 −17·7	30 00 +14·4 −17·4	32 00 −1·5	Jan. 1–Jan. 30	13·8 −6·6	45·5	85 — 8·9
30 46 +14·7 −17·6	31 35 +14·5 −17·3	33 45 −1·4		14·2 −6·7	46·9	90 — 9·2
32 26 +14·8 −17·5	33 20 +14·6 −17·2	35 40 −1·3	°	14·7 −6·8	48·4	95 — 9·5
34 17 +14·9 −17·4	35 17 +14·7 −17·1	37 48 −1·2	60 + 0·1	15·1 −6·9	49·8	
36 20 +15·0 −17·3	37 26 +14·8 −17·0	40 08 −1·1	Jan. 31–June 18	15·5 −7·0	51·3	100 — 9·7
38 36 +15·1 −17·2	39 50 +14·9 −16·9	42 44 −1·0		16·0 −7·1	52·8	105 — 9·9
41 08 +15·2 −17·1	42 31 +15·0 −16·8	45 36 −0·9	°	16·5 −7·2	54·3	110 — 10·2
43 59 +15·3 −17·0	45 31 +15·1 −16·7	48 47 −0·8	41 + 0·2	16·9 −7·3	55·8	115 — 10·4
47 10 +15·4 −16·9	48 55 +15·2 −16·6	52 18 −0·7	75 + 0·1	17·4 −7·4	57·4	120 — 10·6
50 46 +15·5 −16·8	52 44 +15·3 −16·5	56 11 −0·6	June 19–Dec. 31	17·9 −7·5	58·9	125 — 10·8
54 49 +15·6 −16·7	57 02 +15·4 −16·4	60 28 −0·5		18·4 −7·6	60·5	
59 23 +15·7 −16·6	61 51 +15·5 −16·3	65 08 −0·4	°	18·8 −7·7	62·1	130 — 11·1
64 30 +15·8 −16·5	67 17 +15·6 −16·2	70 11 −0·3	60 + 0·1	19·3 −7·8	63·8	135 — 11·3
70 12 +15·9 −16·4	73 16 +15·7 −16·1	75 34 −0·2		19·8 −7·9	65·4	140 — 11·5
76 26 +16·0 −16·3	79 43 +15·8 −16·0	81 13 −0·1		20·4 −8·0	67·1	145 — 11·7
83 05 +16·1 −16·2	86 32 +15·9 −15·9	87 03 0·0		20·9 −8·1	68·8	150 — 11·9
90 00	90 00	90 00 0·0		21·4	70·5	155 — 12·1

App. Alt. = Apparent altitude = Sextant altitude corrected for index error and dip.

ALTITUDE CORRECTION TABLES 0°–35°—MOON

App. Alt.	0°–4° Corrⁿ	5°–9° Corrⁿ	10°–14° Corrⁿ	15°–19° Corrⁿ	20°–24° Corrⁿ	25°–29° Corrⁿ	30°–34° Corrⁿ	App. Alt.
00	0 33.8	5 58.2	10 62.1	15 62.8	20 62.2	25 60.8	30 58.9	00
10	35.9	58.5	62.2	62.8	62.1	60.8	58.8	10
20	37.8	58.7	62.2	62.8	62.1	60.7	58.8	20
30	39.6	58.9	62.3	62.8	62.1	60.7	58.7	30
40	41.2	59.1	62.3	62.8	62.0	60.6	58.6	40
50	42.6	59.3	62.4	62.7	62.0	60.6	58.5	50
00	1 44.0	6 59.5	11 62.4	16 62.7	21 62.0	26 60.5	31 58.5	00
10	45.2	59.7	62.4	62.7	61.9	60.4	58.4	10
20	46.3	59.9	62.5	62.7	61.9	60.4	58.3	20
30	47.3	60.0	62.5	62.7	61.9	60.3	58.2	30
40	48.3	60.2	62.5	62.7	61.8	60.3	58.2	40
50	49.2	60.3	62.6	62.7	61.8	60.2	58.1	50
00	2 50.0	7 60.5	12 62.6	17 62.7	22 61.7	27 60.1	32 58.0	00
10	50.8	60.6	62.6	62.6	61.7	60.1	57.9	10
20	51.4	60.7	62.6	62.6	61.6	60.0	57.8	20
30	52.1	60.9	62.7	62.6	61.6	59.9	57.8	30
40	52.7	61.0	62.7	62.6	61.5	59.9	57.7	40
50	53.3	61.1	62.7	62.6	61.5	59.8	57.6	50
00	3 53.8	8 61.2	13 62.7	18 62.5	23 61.5	28 59.7	33 57.5	00
10	54.3	61.3	62.7	62.5	61.4	59.7	57.4	10
20	54.8	61.4	62.7	62.5	61.4	59.6	57.4	20
30	55.2	61.5	62.8	62.5	61.3	59.6	57.3	30
40	55.6	61.6	62.8	62.4	61.3	59.5	57.2	40
50	56.0	61.6	62.8	62.4	61.2	59.4	57.1	50
00	4 56.4	9 61.7	14 62.8	19 62.4	24 61.2	29 59.3	34 57.0	00
10	56.7	61.8	62.8	62.3	61.1	59.3	56.9	10
20	57.1	61.9	62.8	62.3	61.1	59.2	56.9	20
30	57.4	61.9	62.8	62.3	61.0	59.1	56.8	30
40	57.7	62.0	62.8	62.2	60.9	59.1	56.7	40
50	57.9	62.1	62.8	62.2	60.9	59.0	56.6	50

H.P.	L	U	L	U	L	U	L	U	L	U	L	U	L	U	H.P.
54.0	0.3	0.9	0.3	0.9	0.4	1.0	0.5	1.1	0.6	1.2	0.7	1.3	0.9	1.5	54.0
54.3	0.7	1.1	0.7	1.2	0.7	1.2	0.8	1.3	0.9	1.4	1.1	1.5	1.2	1.7	54.3
54.6	1.1	1.4	1.1	1.4	1.1	1.4	1.2	1.5	1.3	1.6	1.4	1.7	1.5	1.8	54.6
54.9	1.4	1.6	1.5	1.6	1.5	1.6	1.6	1.7	1.6	1.8	1.8	1.9	1.9	2.0	54.9
55.2	1.8	1.8	1.8	1.8	1.9	1.9	1.9	1.9	2.0	2.0	2.1	2.1	2.2	2.2	55.2
55.5	2.2	2.0	2.2	2.0	2.3	2.1	2.3	2.1	2.4	2.2	2.4	2.3	2.5	2.4	55.5
55.8	2.6	2.2	2.6	2.2	2.6	2.3	2.7	2.3	2.7	2.4	2.8	2.4	2.9	2.5	55.8
56.1	3.0	2.4	3.0	2.5	3.0	2.5	3.0	2.5	3.1	2.6	3.1	2.6	3.2	2.7	56.1
56.4	3.4	2.7	3.4	2.7	3.4	2.7	3.4	2.7	3.4	2.8	3.5	2.8	3.5	2.9	56.4
56.7	3.7	2.9	3.7	2.9	3.8	2.9	3.8	2.9	3.8	3.0	3.8	3.0	3.9	3.0	56.7
57.0	4.1	3.1	4.1	3.1	4.1	3.1	4.1	3.1	4.2	3.1	4.2	3.2	4.2	3.2	57.0
57.3	4.5	3.3	4.5	3.3	4.5	3.3	4.5	3.3	4.5	3.3	4.5	3.4	4.6	3.4	57.3
57.6	4.9	3.5	4.9	3.5	4.9	3.5	4.9	3.5	4.9	3.5	4.9	3.5	4.9	3.6	57.6
57.9	5.3	3.8	5.3	3.8	5.2	3.8	5.2	3.7	5.2	3.7	5.2	3.7	5.2	3.7	57.9
58.2	5.6	4.0	5.6	4.0	5.6	4.0	5.6	4.0	5.6	3.9	5.6	3.9	5.6	3.9	58.2
58.5	6.0	4.2	6.0	4.2	6.0	4.2	6.0	4.2	6.0	4.1	5.9	4.1	5.9	4.1	58.5
58.8	6.4	4.4	6.4	4.4	6.4	4.4	6.3	4.4	6.3	4.3	6.3	4.3	6.2	4.2	58.8
59.1	6.8	4.6	6.8	4.6	6.7	4.6	6.7	4.6	6.7	4.5	6.6	4.5	6.6	4.4	59.1
59.4	7.2	4.8	7.1	4.8	7.1	4.8	7.1	4.8	7.0	4.7	7.0	4.7	6.9	4.6	59.4
59.7	7.5	5.1	7.5	5.0	7.5	5.0	7.5	5.0	7.4	4.9	7.3	4.8	7.2	4.7	59.7
60.0	7.9	5.3	7.9	5.3	7.9	5.2	7.8	5.2	7.8	5.1	7.7	5.0	7.6	4.9	60.0
60.3	8.3	5.5	8.3	5.5	8.2	5.4	8.2	5.4	8.1	5.3	8.0	5.2	7.9	5.1	60.3
60.6	8.7	5.7	8.7	5.7	8.6	5.7	8.6	5.6	8.5	5.5	8.4	5.4	8.2	5.3	60.6
60.9	9.1	5.9	9.0	5.9	9.0	5.9	8.9	5.8	8.8	5.7	8.7	5.6	8.6	5.4	60.9
61.2	9.5	6.2	9.4	6.1	9.4	6.1	9.3	6.0	9.2	5.9	9.1	5.8	8.9	5.6	61.2
61.5	9.8	6.4	9.8	6.3	9.7	6.3	9.7	6.2	9.5	6.1	9.4	5.9	9.2	5.8	61.5

DIP

Ht. of Eye (m)	Corrⁿ	Ht. of Eye (ft)	Ht. of Eye (m)	Corrⁿ	Ht. of Eye (ft)
2.4	−2.8	8.0	9.5	−5.5	31.5
2.6	−2.9	8.6	9.9	−5.6	32.7
2.8	−3.0	9.2	10.3	−5.7	33.9
3.0	−3.1	9.8	10.6	−5.8	35.1
3.2	−3.2	10.5	11.0	−5.9	36.3
3.4	−3.3	11.2	11.4	−6.0	37.6
3.6	−3.4	11.9	11.8	−6.1	38.9
3.8	−3.5	12.6	12.2	−6.2	40.1
4.0	−3.6	13.3	12.6	−6.3	41.5
4.3	−3.7	14.1	13.0	−6.4	42.8
4.5	−3.8	14.9	13.4	−6.5	44.2
4.7	−3.9	15.7	13.8	−6.6	45.5
5.0	−4.0	16.5	14.2	−6.7	46.9
5.2	−4.1	17.4	14.7	−6.8	48.4
5.5	−4.2	18.3	15.1	−6.9	49.8
5.8	−4.3	19.1	15.5	−7.0	51.3
6.1	−4.4	20.1	16.0	−7.1	52.8
6.3	−4.5	21.0	16.5	−7.2	54.3
6.6	−4.6	22.0	16.9	−7.3	55.8
6.9	−4.7	22.9	17.4	−7.4	57.4
7.2	−4.8	23.9	17.9	−7.5	58.9
7.5	−4.9	24.9	18.4	−7.6	60.5
7.9	−5.0	26.0	18.8	−7.7	62.1
8.2	−5.1	27.1	19.3	−7.8	63.8
8.5	−5.2	28.1	19.8	−7.9	65.4
8.8	−5.3	29.2	20.4	−8.0	67.1
9.2	−5.4	30.4	20.9	−8.1	68.8
9.5		31.5	21.4		70.5

MOON CORRECTION TABLE

The correction is in two parts; the first correction is taken from the upper part of the table with argument apparent altitude, and the second from the lower part, with argument H.P., in the same column as that from which the first correction was taken. Separate corrections are given in the lower part for lower (L) and upper (U) limbs. All corrections are to be **added** to apparent altitude, *but 30′ is to be subtracted from the altitude of the upper limb.*

For corrections for pressure and temperature see page A4.

For bubble sextant observations ignore dip, take the mean of upper and lower limb corrections and subtract 15′ from the altitude.

App. Alt. = Apparent altitude
Sextant altitude corrected for index error and dip.

ALTITUDE CORRECTION TABLES 35°–90°—MOON

App. Alt.	35°–39° Corrn	40°–44° Corrn	45°–49° Corrn	50°–54° Corrn	55°–59° Corrn	60°–64° Corrn	65°–69° Corrn	70°–74° Corrn	75°–79° Corrn	80°–84° Corrn	85°–89° Corrn	App. Alt.
00	35 56·5	40 53·7	45 50·5	50 46·9	55 43·1	60 38·9	65 34·6	70 30·1	75 25·3	80 20·5	85 15·6	00
10	56·4	53·6	50·4	46·8	42·9	38·8	34·4	29·9	25·2	20·4	15·5	10
20	56·3	53·5	50·2	46·7	42·8	38·7	34·3	29·7	25·0	20·2	15·3	20
30	56·2	53·4	50·1	46·5	42·7	38·5	34·1	29·6	24·9	20·0	15·1	30
40	56·2	53·3	50·0	46·4	42·5	38·4	34·0	29·4	24·7	19·9	15·0	40
50	56·1	53·2	49·9	46·3	42·4	38·2	33·8	29·3	24·5	19·7	14·8	50
00	36 56·0	41 53·1	46 49·8	51 46·2	56 42·3	61 38·1	66 33·7	71 29·1	76 24·4	81 19·6	86 14·6	00
10	55·9	53·0	49·7	46·0	42·1	37·9	33·5	29·0	24·2	19·4	14·5	10
20	55·8	52·8	49·5	45·9	42·0	37·8	33·4	28·8	24·1	19·2	14·3	20
30	55·7	52·7	49·4	45·8	41·8	37·7	33·2	28·7	23·9	19·1	14·1	30
40	55·6	52·6	49·3	45·7	41·7	37·5	33·1	28·5	23·8	18·9	14·0	40
50	55·5	52·5	49·2	45·5	41·6	37·4	32·9	28·3	23·6	18·7	13·8	50
00	37 55·4	42 52·4	47 49·1	52 45·4	57 41·4	62 37·2	67 32·8	72 28·2	77 23·4	82 18·6	87 13·7	00
10	55·3	52·3	49·0	45·3	41·3	37·1	32·6	28·0	23·3	18·4	13·5	10
20	55·2	52·2	48·8	45·2	41·2	36·9	32·5	27·9	23·1	18·2	13·3	20
30	55·1	52·1	48·7	45·0	41·0	36·8	32·3	27·7	22·9	18·1	13·2	30
40	55·0	52·0	48·6	44·9	40·9	36·6	32·2	27·6	22·8	17·9	13·0	40
50	55·0	51·9	48·5	44·8	40·8	36·5	32·0	27·4	22·6	17·8	12·8	50
00	38 54·9	43 51·8	48 48·4	53 44·6	58 40·6	63 36·4	68 31·9	73 27·2	78 22·5	83 17·6	88 12·7	00
10	54·8	51·7	48·2	44·5	40·5	36·2	31·7	27·1	22·3	17·4	12·5	10
20	54·7	51·6	48·1	44·4	40·3	36·1	31·6	26·9	22·1	17·3	12·3	20
30	54·6	51·5	48·0	44·2	40·2	35·9	31·4	26·8	22·0	17·1	12·2	30
40	54·5	51·4	47·9	44·1	40·1	35·8	31·3	26·6	21·8	16·9	12·0	40
50	54·4	51·2	47·8	44·0	39·9	35·6	31·1	26·5	21·7	16·8	11·8	50
00	39 54·3	44 51·1	49 47·6	54 43·9	59 39·8	64 35·5	69 31·0	74 26·3	79 21·5	84 16·6	89 11·7	00
10	54·2	51·0	47·5	43·7	39·6	35·3	30·8	26·1	21·3	16·5	11·5	10
20	54·1	50·9	47·4	43·6	39·5	35·2	30·7	26·0	21·2	16·3	11·4	20
30	54·0	50·8	47·3	43·5	39·4	35·0	30·5	25·8	21·0	16·1	11·2	30
40	53·9	50·7	47·2	43·3	39·2	34·9	30·4	25·7	20·9	16·0	11·0	40
50	53·8	50·6	47·0	43·2	39·1	34·7	30·2	25·5	20·7	15·8	10·9	50

H.P.	L U	L U	L U	L U	L U	L U	L U	L U	L U	L U	L U	H.P.
54·0	1·1 1·7	1·3 1·9	1·5 2·1	1·7 2·4	2·0 2·6	2·3 2·9	2·6 3·2	2·9 3·5	3·2 3·8	3·5 4·1	3·8 4·5	54·0
54·3	1·4 1·8	1·6 2·0	1·8 2·2	2·0 2·5	2·3 2·7	2·5 3·0	2·8 3·2	3·0 3·5	3·3 3·8	3·6 4·1	3·9 4·4	54·3
54·6	1·7 2·0	1·9 2·2	2·1 2·4	2·3 2·6	2·5 2·8	2·7 3·0	3·0 3·3	3·2 3·5	3·5 3·8	3·7 4·1	4·0 4·3	54·6
54·9	2·0 2·2	2·2 2·3	2·3 2·5	2·5 2·7	2·7 2·9	2·9 3·1	3·2 3·3	3·4 3·5	3·6 3·8	3·9 4·0	4·1 4·3	54·9
55·2	2·3 2·3	2·5 2·4	2·6 2·6	2·8 2·8	3·0 2·9	3·2 3·1	3·4 3·3	3·6 3·5	3·8 3·7	4·0 4·0	4·2 4·2	55·2
55·5	2·7 2·5	2·8 2·6	2·9 2·7	3·1 2·9	3·2 3·0	3·4 3·2	3·6 3·4	3·7 3·5	3·9 3·7	4·1 3·9	4·3 4·1	55·5
55·8	3·0 2·6	3·1 2·7	3·2 2·8	3·3 3·0	3·5 3·1	3·6 3·3	3·8 3·4	3·9 3·6	4·1 3·7	4·2 3·9	4·4 4·0	55·8
56·1	3·3 2·8	3·4 2·9	3·5 3·0	3·6 3·1	3·7 3·2	3·8 3·3	4·0 3·4	4·1 3·6	4·2 3·7	4·4 3·8	4·5 4·0	56·1
56·4	3·6 2·9	3·7 3·0	3·8 3·1	3·9 3·2	3·9 3·3	4·0 3·4	4·1 3·5	4·3 3·6	4·4 3·7	4·5 3·8	4·6 3·9	56·4
56·7	3·9 3·1	4·0 3·1	4·1 3·2	4·1 3·3	4·2 3·3	4·3 3·4	4·3 3·5	4·4 3·6	4·5 3·7	4·6 3·8	4·7 3·8	56·7
57·0	4·3 3·2	4·3 3·3	4·3 3·3	4·4 3·4	4·4 3·4	4·5 3·5	4·5 3·5	4·6 3·6	4·6 3·6	4·7 3·7	4·8 3·8	57·0
57·3	4·6 3·4	4·6 3·4	4·6 3·4	4·6 3·5	4·7 3·5	4·7 3·5	4·7 3·6	4·8 3·6	4·8 3·6	5·0 3·6	5·0 3·6	57·3
57·6	4·9 3·6	4·9 3·6	4·9 3·6	4·9 3·6	4·9 3·6	4·9 3·6	4·9 3·6	5·0 3·6	5·0 3·6	5·0 3·6	5·0 3·6	57·6
57·9	5·2 3·7	5·2 3·7	5·2 3·7	5·2 3·7	5·2 3·7	5·1 3·6	5·1 3·6	5·1 3·6	5·1 3·6	5·1 3·6	5·1 3·6	57·9
58·2	5·5 3·9	5·5 3·8	5·5 3·8	5·4 3·8	5·4 3·7	5·4 3·7	5·3 3·7	5·3 3·6	5·2 3·6	5·2 3·5	5·2 3·5	58·2
58·5	5·9 4·0	5·8 4·0	5·8 3·9	5·7 3·9	5·6 3·8	5·6 3·8	5·5 3·7	5·5 3·6	5·4 3·6	5·3 3·5	5·3 3·4	58·5
58·8	6·2 4·2	6·1 4·1	6·0 4·1	6·0 4·0	5·9 3·9	5·8 3·8	5·7 3·7	5·6 3·6	5·5 3·5	5·4 3·5	5·3 3·4	58·8
59·1	6·5 4·3	6·4 4·3	6·3 4·2	6·2 4·1	6·1 4·0	6·0 3·9	5·9 3·8	5·8 3·6	5·7 3·5	5·6 3·4	5·4 3·3	59·1
59·4	6·8 4·5	6·7 4·4	6·6 4·3	6·5 4·2	6·4 4·1	6·2 3·9	6·1 3·8	6·0 3·7	5·8 3·5	5·7 3·4	5·5 3·2	59·4
59·7	7·1 4·6	7·0 4·5	6·9 4·4	6·8 4·3	6·6 4·1	6·5 4·0	6·3 3·8	6·2 3·7	6·0 3·5	5·8 3·3	5·6 3·2	59·7
60·0	7·5 4·8	7·3 4·7	7·2 4·5	7·0 4·4	6·9 4·2	6·7 4·0	6·5 3·9	6·3 3·7	6·1 3·5	5·9 3·3	5·7 3·1	60·0
60·3	7·8 5·0	7·6 4·8	7·5 4·7	7·3 4·5	7·1 4·3	6·9 4·1	6·7 3·9	6·5 3·7	6·3 3·5	6·0 3·2	5·8 3·0	60·3
60·6	8·1 5·1	7·9 5·0	7·7 4·8	7·6 4·6	7·3 4·4	7·1 4·2	6·9 3·9	6·7 3·7	6·4 3·4	6·2 3·2	5·9 2·9	60·6
60·9	8·4 5·3	8·2 5·1	8·0 4·9	7·8 4·7	7·6 4·5	7·3 4·2	7·1 4·0	6·8 3·7	6·6 3·4	6·3 3·2	6·0 2·9	60·9
61·2	8·7 5·4	8·5 5·2	8·3 5·0	8·1 4·8	7·8 4·5	7·6 4·3	7·3 4·0	7·0 3·7	6·7 3·4	6·4 3·1	6·1 2·8	61·2
61·5	9·1 5·6	8·8 5·4	8·6 5·1	8·3 4·9	8·1 4·6	7·8 4·3	7·5 4·0	7·2 3·7	6·9 3·4	6·5 3·1	6·2 2·7	61·5

A4 ALTITUDE CORRECTION TABLES—ADDITIONAL CORRECTIONS
ADDITIONAL REFRACTION CORRECTIONS FOR NON-STANDARD CONDITIONS

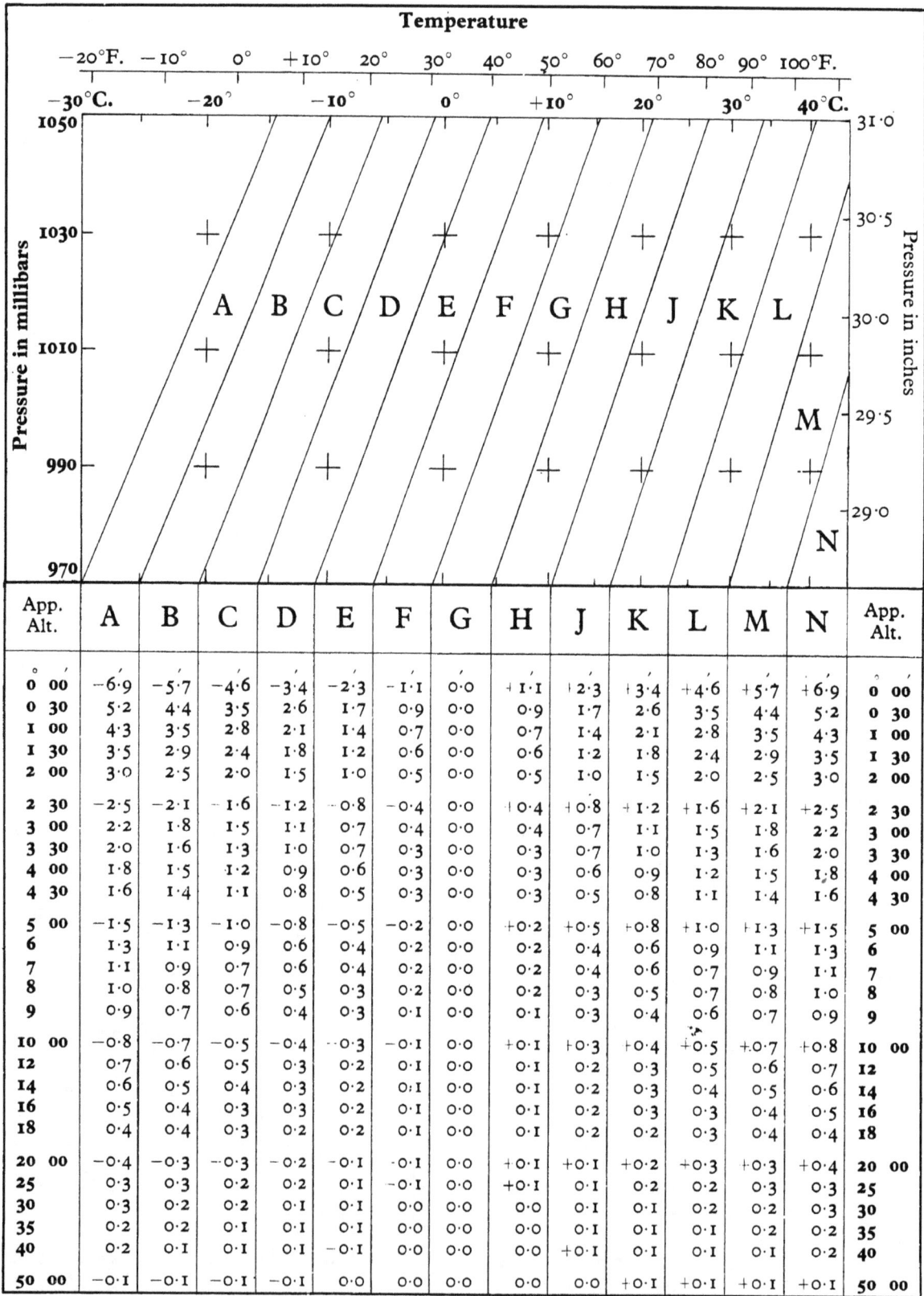

App. Alt.	A	B	C	D	E	F	G	H	J	K	L	M	N	App. Alt.
0 00	−6.9	−5.7	−4.6	−3.4	−2.3	−1.1	0.0	+1.1	+2.3	+3.4	+4.6	+5.7	+6.9	0 00
0 30	5.2	4.4	3.5	2.6	1.7	0.9	0.0	0.9	1.7	2.6	3.5	4.4	5.2	0 30
1 00	4.3	3.5	2.8	2.1	1.4	0.7	0.0	0.7	1.4	2.1	2.8	3.5	4.3	1 00
1 30	3.5	2.9	2.4	1.8	1.2	0.6	0.0	0.6	1.2	1.8	2.4	2.9	3.5	1 30
2 00	3.0	2.5	2.0	1.5	1.0	0.5	0.0	0.5	1.0	1.5	2.0	2.5	3.0	2 00
2 30	−2.5	−2.1	−1.6	−1.2	−0.8	−0.4	0.0	+0.4	+0.8	+1.2	+1.6	+2.1	+2.5	2 30
3 00	2.2	1.8	1.5	1.1	0.7	0.4	0.0	0.4	0.7	1.1	1.5	1.8	2.2	3 00
3 30	2.0	1.6	1.3	1.0	0.7	0.3	0.0	0.3	0.7	1.0	1.3	1.6	2.0	3 30
4 00	1.8	1.5	1.2	0.9	0.6	0.3	0.0	0.3	0.6	0.9	1.2	1.5	1.8	4 00
4 30	1.6	1.4	1.1	0.8	0.5	0.3	0.0	0.3	0.5	0.8	1.1	1.4	1.6	4 30
5 00	−1.5	−1.3	−1.0	−0.8	−0.5	−0.2	0.0	+0.2	+0.5	+0.8	+1.0	+1.3	+1.5	5 00
6	1.3	1.1	0.9	0.6	0.4	0.2	0.0	0.2	0.4	0.6	0.9	1.1	1.3	6
7	1.1	0.9	0.7	0.6	0.4	0.2	0.0	0.2	0.4	0.6	0.7	0.9	1.1	7
8	1.0	0.8	0.7	0.5	0.3	0.2	0.0	0.2	0.3	0.5	0.7	0.8	1.0	8
9	0.9	0.7	0.6	0.4	0.3	0.1	0.0	0.1	0.3	0.4	0.6	0.7	0.9	9
10 00	−0.8	−0.7	−0.5	−0.4	−0.3	−0.1	0.0	+0.1	+0.3	+0.4	+0.5	+0.7	+0.8	10 00
12	0.7	0.6	0.5	0.3	0.2	0.1	0.0	0.1	0.2	0.3	0.5	0.6	0.7	12
14	0.6	0.5	0.4	0.3	0.2	0.1	0.0	0.1	0.2	0.3	0.4	0.5	0.6	14
16	0.5	0.4	0.3	0.3	0.2	0.1	0.0	0.1	0.2	0.3	0.3	0.4	0.5	16
18	0.4	0.4	0.3	0.2	0.2	0.1	0.0	0.1	0.2	0.2	0.3	0.4	0.4	18
20 00	−0.4	−0.3	−0.3	−0.2	−0.1	−0.1	0.0	+0.1	+0.1	+0.2	+0.3	+0.3	+0.4	20 00
25	0.3	0.3	0.2	0.2	0.1	−0.1	0.0	+0.1	0.1	0.2	0.2	0.3	0.3	25
30	0.3	0.2	0.2	0.1	0.1	0.0	0.0	0.0	0.1	0.1	0.2	0.2	0.3	30
35	0.2	0.2	0.1	0.1	0.1	0.0	0.0	0.0	0.1	0.1	0.1	0.2	0.2	35
40	0.2	0.1	0.1	0.1	−0.1	0.0	0.0	0.0	+0.1	0.1	0.1	0.1	0.2	40
50 00	−0.1	−0.1	−0.1	−0.1	0.0	0.0	0.0	0.0	0.0	+0.1	+0.1	+0.1	+0.1	50 00

The graph is entered with arguments temperature and pressure to find a zone letter; using as arguments this zone letter and apparent altitude (sextant altitude corrected for dip), a correction is taken from the table. This correction is to be applied to the sextant altitude in addition to the corrections for standard conditions (for the Sun, stars and planets from page A2 and for the Moon from pages xxxiv and xxxv).

POLARIS (POLE STAR) TABLES, 1982
FOR DETERMINING LATITUDE FROM SEXTANT ALTITUDE AND FOR AZIMUTH

L.H.A. ARIES	0°–9°	10°–19°	20°–29°	30°–39°	40°–49°	50°–59°	60°–69°	70°–79°	80°–89°	90°–99°	100°–109°	110°–119°
	a_0	a_0	a_0	a_0	a_0	a_0	a_0	a_0	a_0	a_0	a_0	a_0
°	° ′	° ′	° ′	° ′	° ′	° ′	° ′	° ′	° ′	° ′	° ′	° ′
0	0 18.1	0 14.0	0 11.3	0 10.0	0 10.2	0 12.0	0 15.1	0 19.6	0 25.4	0 32.1	0 39.7	0 47.8
1	17.7	13.7	11.1	09.9	10.3	12.2	15.5	20.2	26.0	32.8	40.5	48.6
2	17.2	13.4	10.9	09.9	10.4	12.5	15.9	20.7	26.6	33.6	41.3	49.5
3	16.8	13.0	10.7	09.9	10.6	12.8	16.3	21.2	27.3	34.3	42.1	50.3
4	16.3	12.7	10.6	09.9	10.7	13.1	16.8	21.8	28.0	35.0	42.9	51.1
5	0 15.9	0 12.5	0 10.4	0 09.9	0 10.9	0 13.4	0 17.2	0 22.4	0 28.6	0 35.8	0 43.7	0 52.0
6	15.5	12.2	10.3	09.9	11.1	13.7	17.7	22.9	29.3	36.6	44.5	52.8
7	15.1	11.9	10.2	10.0	11.3	14.0	18.2	23.5	30.0	37.3	45.3	53.7
8	14.7	11.7	10.1	10.1	11.5	14.4	18.6	24.1	30.7	38.1	46.1	54.5
9	14.4	11.5	10.1	10.1	11.7	14.7	19.1	24.7	31.4	38.9	47.0	55.4
10	0 14.0	0 11.3	0 10.0	0 10.2	0 12.0	0 15.1	0 19.6	0 25.4	0 32.1	0 39.7	0 47.8	0 56.2

Lat.	a_1	a_1	a_1	a_1	a_1	a_1	a_1	a_1	a_1	a_1	a_1	a_1
°	′	′	′	′	′	′	′	′	′	′	′	′
0	0.5	0.6	0.6	0.6	0.6	0.5	0.5	0.4	0.3	0.3	0.2	0.2
10	.5	.6	.6	.6	.6	.6	.5	.4	.4	.3	.3	.3
20	.5	.6	.6	.6	.6	.6	.5	.5	.4	.4	.3	.3
30	.6	.6	.6	.6	.6	.6	.5	.5	.5	.4	.4	.4
40	0.6	0.6	0.6	0.6	0.6	0.6	0.6	0.5	0.5	0.5	0.5	0.5
45	.6	.6	.6	.6	.6	.6	.6	.6	.6	.5	.5	.5
50	.6	.6	.6	.6	.6	.6	.6	.6	.6	.6	.6	.6
55	.6	.6	.6	.6	.6	.6	.6	.7	.7	.7	.7	.7
60	.6	.6	.6	.6	.6	.6	.7	.7	.7	.7	.8	.8
62	0.7	0.6	0.6	0.6	0.6	0.6	0.7	0.7	0.7	0.8	0.8	0.8
64	.7	.6	.6	.6	.6	.6	.7	.7	.8	.8	.9	0.9
66	.7	.6	.6	.6	.6	.6	.7	.8	.8	.9	0.9	1.0
68	0.7	0.6	0.6	0.6	0.6	0.7	0.7	0.8	0.9	0.9	1.0	1.0

Month	a_2	a_2	a_2	a_2	a_2	a_2	a_2	a_2	a_2	a_2	a_2	a_2
	′	′	′	′	′	′	′	′	′	′	′	′
Jan.	0.7	0.7	0.7	0.7	0.7	0.7	0.7	0.7	0.7	0.7	0.6	0.6
Feb.	.6	.6	.7	.7	.7	.7	.8	.8	.8	.8	.8	.8
Mar.	.5	.5	.6	.6	.7	.7	.7	.8	.8	.9	.9	.9
Apr.	0.3	0.4	0.4	0.5	0.5	0.6	0.7	0.7	0.8	0.8	0.9	0.9
May	.2	.2	.3	.3	.4	.5	.5	.6	.7	.7	.8	.9
June	.2	.2	.2	.2	.3	.3	.4	.5	.5	.6	.7	.8
July	0.2	0.2	0.2	0.2	0.2	0.2	0.3	0.3	0.4	0.5	0.5	0.6
Aug.	.3	.3	.3	.2	.2	.2	.2	.3	.3	.3	.4	.4
Sept.	.5	.5	.4	.4	.3	.3	.3	.3	.3	.3	.3	.3
Oct.	0.7	0.6	0.6	0.5	0.5	0.4	0.4	0.3	0.3	0.3	0.3	0.3
Nov.	0.9	0.8	.8	.7	.6	.6	.5	.5	.4	.4	.3	.3
Dec.	1.0	1.0	0.9	0.9	0.8	0.8	0.7	0.6	0.6	0.5	0.4	0.4

Lat.	AZIMUTH											
°	°	°	°	°	°	°	°	°	°	°	°	°
0	0.4	0.3	0.1	0.0	359.8	359.7	359.6	359.5	359.4	359.3	359.2	359.2
20	0.4	0.3	0.1	0.0	359.8	359.7	359.5	359.4	359.3	359.2	359.2	359.1
40	0.5	0.3	0.2	0.0	359.8	359.6	359.4	359.3	359.2	359.1	359.0	358.9
50	0.6	0.4	0.2	0.0	359.7	359.5	359.3	359.1	359.0	358.9	358.8	358.7
55	0.7	0.5	0.2	0.0	359.7	359.5	359.2	359.0	358.9	358.7	358.6	358.6
60	0.8	0.5	0.2	0.0	359.7	359.4	359.1	358.9	358.7	358.6	358.4	358.4
65	0.9	0.6	0.3	359.9	359.6	359.3	359.0	358.7	358.5	358.3	358.2	358.1

Latitude = Apparent altitude (corrected for refraction) $-1° + a_0 + a_1 + a_2$

The table is entered with L.H.A. Aries to determine the column to be used; each column refers to a range of 10°. a_0 is taken, with mental interpolation, from the upper table with the units of L.H.A. Aries in degrees as argument; a_1, a_2 are taken, without interpolation, from the second and third tables with arguments latitude and month respectively. a_0, a_1, a_2 are always positive. The final table gives the azimuth of *Polaris*.

POLARIS (POLE STAR) TABLES, 1982

FOR DETERMINING LATITUDE FROM SEXTANT ALTITUDE AND FOR AZIMUTH

L.H.A. ARIES	120°–129°	130°–139°	140°–149°	150°–159°	160°–169°	170°–179°	180°–189°	190°–199°	200°–209°	210°–219°	220°–229°	230°–239°
	a_0	a_0	a_0	a_0	a_0	a_0	a_0	a_0	a_0	a_0	a_0	a_0
0	0 56.2	1 04.8	1 13.1	1 21.0	1 28.2	1 34.5	1 39.7	1 43.7	1 46.4	1 47.6	1 47.4	1 45.7
1	57.1	05.6	13.9	21.7	28.8	35.1	40.2	44.0	46.6	47.7	47.3	45.5
2	57.9	06.4	14.7	22.5	29.5	35.6	40.6	44.4	46.7	47.7	47.2	45.2
3	58.8	07.3	15.5	23.2	30.2	36.2	41.0	44.7	46.9	47.7	47.0	44.9
4	0 59.7	08.1	16.3	23.9	30.8	36.7	41.5	44.9	47.0	47.7	46.9	44.6
5	1 00.5	1 09.0	1 17.1	1 24.7	1 31.4	1 37.2	1 41.9	1 45.2	1 47.2	1 47.7	1 46.7	1 44.3
6	01.4	09.8	17.9	25.4	32.1	37.8	42.3	45.5	47.3	47.7	46.6	44.0
7	02.2	10.6	18.7	26.1	32.7	38.3	42.7	45.7	47.4	47.6	46.4	43.7
8	03.1	11.4	19.4	26.8	33.3	38.8	43.0	46.0	47.5	47.6	46.2	43.4
9	03.9	12.3	20.2	27.5	33.9	39.2	43.4	46.2	47.6	47.5	45.9	43.0
10	1 04.8	1 13.1	1 21.0	1 28.2	1 34.5	1 39.7	1 43.7	1 46.4	1 47.6	1 47.4	1 45.7	1 42.6
Lat.	a_1	a_1	a_1	a_1	a_1	a_1	a_1	a_1	a_1	a_1	a_1	a_1
0	0.2	0.2	0.2	0.3	0.4	0.4	0.5	0.6	0.6	0.6	0.6	0.5
10	.2	.3	.3	.3	.4	.5	.5	.6	.6	.6	.6	.6
20	.3	.3	.4	.4	.4	.5	.5	.6	.6	.6	.6	.6
30	.4	.4	.4	.4	.5	.5	.6	.6	.6	.6	.6	.6
40	0.5	0.5	0.5	0.5	0.5	0.6	0.6	0.6	0.6	0.6	0.6	0.6
45	.5	.5	.5	.6	.6	.6	.6	.6	.6	.6	.6	.6
50	.6	.6	.6	.6	.6	.6	.6	.6	.6	.6	.6	.6
55	.7	.7	.7	.7	.6	.6	.6	.6	.6	.6	.6	.6
60	.8	.8	.8	.7	.7	.7	.6	.6	.6	.6	.6	.6
62	0.8	0.8	0.8	0.8	0.7	0.7	0.7	0.6	0.6	0.6	0.6	0.6
64	0.9	0.9	.9	.8	.8	.7	.7	.6	.6	.6	.6	.6
66	1.0	1.0	0.9	.9	.8	.7	.7	.6	.6	.6	.6	.6
68	1.0	1.0	1.0	0.9	0.9	0.8	0.7	0.6	0.6	0.6	0.6	0.7
Month	a_2	a_2	a_2	a_2	a_2	a_2	a_2	a_2	a_2	a_2	a_2	a_2
Jan.	0.6	0.6	0.6	0.6	0.6	0.6	0.5	0.5	0.5	0.5	0.5	0.5
Feb.	.8	.8	.7	.7	.7	.6	.6	.6	.5	.5	.5	.5
Mar.	0.9	0.9	0.9	0.9	0.8	.8	.7	.7	.6	.6	.5	.5
Apr.	1.0	1.0	1.0	1.0	1.0	0.9	0.9	0.8	0.8	0.7	0.7	0.6
May	0.9	1.0	1.0	1.0	1.0	1.0	1.0	1.0	0.9	0.9	.8	.7
June	.8	0.9	0.9	1.0	1.0	1.0	1.0	1.0	1.0	1.0	0.9	0.9
July	0.7	0.7	0.8	0.9	0.9	1.0	1.0	1.0	1.0	1.0	1.0	1.0
Aug.	.5	.6	.6	.7	.8	0.8	0.9	0.9	0.9	1.0	1.0	1.0
Sept.	.4	.4	.5	.5	.6	.6	.7	.7	.8	0.8	0.9	0.9
Oct.	0.3	0.3	0.3	0.4	0.4	0.4	0.5	0.6	0.6	0.7	0.7	0.8
Nov.	.3	.2	.2	.2	.3	.3	.3	.4	.4	.5	.6	.6
Dec.	0.3	0.3	0.2	0.2	0.2	0.2	0.2	0.2	0.3	0.3	0.4	0.4
Lat.	AZIMUTH											
0	359.2	359.2	359.2	359.3	359.4	359.5	359.6	359.7	359.9	0.0	0.2	0.3
20	359.1	359.2	359.2	359.3	359.4	359.5	359.6	359.7	359.9	0.0	0.2	0.3
40	358.9	359.0	359.0	359.1	359.2	359.3	359.5	359.7	359.8	0.0	0.2	0.4
50	358.7	358.8	358.8	358.9	359.1	359.2	359.4	359.6	359.8	0.0	0.2	0.5
55	358.6	358.6	358.7	358.8	359.0	359.1	359.3	359.6	359.8	0.0	0.3	0.5
60	358.4	358.4	358.5	358.6	358.8	359.0	359.2	359.5	359.8	0.0	0.3	0.6
65	358.1	358.1	358.2	358.4	358.6	358.8	359.1	359.4	359.7	0.0	0.4	0.7

ILLUSTRATION

On 1982 April 21 at G.M.T. 23ʰ 18ᵐ 56ˢ in longitude W. 37° 14′ the apparent altitude (corrected for refraction), H_o, of *Polaris* was 49° 31′·6.

From the daily pages :			
G.H.A. Aries (23ʰ)	194 41.0	H_o	49 31.6
Increment (18ᵐ 56ˢ)	4 44.8	a_0 (argument 162° 12′)	1 29.6
Longitude (west)	−37 14	a_1 (lat. 50° approx.)	0.6
		a_2 (April)	1.0
L.H.A. Aries	162 12	Sum −1° = Lat. =	50 02.8

POLARIS (POLE STAR) TABLES, 1982

FOR DETERMINING LATITUDE FROM SEXTANT ALTITUDE AND FOR AZIMUTH

L.H.A. ARIES	240°– 249°	250°– 259°	260°– 269°	270°– 279°	280°– 289°	290°– 299°	300°– 309°	310°– 319°	320°– 329°	330°– 339°	340°– 349°	350°– 359°
	a_0	a_0	a_0	a_0	a_0	a_0	a_0	a_0	a_0	a_0	a_0	a_0
°	° ′	° ′	° ′	° ′	° ′	° ′	° ′	° ′	° ′	° ′	° ′	° ′
0	1 42·6	1 38·2	1 32·7	1 26·1	1 18·6	1 10·6	1 02·2	0 53·7	0 45·3	0 37·3	0 30·0	0 23·5
1	42·3	37·7	32·1	25·4	17·9	09·8	01·3	52·8	44·5	36·5	29·3	22·9
2	41·9	37·2	31·4	24·6	17·1	08·9	1 00·5	52·0	43·6	35·8	28·6	22·3
3	41·5	36·7	30·8	23·9	16·3	08·1	0 59·6	51·1	42·8	35·0	27·9	21·8
4	41·0	36·1	30·1	23·2	15·5	07·3	58·8	50·3	42·0	34·3	27·3	21·2
5	1 40·6	1 35·6	1 29·5	1 22·4	1 14·7	1 06·4	0 57·9	0 49·4	0 41·2	0 33·5	0 26·6	0 20·7
6	40·2	35·0	28·8	21·7	13·9	05·6	57·1	48·6	40·4	32·8	26·0	20·1
7	39·7	34·5	28·1	20·9	13·1	04·7	56·2	47·8	39·6	32·1	25·3	19·6
8	39·2	33·9	27·5	20·2	12·2	03·9	55·4	46·9	38·9	31·4	24·7	19·1
9	38·7	33·3	26·8	19·4	11·4	03·0	54·5	46·1	38·1	30·7	24·1	18·6
10	1 38·2	1 32·7	1 26·1	1 18·6	1 10·6	1 02·2	0 53·7	0 45·3	0 37·3	0 30·0	0 23·5	0 18·1
Lat.	a_1	a_1	a_1	a_1	a_1	a_1	a_1	a_1	a_1	a_1	a_1	a_1
°	′	′	′	′	′	′	′	′	′	′	′	′
0	0·5	0·4	0·3	0·3	0·2	0·2	0·2	0·2	0·2	0·3	0·4	0·4
10	·5	·4	·4	·3	·3	·3	·2	·3	·3	·3	·4	·5
20	·5	·5	·4	·4	·3	·3	·3	·3	·4	·4	·4	·5
30	·5	·5	·5	·4	·4	·4	·4	·4	·4	·4	·5	·5
40	0·6	0·5	0·5	0·5	0·5	0·5	0·5	0·5	0·5	0·5	0·5	0·6
45	·6	·6	·6	·5	·5	·5	·5	·5	·5	·6	·6	·6
50	·6	·6	·6	·6	·6	·6	·6	·6	·6	·6	·6	·6
55	·6	·6	·7	·7	·7	·7	·7	·7	·7	·7	·6	·6
60	·7	·7	·7	·7	·8	·8	·8	·8	·8	·7	·7	·7
62	0·7	0·7	0·7	0·8	0·8	0·8	0·8	0·8	0·8	0·8	0·7	0·7
64	·7	·7	·8	·8	·9	0·9	0·9	0·9	·9	·8	·8	·7
66	·7	·8	·8	·9	0·9	1·0	1·0	1·0	0·9	·9	·8	·7
68	0·7	0·8	0·9	0·9	1·0	1·0	1·0	1·0	1·0	0·9	0·9	0·8
Month	a_2	a_2	a_2	a_2	a_2	a_2	a_2	a_2	a_2	a_2	a_2	a_2
	′	′	′	′	′	′	′	′	′	′	′	′
Jan.	0·5	0·5	0·5	0·5	0·6	0·6	0·6	0·6	0·6	0·6	0·6	0·6
Feb.	·4	·4	·4	·4	·4	·4	·4	·4	·5	·5	·5	·6
Mar.	·5	·4	·4	·3	·3	·3	·3	·3	·3	·3	·4	·4
Apr.	0·5	0·5	0·4	0·4	0·3	0·3	0·2	0·2	0·2	0·2	0·2	0·3
May	·7	·6	·5	·5	·4	·3	·3	·2	·2	·2	·2	·2
June	·8	·7	·7	·6	·5	·4	·4	·3	·3	·2	·2	·2
July	0·9	0·9	0·8	0·7	0·7	0·6	0·5	0·5	0·4	0·3	0·3	0·2
Aug.	1·0	·9	·9	·9	·8	·8	·7	·6	·6	·5	·4	·4
Sept.	0·9	·9	·9	·9	·9	·9	·8	·8	·7	·7	·6	·6
Oct.	0·8	0·9	0·9	0·9	0·9	0·9	0·9	0·9	0·9	0·8	0·8	0·8
Nov.	·7	·7	·8	·8	·9	·9	·9	1·0	1·0	1·0	0·9	0·9
Dec.	0·5	0·6	0·6	0·7	0·8	0·8	0·9	0·9	1·0	1·0	1·0	1·0
Lat.	AZIMUTH											
°	°	°	°	°	°	°	°	°	°	°	°	°
0	0·4	0·5	0·6	0·7	0·8	0·8	0·8	0·8	0·8	0·7	0·6	0·5
20	0·5	0·6	0·7	0·8	0·8	0·9	0·9	0·9	0·8	0·7	0·7	0·5
40	0·6	0·7	0·8	0·9	1·0	1·1	1·1	1·0	1·0	0·9	0·8	0·7
50	0·7	0·8	1·0	1·1	1·2	1·3	1·3	1·2	1·2	1·1	1·0	0·8
55	0·7	0·9	1·1	1·2	1·3	1·4	1·4	1·4	1·3	1·2	1·1	0·9
60	0·8	1·1	1·3	1·4	1·5	1·6	1·6	1·6	1·5	1·4	1·2	1·0
65	1·0	1·2	1·5	1·7	1·8	1·9	1·9	1·9	1·8	1·7	1·5	1·2

$$\text{Latitude} = \text{Apparent altitude (corrected for refraction)} - 1° + a_0 + a_1 + a_2$$

The table is entered with L.H.A. Aries to determine the column to be used; each column refers to a range of 10°. a_0 is taken, with mental interpolation, from the upper table with the units of L.H.A. Aries in degrees as argument; a_1, a_2 are taken, without interpolation, from the second and third tables with arguments latitude and month respectively. a_0, a_1, a_2 are always positive. The final table gives the azimuth of *Polaris*.

TABLES FOR INTERPOLATING SUNRISE, MOONRISE, ETC.

TABLE I—FOR LATITUDE

Tabular Interval 10°	5°	2°	Difference between the times for consecutive latitudes 5m	10m	15m	20m	25m	30m	35m	40m	45m	50m	55m	60m	1h 05m	1h 10m	1h 15m	1h 20m
0 30	0 15	0 06	0	0	1	1	1	1	1	2	2	2	2	2	0 02	0 02	0 02	0 02
1 00	0 30	0 12	0	1	1	2	2	3	3	3	4	4	4	5	05	05	05	05
1 30	0 45	0 18	1	1	2	3	3	4	4	5	5	6	7	7	07	07	07	07
2 00	1 00	0 24	1	2	3	4	5	5	6	7	7	8	9	10	10	10	10	10
2 30	1 15	0 30	1	2	4	5	6	7	8	9	9	10	11	12	12	13	13	13
3 00	1 30	0 36	1	3	4	6	7	8	9	10	11	12	13	14	0 15	0 15	0 16	0 16
3 30	1 45	0 42	2	3	5	7	8	10	11	12	13	14	16	17	18	18	19	19
4 00	2 00	0 48	2	4	6	8	9	11	13	14	15	16	18	19	20	21	22	22
4 30	2 15	0 54	2	4	7	9	11	13	15	16	18	19	21	22	23	24	25	26
5 00	2 30	1 00	2	5	7	10	12	14	16	18	20	22	23	25	26	27	28	29
5 30	2 45	1 06	3	5	8	11	13	16	18	20	22	24	26	28	0 29	0 30	0 31	0 32
6 00	3 00	1 12	3	6	9	12	14	17	20	22	24	26	29	31	32	33	34	36
6 30	3 15	1 18	3	6	10	13	16	19	22	24	26	29	31	34	36	37	38	40
7 00	3 30	1 24	3	7	10	14	17	20	23	26	29	31	34	37	39	41	42	44
7 30	3 45	1 30	4	7	11	15	18	22	25	28	31	34	37	40	43	44	46	48
8 00	4 00	1 36	4	8	12	16	20	23	27	30	34	37	41	44	0 47	0 48	0 51	0 53
8 30	4 15	1 42	4	8	13	17	21	25	29	33	36	40	44	48	0 51	0 53	0 56	0 58
9 00	4 30	1 48	4	9	13	18	22	27	31	35	39	43	47	52	0 55	0 58	1 01	1 04
9 30	4 45	1 54	5	9	14	19	24	28	33	38	42	47	51	56	1 00	1 04	1 08	1 12
10 00	5 00	2 00	5	10	15	20	25	30	35	40	45	50	55	60	1 05	1 10	1 15	1 20

Table I is for interpolating the L.M.T. of sunrise, twilight, moonrise, etc., for latitude. It is to be entered, in the appropriate column on the left, with the difference between true latitude and the nearest tabular latitude which is *less* than the true latitude; and with the argument at the top which is the nearest value of the difference between the times for the tabular latitude and the next higher one; the correction so obtained is applied to the time for the tabular latitude; the sign of the correction can be seen by inspection. It is to be noted that the interpolation is not linear, so that when using this table it is essential to take out the tabular phenomenon for the latitude *less* than the true latitude.

TABLE II—FOR LONGITUDE

Long. East or West	Difference between the times for given date and preceding date (for east longitude) or for given date and following date (for west longitude) 10m	20m	30m	40m	50m	60m	1h + 10m	20m	30m	1h + 40m	50m	60m	2h 10m	2h 20m	2h 30m	2h 40m	2h 50m	3h 00m
0	0	0	0	0	0	0	0	0	0	0	0	0	0 00	0 00	0 00	0 00	0 00	0 00
10	0	1	1	1	1	2	2	2	2	3	3	3	04	04	04	04	05	05
20	1	1	2	2	3	3	4	4	5	6	6	7	07	08	08	09	09	10
30	1	2	2	3	4	5	6	7	7	8	9	10	11	12	12	13	14	15
40	1	2	3	4	6	7	8	9	10	11	12	13	14	16	17	18	19	20
50	1	3	4	6	7	8	10	11	12	14	15	17	0 18	0 19	0 21	0 22	0 24	0 25
60	2	3	5	7	8	10	12	13	15	17	18	20	22	23	25	27	28	30
70	2	4	6	8	10	12	14	16	17	19	21	23	25	27	29	31	33	35
80	2	4	7	9	11	13	16	18	20	22	24	27	29	31	33	36	38	40
90	2	5	7	10	12	15	17	20	22	25	27	30	32	35	37	40	42	45
100	3	6	8	11	14	17	19	22	25	28	31	33	0 36	0 39	0 42	0 44	0 47	0 50
110	3	6	9	12	15	18	21	24	27	31	34	37	40	43	46	49	0 52	0 55
120	3	7	10	13	17	20	23	27	30	33	37	40	43	47	50	53	0 57	1 00
130	4	7	11	14	18	22	25	29	32	36	40	43	47	51	54	0 58	1 01	1 05
140	4	8	12	16	19	23	27	31	35	39	43	47	51	54	0 58	1 02	1 06	1 10
150	4	8	13	17	21	25	29	33	38	42	46	50	0 54	0 58	1 03	1 07	1 11	1 15
160	4	9	13	18	22	27	31	36	40	44	49	53	0 58	1 02	1 07	1 11	1 16	1 20
170	5	9	14	19	24	28	33	38	42	47	52	57	1 01	1 06	1 11	1 16	1 20	1 25
180	5	10	15	20	25	30	35	40	45	50	55	60	1 05	1 10	1 15	1 20	1 25	1 30

Table II is for interpolating the L.M.T. of moonrise, moonset and the Moon's meridian passage for longitude. It is entered with longitude and with the difference between the times for the given date and for the preceding date (in east longitudes) or following date (in west longitudes). The correction is normally *added* for west longitudes and *subtracted* for east longitudes, but if, as occasionally happens, the times become earlier each day instead of later, the signs of the corrections must be reversed.

CONVERSION OF ARC TO TIME

0°–59° °	h m	60°–119° °	h m	120°–179° °	h m	180°–239° °	h m	240°–299° °	h m	300°–359° °	h m	′	0′.00 m s	0′.25 m s	0′.50 m s	0′.75 m s
0	0 00	60	4 00	120	8 00	180	12 00	240	16 00	300	20 00	0	0 00	0 01	0 02	0 03
1	0 04	61	4 04	121	8 04	181	12 04	241	16 04	301	20 04	1	0 04	0 05	0 06	0 07
2	0 08	62	4 08	122	8 08	182	12 08	242	16 08	302	20 08	2	0 08	0 09	0 10	0 11
3	0 12	63	4 12	123	8 12	183	12 12	243	16 12	303	20 12	3	0 12	0 13	0 14	0 15
4	0 16	64	4 16	124	8 16	184	12 16	244	16 16	304	20 16	4	0 16	0 17	0 18	0 19
5	0 20	65	4 20	125	8 20	185	12 20	245	16 20	305	20 20	5	0 20	0 21	0 22	0 23
6	0 24	66	4 24	126	8 24	186	12 24	246	16 24	306	20 24	6	0 24	0 25	0 26	0 27
7	0 28	67	4 28	127	8 28	187	12 28	247	16 28	307	20 28	7	0 28	0 29	0 30	0 31
8	0 32	68	4 32	128	8 32	188	12 32	248	16 32	308	20 32	8	0 32	0 33	0 34	0 35
9	0 36	69	4 36	129	8 36	189	12 36	249	16 36	309	20 36	9	0 36	0 37	0 38	0 39
10	0 40	70	4 40	130	8 40	190	12 40	250	16 40	310	20 40	10	0 40	0 41	0 42	0 43
11	0 44	71	4 44	131	8 44	191	12 44	251	16 44	311	20 44	11	0 44	0 45	0 46	0 47
12	0 48	72	4 48	132	8 48	192	12 48	252	16 48	312	20 48	12	0 48	0 49	0 50	0 51
13	0 52	73	4 52	133	8 52	193	12 52	253	16 52	313	20 52	13	0 52	0 53	0 54	0 55
14	0 56	74	4 56	134	8 56	194	12 56	254	16 56	314	20 56	14	0 56	0 57	0 58	0 59
15	1 00	75	5 00	135	9 00	195	13 00	255	17 00	315	21 00	15	1 00	1 01	1 02	1 03
16	1 04	76	5 04	136	9 04	196	13 04	256	17 04	316	21 04	16	1 04	1 05	1 06	1 07
17	1 08	77	5 08	137	9 08	197	13 08	257	17 08	317	21 08	17	1 08	1 09	1 10	1 11
18	1 12	78	5 12	138	9 12	198	13 12	258	17 12	318	21 12	18	1 12	1 13	1 14	1 15
19	1 16	79	5 16	139	9 16	199	13 16	259	17 16	319	21 16	19	1 16	1 17	1 18	1 19
20	1 20	80	5 20	140	9 20	200	13 20	260	17 20	320	21 20	20	1 20	1 21	1 22	1 23
21	1 24	81	5 24	141	9 24	201	13 24	261	17 24	321	21 24	21	1 24	1 25	1 26	1 27
22	1 28	82	5 28	142	9 28	202	13 28	262	17 28	322	21 28	22	1 28	1 29	1 30	1 31
23	1 32	83	5 32	143	9 32	203	13 32	263	17 32	323	21 32	23	1 32	1 33	1 34	1 35
24	1 36	84	5 36	144	9 36	204	13 36	264	17 36	324	21 36	24	1 36	1 37	1 38	1 39
25	1 40	85	5 40	145	9 40	205	13 40	265	17 40	325	21 40	25	1 40	1 41	1 42	1 43
26	1 44	86	5 44	146	9 44	206	13 44	266	17 44	326	21 44	26	1 44	1 45	1 46	1 47
27	1 48	87	5 48	147	9 48	207	13 48	267	17 48	327	21 48	27	1 48	1 49	1 50	1 51
28	1 52	88	5 52	148	9 52	208	13 52	268	17 52	328	21 52	28	1 52	1 53	1 54	1 55
29	1 56	89	5 56	149	9 56	209	13 56	269	17 56	329	21 56	29	1 56	1 57	1 58	1 59
30	2 00	90	6 00	150	10 00	210	14 00	270	18 00	330	22 00	30	2 00	2 01	2 02	2 03
31	2 04	91	6 04	151	10 04	211	14 04	271	18 04	331	22 04	31	2 04	2 05	2 06	2 07
32	2 08	92	6 08	152	10 08	212	14 08	272	18 08	332	22 08	32	2 08	2 09	2 10	2 11
33	2 12	93	6 12	153	10 12	213	14 12	273	18 12	333	22 12	33	2 12	2 13	2 14	2 15
34	2 16	94	6 16	154	10 16	214	14 16	274	18 16	334	22 16	34	2 16	2 17	2 18	2 19
35	2 20	95	6 20	155	10 20	215	14 20	275	18 20	335	22 20	35	2 20	2 21	2 22	2 23
36	2 24	96	6 24	156	10 24	216	14 24	276	18 24	336	22 24	36	2 24	2 25	2 26	2 27
37	2 28	97	6 28	157	10 28	217	14 28	277	18 28	337	22 28	37	2 28	2 29	2 30	2 31
38	2 32	98	6 32	158	10 32	218	14 32	278	18 32	338	22 32	38	2 32	2 33	2 34	2 35
39	2 36	99	6 36	159	10 36	219	14 36	279	18 36	339	22 36	39	2 36	2 37	2 38	2 39
40	2 40	100	6 40	160	10 40	220	14 40	280	18 40	340	22 40	40	2 40	2 41	2 42	2 43
41	2 44	101	6 44	161	10 44	221	14 44	281	18 44	341	22 44	41	2 44	2 45	2 46	2 47
42	2 48	102	6 48	162	10 48	222	14 48	282	18 48	342	22 48	42	2 48	2 49	2 50	2 51
43	2 52	103	6 52	163	10 52	223	14 52	283	18 52	343	22 52	43	2 52	2 53	2 54	2 55
44	2 56	104	6 56	164	10 56	224	14 56	284	18 56	344	22 56	44	2 56	2 57	2 58	2 59
45	3 00	105	7 00	165	11 00	225	15 00	285	19 00	345	23 00	45	3 00	3 01	3 02	3 03
46	3 04	106	7 04	166	11 04	226	15 04	286	19 04	346	23 04	46	3 04	3 05	3 06	3 07
47	3 08	107	7 08	167	11 08	227	15 08	287	19 08	347	23 08	47	3 08	3 09	3 10	3 11
48	3 12	108	7 12	168	11 12	228	15 12	288	19 12	348	23 12	48	3 12	3 13	3 14	3 15
49	3 16	109	7 16	169	11 16	229	15 16	289	19 16	349	23 16	49	3 16	3 17	3 18	3 19
50	3 20	110	7 20	170	11 20	230	15 20	290	19 20	350	23 20	50	3 20	3 21	3 22	3 23
51	3 24	111	7 24	171	11 24	231	15 24	291	19 24	351	23 24	51	3 24	3 25	3 26	3 27
52	3 28	112	7 28	172	11 28	232	15 28	292	19 28	352	23 28	52	3 28	3 29	3 30	3 31
53	3 32	113	7 32	173	11 32	233	15 32	293	19 32	353	23 32	53	3 32	3 33	3 34	3 35
54	3 36	114	7 36	174	11 36	234	15 36	294	19 36	354	23 36	54	3 36	3 37	3 38	3 39
55	3 40	115	7 40	175	11 40	235	15 40	295	19 40	355	23 40	55	3 40	3 41	3 42	3 43
56	3 44	116	7 44	176	11 44	236	15 44	296	19 44	356	23 44	56	3 44	3 45	3 46	3 47
57	3 48	117	7 48	177	11 48	237	15 48	297	19 48	357	23 48	57	3 48	3 49	3 50	3 51
58	3 52	118	7 52	178	11 52	238	15 52	298	19 52	358	23 52	58	3 52	3 53	3 54	3 55
59	3 56	119	7 56	179	11 56	239	15 56	299	19 56	359	23 56	59	3 56	3 57	3 58	3 59

The above table is for converting expressions in arc to their equivalent in time ; its main use in this Almanac is for the conversion of longitude for application to L.M.T. (*added* if *west*, *subtracted* if *east*) to give G.M.T. or vice versa, particularly in the case of sunrise, sunset, etc.

Daily Pages

1982 JULY 3, 4, 5 (SAT., SUN., MON.)

G.M.T.	ARIES G.H.A.	VENUS −3.4 G.H.A.	Dec.	MARS +0.5 G.H.A.	Dec.	JUPITER −1.8 G.H.A.	Dec.	SATURN +1.0 G.H.A.	Dec.	STARS Name	S.H.A.	Dec.
3 00	280 41.5	213 16.8 N20	17.8	88 02.8 S 5	42.3	71 53.3 S10	29.6	85 16.9 S 3	50.5	Acamar	315 36.5	S40 22.4
01	295 43.9	228 16.2	18.3	103 04.2	42.8	86 55.8	29.6	100 19.3	50.5	Achernar	335 44.4	S57 19.3
02	310 46.4	243 15.5	18.9	118 05.7	43.2	101 58.2	29.7	115 21.7	50.6	Acrux	173 36.0	S63 00.3
03	325 48.8	258 14.9 ··	19.4	133 07.1 ··	43.7	117 00.6 ··	29.7	130 24.1 ··	50.6	Adhara	255 31.5	S28 56.9
04	340 51.3	273 14.2	20.0	148 08.6	44.2	132 03.0	29.7	145 26.5	50.6	Aldebaran	291 16.9	N16 28.4
05	355 53.8	288 13.6	20.5	163 10.0	44.7	147 05.5	29.7	160 28.9	50.7			
06	10 56.2	303 12.9 N20	21.0	178 11.5 S 5	45.2	162 07.9 S10	29.8	175 31.3 S 3	50.7	Alioth	166 41.3	N56 03.7
07	25 58.7	318 12.3	21.6	193 12.9	45.7	177 10.3	29.8	190 33.7	50.7	Alkaid	153 17.3	N49 24.4
S 08	41 01.2	333 11.6	22.1	208 14.4	46.1	192 12.8	29.8	205 36.2	50.8	Al Na'ir	28 13.0	S47 02.6
A 09	56 03.6	348 11.0 ··	22.6	223 15.8 ··	46.6	207 15.2 ··	29.8	220 38.6 ··	50.8	Alnilam	276 10.7	S 1 12.8
T 10	71 06.1	3 10.3	23.2	238 17.3	47.1	222 17.6	29.9	235 41.0	50.8	Alphard	218 19.6	S 8 34.9
U 11	86 08.6	18 09.7	23.7	253 18.7	47.6	237 20.0	29.9	250 43.4	50.9			
R 12	101 11.0	33 09.0 N20	24.2	268 20.2 S 5	48.1	252 22.5 S10	29.9	265 45.8 S 3	50.9	Alphecca	126 30.8	N26 46.6
D 13	116 13.5	48 08.4	24.8	283 21.6	48.6	267 24.9	29.9	280 48.2	50.9	Alpheratz	358 08.0	N28 59.4
A 14	131 16.0	63 07.7	25.3	298 23.1	49.0	282 27.3	30.0	295 50.6	51.0	Altair	62 31.0	N 8 49.3
Y 15	146 18.4	78 07.0 ··	25.8	313 24.5 ··	49.5	297 29.8 ··	30.0	310 53.0 ··	51.0	Ankaa	353 38.9	S42 23.9
16	161 20.9	93 06.4	26.3	328 26.0	50.0	312 32.2	30.0	325 55.4	51.0	Antares	112 55.0	S26 23.6
17	176 23.3	108 05.7	26.9	343 27.4	50.5	327 34.6	30.0	340 57.9	51.1			
18	191 25.8	123 05.1 N20	27.4	358 28.8 S 5	51.0	342 37.0 S10	30.1	356 00.3 S 3	51.1	Arcturus	146 17.2	N19 16.6
19	206 28.3	138 04.4	27.9	13 30.3	51.5	357 39.5	30.1	11 02.7	51.2	Atria	108 17.6	S68 59.9
20	221 30.7	153 03.8	28.4	28 31.7	51.9	12 41.9	30.1	26 05.1	51.2	Avior	234 28.3	S59 27.3
21	236 33.2	168 03.1 ··	29.0	43 33.2 ··	52.4	27 44.3 ··	30.1	41 07.5 ··	51.2	Bellatrix	278 57.7	N 6 20.0
22	251 35.7	183 02.4	29.5	58 34.6	52.9	42 46.7	30.2	56 09.9	51.3	Betelgeuse	271 27.2	N 7 24.3
23	266 38.1	198 01.8	30.0	73 36.0	53.4	57 49.2	30.2	71 12.3	51.3			
4 00	281 40.6	213 01.1 N20	30.5	88 37.5 S 5	53.9	72 51.6 S10	30.2	86 14.7 S 3	51.3	Canopus	264 07.2	S52 41.1
01	296 43.1	228 00.5	31.1	103 38.9	54.4	87 54.0	30.3	101 17.1	51.4	Capella	281 09.9	N45 58.8
02	311 45.5	242 59.8	31.6	118 40.4	54.9	102 56.4	30.3	116 19.5	51.4	Deneb	49 47.2	N45 12.9
03	326 48.0	257 59.1 ··	32.1	133 41.8 ··	55.3	117 58.9 ··	30.3	131 21.9 ··	51.4	Denebola	182 57.8	N14 40.4
04	341 50.5	272 58.5	32.6	148 43.2	55.8	133 01.3	30.3	146 24.4	51.5	Diphda	349 19.6	S18 04.9
05	356 52.9	287 57.8	33.1	163 44.7	56.3	148 03.7	30.4	161 26.8	51.5			
06	11 55.4	302 57.2 N20	33.6	178 46.1 S 5	56.8	163 06.1 S10	30.4	176 29.2 S 3	51.5	Dubhe	194 20.8	N61 51.1
07	26 57.8	317 56.5	34.2	193 47.5	57.3	178 08.5	30.4	191 31.6	51.6	Elnath	278 42.9	N28 35.5
08	42 00.3	332 55.8	34.7	208 49.0	57.8	193 11.0	30.4	206 34.0	51.6	Eltanin	90 56.6	N51 29.6
S 09	57 02.8	347 55.2 ··	35.2	223 50.4 ··	58.3	208 13.4 ··	30.5	221 36.4 ··	51.6	Enif	34 10.1	N 9 47.6
U 10	72 05.2	2 54.5	35.7	238 51.8	58.7	223 15.8	30.5	236 38.8	51.7	Fomalhaut	15 49.8	S29 42.8
N 11	87 07.7	17 53.8	36.2	253 53.3	59.2	238 18.2	30.5	251 41.2	51.7			
D 12	102 10.2	32 53.2 N20	36.7	268 54.7 S 5	59.7	253 20.6 S10	30.6	266 43.6 S 3	51.7	Gacrux	172 27.4	S57 01.1
A 13	117 12.6	47 52.5	37.2	283 56.1	6 00.2	268 23.1	30.6	281 46.0	51.8	Gienah	176 16.7	S17 26.7
Y 14	132 15.1	62 51.8	37.7	298 57.6	00.7	283 25.5	30.6	296 48.4	51.8	Hadar	149 21.4	S60 17.5
15	147 17.6	77 51.2 ··	38.2	313 59.0 ··	01.2	298 27.9 ··	30.6	311 50.8 ··	51.8	Hamal	328 27.6	N23 22.6
16	162 20.0	92 50.5	38.7	329 00.4	01.7	313 30.3	30.7	326 53.2	51.9	Kaus Aust.	84 14.8	S34 23.6
17	177 22.5	107 49.8	39.2	344 01.9	02.2	328 32.7	30.7	341 55.6	51.9			
18	192 24.9	122 49.2 N20	39.8	359 03.3 S 6	02.6	343 35.2 S10	30.7	356 58.1 S 3	52.0	Kochab	137 18.3	N74 14.0
19	207 27.4	137 48.5	40.3	14 04.7	03.1	358 37.6	30.8	12 00.5	52.0	Markab	14 01.8	N15 06.5
20	222 29.9	152 47.8	40.8	29 06.2	03.6	13 40.0	30.8	27 02.9	52.0	Menkar	314 40.0	N 4 01.2
21	237 32.3	167 47.2 ··	41.3	44 07.6 ··	04.1	28 42.4 ··	30.8	42 05.3 ··	52.1	Menkent	148 35.4	S36 17.1
22	252 34.8	182 46.5	41.8	59 09.0	04.6	43 44.8	30.8	57 07.7	52.1	Miaplacidus	221 45.5	S69 38.8
23	267 37.3	197 45.8	42.3	74 10.4	05.1	58 47.2	30.9	72 10.1	52.1			
5 00	282 39.7	212 45.2 N20	42.8	89 11.9 S 6	05.6	73 49.7 S10	30.9	87 12.5 S 3	52.2	Mirfak	309 14.7	N49 47.7
01	297 42.2	227 44.5	43.3	104 13.3	06.1	88 52.1	30.9	102 14.9	52.2	Nunki	76 27.2	S26 19.1
02	312 44.7	242 43.8	43.8	119 14.7	06.5	103 54.5	31.0	117 17.3	52.2	Peacock	53 55.8	S56 47.4
03	327 47.1	257 43.2 ··	44.2	134 16.2 ··	07.0	118 56.9 ··	31.0	132 19.7 ··	52.3	Pollux	243 57.0	N28 04.2
04	342 49.6	272 42.5	44.7	149 17.6	07.5	133 59.3	31.0	147 22.1	52.3	Procyon	245 24.8	N 5 16.3
05	357 52.1	287 41.8	45.2	164 19.0	08.0	149 01.7	31.1	162 24.5	52.3			
06	12 54.5	302 41.1 N20	45.7	179 20.4 S 6	08.5	164 04.2 S10	31.1	177 26.9 S 3	52.4	Rasalhague	96 28.1	N12 34.4
07	27 57.0	317 40.5	46.2	194 21.9	09.0	179 06.6	31.1	192 29.3	52.4	Regulus	208 08.9	N12 03.3
08	42 59.4	332 39.8	46.7	209 23.3	09.5	194 09.0	31.1	207 31.7	52.5	Rigel	281 35.1	S 8 13.3
M 09	58 01.9	347 39.1 ··	47.2	224 24.7 ··	10.0	209 11.4 ··	31.2	222 34.1 ··	52.5	Rigil Kent.	140 23.8	S60 45.9
O 10	73 04.4	2 38.4	47.7	239 26.1	10.5	224 13.8	31.2	237 36.5	52.5	Sabik	102 39.4	S15 42.2
N 11	88 06.8	17 37.8	48.2	254 27.5	10.9	239 16.2	31.2	252 38.9	52.6			
D 12	103 09.3	32 37.1 N20	48.7	269 29.0 S 6	11.4	254 18.6 S10	31.3	267 41.3 S 3	52.6	Schedar	350 07.6	N56 26.1
A 13	118 11.8	47 36.4	49.2	284 30.4	11.9	269 21.1	31.3	282 43.7	52.6	Shaula	96 53.6	S37 05.5
Y 14	133 14.2	62 35.7	49.6	299 31.8	12.4	284 23.5	31.3	297 46.1	52.7	Sirius	258 54.9	S16 41.5
15	148 16.7	77 35.1 ··	50.1	314 33.2 ··	12.9	299 25.9 ··	31.4	312 48.5 ··	52.7	Spica	158 56.2	S11 04.1
16	163 19.2	92 34.4	50.6	329 34.6	13.4	314 28.3	31.4	327 50.9	52.7	Suhail	223 10.3	S43 21.8
17	178 21.6	107 33.7	51.1	344 36.1	13.9	329 30.7	31.4	342 53.3	52.8			
18	193 24.1	122 33.0 N20	51.6	359 37.5 S 6	14.4	344 33.1 S10	31.4	357 55.7 S 3	52.8	Vega	80 54.6	N38 46.1
19	208 26.6	137 32.4	52.1	14 38.9	14.9	359 35.5	31.5	12 58.2	52.9	Zuben'ubi	137 31.5	S15 58.1
20	223 29.0	152 31.7	52.5	29 40.3	15.4	14 37.9	31.5	28 00.6	52.9		S.H.A.	Mer. Pass.
21	238 31.5	167 31.0 ··	53.0	44 41.7 ··	15.9	29 40.4 ··	31.5	43 03.0 ··	52.9		° ′	h m
22	253 33.9	182 30.3	53.5	59 43.2	16.3	44 42.8	31.6	58 05.4	53.0	Venus	291 20.5	9 48
23	268 36.4	197 29.6	54.0	74 44.6	16.8	59 45.2	31.6	73 07.8	53.0	Mars	166 56.9	18 04
Mer. Pass.	h m 5 12.4	v −0.7	d 0.5	v 1.4	d 0.5	v 2.4	d 0.0	v 2.4	d 0.0	Jupiter	151 11.0	19 05
										Saturn	164 34.1	18 12

1982 JULY 3, 4, 5 (SAT., SUN., MON.)

SUN and MOON

G.M.T.	SUN G.H.A.	SUN Dec.	MOON G.H.A.	v	MOON Dec.	d	H.P.
3 00	178 59.6	N23 00.3	37 15.8	13.2	S17 50.0	7.4	54.2
01	193 59.5	23 00.1	51 48.0	13.1	17 57.4	7.3	54.2
02	208 59.4	22 59.9	66 20.1	13.1	18 04.7	7.2	54.2
03	223 59.3	·· 59.7	80 52.2	13.1	18 11.9	7.1	54.2
04	238 59.2	59.5	95 24.3	13.1	18 19.0	7.0	54.2
05	253 59.0	59.3	109 56.4	13.0	18 26.0	7.0	54.2
06	268 58.9	N22 59.1	124 28.4	13.0	S18 33.0	6.8	54.1
07	283 58.8	58.9	139 00.4	12.9	18 39.8	6.8	54.1
S 08	298 58.7	58.7	153 32.3	12.9	18 46.6	6.7	54.1
A 09	313 58.6	·· 58.5	168 04.2	12.9	18 53.3	6.6	54.1
T 10	328 58.5	58.4	182 36.1	12.8	18 59.9	6.6	54.1
U 11	343 58.4	58.2	197 07.9	12.8	19 06.5	6.4	54.1
R 12	358 58.2	N22 58.0	211 39.7	12.8	S19 12.9	6.4	54.1
D 13	13 58.1	57.8	226 11.5	12.7	19 19.3	6.2	54.1
A 14	28 58.0	57.5	240 43.2	12.7	19 25.5	6.2	54.1
Y 15	43 57.9	·· 57.3	255 14.9	12.7	19 31.7	6.1	54.1
16	58 57.8	57.1	269 46.6	12.6	19 37.8	6.0	54.1
17	73 57.7	56.9	284 18.2	12.6	19 43.8	6.0	54.1
18	88 57.5	N22 56.7	298 49.8	12.6	S19 49.8	5.8	54.1
19	103 57.4	56.5	313 21.4	12.5	19 55.6	5.7	54.1
20	118 57.3	56.3	327 52.9	12.5	20 01.3	5.7	54.1
21	133 57.2	·· 56.1	342 24.4	12.5	20 07.0	5.6	54.1
22	148 57.1	55.9	356 55.9	12.4	20 12.6	5.4	54.0
23	163 57.0	55.7	11 27.3	12.4	20 18.0	5.4	54.0
4 00	178 56.9	N22 55.5	25 58.7	12.4	S20 23.4	5.3	54.0
01	193 56.8	55.3	40 30.1	12.3	20 28.7	5.2	54.0
02	208 56.6	55.1	55 01.4	12.3	20 33.9	5.1	54.0
03	223 56.5	·· 54.9	69 32.7	12.3	20 39.0	5.0	54.0
04	238 56.4	54.7	84 04.0	12.2	20 44.0	4.9	54.0
05	253 56.3	54.4	98 35.2	12.2	20 48.9	4.8	54.0
06	268 56.2	N22 54.2	113 06.4	12.2	S20 53.7	4.7	54.0
07	283 56.1	54.0	127 37.6	12.1	20 58.4	4.7	54.0
08	298 56.0	53.8	142 08.7	12.1	21 03.1	4.5	54.0
S 09	313 55.9	·· 53.6	156 39.8	12.1	21 07.6	4.4	54.0
U 10	328 55.7	53.4	171 10.9	12.0	21 12.0	4.4	54.0
N 11	343 55.6	53.2	185 41.9	12.1	21 16.4	4.2	54.0
D 12	358 55.5	N22 52.9	200 13.0	12.0	S21 20.6	4.1	54.0
A 13	13 55.4	52.7	214 44.0	11.9	21 24.7	4.1	54.0
Y 14	28 55.3	52.5	229 14.9	12.0	21 28.8	3.9	54.0
15	43 55.2	·· 52.3	243 45.9	11.9	21 32.7	3.9	54.0
16	58 55.1	52.1	258 16.8	11.8	21 36.6	3.7	54.0
17	73 55.0	51.8	272 47.6	11.9	21 40.3	3.7	54.0
18	88 54.9	N22 51.6	287 18.5	11.8	S21 44.0	3.5	54.0
19	103 54.7	51.4	301 49.3	11.8	21 47.5	3.5	54.0
20	118 54.6	51.2	316 20.1	11.8	21 51.0	3.3	54.0
21	133 54.5	·· 51.0	330 50.9	11.7	21 54.3	3.3	54.0
22	148 54.4	50.7	345 21.6	11.8	21 57.6	3.1	54.0
23	163 54.3	50.5	359 52.4	11.7	22 00.7	3.1	54.0
5 00	178 54.2	N22 50.3	14 23.1	11.6	S22 03.8	2.9	54.0
01	193 54.1	50.1	28 53.7	11.7	22 06.7	2.8	54.0
02	208 54.0	49.8	43 24.4	11.6	22 09.5	2.8	54.0
03	223 53.9	·· 49.6	57 55.0	11.6	22 12.3	2.6	54.0
04	238 53.8	49.4	72 25.6	11.6	22 14.9	2.5	54.0
05	253 53.6	49.2	86 56.2	11.6	22 17.4	2.4	54.0
06	268 53.5	N22 48.9	101 26.8	11.6	S22 19.8	2.4	54.0
07	283 53.4	48.7	115 57.4	11.5	22 22.2	2.2	54.0
08	298 53.3	48.5	130 27.9	11.5	22 24.4	2.1	54.0
M 09	313 53.2	·· 48.2	144 58.4	11.5	22 26.5	2.0	54.0
O 10	328 53.1	48.0	159 28.9	11.5	22 28.5	1.9	54.0
N 11	343 53.0	47.8	173 59.4	11.4	22 30.4	1.7	54.0
D 12	358 52.9	N22 47.5	188 29.8	11.5	S22 32.2	1.7	54.0
A 13	13 52.8	47.3	203 00.3	11.4	22 33.9	1.6	54.0
Y 14	28 52.7	47.1	217 30.7	11.4	22 35.5	1.5	54.0
15	43 52.6	·· 46.8	232 01.1	11.4	22 37.0	1.3	54.0
16	58 52.5	46.6	246 31.5	11.4	22 38.3	1.3	54.0
17	73 52.4	46.4	261 01.9	11.3	22 39.6	1.2	54.0
18	88 52.2	N22 46.1	275 32.2	11.4	S22 40.8	1.0	54.0
19	103 52.1	45.9	290 02.6	11.4	22 41.8	1.0	54.0
20	118 52.0	45.6	304 33.0	11.3	22 42.8	0.8	54.0
21	133 51.9	·· 45.4	319 03.3	11.3	22 43.6	0.8	54.0
22	148 51.8	45.2	333 33.6	11.3	22 44.4	0.6	54.0
23	163 51.7	44.9	348 03.9	11.3	22 45.0	0.5	54.0
	S.D. 15.8	d 0.2	S.D. 14.7		14.7		14.7

Twilight, Sunrise, Moonrise

Lat.	Naut.	Civil	Sunrise	Moonrise 3	4	5	6
N 72	□	□	□	■	■	■	■
N 70	□	□	□	■	■	■	■
68	□	□	□	20 31	■	■	■
66	////	////	00 39	19 49	21 18	22 31	23 11
64	////	////	01 46	19 21	20 39	21 44	22 28
62	////	////	02 20	19 00	20 12	21 14	21 59
60	////	01 10	02 45	18 42	19 51	20 51	21 37
N 58	////	01 52	03 04	18 28	19 34	20 32	21 19
56	////	02 20	03 21	18 15	19 20	20 17	21 04
54	01 04	02 41	03 34	18 05	19 07	20 03	20 51
52	01 43	02 58	03 46	17 55	18 56	19 52	20 40
50	02 09	03 13	03 57	17 47	18 47	19 42	20 30
45	02 53	03 42	04 19	17 29	18 26	19 20	20 08
N 40	03 22	04 04	04 36	17 14	18 10	19 03	19 51
35	03 45	04 21	04 51	17 01	17 56	18 48	19 37
30	04 03	04 36	05 03	16 51	17 44	18 35	19 24
20	04 31	05 00	05 25	16 32	17 23	18 14	19 03
N 10	04 54	05 20	05 43	16 16	17 05	17 55	18 44
0	05 12	05 38	06 01	16 01	16 49	17 37	18 27
S 10	05 29	05 55	06 18	15 46	16 32	17 20	18 09
20	05 44	06 12	06 36	15 31	16 15	17 01	17 51
30	06 00	06 30	06 56	15 13	15 54	16 40	17 29
35	06 09	06 40	07 08	15 02	15 42	16 27	17 17
40	06 18	06 52	07 22	14 50	15 29	16 13	17 02
45	06 28	07 05	07 39	14 36	15 13	15 56	16 45
S 50	06 39	07 21	07 59	14 19	14 53	15 35	16 24
52	06 44	07 28	08 08	14 11	14 44	15 25	16 13
54	06 50	07 36	08 19	14 02	14 33	15 13	16 02
56	06 56	07 44	08 31	13 52	14 22	15 00	15 49
58	07 02	07 54	08 45	13 40	14 08	14 45	15 34
S 60	07 09	08 05	09 02	13 27	13 52	14 27	15 16

Sunset, Twilight, Moonset

Lat.	Sunset	Civil	Naut.	Moonset 3	4	5	6
N 72	□	□	□	■	■	■	■
N 70	□	□	□	■	■	■	■
68	□	□	□	23 46	■	■	■
66	23 24	////	////	00 25	00 28	00 38	01 07
64	22 21	////	////	00 45	00 57	01 18	01 54
62	21 47	////	////	01 02	01 19	01 45	02 25
60	21 23	22 56	////	01 15	01 36	02 06	02 48
N 58	21 03	22 15	////	01 27	01 51	02 23	03 06
56	20 47	21 48	////	01 38	02 04	02 38	03 22
54	20 34	21 27	23 02	01 47	02 15	02 51	03 35
52	20 22	21 10	22 24	01 55	02 25	03 02	03 46
50	20 12	20 55	21 59	02 02	02 34	03 12	03 57
45	19 50	20 27	21 15	02 18	02 52	03 32	04 18
N 40	19 32	20 05	20 46	02 31	03 08	03 49	04 36
35	19 18	19 47	20 24	02 42	03 21	04 03	04 50
30	19 05	19 32	20 05	02 52	03 32	04 16	05 03
20	18 44	19 08	19 37	03 09	03 51	04 37	05 25
N 10	18 25	18 48	19 15	03 24	04 08	04 55	05 44
0	18 08	18 30	18 57	03 37	04 24	05 12	06 01
S 10	17 51	18 14	18 40	03 51	04 40	05 29	06 19
20	17 33	17 57	18 24	04 06	04 57	05 48	06 38
30	17 12	17 39	18 08	04 23	05 17	06 09	06 59
35	17 00	17 28	18 00	04 33	05 28	06 21	07 12
40	16 46	17 17	17 51	04 44	05 41	06 36	07 26
45	16 30	17 04	17 41	04 57	05 57	06 53	07 44
S 50	16 10	16 48	17 29	05 14	06 16	07 13	08 05
52	16 01	16 41	17 24	05 22	06 25	07 23	08 15
54	15 50	16 33	17 19	05 30	06 35	07 35	08 27
56	15 38	16 24	17 13	05 40	06 47	07 48	08 40
58	15 24	16 15	17 07	05 51	07 00	08 02	08 55
S 60	15 07	16 03	17 00	06 03	07 16	08 20	09 13

SUN and MOON

Day	SUN Eqn. of Time 00h	12h	Mer. Pass.	MOON Mer. Pass. Upper	Lower	Age	Phase
	m s	m s	h m	h m	h m	d	
3	04 01	04 07	12 04	22 13	09 49	12	
4	04 12	04 18	12 04	23 01	10 36	13	
5	04 23	04 28	12 04	23 49	11 25	14	○

1982 JULY 6, 7, 8 (TUES., WED., THURS.)

G.M.T.	ARIES G.H.A.	VENUS −3.4 G.H.A.	Dec.	MARS +0.5 G.H.A.	Dec.	JUPITER −1.7 G.H.A.	Dec.	SATURN +1.0 G.H.A.	Dec.	STARS Name	S.H.A.	Dec.
6 00	283 38.9	212 29.0	N20 54.4	89 46.0	S 6 17.3	74 47.6	S10 31.6	88 10.2	S 3 53.0	Acamar	315 36.5	S40 22.4
01	298 41.3	227 28.3	54.9	104 47.4	17.8	89 50.0	31.7	103 12.6	53.1	Achernar	335 44.4	S57 19.3
02	313 43.8	242 27.6	55.4	119 48.8	18.3	104 52.4	31.7	118 15.0	53.1	Acrux	173 36.0	S63 00.3
03	328 46.3	257 26.9 ··	55.9	134 50.2 ··	18.8	119 54.8 ··	31.7	133 17.4 ··	53.2	Adhara	255 31.5	S28 56.8
04	343 48.7	272 26.2	56.3	149 51.6	19.3	134 57.2	31.8	148 19.8	53.2	Aldebaran	291 16.8	N16 28.4
05	358 51.2	287 25.6	56.8	164 53.1	19.8	149 59.6	31.8	163 22.2	53.2			
06	13 53.7	302 24.9	N20 57.3	179 54.5	S 6 20.3	165 02.0	S10 31.8	178 24.6	S 3 53.3	Alioth	166 41.3	N56 03.7
07	28 56.1	317 24.2	57.8	194 55.9	20.8	180 04.4	31.9	193 27.0	53.3	Alkaid	153 17.3	N49 24.4
08	43 58.6	332 23.5	58.2	209 57.3	21.3	195 06.8	31.9	208 29.4	53.3	Al Na'ir	28 13.0	S47 02.6
09	59 01.0	347 22.8 ··	58.7	224 58.7 ··	21.8	210 09.3 ··	31.9	223 31.8 ··	53.4	Alnilam	276 10.7	S 1 12.7
10	74 03.5	2 22.1	59.2	240 00.1	22.3	225 11.7	32.0	238 34.2	53.4	Alphard	218 19.6	S 8 34.9
11	89 06.0	17 21.5	20 59.6	255 01.5	22.7	240 14.1	32.0	253 36.6	53.5			
12	104 08.4	32 20.8	N21 00.1	270 02.9	S 6 23.2	255 16.5	S10 32.0	268 39.0	S 3 53.5	Alphecca	126 30.8	N26 46.6
13	119 10.9	47 20.1	00.6	285 04.3	23.7	270 18.9	32.1	283 41.4	53.5	Alpheratz	358 07.9	N28 59.4
14	134 13.4	62 19.4	01.0	300 05.7	24.2	285 21.3	32.1	298 43.8	53.6	Altair	62 31.0	N 8 49.3
15	149 15.8	77 18.7 ··	01.5	315 07.2 ··	24.7	300 23.7 ··	32.1	313 46.2 ··	53.6	Ankaa	353 38.9	S42 23.9
16	164 18.3	92 18.0	01.9	330 08.6	25.2	315 26.1	32.2	328 48.6	53.7	Antares	112 55.0	S26 23.6
17	179 20.8	107 17.3	02.4	345 10.0	25.7	330 28.5	32.2	343 51.0	53.7			
18	194 23.2	122 16.7	N21 02.9	0 11.4	S 6 26.2	345 30.9	S10 32.2	358 53.4	S 3 53.7	Arcturus	146 17.2	N19 16.6
19	209 25.7	137 16.0	03.3	15 12.8	26.7	0 33.3	32.3	13 55.8	53.8	Atria	108 17.6	S68 59.9
20	224 28.2	152 15.3	03.8	30 14.2	27.2	15 35.7	32.3	28 58.2	53.8	Avior	234 28.3	S59 27.2
21	239 30.6	167 14.6 ··	04.2	45 15.6 ··	27.7	30 38.1 ··	32.3	44 00.5 ··	53.8	Bellatrix	278 57.7	N 6 20.0
22	254 33.1	182 13.9	04.7	60 17.0	28.2	45 40.5	32.4	59 02.9	53.9	Betelgeuse	271 27.2	N 7 24.3
23	269 35.5	197 13.2	05.1	75 18.4	28.7	60 42.9	32.4	74 05.3	53.9			
7 00	284 38.0	212 12.5	N21 05.6	90 19.8	S 6 29.2	75 45.3	S10 32.4	89 07.7	S 3 54.0	Canopus	264 07.2	S52 41.1
01	299 40.5	227 11.8	06.1	105 21.2	29.7	90 47.7	32.5	104 10.1	54.0	Capella	281 09.9	N45 58.8
02	314 42.9	242 11.1	06.5	120 22.6	30.2	105 50.1	32.5	119 12.5	54.0	Deneb	49 47.2	N45 12.9
03	329 45.4	257 10.4 ··	07.0	135 24.0 ··	30.6	120 52.5 ··	32.6	134 14.9 ··	54.1	Denebola	182 57.8	N14 40.4
04	344 47.9	272 09.8	07.4	150 25.4	31.1	135 54.9	32.6	149 17.3	54.1	Diphda	349 19.6	S18 04.9
05	359 50.3	287 09.1	07.9	165 26.8	31.6	150 57.3	32.6	164 19.7	54.2			
06	14 52.8	302 08.4	N21 08.3	180 28.2	S 6 32.1	165 59.7	S10 32.6	179 22.1	S 3 54.2	Dubhe	194 20.8	N61 51.1
07	29 55.3	317 07.7	08.8	195 29.6	32.6	181 02.1	32.7	194 24.5	54.2	Elnath	278 42.9	N28 35.5
08	44 57.7	332 07.0	09.2	210 31.0	33.1	196 04.5	32.7	209 26.9	54.3	Eltanin	90 56.6	N51 29.6
09	60 00.2	347 06.3 ··	09.6	225 32.4 ··	33.6	211 06.9 ··	32.8	224 29.3 ··	54.3	Enif	34 10.1	N 9 47.6
10	75 02.7	2 05.6	10.1	240 33.8	34.1	226 09.3	32.8	239 31.7	54.4	Fomalhaut	15 49.8	S29 42.8
11	90 05.1	17 04.9	10.5	255 35.2	34.6	241 11.7	32.8	254 34.1	54.4			
12	105 07.6	32 04.2	N21 11.0	270 36.6	S 6 35.1	256 14.1	S10 32.9	269 36.5	S 3 54.4	Gacrux	172 27.5	S57 01.1
13	120 10.0	47 03.5	11.4	285 38.0	35.6	271 16.5	32.9	284 38.9	54.5	Gienah	176 16.7	S17 26.7
14	135 12.5	62 02.8	11.9	300 39.4	36.1	286 18.9	32.9	299 41.3	54.5	Hadar	149 21.4	S60 17.5
15	150 15.0	77 02.1 ··	12.3	315 40.8 ··	36.6	301 21.3 ··	33.0	314 43.7 ··	54.6	Hamal	328 27.6	N23 22.6
16	165 17.4	92 01.4	12.7	330 42.2	37.1	316 23.7	33.0	329 46.1	54.6	Kaus Aust.	84 14.8	S34 23.6
17	180 19.9	107 00.7	13.2	345 43.6	37.6	331 26.1	33.0	344 48.5	54.6			
18	195 22.4	122 00.0	N21 13.6	0 45.0	S 6 38.1	346 28.5	S10 33.1	359 50.9	S 3 54.7	Kochab	137 18.4	N74 14.0
19	210 24.8	136 59.3	14.0	15 46.4	38.6	1 30.9	33.1	14 53.3	54.7	Markab	14 01.7	N15 06.5
20	225 27.3	151 58.6	14.5	30 47.8	39.1	16 33.3	33.1	29 55.7	54.8	Menkar	314 40.0	N 4 01.2
21	240 29.8	166 57.9 ··	14.9	45 49.2 ··	39.6	31 35.7 ··	33.2	44 58.1 ··	54.8	Menkent	148 35.4	S36 17.1
22	255 32.2	181 57.2	15.3	60 50.6	40.1	46 38.1	33.2	60 00.4	54.8	Miaplacidus	221 45.5	S69 38.8
23	270 34.7	196 56.5	15.8	75 52.0	40.6	61 40.5	33.3	75 02.8	54.9			
8 00	285 37.1	211 55.8	N21 16.2	90 53.3	S 6 41.1	76 42.9	S10 33.3	90 05.2	S 3 54.9	Mirfak	309 14.6	N49 47.7
01	300 39.6	226 55.1	16.6	105 54.7	41.6	91 45.3	33.3	105 07.6	55.0	Nunki	76 27.2	S26 19.1
02	315 42.1	241 54.4	17.1	120 56.1	42.1	106 47.7	33.4	120 10.0	55.0	Peacock	53 55.8	S56 47.4
03	330 44.5	256 53.7 ··	17.5	135 57.5 ··	42.6	121 50.1 ··	33.4	135 12.4 ··	55.0	Pollux	243 57.0	N28 04.2
04	345 47.0	271 53.0	17.9	150 58.9	43.1	136 52.5	33.4	150 14.8	55.1	Procyon	245 24.8	N 5 16.3
05	0 49.5	286 52.3	18.3	166 00.3	43.6	151 54.9	33.5	165 17.2	55.1			
06	15 51.9	301 51.6	N21 18.8	181 01.7	S 6 44.1	166 57.3	S10 33.5	180 19.6	S 3 55.2	Rasalhague	96 28.1	N12 34.4
07	30 54.4	316 50.9	19.2	196 03.1	44.6	181 59.7	33.6	195 22.0	55.2	Regulus	208 08.9	N12 03.3
08	45 56.9	331 50.2	19.6	211 04.5	45.1	197 02.1	33.6	210 24.4	55.2	Rigel	281 35.1	S 8 13.3
09	60 59.3	346 49.5 ··	20.0	226 05.9 ··	45.6	212 04.5 ··	33.6	225 26.8 ··	55.3	Rigil Kent.	140 23.9	S60 45.9
10	76 01.8	1 48.8	20.5	241 07.2	46.1	227 06.8	33.7	240 29.2	55.3	Sabik	102 39.4	S15 42.2
11	91 04.3	16 48.1	20.9	256 08.6	46.6	242 09.2	33.7	255 31.6	55.4			
12	106 06.7	31 47.4	N21 21.3	271 10.0	S 6 47.0	257 11.6	S10 33.7	270 34.0	S 3 55.4	Schedar	350 07.6	N56 26.1
13	121 09.2	46 46.7	21.7	286 11.4	47.5	272 14.0	33.8	285 36.3	55.4	Shaula	96 53.6	S37 05.5
14	136 11.6	61 46.0	22.1	301 12.8	48.0	287 16.4	33.8	300 38.7	55.5	Sirius	258 54.9	S16 41.5
15	151 14.1	76 45.3 ··	22.6	316 14.2 ··	48.5	302 18.8 ··	33.9	315 41.1 ··	55.5	Spica	158 56.2	S11 04.1
16	166 16.6	91 44.6	23.0	331 15.6	49.0	317 21.2	33.9	330 43.5	55.6	Suhail	223 10.3	S43 21.7
17	181 19.0	106 43.9	23.4	346 16.9	49.5	332 23.6	33.9	345 45.9	55.6			
18	196 21.5	121 43.2	N21 23.8	1 18.3	S 6 50.0	347 26.0	S10 34.0	0 48.3	S 3 55.7	Vega	80 54.5	N38 46.1
19	211 24.0	136 42.5	24.2	16 19.7	50.5	2 28.4	34.0	15 50.7	55.7	Zuben'ubi	137 31.5	S15 58.1
20	226 26.4	151 41.7	24.6	31 21.1	51.0	17 30.8	34.1	30 53.1	55.7			
21	241 28.9	166 41.0 ··	25.0	46 22.5 ··	51.5	32 33.2 ··	34.1	45 55.5 ··	55.8		S.H.A.	Mer. Pass.
22	256 31.4	181 40.3	25.4	61 23.9	52.0	47 35.5	34.1	60 57.9	55.8	Venus	287 34.5	9 52
23	271 33.8	196 39.6	25.8	76 25.2	52.5	62 37.9	34.2	76 00.3	55.9	Mars	165 41.8	17 57
Mer. Pass.	5 00.6	*v* −0.7 *d* 0.4		*v* 1.4 *d* 0.5		*v* 2.4 *d* 0.0		*v* 2.4 *d* 0.0		Jupiter	151 07.3	18 54
										Saturn	164 29.7	18 01

1982 JULY 6, 7, 8 (TUES., WED., THURS.)

G.M.T.	SUN G.H.A.	SUN Dec.	MOON G.H.A.	v	Dec.	d	H.P.
6 00	178 51.6	N22 44.7	2 34.2	11.3	S22 45.5	0.4	54.0
01	193 51.5	44.4	17 04.5	11.3	22 45.9	0.3	54.0
02	208 51.4	44.2	31 34.8	11.3	22 46.2	0.2	54.0
03	223 51.3 ··	44.0	46 05.1	11.3	22 46.4	0.1	54.0
04	238 51.2	43.7	60 35.4	11.3	22 46.5	0.0	54.0
05	253 51.1	43.5	75 05.7	11.2	22 46.5	0.1	54.0
06	268 51.0	N22 43.2	89 35.9	11.3	S22 46.4	0.3	54.0
07	283 50.9	43.0	104 06.2	11.3	22 46.1	0.3	54.1
08	298 50.8	42.7	118 36.5	11.2	22 45.8	0.4	54.1
09	313 50.7 ··	42.5	133 06.7	11.3	22 45.4	0.6	54.1
10	328 50.6	42.2	147 37.0	11.2	22 44.8	0.7	54.1
11	343 50.5	42.0	162 07.2	11.3	22 44.1	0.7	54.1
12	358 50.3	N22 41.7	176 37.5	11.2	S22 43.4	0.9	54.1
13	13 50.2	41.5	191 07.7	11.3	22 42.5	1.0	54.1
14	28 50.1	41.2	205 38.0	11.2	22 41.5	1.1	54.1
15	43 50.0 ··	41.0	220 08.2	11.3	22 40.4	1.2	54.1
16	58 49.9	40.7	234 38.5	11.3	22 39.2	1.3	54.1
17	73 49.8	40.5	249 08.8	11.2	22 37.9	1.4	54.1
18	88 49.7	N22 40.2	263 39.0	11.3	S22 36.5	1.5	54.1
19	103 49.6	40.0	278 09.3	11.3	22 35.0	1.7	54.1
20	118 49.5	39.7	292 39.6	11.3	22 33.3	1.7	54.1
21	133 49.4 ··	39.5	307 09.9	11.3	22 31.6	1.8	54.1
22	148 49.3	39.2	321 40.2	11.3	22 29.8	2.0	54.1
23	163 49.2	38.9	336 10.5	11.3	22 27.8	2.1	54.1
7 00	178 49.1	N22 38.7	350 40.8	11.3	S22 25.7	2.1	54.2
01	193 49.0	38.4	5 11.1	11.3	22 23.6	2.3	54.2
02	208 48.9	38.2	19 41.4	11.3	22 21.3	2.4	54.2
03	223 48.8 ··	37.9	34 11.7	11.4	22 18.9	2.5	54.2
04	238 48.7	37.6	48 42.1	11.3	22 16.4	2.5	54.2
05	253 48.6	37.4	63 12.4	11.4	22 13.9	2.7	54.2
06	268 48.5	N22 37.1	77 42.8	11.4	S22 11.2	2.8	54.2
07	283 48.4	36.9	92 13.2	11.4	22 08.4	2.9	54.2
08	298 48.3	36.6	106 43.6	11.4	22 05.5	3.1	54.2
09	313 48.2 ··	36.3	121 14.0	11.4	22 02.4	3.1	54.2
10	328 48.1	36.1	135 44.4	11.4	21 59.3	3.2	54.2
11	343 48.0	35.8	150 14.8	11.5	21 56.1	3.3	54.2
12	358 47.9	N22 35.5	164 45.3	11.4	S21 52.8	3.4	54.2
13	13 47.8	35.3	179 15.7	11.5	21 49.4	3.6	54.3
14	28 47.7	35.0	193 46.2	11.5	21 45.8	3.6	54.3
15	43 47.6 ··	34.7	208 16.7	11.5	21 42.2	3.7	54.3
16	58 47.5	34.5	222 47.2	11.6	21 38.5	3.9	54.3
17	73 47.4	34.2	237 17.8	11.5	21 34.6	3.9	54.3
18	88 47.3	N22 33.9	251 48.3	11.6	S21 30.7	4.1	54.3
19	103 47.2	33.7	266 18.9	11.6	21 26.6	4.1	54.3
20	118 47.1	33.4	280 49.5	11.6	21 22.5	4.3	54.3
21	133 47.0 ··	33.1	295 20.1	11.6	21 18.2	4.3	54.3
22	148 46.9	32.8	309 50.7	11.7	21 13.9	4.5	54.3
23	163 46.8	32.6	324 21.4	11.7	21 09.4	4.5	54.4
8 00	178 46.7	N22 32.3	338 52.1	11.7	S21 04.9	4.7	54.4
01	193 46.6	32.0	353 22.8	11.7	21 00.2	4.7	54.4
02	208 46.5	31.7	7 53.5	11.7	20 55.5	4.9	54.4
03	223 46.4 ··	31.5	22 24.2	11.8	20 50.6	4.9	54.4
04	238 46.3	31.2	36 55.0	11.8	20 45.7	5.1	54.4
05	253 46.2	30.9	51 25.8	11.8	20 40.6	5.1	54.4
06	268 46.1	N22 30.6	65 56.6	11.8	S20 35.5	5.3	54.4
07	283 46.0	30.4	80 27.4	11.9	20 30.2	5.3	54.4
08	298 45.9	30.1	94 58.3	11.9	20 24.9	5.5	54.5
09	313 45.8 ··	29.8	109 29.2	11.9	20 19.4	5.5	54.5
10	328 45.7	29.5	124 00.1	11.9	20 13.9	5.6	54.5
11	343 45.6	29.2	138 31.0	12.0	20 08.3	5.8	54.5
12	358 45.5	N22 28.9	153 02.0	12.0	S20 02.5	5.8	54.5
13	13 45.4	28.7	167 33.0	12.0	19 56.7	5.9	54.5
14	28 45.4	28.4	182 04.0	12.0	19 50.8	6.0	54.5
15	43 45.3 ··	28.1	196 35.0	12.1	19 44.8	6.1	54.5
16	58 45.2	27.8	211 06.1	12.1	19 38.7	6.2	54.6
17	73 45.1	27.5	225 37.2	12.1	19 32.5	6.3	54.6
18	88 45.0	N22 27.2	240 08.3	12.2	S19 26.2	6.4	54.6
19	103 44.9	27.0	254 39.5	12.1	19 19.8	6.5	54.6
20	118 44.8	26.7	269 10.6	12.3	19 13.3	6.5	54.6
21	133 44.7 ··	26.4	283 41.9	12.2	19 06.8	6.7	54.6
22	148 44.6	26.1	298 13.1	12.3	19 00.1	6.8	54.6
23	163 44.5	25.8	312 44.4	12.2	18 53.3	6.8	54.7
	S.D. 15.8	d 0.3	S.D. 14.7		14.8		14.9

Lat.	Twilight Naut.	Twilight Civil	Sunrise	Moonrise 6	7	8	9
N 72	□	□	□	■	■	■	■
N 70	□	□	□	■	■	■	00 49
68	□	□	□	■	■	00 18	{00 02 / 23 53}
66	////	////	00 56	23 11	23 26	23 32	23 33
64	////	////	01 53	22 28	22 54	23 09	23 17
62	////	////	02 25	21 59	22 30	22 50	23 04
60	////	01 18	02 49	21 37	22 11	22 35	22 52
N 58	////	01 58	03 08	21 19	21 55	22 22	22 43
56	////	02 24	03 24	21 04	21 42	22 11	22 34
54	01 12	02 45	03 37	20 51	21 30	22 01	22 26
52	01 48	03 01	03 49	20 40	21 20	21 52	22 19
50	02 13	03 16	03 59	20 30	21 10	21 44	22 13
45	02 55	03 44	04 21	20 08	20 51	21 28	21 59
N 40	03 24	04 05	04 38	19 51	20 35	21 14	21 48
35	03 47	04 23	04 52	19 37	20 21	21 02	21 39
30	04 05	04 38	05 05	19 24	20 10	20 52	21 30
20	04 33	05 02	05 26	19 03	19 50	20 34	21 16
N 10	04 54	05 21	05 44	18 44	19 32	20 18	21·03
0	05 13	05 39	06 01	18 27	19 16	20 04	20 51
S 10	05 29	05 55	06 18	18 09	18 59	19 49	20 39
20	05 45	06 12	06 36	17 51	18 42	19 34	20 26
30	06 00	06 30	06 56	17 29	18 21	19 16	20 11
35	06 09	06 40	07 08	17 17	18 10	19 05	20 03
40	06 18	06 51	07 22	17 02	17 56	18 53	19 53
45	06 27	07 04	07 38	16 45	17 40	18 39	19 41
S 50	06 38	07 19	07 57	16 24	17 20	18 22	19 27
52	06 43	07 27	08 07	16 13	17 10	18 13	19 20
54	06 49	07 34	08 17	16 02	17 00	18 04	19 13
56	06 54	07 43	08 29	15 49	16 48	17 54	19 05
58	07 01	07 52	08 43	15 34	16 34	17 42	18 56
S 60	07 08	08 03	08 59	15 16	16 17	17 28	18 45

Lat.	Sunset	Twilight Civil	Twilight Naut.	Moonset 6	7	8	9
N 72	□	□	□	■	■	■	■
N 70	□	□	□	■	■	■	03 54
68	□	□	□	■	■	02 44	04 40
66	23 10	////	////	01 07	02 09	03 36	05 09
64	22 15	////	////	01 54	02 52	04 07	05 32
62	21 43	////	////	02 25	03 21	04 31	05 49
60	21 19	22 49	////	02 48	03 43	04 49	06 04
N 58	21 01	22 10	////	03 06	04 00	05 05	06 16
56	20 45	21 44	////	03 22	04 15	05 18	06 27
54	20 32	21 24	22 55	03 35	04 28	05 30	06 37
52	20 20	21 08	22 20	03 46	04 39	05 40	06 45
50	20 10	20 53	21 56	03 57	04 49	05 49	06 53
45	19 49	20 25	21 14	04 18	05 10	06 08	07 08
N 40	19 32	20 04	20 45	04 36	05 27	06 23	07 22
35	19 17	19 46	20 20	04 50	05 42	06 36	07 33
30	19 05	19 32	20 05	05 03	05 54	06 47	07 42
20	18 44	19 08	19 37	05 25	06 15	07 07	07 59
N 10	18 25	18 48	19 15	05 44	06 33	07 23	08 13
0	18 08	18 31	18 57	06 01	06 50	07 39	08 27
S 10	17 52	18 14	18 41	06 19	07 07	07 55	08 40
20	17 34	17 58	18 25	06 38	07 26	08 11	08 54
30	17 14	17 40	18 09	06 59	07 46	08 30	09 10
35	17 02	17 30	18 01	07 12	07 59	08 41	09 20
40	16 48	17 18	17 43	07 26	08 13	08 54	09 30
45	16 32	17 06	17 43	07 44	08 29	09 09	09 43
S 50	16 12	16 50	17 31	08 05	08 49	09 27	09 58
52	16 03	16 43	17 27	08 15	08 59	09 35	10 05
54	15 53	16 36	17 21	08 27	09 10	09 45	10 13
56	15 41	16 27	17 16	08 40	09 22	09 56	10 21
58	15 27	16 17	17 09	08 55	09 37	10 08	10 31
S 60	15 11	16 07	17 02	09 13	09 53	10 22	10 42

Day	SUN Eqn. of Time 00h	12h	Mer. Pass.	MOON Mer. Pass. Upper	Lower	Age	Phase
	m s	m s	h m	h m	h m	d	
6	04 33	04 38	12 05	24 39	12 14	15	○
7	04 43	04 48	12 05	00 39	13 03	16	
8	04 53	04 58	12 05	01 27	13 51	17	

1982 JULY 9, 10, 11 (FRI., SAT., SUN.)

G.M.T.	ARIES G.H.A.	VENUS −3.4 G.H.A.	Dec.	MARS +0.5 G.H.A.	Dec.	JUPITER −1.7 G.H.A.	Dec.	SATURN +1.0 G.H.A.	Dec.	STARS Name	S.H.A.	Dec.
9 00	286 36.3	211 38.9 N21	26.3	91 26.6 S 6	53.0	77 40.3 S10	34.2	91 02.6 S 3	55.9	Acamar	315 36.5	S40 22.3
01	301 38.8	226 38.2	26.7	106 28.0	53.5	92 42.7	34.3	106 05.0	55.9	Achernar	335 44.3	S57 19.3
02	316 41.2	241 37.5	27.1	121 29.4	54.0	107 45.1	34.3	121 07.4	56.0	Acrux	173 36.0	S63 00.3
03	331 43.7	256 36.8 ··	27.5	136 30.8 ··	54.5	122 47.5 ··	34.3	136 09.8 ··	56.0	Adhara	255 31.5	S28 56.8
04	346 46.1	271 36.1	27.9	151 32.1	55.0	137 49.9	34.4	151 12.2	56.1	Aldebaran	291 16.8	N16 28.4
05	1 48.6	286 35.4	28.3	166 33.5	55.6	152 52.3	34.4	166 14.6	56.1			
06	16 51.1	301 34.6 N21	28.7	181 34.9 S 6	56.1	167 54.6 S10	34.5	181 17.0 S 3	56.2	Alioth	166 41.4	N56 03.7
07	31 53.5	316 33.9	29.1	196 36.3	56.6	182 57.0	34.5	196 19.4	56.2	Alkaid	153 17.4	N49 24.4
08	46 56.0	331 33.2	29.5	211 37.6	57.1	197 59.4	34.5	211 21.8	56.2	Al Na'ir	28 12.9	S47 02.6
F 09	61 58.5	346 32.5 ··	29.9	226 39.0 ··	57.6	213 01.8 ··	34.6	226 24.1 ··	56.3	Alnilam	276 10.7	S 1 12.7
R 10	77 00.9	1 31.8	30.3	241 40.4	58.1	228 04.2	34.6	241 26.5	56.3	Alphard	218 19.6	S 8 34.9
I 11	92 03.4	16 31.1	30.7	256 41.8	58.6	243 06.6	34.7	256 28.9	56.4			
D 12	107 05.9	31 30.4 N21	31.1	271 43.1 S 6	59.1	258 09.0 S10	34.7	271 31.3 S 3	56.4	Alphecca	126 30.8	N26 46.6
A 13	122 08.3	46 29.7	31.5	286 44.5	59.6	273 11.3	34.7	286 33.7	56.5	Alpheratz	358 07.9	N28 59.4
Y 14	137 10.8	61 28.9	31.9	301 45.9	7 00.1	288 13.7	34.8	301 36.1	56.5	Altair	62 31.0	N 8 49.3
15	152 13.2	76 28.2 ··	32.3	316 47.3 ··	00.6	303 16.1 ··	34.8	316 38.5 ··	56.5	Ankaa	353 38.9	S42 23.9
16	167 15.7	91 27.5	32.6	331 48.6	01.1	318 18.5	34.9	331 40.9	56.6	Antares	112 55.0	S26 23.6
17	182 18.2	106 26.8	33.0	346 50.0	01.6	333 20.9	34.9	346 43.3	56.6			
18	197 20.6	121 26.1 N21	33.4	1 51.4 S 7	02.1	348 23.3 S10	34.9	1 45.6 S 3	56.7	Arcturus	146 17.2	N19 16.6
19	212 23.1	136 25.4	33.8	16 52.8	02.6	3 25.7	35.0	16 48.0	56.7	Atria	108 17.6	S68 59.9
20	227 25.6	151 24.6	34.2	31 54.1	03.1	18 28.0	35.0	31 50.4	56.8	Avior	234 28.3	S59 27.2
21	242 28.0	166 23.9 ··	34.6	46 55.5 ··	03.6	33 30.4 ··	35.1	46 52.8 ··	56.8	Bellatrix	278 57.7	N 6 20.1
22	257 30.5	181 23.2	35.0	61 56.9	04.1	48 32.8	35.1	61 55.2	56.8	Betelgeuse	271 27.2	N 7 24.3
23	272 33.0	196 22.5	35.4	76 58.2	04.6	63 35.2	35.2	76 57.6	56.9			
10 00	287 35.4	211 21.8 N21	35.7	91 59.6 S 7	05.1	78 37.6 S10	35.2	92 00.0 S 3	56.9	Canopus	264 07.2	S52 41.1
01	302 37.9	226 21.1	36.1	107 01.0	05.6	93 39.9	35.2	107 02.3	57.0	Capella	281 09.8	N45 58.8
02	317 40.4	241 20.3	36.5	122 02.3	06.1	108 42.3	35.3	122 04.7	57.0	Deneb	49 47.2	N45 12.9
03	332 42.8	256 19.6 ··	36.9	137 03.7 ··	06.6	123 44.7 ··	35.3	137 07.1 ··	57.1	Denebola	182 57.9	N14 40.4
04	347 45.3	271 18.9	37.3	152 05.1	07.1	138 47.1	35.4	152 09.5	57.1	Diphda	349 19.5	S18 04.9
05	2 47.7	286 18.2	37.6	167 06.4	07.6	153 49.5	35.4	167 11.9	57.2			
06	17 50.2	301 17.4 N21	38.0	182 07.8 S 7	08.1	168 51.8 S10	35.5	182 14.3 S 3	57.2	Dubhe	194 20.9	N61 51.1
07	32 52.7	316 16.7	38.4	197 09.2	08.6	183 54.2	35.5	197 16.7	57.2	Elnath	278 42.9	N28 35.5
S 08	47 55.1	331 16.0	38.8	212 10.5	09.1	198 56.6	35.5	212 19.0	57.3	Eltanin	90 56.6	N51 29.6
A 09	62 57.6	346 15.3 ··	39.2	227 11.9 ··	09.6	213 59.0 ··	35.6	227 21.4 ··	57.3	Enif	34 10.1	N 9 47.6
T 10	78 00.1	1 14.6	39.5	242 13.3	10.1	229 01.4	35.6	242 23.8	57.4	Fomalhaut	15 49.8	S29 42.8
U 11	93 02.5	16 13.8	39.9	257 14.6	10.6	244 03.7	35.7	257 26.2	57.4			
R 12	108 05.0	31 13.1 N21	40.3	272 16.0 S 7	11.1	259 06.1 S10	35.7	272 28.6 S 3	57.5	Gacrux	172 27.5	S57 01.1
D 13	123 07.5	46 12.4	40.6	287 17.4	11.6	274 08.5	35.8	287 31.0	57.5	Gienah	176 16.7	S17 26.6
A 14	138 09.9	61 11.7	41.0	302 18.7	12.1	289 10.9	35.8	302 33.4	57.5	Hadar	149 21.4	S60 17.5
Y 15	153 12.4	76 10.9 ··	41.4	317 20.1 ··	12.7	304 13.3 ··	35.8	317 35.7 ··	57.6	Hamal	328 27.6	N23 22.6
16	168 14.9	91 10.2	41.7	332 21.4	13.2	319 15.6	35.9	332 38.1	57.6	Kaus Aust.	84 14.7	S34 23.6
17	183 17.3	106 09.5	42.1	347 22.8	13.7	334 18.0	35.9	347 40.5	57.7			
18	198 19.8	121 08.8 N21	42.5	2 24.2 S 7	14.2	349 20.4 S10	36.0	2 42.9 S 3	57.7	Kochab	137 18.4	N74 14.0
19	213 22.2	136 08.0	42.8	17 25.5	14.7	4 22.8	36.0	17 45.3	57.8	Markab	14 01.7	N15 06.5
20	228 24.7	151 07.3	43.2	32 26.9	15.2	19 25.1	36.1	32 47.7	57.8	Menkar	314 40.0	N 4 01.2
21	243 27.2	166 06.6 ··	43.6	47 28.2 ··	15.7	34 27.5 ··	36.1	47 50.0 ··	57.9	Menkent	148 35.4	S36 17.1
22	258 29.6	181 05.9	43.9	62 29.6	16.2	49 29.9	36.1	62 52.4	57.9	Miaplacidus	221 45.6	S69 38.8
23	273 32.1	196 05.1	44.3	77 31.0	16.7	64 32.3	36.2	77 54.8	57.9			
11 00	288 34.6	211 04.4 N21	44.7	92 32.3 S 7	17.2	79 34.6 S10	36.2	92 57.2 S 3	58.0	Mirfak	309 14.6	N49 47.7
01	303 37.0	226 03.7	45.0	107 33.7	17.7	94 37.0	36.3	107 59.6	58.0	Nunki	76 27.2	S26 19.1
02	318 39.5	241 03.0	45.4	122 35.0	18.2	109 39.4	36.3	123 02.0	58.1	Peacock	53 55.8	S56 47.4
03	333 42.0	256 02.2 ··	45.7	137 36.4 ··	18.7	124 41.8 ··	36.4	138 04.3 ··	58.1	Pollux	243 57.0	N28 04.2
04	348 44.4	271 01.5	46.1	152 37.7	19.2	139 44.1	36.4	153 06.7	58.2	Procyon	245 24.8	N 5 16.3
05	3 46.9	286 00.8	46.4	167 39.1	19.7	154 46.5	36.5	168 09.1	58.2			
06	18 49.3	301 00.0 N21	46.8	182 40.5 S 7	20.2	169 48.9 S10	36.5	183 11.5 S 3	58.3	Rasalhague	96 28.1	N12 34.4
07	33 51.8	315 59.3	47.1	197 41.8	20.7	184 51.3	36.6	198 13.9	58.3	Regulus	208 08.9	N12 03.4
08	48 54.3	330 58.6	47.5	212 43.2	21.3	199 53.6	36.6	213 16.2	58.4	Rigel	281 35.1	S 8 13.3
S 09	63 56.7	345 57.8 ··	47.8	227 44.5 ··	21.8	214 56.0 ··	36.6	228 18.6 ··	58.4	Rigil Kent.	140 23.9	S60 45.9
U 10	78 59.2	0 57.1	48.2	242 45.9	22.3	229 58.4	36.7	243 21.0	58.4	Sabik	102 39.4	S15 42.2
N 11	94 01.7	15 56.4	48.5	257 47.2	22.8	245 00.7	36.7	258 23.4	58.5			
D 12	109 04.1	30 55.7 N21	48.9	272 48.6 S 7	23.3	260 03.1 S10	36.8	273 25.8 S 3	58.5	Schedar	350 07.5	N56 26.1
A 13	124 06.6	45 54.9	49.2	287 49.9	23.8	275 05.5	36.8	288 28.2	58.6	Shaula	96 53.6	S37 05.5
Y 14	139 09.1	60 54.2	49.6	302 51.3	24.3	290 07.9	36.9	303 30.5	58.6	Sirius	258 54.9	S16 41.5
15	154 11.5	75 53.5 ··	49.9	317 52.6 ··	24.8	305 10.2 ··	36.9	318 32.9 ··	58.7	Spica	158 56.2	S11 04.1
16	169 14.0	90 52.7	50.3	332 54.0	25.3	320 12.6	37.0	333 35.3	58.7	Suhail	223 10.3	S43 21.7
17	184 16.5	105 52.0	50.6	347 55.3	25.8	335 15.0	37.0	348 37.7	58.8			
18	199 18.9	120 51.3 N21	51.0	2 56.7 S 7	26.3	350 17.3 S10	37.1	3 40.1 S 3	58.8	Vega	80 54.5	N38 46.1
19	214 21.4	135 50.5	51.3	17 58.0	26.8	5 19.7	37.1	18 42.4	58.9	Zuben'ubi	137 31.5	S15 58.1
20	229 23.8	150 49.8	51.6	32 59.4	27.3	20 22.1	37.1	33 44.8	58.9			
21	244 26.3	165 49.1 ··	52.0	48 00.7 ··	27.9	35 24.5 ··	37.2	48 47.2 ··	59.0		S.H.A.	Mer. Pass.
22	259 28.8	180 48.3	52.3	63 02.1	28.4	50 26.8	37.2	63 49.6	59.0	Venus	283 46.3	9 55
23	274 31.2	195 47.6	52.7	78 03.4	28.9	65 29.2	37.3	78 52.0	59.0	Mars	164 24.2	17 50
										Jupiter	151 02.1	18 43
Mer. Pass. 4 48.8		v 0.7	d 0.4	v 1.4	d 0.5	v 2.4	d 0.0	v 2.4	d 0.0	Saturn	164 24.5	17 49

1982 JULY 9, 10, 11 (FRI., SAT., SUN.)

G.M.T.	SUN G.H.A.	SUN Dec.	MOON G.H.A.	v	Dec.	d	H.P.
9 00	178 44.4	N22 25.5	327 15.6	12.4	S18 46.5	6.9	54.7
01	193 44.3	25.2	341 47.0	12.3	18 39.6	7.0	54.7
02	208 44.2	24.9	356 18.3	12.4	18 32.6	7.1	54.7
03	223 44.1 ··	24.6	10 49.7	12.4	18 25.5	7.2	54.7
04	238 44.0	24.3	25 21.1	12.4	18 18.3	7.3	54.7
05	253 43.9	24.0	39 52.5	12.5	18 11.0	7.4	54.7
06	268 43.8	N22 23.8	54 24.0	12.5	S18 03.6	7.4	54.8
07	283 43.7	23.5	68 55.5	12.5	17 56.2	7.6	54.8
08	298 43.7	23.2	83 27.0	12.5	17 48.6	7.6	54.8
F 09	313 43.6 ··	22.9	97 58.5	12.6	17 41.0	7.7	54.8
R 10	328 43.5	22.6	112 30.1	12.6	17 33.3	7.8	54.8
I 11	343 43.4	22.3	127 01.7	12.6	17 25.5	7.9	54.8
D 12	358 43.3	N22 22.0	141 33.3	12.7	S17 17.6	7.9	54.9
A 13	13 43.2	21.7	156 05.0	12.7	17 09.7	8.0	54.9
Y 14	28 43.1	21.4	170 36.7	12.7	17 01.7	8.2	54.9
15	43 43.0 ··	21.1	185 08.4	12.8	16 53.5	8.2	54.9
16	58 42.9	20.8	199 40.2	12.7	16 45.3	8.2	54.9
17	73 42.8	20.5	214 11.9	12.8	16 37.1	8.4	54.9
18	88 42.7	N22 20.2	228 43.7	12.9	S16 28.7	8.4	55.0
19	103 42.6	19.9	243 15.6	12.8	16 20.3	8.6	55.0
20	118 42.6	19.6	257 47.4	12.9	16 11.7	8.6	55.0
21	133 42.5 ··	19.3	272 19.3	12.9	16 03.1	8.6	55.0
22	148 42.4	18.9	286 51.2	12.9	15 54.5	8.8	55.0
23	163 42.3	18.6	301 23.1	13.0	15 45.7	8.8	55.0
10 00	178 42.2	N22 18.3	315 55.1	13.0	S15 36.9	8.9	55.1
01	193 42.1	18.0	330 27.1	13.0	15 28.0	9.0	55.1
02	208 42.0	17.7	344 59.1	13.0	15 19.0	9.0	55.1
03	223 41.9 ··	17.4	359 31.1	13.1	15 10.0	9.1	55.1
04	238 41.8	17.1	14 03.2	13.1	15 00.9	9.2	55.1
05	253 41.7	16.8	28 35.3	13.1	14 51.7	9.3	55.2
06	268 41.7	N22 16.5	43 07.4	13.1	S14 42.4	9.4	55.2
07	283 41.6	16.2	57 39.5	13.2	14 33.1	9.4	55.2
S 08	298 41.5	15.9	72 11.7	13.2	14 23.7	9.5	55.2
A 09	313 41.4 ··	15.5	86 43.9	13.2	14 14.2	9.6	55.2
T 10	328 41.3	15.2	101 16.1	13.2	14 04.6	9.6	55.2
U 11	343 41.2	14.9	115 48.3	13.3	13 55.0	9.7	55.3
R 12	358 41.1	N22 14.6	130 20.6	13.3	S13 45.3	9.7	55.3
D 13	13 41.0	14.3	144 52.9	13.3	13 35.6	9.9	55.3
A 14	28 40.9	14.0	159 25.2	13.3	13 25.7	9.8	55.3
Y 15	43 40.9 ··	13.7	173 57.5	13.3	13 15.9	10.0	55.4
16	58 40.8	13.3	188 29.8	13.4	13 05.9	10.0	55.4
17	73 40.7	13.0	203 02.2	13.4	12 55.9	10.1	55.4
18	88 40.6	N22 12.7	217 34.6	13.4	S12 45.8	10.1	55.4
19	103 40.5	12.4	232 07.0	13.4	12 35.7	10.2	55.4
20	118 40.4	12.1	246 39.4	13.4	12 25.5	10.3	55.5
21	133 40.3 ··	11.7	261 11.8	13.5	12 15.2	10.3	55.5
22	148 40.3	11.4	275 44.3	13.5	12 04.9	10.4	55.5
23	163 40.2	11.1	290 16.8	13.4	11 54.5	10.5	55.5
11 00	178 40.1	N22 10.8	304 49.2	13.5	S11 44.0	10.5	55.5
01	193 40.0	10.5	319 21.7	13.6	11 33.5	10.6	55.6
02	208 39.9	10.1	333 54.3	13.5	11 22.9	10.6	55.6
03	223 39.8 ··	09.8	348 26.8	13.5	11 12.3	10.7	55.6
04	238 39.7	09.5	2 59.3	13.6	11 01.6	10.7	55.6
05	253 39.7	09.2	17 31.9	13.6	10 50.9	10.8	55.6
06	268 39.6	N22 08.8	32 04.5	13.6	S10 40.1	10.9	55.7
07	283 39.5	08.5	46 37.1	13.6	10 29.2	10.9	55.7
08	298 39.4	08.2	61 09.7	13.6	10 18.3	11.0	55.7
S 09	313 39.3 ··	07.8	75 42.3	13.6	10 07.3	11.0	55.8
U 10	328 39.2	07.5	90 14.9	13.6	9 56.3	11.1	55.8
N 11	343 39.2	07.2	104 47.5	13.7	9 45.2	11.1	55.8
D 12	358 39.1	N22 06.9	119 20.2	13.6	S 9 34.1	11.2	55.8
A 13	13 39.0	06.5	133 52.8	13.7	9 22.9	11.2	55.9
Y 14	28 38.9	06.2	148 25.5	13.7	9 11.7	11.3	55.9
15	43 38.8 ··	05.9	162 58.2	13.6	9 00.4	11.3	55.9
16	58 38.7	05.5	177 30.8	13.7	8 49.1	11.4	55.9
17	73 38.7	05.2	192 03.5	13.7	8 37.7	11.4	56.0
18	88 38.6	N22 04.9	206 36.2	13.7	S 8 26.3	11.5	56.0
19	103 38.5	04.5	221 08.9	13.7	8 14.8	11.5	56.0
20	118 38.4	04.2	235 41.6	13.7	8 03.3	11.5	56.0
21	133 38.3 ··	03.8	250 14.3	13.7	7 51.8	11.7	56.1
22	148 38.2	03.5	264 47.0	13.7	7 40.1	11.6	56.1
23	163 38.2	03.2	279 19.7	13.7	7 28.5	11.7	56.1
	S.D. 15.8 d 0.3		S.D. 14.9		15.1		15.2

Lat.	Twilight Naut.	Twilight Civil	Sunrise	Moonrise 9	10	11	12
N 72	☐	☐	☐	■	00 55	{00 21 / 23 59}	23 40
N 70	☐	☐	☐	00 49	00 19	{00 01 / 23 48}	23 37
68	☐	☐	☐	{00 02 / 23 53}	23 46	23 40	23 34
66	////	////	01 10	23 33	23 33	23 32	23 31
64	////	////	02 00	23 17	23 23	23 26	23 29
62	////	////	02 31	23 04	23 13	23 21	23 27
60	////	01 27	02 54	22 52	23 06	23 16	23 26
N 58	////	02 04	03 12	22 43	22 59	23 12	23 24
56	////	02 29	03 27	22 34	22 52	23 08	23 23
54	01 20	02 49	03 40	22 26	22 47	23 05	23 22
52	01 54	03 05	03 52	22 19	22 42	23 02	23 21
50	02 17	03 19	04 02	22 13	22 37	22 59	23 20
45	02 58	03 46	04 23	21 59	22 28	22 53	23 18
N 40	03 27	04 07	04 40	21 48	22 19	22 48	23 16
35	03 49	04 25	04 54	21 39	22 12	22 44	23 15
30	04 06	04 39	05 06	21 30	22 06	22 40	23 13
20	04 34	05 03	05 27	21 16	21 55	22 33	23 11
N 10	04 55	05 22	05 45	21 03	21 46	22 28	23 09
0	05 13	05 39	06 02	20 51	21 37	22 22	23 07
S 10	05 29	05 55	06 18	20 39	21 28	22 16	23 05
20	05 45	06 12	06 36	20 26	21 18	22 10	23 03
30	06 00	06 30	06 56	20 11	21 07	22 03	23 01
35	06 08	06 39	07 07	20 03	21 01	22 00	23 00
40	06 17	06 50	07 21	19 53	20 54	21 55	22 58
45	06 26	07 03	07 36	19 41	20 45	21 50	22 57
S 50	06 37	07 18	07 56	19 27	20 35	21 44	22 54
52	06 42	07 25	08 05	19 20	20 30	21 41	22 54
54	06 47	07 32	08 15	19 13	20 25	21 38	22 52
56	06 53	07 41	08 27	19 05	20 19	21 34	22 51
58	06 59	07 50	08 40	18 56	20 12	21 30	22 50
S 60	07 05	08 01	08 56	18 45	20 05	21 26	22 49

Lat.	Sunset	Twilight Civil	Naut.	Moonset 9	10	11	12
N 72	☐	☐	☐	■	05 27	07 36	09 33
N 70	☐	☐	☐	03 54	06 01	07 54	09 41
68	☐	☐	☐	04 40	06 26	08 08	09 48
66	22 56	////	////	05 09	06 44	08 19	09 53
64	22 08	////	////	05 32	07 00	08 28	09 58
62	21 38	////	////	05 49	07 12	08 36	10 02
60	21 16	22 40	////	06 04	07 23	08 43	10 05
N 58	20 57	22 05	////	06 16	07 32	08 49	10 08
56	20 42	21 40	////	06 27	07 40	08 55	10 11
54	20 29	21 21	22 48	06 37	07 47	08 59	10 13
52	20 18	21 05	22 15	06 45	07 53	09 04	10 15
50	20 08	20 51	21 52	06 53	07 59	09 08	10 17
45	19 47	20 24	21 11	07 08	08 12	09 16	10 22
N 40	19 30	20 03	20 43	07 22	08 22	09 23	10 25
35	19 16	19 46	20 21	07 33	08 30	09 29	10 28
30	19 04	19 31	20 04	07 42	08 38	09 34	10 31
20	18 43	19 08	19 37	07 59	08 51	09 43	10 36
N 10	18 25	18 48	19 15	08 13	09 02	09 51	10 40
0	18 09	18 31	18 57	08 27	09 13	09 59	10 44
S 10	17 52	18 15	18 41	08 40	09 24	10 06	10 47
20	17 35	17 59	18 26	08 54	09 35	10 14	10 51
30	17 15	17 41	18 11	09 10	09 47	10 22	10 56
35	17 03	17 31	18 03	09 20	09 55	10 27	10 58
40	16 50	17 20	17 54	09 30	10 03	10 33	11 01
45	16 34	17 08	17 44	09 43	10 13	10 39	11 04
S 50	16 15	16 53	17 34	09 58	10 24	10 47	11 08
52	16 06	16 46	17 29	10 05	10 30	10 51	11 10
54	15 56	16 38	17 24	10 13	10 35	10 55	11 12
56	15 44	16 30	17 18	10 21	10 42	10 59	11 14
58	15 31	16 21	17 12	10 31	10 49	11 04	11 17
S 60	15 15	16 10	17 05	10 42	10 57	11 09	11 19

Day	SUN Eqn. of Time 00h	12h	Mer. Pass.	MOON Mer. Pass. Upper	Lower	Age	Phase
9	05 02	05 07	12 05	02 15	14 39	18	
10	05 11	05 15	12 05	03 02	15 25	19	
11	05 19	05 24	12 05	03 48	16 10	20	◐

1982 JULY 12, 13, 14 (MON., TUES., WED.)

G.M.T.	ARIES G.H.A.	VENUS −3.3 G.H.A.	VENUS Dec.	MARS +0.6 G.H.A.	MARS Dec.	JUPITER −1.7 G.H.A.	JUPITER Dec.	SATURN +1.0 G.H.A.	SATURN Dec.	STARS Name	S.H.A.	Dec.
12 00	289 33.7	210 46.8 N21	53.0	93 04.8 S 7	29.4	80 31.6 S10	37.3	93 54.3 S 3	59.1	Acamar	315 36.4	S40 22.3
01	304 36.2	225 46.1	53.3	108 06.1	29.9	95 33.9	37.4	108 56.7	59.1	Achernar	335 44.3	S57 19.3
02	319 38.6	240 45.4	53.7	123 07.4	30.4	110 36.3	37.4	123 59.1	59.2	Acrux	173 36.0	S63 00.3
03	334 41.1	255 44.6 ··	54.0	138 08.8 ··	30.9	125 38.7 ··	37.5	139 01.5 ··	59.2	Adhara	255 31.5	S28 56.8
04	349 43.6	270 43.9	54.3	153 10.1	31.4	140 41.0	37.5	154 03.8	59.3	Aldebaran	291 16.8	N16 28.4
05	4 46.0	285 43.2	54.7	168 11.5	31.9	155 43.4	37.6	169 06.2	59.3			
06	19 48.5	300 42.4 N21	55.0	183 12.8 S 7	32.4	170 45.8 S10	37.6	184 08.6 S 3	59.4	Alioth	166 41.4	N56 03.7
07	34 51.0	315 41.7	55.3	198 14.2	32.9	185 48.1	37.7	199 11.0	59.4	Alkaid	153 17.4	N49 24.4
08	49 53.4	330 40.9	55.6	213 15.5	33.4	200 50.5	37.7	214 13.4	59.5	Al Na'ir	28 12.9	S47 02.6
M 09	64 55.9	345 40.2 ··	56.0	228 16.9 ··	34.0	215 52.9 ··	37.8	229 15.7 ··	59.5	Alnilam	276 10.7	S 1 12.7
O 10	79 58.3	0 39.5	56.3	243 18.2	34.5	230 55.2	37.8	244 18.1	59.6	Alphard	218 19.6	S 8 34.9
N 11	95 00.8	15 38.7	56.6	258 19.5	35.0	245 57.6	37.9	259 20.5	59.6			
D 12	110 03.3	30 38.0 N21	56.9	273 20.9 S 7	35.5	261 00.0 S10	37.9	274 22.9 S 3	59.7	Alphecca	126 30.8	N26 46.6
A 13	125 05.7	45 37.2	57.3	288 22.2	36.0	276 02.3	38.0	289 25.2	59.7	Alpheratz	358 07.9	N28 59.4
Y 14	140 08.2	60 36.5	57.6	303 23.6	36.5	291 04.7	38.0	304 27.6	59.7	Altair	62 30.9	N 8 49.3
15	155 10.7	75 35.8 ··	57.9	318 24.9 ··	37.0	306 07.0 ··	38.1	319 30.0 ··	59.8	Ankaa	353 38.8	S42 23.9
16	170 13.1	90 35.0	58.2	333 26.2	37.5	321 09.4	38.1	334 32.4	59.8	Antares	112 55.0	S26 23.6
17	185 15.6	105 34.3	58.5	348 27.6	38.0	336 11.8	38.2	349 34.8	59.9			
18	200 18.1	120 33.5 N21	58.9	3 28.9 S 7	38.5	351 14.1 S10	38.2	4 37.1 S 3	59.9	Arcturus	146 17.2	N19 16.6
19	215 20.5	135 32.8	59.2	18 30.2	39.1	6 16.5	38.2	19 39.5	4 00.0	Atria	108 17.7	S68 59.9
20	230 23.0	150 32.1	59.5	33 31.6	39.6	21 18.9	38.3	34 41.9	00.0	Avior	234 28.4	S59 27.2
21	245 25.4	165 31.3 21	59.8	48 32.9 ··	40.1	36 21.2 ··	38.3	49 44.3 ··	00.1	Bellatrix	278 57.7	N 6 20.1
22	260 27.9	180 30.6 22	00.1	63 34.3	40.6	51 23.6	38.4	64 46.6	00.1	Betelgeuse	271 27.2	N 7 24.3
23	275 30.4	195 29.8	00.4	78 35.6	41.1	66 25.9	38.4	79 49.0	00.2			
13 00	290 32.8	210 29.1 N22	00.7	93 36.9 S 7	41.6	81 28.3 S10	38.5	94 51.4 S 4	00.2	Canopus	264 07.2	S52 41.1
01	305 35.3	225 28.3	01.0	108 38.3	42.1	96 30.7	38.5	109 53.8	00.3	Capella	281 09.8	N45 58.7
02	320 37.8	240 27.6	01.4	123 39.6	42.6	111 33.0	38.6	124 56.1	00.3	Deneb	49 47.2	N45 13.0
03	335 40.2	255 26.8 ··	01.7	138 40.9 ··	43.1	126 35.4 ··	38.6	139 58.5 ··	00.4	Denebola	182 57.9	N14 40.4
04	350 42.7	270 26.1	02.0	153 42.3	43.7	141 37.7	38.7	155 00.9	00.4	Diphda	349 19.5	S18 04.9
05	5 45.2	285 25.4	02.3	168 43.6	44.2	156 40.1	38.7	170 03.3	00.5			
06	20 47.6	300 24.6 N22	02.6	183 44.9 S 7	44.7	171 42.5 S10	38.8	185 05.6 S 4	00.5	Dubhe	194 20.9	N61 51.1
07	35 50.1	315 23.9	02.9	198 46.3	45.2	186 44.8	38.8	200 08.0	00.6	Elnath	278 42.9	N28 35.5
08	50 52.6	330 23.1	03.2	213 47.6	45.7	201 47.2	38.9	215 10.4	00.6	Eltanin	90 56.6	N51 29.6
T 09	65 55.0	345 22.4 ··	03.5	228 48.9 ··	46.2	216 49.5 ··	38.9	230 12.8 ··	00.7	Enif	34 10.1	N 9 47.6
U 10	80 57.5	0 21.6	03.8	243 50.3	46.7	231 51.9	39.0	245 15.1	00.7	Fomalhaut	15 49.8	S29 42.8
E 11	95 59.9	15 20.9	04.1	258 51.6	47.2	246 54.3	39.0	260 17.5	00.8			
S 12	111 02.4	30 20.1 N22	04.4	273 52.9 S 7	47.7	261 56.6 S10	39.1	275 19.9 S 4	00.8	Gacrux	172 27.5	S57 01.1
D 13	126 04.9	45 19.4	04.7	288 54.2	48.3	276 59.0	39.1	290 22.3	00.9	Gienah	176 16.8	S17 26.6
A 14	141 07.3	60 18.6	05.0	303 55.6	48.8	292 01.3	39.2	305 24.6	00.9	Hadar	149 21.5	S60 17.5
Y 15	156 09.8	75 17.9 ··	05.3	318 56.9 ··	49.3	307 03.7 ··	39.2	320 27.0 ··	00.9	Hamal	328 27.6	N23 22.6
16	171 12.3	90 17.1	05.6	333 58.2	49.8	322 06.0	39.3	335 29.4	01.0	Kaus Aust.	84 14.7	S34 23.6
17	186 14.7	105 16.4	05.9	348 59.6	50.3	337 08.4	39.4	350 31.7	01.0			
18	201 17.2	120 15.6 N22	06.2	4 00.9 S 7	50.8	352 10.8 S10	39.4	5 34.1 S 4	01.1	Kochab	137 18.5	N74 14.0
19	216 19.7	135 14.9	06.4	19 02.2	51.3	7 13.1	39.5	20 36.5	01.1	Markab	14 01.7	N15 06.5
20	231 22.1	150 14.1	06.7	34 03.5	51.8	22 15.5	39.5	35 38.9	01.2	Menkar	314 39.9	N 4 01.2
21	246 24.6	165 13.4 ··	07.0	49 04.9 ··	52.4	37 17.8 ··	39.6	50 41.2 ··	01.2	Menkent	148 35.4	S36 17.1
22	261 27.1	180 12.6	07.3	64 06.2	52.9	52 20.2	39.6	65 43.6	01.3	Miaplacidus	221 45.6	S69 38.8
23	276 29.5	195 11.9	07.6	79 07.5	53.4	67 22.5	39.7	80 46.0	01.3			
14 00	291 32.0	210 11.1 N22	07.9	94 08.8 S 7	53.9	82 24.9 S10	39.7	95 48.4 S 4	01.4	Mirfak	309 14.6	N49 47.7
01	306 34.4	225 10.4	08.2	109 10.2	54.4	97 27.2	39.8	110 50.7	01.4	Nunki	76 27.2	S26 19.1
02	321 36.9	240 09.6	08.5	124 11.5	54.9	112 29.6	39.8	125 53.1	01.5	Peacock	53 55.7	S56 47.5
03	336 39.4	255 08.9 ··	08.7	139 12.8 ··	55.4	127 32.0 ··	39.9	140 55.5 ··	01.5	Pollux	243 57.0	N28 04.2
04	351 41.8	270 08.1	09.0	154 14.1	56.0	142 34.3	39.9	155 57.8	01.6	Procyon	245 24.8	N 5 16.3
05	6 44.3	285 07.4	09.3	169 15.4	56.5	157 36.7	40.0	171 00.2	01.6			
06	21 46.8	300 06.6 N22	09.6	184 16.8 S 7	57.0	172 39.0 S10	40.0	186 02.6 S 4	01.7	Rasalhague	96 28.1	N12 34.4
07	36 49.2	315 05.8	09.9	199 18.1	57.5	187 41.4	40.1	201 05.0	01.7	Regulus	208 08.9	N12 03.4
W 08	51 51.7	330 05.1	10.1	214 19.4	58.0	202 43.7	40.1	216 07.3	01.8	Rigel	281 35.1	S 8 13.2
E 09	66 54.2	345 04.3 ··	10.4	229 20.7 ··	58.5	217 46.1 ··	40.2	231 09.7 ··	01.8	Rigil Kent.	140 23.9	S60 45.9
D 10	81 56.6	0 03.6	10.7	244 22.0	59.0	232 48.4	40.2	246 12.1	01.9	Sabik	102 39.4	S15 42.2
N 11	96 59.1	15 02.8	11.0	259 23.4	7 59.6	247 50.8	40.3	261 14.4	01.9			
E 12	112 01.5	30 02.1 N22	11.2	274 24.7 S 8	00.1	262 53.1 S10	40.3	276 16.8 S 4	02.0	Schedar	350 07.5	N56 26.1
S 13	127 04.0	45 01.3	11.5	289 26.0	00.6	277 55.5	40.4	291 19.2	02.0	Shaula	96 53.6	S37 05.5
D 14	142 06.5	60 00.6	11.8	304 27.3	01.1	292 57.8	40.4	306 21.5	02.1	Sirius	258 54.9	S16 41.5
A 15	157 08.9	74 59.8 ··	12.0	319 28.6 ··	01.6	308 00.2 ··	40.5	321 23.9 ··	02.1	Spica	158 56.2	S11 04.1
Y 16	172 11.4	89 59.0	12.3	334 29.9	02.1	323 02.5	40.6	336 26.3	02.2	Suhail	223 10.3	S43 21.7
17	187 13.9	104 58.3	12.6	349 31.3	02.6	338 04.9	40.6	351 28.7	02.2			
18	202 16.3	119 57.5 N22	12.9	4 32.6 S 8	03.2	353 07.2 S10	40.7	6 31.0 S 4	02.3	Vega	80 54.5	N38 46.1
19	217 18.8	134 56.8	13.1	19 33.9	03.7	8 09.6	40.7	21 33.4	02.3	Zuben'ubi	137 31.5	S15 58.1
20	232 21.3	149 56.0	13.4	34 35.2	04.2	23 11.9	40.8	36 35.8	02.4		S.H.A.	Mer. Pass.
21	247 23.7	164 55.3 ··	13.6	49 36.5 ··	04.7	38 14.3 ··	40.8	51 38.1 ··	02.4		° '	h m
22	262 26.2	179 54.5	13.9	64 37.8	05.2	53 16.6	40.9	66 40.5	02.5	Venus	279 56.2	9 59
23	277 28.7	194 53.7	14.2	79 39.1	05.7	68 19.0	40.9	81 42.9	02.5	Mars	163 04.1	17 44
	h m									Jupiter	150 55.5	18 31
Mer. Pass.	4 37.1	v −0.7	d 0.3	v 1.3	d 0.5	v 2.4	d 0.1	v 2.4	d 0.0	Saturn	164 18.5	17 38

1982 JULY 12, 13, 14 (MON., TUES., WED.)

SUN / MOON

G.M.T.		SUN G.H.A.	Dec.	MOON G.H.A.	v	Dec.	d	H.P.
12	00	178 38.1	N22 02.8	293 52.4	13.7	S 7 16.8	11.7	56.1
	01	193 38.0	02.5	308 25.1	13.7	7 05.1	11.8	56.2
	02	208 37.9	02.2	322 57.8	13.7	6 53.3	11.8	56.2
	03	223 37.8	·· 01.8	337 30.5	13.6	6 41.5	11.9	56.2
	04	238 37.8	01.5	352 03.1	13.7	6 29.6	11.9	56.2
	05	253 37.7	01.1	6 35.8	13.7	6 17.7	11.9	56.3
	06	268 37.6	N22 00.8	21 08.5	13.7	S 6 05.8	12.0	56.3
	07	283 37.5	00.4	35 41.2	13.7	5 53.8	12.0	56.3
M	08	298 37.4	22 00.1	50 13.9	13.6	5 41.8	12.1	56.4
O	09	313 37.4	21 59.8	64 46.5	13.7	5 29.7	12.1	56.4
N	10	328 37.3	59.4	79 19.2	13.6	5 17.6	12.1	56.4
D	11	343 37.2	59.1	93 51.8	13.7	5 05.5	12.2	56.4
A	12	358 37.1	N21 58.7	108 24.5	13.6	S 4 53.3	12.1	56.5
Y	13	13 37.0	58.4	122 57.1	13.6	4 41.2	12.3	56.5
	14	28 37.0	58.0	137 29.7	13.6	4 28.9	12.2	56.5
	15	43 36.9	·· 57.7	152 02.3	13.6	4 16.7	12.3	56.5
	16	58 36.8	57.3	166 34.9	13.6	4 04.4	12.3	56.6
	17	73 36.7	57.0	181 07.5	13.6	3 52.1	12.4	56.6
	18	88 36.6	N21 56.6	195 40.1	13.5	S 3 39.7	12.4	56.6
	19	103 36.6	56.3	210 12.6	13.5	3 27.3	12.4	56.7
	20	118 36.5	55.9	224 45.1	13.5	3 14.9	12.4	56.7
	21	133 36.4	·· 55.6	239 17.6	13.5	3 02.5	12.5	56.7
	22	148 36.3	55.2	253 50.1	13.5	2 50.0	12.4	56.8
	23	163 36.3	54.9	268 22.6	13.5	2 37.6	12.5	56.8
13	00	178 36.2	N21 54.5	282 55.1	13.4	S 2 25.1	12.6	56.8
	01	193 36.1	54.2	297 27.5	13.4	2 12.5	12.5	56.8
	02	208 36.0	53.8	311 59.9	13.4	2 00.0	12.6	56.9
	03	223 36.0	·· 53.4	326 32.3	13.3	1 47.4	12.6	56.9
	04	238 35.9	53.1	341 04.6	13.4	1 34.8	12.6	56.9
	05	253 35.8	52.7	355 37.0	13.3	1 22.2	12.7	57.0
	06	268 35.7	N21 52.4	10 09.3	13.3	S 1 09.5	12.6	57.0
T	07	283 35.6	52.0	24 41.6	13.2	0 56.9	12.7	57.0
U	08	298 35.6	51.7	39 13.8	13.2	0 44.2	12.7	57.1
E	09	313 35.5	·· 51.3	53 46.0	13.2	0 31.5	12.7	57.1
S	10	328 35.4	50.9	68 18.2	13.2	0 18.8	12.7	57.1
D	11	343 35.3	50.6	82 50.4	13.1	S 0 06.1	12.8	57.2
A	12	358 35.3	N21 50.2	97 22.5	13.1	N 0 06.7	12.7	57.2
Y	13	13 35.2	49.9	111 54.6	13.1	0 19.4	12.8	57.2
	14	28 35.1	49.5	126 26.7	13.0	0 32.2	12.8	57.3
	15	43 35.0	·· 49.1	140 58.7	13.0	0 45.0	12.8	57.3
	16	58 35.0	48.8	155 30.7	12.9	0 57.8	12.8	57.3
	17	73 34.9	48.4	170 02.6	12.9	1 10.6	12.8	57.4
	18	88 34.8	N21 48.0	184 34.5	12.9	N 1 23.4	12.8	57.4
	19	103 34.8	47.7	199 06.4	12.8	1 36.2	12.8	57.4
	20	118 34.7	47.3	213 38.2	12.8	1 49.0	12.8	57.4
	21	133 34.6	·· 46.9	228 10.0	12.8	2 01.8	12.9	57.5
	22	148 34.5	46.6	242 41.8	12.7	2 14.7	12.8	57.5
	23	163 34.5	46.2	257 13.5	12.6	2 27.5	12.8	57.5
14	00	178 34.4	N21 45.8	271 45.1	12.6	N 2 40.3	12.9	57.6
	01	193 34.3	45.4	286 16.7	12.6	2 53.2	12.8	57.6
	02	208 34.2	45.1	300 48.3	12.5	3 06.0	12.9	57.6
	03	223 34.2	·· 44.7	315 19.8	12.4	3 18.9	12.8	57.7
	04	238 34.1	44.3	329 51.2	12.5	3 31.7	12.8	57.7
	05	253 34.0	44.0	344 22.7	12.3	3 44.5	12.9	57.7
	06	268 34.0	N21 43.6	358 54.0	12.3	N 3 57.4	12.8	57.8
	07	283 33.9	43.2	13 25.3	12.3	4 10.2	12.8	57.8
W	08	298 33.8	42.8	27 56.6	12.2	4 23.0	12.9	57.9
E	09	313 33.8	·· 42.5	42 27.8	12.1	4 35.9	12.8	57.9
D	10	328 33.7	42.1	56 58.9	12.1	4 48.7	12.8	57.9
N	11	343 33.6	41.7	71 30.0	12.0	5 01.5	12.8	57.9
E	12	358 33.5	N21 41.3	86 01.0	12.0	N 5 14.3	12.7	58.0
S	13	13 33.5	41.0	100 32.0	11.9	5 27.0	12.8	58.0
D	14	28 33.4	40.6	115 02.9	11.9	5 39.8	12.8	58.1
A	15	43 33.3	·· 40.2	129 33.8	11.8	5 52.6	12.7	58.1
Y	16	58 33.3	39.8	144 04.6	11.7	6 05.3	12.7	58.1
	17	73 33.2	39.4	158 35.3	11.6	6 18.0	12.7	58.2
	18	88 33.1	N21 39.1	173 05.9	11.6	N 6 30.7	12.7	58.2
	19	103 33.1	38.7	187 36.5	11.6	6 43.4	12.7	58.2
	20	118 33.0	38.3	202 07.1	11.4	6 56.1	12.7	58.3
	21	133 32.9	·· 37.9	216 37.5	11.4	7 08.8	12.6	58.3
	22	148 32.9	37.5	231 07.9	11.4	7 21.4	12.6	58.3
	23	163 32.8	37.1	245 38.3	11.2	7 34.0	12.6	58.4
		S.D. 15.8	d 0.4	S.D. 15.4		15.6		15.8

Twilight, Sunrise, Moonrise

Lat.	Naut.	Civil	Sunrise	Moonrise 12	13	14	15
N 72	□	□	□	23 40	23 22	23 03	22 39
N 70	□	□	□	23 37	23 25	23 13	23 00
68	□	□	□	23 34	23 28	23 22	23 16
66	////	////	01 24	23 31	23 30	23 29	23 29
64	////	////	02 08	23 29	23 32	23 34	23 41
62	////	00 25	02 37	23 27	23 34	23 41	23 50
60	//// ·	01 37	02 59	23 26	23 35	23 46	23 59
N 58	////	02 10	03 17	23 24	23 37	23 50	24 06
56	00 24	02 34	03 31	23 23	23 38	23 54	24 12
54	01 29	02 53	03 44	23 22	23 39	23 57	24 18
52	02 00	03 09	03 55	23 21	23 40	24 00	00 00
50	02 22	03 22	04 05	23 20	23 41	24 03	00 03
45	03 02	03 49	04 25	23 18	23 43	24 09	00 09
N 40	03 30	04 10	04 42	23 16	23 44	24 14	00 14
35	03 51	04 27	04 56	23 15	23 46	24 19	00 19
30	04 08	04 41	05 08	23 13	23 47	24 23	00 23
20	04 35	05 04	05 28	23 11	23 49	24 29	00 29
N 10	04 56	05 23	05 46	23 09	23 51	24 36	00 36
0	05 14	05 40	06 02	23 07	23 53	24 41	00 41
S 10	05 30	05 56	06 18	23 05	23 55	24 47	00 47
20	05 44	06 12	06 35	23 03	23 57	24 53	00 53
30	05 59	06 29	06 55	23 01	24 00	00 00	01 01
35	06 07	06 39	07 06	23 00	24 01	00 01	01 05
40	06 16	06 49	07 19	22 58	24 03	00 03	01 10
45	06 25	07 02	07 35	22 57	24 05	00 05	01 15
S 50	06 35	07 16	07 54	22 54	24 07	00 07	01 22
52	06 40	07 23	08 02	22 54	24 08	00 08	01 25
54	06 45	07 30	08 12	22 52	24 09	00 09	01 28
56	06 50	07 38	08 24	22 51	24 10	00 10	01 32
58	06 56	07 47	08 37	22 50	24 12	00 12	01 36
S 60	07 03	07 58	08 52	22 49	24 13	00 13	01 41

Sunset, Twilight, Moonset

Lat.	Sunset	Civil	Naut.	Moonset 12	13	14	15
N 72	□	□	□	09 33	11 28	13 26	15 35
N 70	□	□	□	09 41	11 28	13 18	15 16
68	□	□	□	09 48	11 28	13 12	15 01
66	22 43	////	////	09 53	11 28	13 06	14 50
64	22 01	////	////	09 58	11 28	13 02	14 40
62	21 32	23 34	////	10 02	11 28	12 58	14 31
60	21 11	22 32	////	10 05	11 29	12 54	14 24
N 58	20 54	21 59	////	10 08	11 29	12 51	14 18
56	20 39	21 36	23 37	10 11	11 29	12 49	14 12
54	20 27	21 17	22 40	10 13	11 29	12 46	14 07
52	20 16	21 02	22 10	10 15	11 29	12 44	14 03
50	20 06	20 48	21 48	10 17	11 29	12 42	13 59
45	19 46	20 22	21 09	10 22	11 29	12 38	13 50
N 40	19 29	20 01	20 41	10 25	11 29	12 34	13 42
35	19 15	19 44	20 20	10 28	11 29	12 31	13 36
30	19 03	19 30	20 03	10 31	11 29	12 29	13 31
20	18 43	19 07	19 36	10 36	11 29	12 24	13 21
N 10	18 26	18 48	19 15	10 40	11 29	12 20	13 13
0	18 09	18 32	18 57	10 44	11 29	12 16	13 05
S 10	17 53	18 16	18 42	10 47	11 29	12 12	12 58
20	17 36	18 00	18 27	10 51	11 29	12 08	12 49
30	17 17	17 42	18 12	10 56	11 29	12 03	12 40
35	17 05	17 33	18 04	10 58	11 29	12 01	12 35
40	16 52	17 22	17 56	11 01	11 29	11 58	12 29
45	16 37	17 10	17 47	11 04	11 29	11 54	12 21
S 50	16 18	16 55	17 36	11 08	11 29	11 50	12 13
52	16 09	16 49	17 32	11 10	11 29	11 48	12 09
54	15 59	16 41	17 27	11 12	11 29	11 46	12 05
56	15 48	16 33	17 21	11 14	11 29	11 44	12 00
58	15 35	16 24	17 15	11 17	11 29	11 41	11 55
S 60	15 20	16 14	17 09	11 19	11 29	11 38	11 49

SUN / MOON

Day	SUN Eqn. of Time 00h	12h	Mer. Pass.	MOON Mer. Pass. Upper	Lower	Age	Phase
	m s	m s	h m	h m	h m	d	
12	05 28	05 31	12 06	04 33	16 55	21	
13	05 35	05 39	12 06	05 18	17 41	22	
14	05 42	05 46	12 06	06 05	18 29	23	◑

1982 JULY 15, 16, 17 (THURS., FRI., SAT.)

G.M.T.	ARIES G.H.A.	VENUS −3.3 G.H.A.	VENUS Dec.	MARS +0.6 G.H.A.	MARS Dec.	JUPITER −1.7 G.H.A.	JUPITER Dec.	SATURN +1.0 G.H.A.	SATURN Dec.	STARS Name	S.H.A.	Dec.
15 00	292 31.1	209 53.0	N22 14.4	94 40.5	S 8 06.2	83 21.3	S10 41.0	96 45.2	S 4 02.6	Acamar	315 36.4	S40 22.3
01	307 33.6	224 52.2	14.7	109 41.8	06.8	98 23.7	41.0	111 47.6	02.6	Achernar	335 44.3	S57 19.3
02	322 36.0	239 51.5	15.0	124 43.1	07.3	113 26.0	41.1	126 50.0	02.7	Acrux	173 36.1	S63 00.3
03	337 38.5	254 50.7 ··	15.2	139 44.4 ··	07.8	128 28.4 ··	41.1	141 52.3 ··	02.7	Adhara	255 31.5	S28 56.8
04	352 41.0	269 49.9	15.5	154 45.7	08.3	143 30.7	41.2	156 54.7	02.8	Aldebaran	291 16.8	N16 28.4
05	7 43.4	284 49.2	15.7	169 47.0	08.8	158 33.0	41.3	171 57.1	02.8			
06	22 45.9	299 48.4	N22 16.0	184 48.3	S 8 09.3	173 35.4	S10 41.3	186 59.4	S 4 02.9	Alioth	166 41.4	N56 03.7
07	37 48.4	314 47.7	16.2	199 49.6	09.9	188 37.7	41.4	202 01.8	02.9	Alkaid	153 17.4	N49 24.4
T 08	52 50.8	329 46.9	16.5	214 50.9	10.4	203 40.1	41.4	217 04.2	03.0	Al Na'ir	28 12.9	S47 02.7
H 09	67 53.3	344 46.1 ··	16.7	229 52.3 ··	10.9	218 42.4 ··	41.5	232 06.5 ··	03.0	Alnilam	276 10.7	S 1 12.7
U 10	82 55.8	359 45.4	17.0	244 53.6	11.4	233 44.8	41.5	247 08.9	03.1	Alphard	218 19.6	S 8 34.9
R 11	97 58.2	14 44.6	17.2	259 54.9	11.9	248 47.1	41.6	262 11.3	03.2			
S 12	113 00.7	29 43.9	N22 17.5	274 56.2	S 8 12.4	263 49.5	S10 41.6	277 13.6	S 4 03.2	Alphecca	126 30.8	N26 46.6
D 13	128 03.2	44 43.1	17.7	289 57.5	13.0	278 51.8	41.7	292 16.0	03.3	Alpheratz	358 07.9	N28 59.4
A 14	143 05.6	59 42.3	18.0	304 58.8	13.5	293 54.2	41.8	307 18.4	03.3	Altair	62 30.9	N 8 49.3
Y 15	158 08.1	74 41.6 ··	18.2	320 00.1 ··	14.0	308 56.5 ··	41.8	322 20.7 ··	03.4	Ankaa	353 38.8	S42 23.9
16	173 10.5	89 40.8	18.5	335 01.4	14.5	323 58.8	41.9	337 23.1	03.4	Antares	112 55.0	S26 23.6
17	188 13.0	104 40.0	18.7	350 02.7	15.0	339 01.2	41.9	352 25.5	03.5			
18	203 15.5	119 39.3	N22 18.9	5 04.0	S 8 15.5	354 03.5	S10 42.0	7 27.8	S 4 03.5	Arcturus	146 17.2	N19 16.6
19	218 17.9	134 38.5	19.2	20 05.3	16.1	9 05.9	42.0	22 30.2	03.6	Atria	108 17.7	S69 00.0
20	233 20.4	149 37.7	19.4	35 06.6	16.6	24 08.2	42.1	37 32.6	03.6	Avior	234 28.4	S59 27.2
21	248 22.9	164 37.0 ··	19.7	50 07.9 ··	17.1	39 10.6 ··	42.1	52 34.9 ··	03.7	Bellatrix	278 57.7	N 6 20.1
22	263 25.3	179 36.2	19.9	65 09.2	17.6	54 12.9	42.2	67 37.3	03.7	Betelgeuse	271 27.2	N 7 24.3
23	278 27.8	194 35.4	20.1	80 10.5	18.1	69 15.2	42.3	82 39.7	03.8			
16 00	293 30.3	209 34.7	N22 20.4	95 11.8	S 8 18.6	84 17.6	S10 42.3	97 42.0	S 4 03.8	Canopus	264 07.2	S52 41.1
01	308 32.7	224 33.9	20.6	110 13.1	19.2	99 19.9	42.4	112 44.4	03.9	Capella	281 09.8	N45 58.7
02	323 35.2	239 33.1	20.8	125 14.4 ·	19.7	114 22.3	42.4	127 46.8	03.9	Deneb	49 47.2	N45 13.0
03	338 37.6	254 32.4 ··	21.1	140 15.7 ··	20.2	129 24.6 ··	42.5	142 49.1 ··	04.0	Denebola	182 57.9	N14 40.4
04	353 40.1	269 31.6	21.3	155 17.0	20.7	144 26.9	42.5	157 51.5	04.0	Diphda	349 19.5	S18 04.9
05	8 42.6	284 30.8	21.5	170 18.3	21.2	159 29.3	42.6	172 53.9	04.1			
06	23 45.0	299 30.1	N22 21.8	185 19.6	S 8 21.8	174 31.6	S10 42.7	187 56.2	S 4 04.1	Dubhe	194 20.9	N61 51.1
07	38 47.5	314 29.3	22.0	200 20.9	22.3	189 34.0	42.7	202 58.6	04.2	Elnath	278 42.8	N28 35.5
08	53 50.0	329 28.5	22.2	215 22.2	22.8	204 36.3	42.8	218 00.9	04.2	Eltanin	90 56.6	N51 29.6
F 09	68 52.4	344 27.8 ··	22.4	230 23.5 ··	23.3	219 38.6 ··	42.8	233 03.3 ··	04.3	Enif	34 10.0	N 9 47.6
R 10	83 54.9	359 27.0	22.7	245 24.8	23.8	234 41.0	42.9	248 05.7	04.3	Fomalhaut	15 49.7	S29 42.8
I 11	98 57.4	14 26.2	22.9	260 26.1	24.3	249 43.3	42.9	263 08.0	04.4			
D 12	113 59.8	29 25.5	N22 23.1	275 27.4	S 8 24.9	264 45.6	S10 43.0	278 10.4	S 4 04.5	Gacrux	172 27.5	S57 01.1
A 13	129 02.3	44 24.7	23.3	290 28.7	25.4	279 48.0	43.1	293 12.8	04.5	Gienah	176 16.8	S17 26.6
Y 14	144 04.8	59 23.9	23.6	305 30.0	25.9	294 50.3	43.1	308 15.1	04.6	Hadar	149 21.5	S60 17.5
15	159 07.2	74 23.2 ··	23.8	320 31.3 ··	26.4	309 52.7 ··	43.2	323 17.5 ··	04.6	Hamal	328 27.5	N23 22.6
16	174 09.7	89 22.4	24.0	335 32.6	26.9	324 55.0	43.2	338 19.9	04.7	Kaus Aust.	84 14.7	S34 23.6
17	189 12.1	104 21.6	24.2	350 33.9	27.5	339 57.3	43.3	353 22.2	04.7			
18	204 14.6	119 20.9	N22 24.4	5 35.2	S 8 28.0	354 59.7	S10 43.4	8 24.6	S 4 04.8	Kochab	137 18.5	N74 14.0
19	219 17.1	134 20.1	24.6	20 36.5	28.5	10 02.0	43.4	23 26.9	04.8	Markab	14 01.7	N15 06.6
20	234 19.5	149 19.3	24.9	35 37.8	29.0	25 04.3	43.5	38 29.3	04.9	Menkar	314 39.9	N 4 01.2
21	249 22.0	164 18.5 ··	25.1	50 39.1 ··	29.5	40 06.7 ··	43.5	53 31.7 ··	04.9	Menkent	148 35.5	S36 17.1
22	264 24.5	179 17.8	25.3	65 40.3	30.1	55 09.0	43.6	68 34.0	05.0	Miaplacidus	221 45.6	S69 38.8
23	279 26.9	194 17.0	25.5	80 41.6	30.6	70 11.3	43.6	83 36.4	05.0			
17 00	294 29.4	209 16.2	N22 25.7	95 42.9	S 8 31.1	85 13.7	S10 43.7	98 38.7	S 4 05.1	Mirfak	309 14.5	N49 47.7
01	309 31.9	224 15.4	25.9	110 44.2	31.6	100 16.0	43.8	113 41.1	05.1	Nunki	76 27.2	S26 19.1
02	324 34.3	239 14.7	26.1	125 45.5	32.1	115 18.3	43.8	128 43.5	05.2	Peacock	53 55.7	S56 47.5
03	339 36.8	254 13.9 ··	26.3	140 46.8 ··	32.6	130 20.7 ··	43.9	143 45.8 ··	05.3	Pollux	243 57.0	N28 04.2
04	354 39.3	269 13.1	26.5	155 48.1	33.2	145 23.0	43.9	158 48.2	05.3	Procyon	245 24.8	N 5 16.3
05	9 41.7	284 12.4	26.7	170 49.4	33.7	160 25.3	44.0	173 50.6	05.4			
06	24 44.2	299 11.6	N22 26.9	185 50.7	S 8 34.2	175 27.7	S10 44.1	188 52.9	S 4 05.4	Rasalhague	96 28.1	N12 34.5
07	39 46.6	314 10.8	27.1	200 52.0	34.7	190 30.0	44.1	203 55.3	05.5	Regulus	208 08.9	N12 03.4
S 08	54 49.1	329 10.0	27.3	215 53.2	35.2	205 32.3	44.2	218 57.6	05.5	Rigel	281 35.1	S 8 13.2
A 09	69 51.6	344 09.3 ··	27.5	230 54.5 ··	35.8	220 34.7 ··	44.2	234 00.0 ··	05.6	Rigil Kent.	140 23.9	S60 45.9
T 10	84 54.0	359 08.5	27.7	245 55.8	36.3	235 37.0	44.3	249 02.4	05.6	Sabik	102 39.4	S15 42.2
U 11	99 56.5	14 07.7	27.9	260 57.1	36.8	250 39.3	44.4	264 04.7	05.7			
R 12	114 59.0	29 06.9	N22 28.1	275 58.4	S 8 37.3	265 41.7	S10 44.4	279 07.1	S 4 05.7	Schedar	350 07.5	N56 26.2
D 13	130 01.4	44 06.2	28.3	290 59.7	37.9	280 44.0	44.5	294 09.4	05.8	Shaula	96 53.6	S37 05.5
A 14	145 03.9	59 05.4	28.5	306 00.9	38.4	295 46.3	44.5	309 11.8	05.8	Sirius	258 54.9	S16 41.5
Y 15	160 06.4	74 04.6 ··	28.7	321 02.2 ··	38.9	310 48.7 ··	44.6	324 14.1 ··	05.9	Spica	158 56.2	S11 04.1
16	175 08.8	89 03.8	28.9	336 03.5	39.4	325 51.0	44.6	339 16.5	06.0	Suhail	223 10.3	S43 21.7
17	190 11.3	104 03.1	29.1	351 04.8	39.9	340 53.3	44.7	354 18.9	06.0			
18	205 13.8	119 02.3	N22 29.3	6 06.1	S 8 40.5	355 55.6	S10 44.8	9 21.2	S 4 06.1	Vega	80 54.5	N38 46.1
19	220 16.2	134 01.5	29.5	21 07.4	41.0	10 58.0	44.8	24 23.6	06.1	Zuben'ubi	137 31.5	S15 58.1
20	235 18.7	149 00.7	29.7	36 08.6	41.5	26 00.3	44.9	39 25.9	06.2			
21	250 21.1	163 59.9 ··	29.9	51 09.9 ··	42.0	41 02.6 ··	45.0	54 28.3 ··	06.2		S.H.A.	Mer. Pass.
22	265 23.6	178 59.2	30.0	66 11.2	42.5	56 05.0	45.0	69 30.7	06.3	Venus	276 04.4	10 02
23	280 26.1	193 58.4	30.2	81 12.5	43.1	71 07.3	45.1	84 33.0	06.3	Mars	161 41.6	17 38
										Jupiter	150 47.3	18 20
Mer. Pass.	4 25.3	v −0.8	d 0.2	v 1.3	d 0.5	v 2.3	d 0.1	v 2.4	d 0.1	Saturn	164 11.8	17 26

1982 JULY 15, 16, 17 (THURS., FRI., SAT.)

SUN / MOON

G.M.T.	SUN G.H.A.	SUN Dec.	MOON G.H.A.	v	MOON Dec.	d	H.P.
15 00	178 32.7	N21 36.8	260 08.5	11.2	N 7 46.6	12.5	58.4
01	193 32.7	36.4	274 38.7	11.1	7 59.1	12.6	58.4
02	208 32.6	36.0	289 08.8	11.0	8 11.7	12.5	58.5
03	223 32.5 ··	35.6	303 38.8	11.0	8 24.2	12.4	58.5
04	238 32.5	35.2	318 08.8	10.9	8 36.6	12.5	58.5
05	253 32.4	34.8	332 38.7	10.8	8 49.1	12.4	58.6
06	268 32.3	N21 34.4	347 08.5	10.7	N 9 01.5	12.4	58.6
07	283 32.3	34.0	1 38.2	10.7	9 13.9	12.3	58.6
T 08	298 32.2	33.6	16 07.9	10.6	9 26.2	12.3	58.7
H 09	313 32.1 ··	33.3	30 37.5	10.5	9 38.5	12.3	58.7
U 10	328 32.1	32.9	45 07.0	10.4	9 50.8	12.2	58.7
R 11	343 32.0	32.5	59 36.4	10.3	10 03.0	12.3	58.7
S 12	358 31.9	N21 32.1	74 05.7	10.3	N10 15.2	12.2	58.8
D 13	13 31.9	31.7	88 35.0	10.1	10 27.4	12.1	58.8
A 14	28 31.8	31.3	103 04.1	10.1	10 39.5	12.0	58.9
Y 15	43 31.7 ··	30.9	117 33.2	10.0	10 51.5	12.1	58.9
16	58 31.7	30.5	132 02.2	9.9	11 03.6	11.9	59.0
17	73 31.6	30.1	146 31.1	9.9	11 15.5	12.0	59.0
18	88 31.5	N21 29.7	161 00.0	9.7	N11 27.5	11.8	59.0
19	103 31.5	29.3	175 28.7	9.7	11 39.3	11.9	59.1
20	118 31.4	28.9	189 57.4	9.5	11 51.2	11.7	59.1
21	133 31.3 ··	28.5	204 25.9	9.5	12 02.9	11.7	59.1
22	148 31.3	28.1	218 54.4	9.4	12 14.6	11.7	59.2
23	163 31.2	27.7	233 22.8	9.3	12 26.3	11.6	59.2
16 00	178 31.2	N21 27.3	247 51.1	9.2	N12 37.9	11.5	59.2
01	193 31.1	26.9	262 19.3	9.1	12 49.4	11.5	59.3
02	208 31.0	26.5	276 47.4	9.0	13 00.9	11.4	59.3
03	223 31.0 ··	26.1	291 15.4	8.9	13 12.3	11.4	59.3
04	238 30.9	25.7	305 43.3	8.8	13 23.7	11.3	59.4
05	253 30.9	25.3	320 11.1	8.7	13 35.0	11.2	59.4
06	268 30.8	N21 24.9	334 38.8	8.7	N13 46.2	11.2	59.4
07	283 30.7	24.5	349 06.5	8.5	13 57.4	11.1	59.5
08	298 30.7	24.1	3 34.0	8.4	14 08.5	11.0	59.5
F 09	313 30.6 ··	23.7	18 01.4	8.4	14 19.5	10.9	59.5
R 10	328 30.5	23.3	32 28.8	8.2	14 30.4	10.9	59.6
I 11	343 30.5	22.9	46 56.0	8.1	14 41.3	10.8	59.6
D 12	358 30.4	N21 22.5	61 23.1	8.1	N14 52.1	10.7	59.6
A 13	13 30.4	22.0	75 50.2	7.9	15 02.8	10.6	59.6
Y 14	28 30.3	21.6	90 17.1	7.9	15 13.4	10.5	59.7
15	43 30.3 ··	21.2	104 44.0	7.7	15 23.9	10.5	59.7
16	58 30.2	20.8	119 10.7	7.7	15 34.4	10.4	59.7
17	73 30.1	20.4	133 37.4	7.5	15 44.8	10.3	59.8
18	88 30.1	N21 20.0	148 03.9	7.5	N15 55.1	10.2	59.8
19	103 30.0	19.6	162 30.4	7.3	16 05.3	10.1	59.8
20	118 30.0	19.2	176 56.7	7.2	16 15.4	10.0	59.9
21	133 29.9 ··	18.8	191 22.9	7.2	16 25.4	10.0	59.9
22	148 29.8	18.3	205 49.1	7.0	16 35.4	9.8	59.9
23	163 29.8	17.9	220 15.1	7.0	16 45.2	9.8	60.0
17 00	178 29.7	N21 17.5	234 41.1	6.8	N16 55.0	9.6	60.0
01	193 29.7	17.1	249 06.9	6.7	17 04.6	9.5	60.0
02	208 29.6	16.7	263 32.6	6.7	17 14.1	9.5	60.0
03	223 29.6 ··	16.3	277 58.3	6.5	17 23.6	9.3	60.1
04	238 29.5	15.8	292 23.8	6.5	17 32.9	9.3	60.1
05	253 29.4	15.4	306 49.3	6.3	17 42.2	9.1	60.1
06	268 29.4	N21 15.0	321 14.6	6.2	N17 51.3	9.0	60.2
07	283 29.3	14.6	335 39.8	6.2	18 00.3	8.9	60.2
S 08	298 29.3	14.2	350 05.0	6.0	18 09.2	8.8	60.2
A 09	313 29.2 ··	13.7	4 30.0	5.9	18 18.0	8.7	60.2
T 10	328 29.2	13.3	18 54.9	5.9	18 26.7	8.6	60.3
U 11	343 29.1	12.9	33 19.8	5.7	18 35.3	8.4	60.3
R 12	358 29.1	N21 12.5	47 44.5	5.7	N18 43.7	8.3	60.3
D 13	13 29.0	12.1	62 09.2	5.5	18 52.0	8.2	60.3
A 14	28 28.9	11.6	76 33.7	5.4	19 00.2	8.1	60.4
Y 15	43 28.9 ··	11.2	90 58.1	5.4	19 08.3	8.0	60.4
16	58 28.8	10.8	105 22.5	5.3	19 16.3	7.8	60.4
17	73 28.8	10.3	119 46.8	5.1	19 24.1	7.8	60.4
18	88 28.7	N21 09.9	134 10.9	5.1	N19 31.9	7.6	60.5
19	103 28.7	09.5	148 35.0	5.0	19 39.5	7.4	60.5
20	118 28.6	09.1	162 59.0	4.8	19 46.9	7.3	60.5
21	133 28.6 ··	08.6	177 22.8	4.8	19 54.2	7.2	60.5
22	148 28.5	08.2	191 46.6	4.7	20 01.4	7.1	60.6
23	163 28.5	07.8	206 10.3	4.7	20 08.5	6.9	60.6
	S.D. 15.8	d 0.4	S.D. 16.0		16.2		16.4

Twilight / Sunrise / Moonrise

Lat.	Naut.	Civil	Sunrise	Moonrise 15	16	17	18
N 72	□	⊔	⊔	22 39	21 56	⊔	⊔
N 70	□	⊔	⊔	23 00	22 40	21 44	□
68	□	□	□	23 16	23 09	22 59	□
66	////	////	01 38	23 29	23 31	23 37	23 54
64	////	////	02 17	23 41	23 49	24 04	00 04
62	////	00 54	02 44	23 50	24 03	00 03	00 24
60	////	01 47	03 05	23 59	24 16	00 16	00 42
N 58	////	02 17	03 21	24 06	00 06	00 27	00 56
56	00 50	02 40	03 36	24 12	00 12	00 36	01 08
54	01 38	02 58	03 48	24 18	00 18	00 44	01 19
52	02 06	03 13	03 59	00 00	00 23	00 52	01 29
50	02 27	03 26	04 08	00 03	00 28	00 59	01 37
45	03 05	03 52	04 28	00 09	00 39	01 13	01 56
N 40	03 32	04 12	04 44	00 14	00 47	01 25	02 11
35	03 53	04 29	04 58	00 19	00 55	01 36	02 24
30	04 10	04 42	05 09	00 23	01 01	01 45	02 35
20	04 36	05 05	05 29	00 29	01 13	02 01	02 54
N 10	04 57	05 24	05 46	00 36	01 23	02 14	03 11
0	05 14	05 40	06 02	00 41	01 32	02 28	03 27
S 10	05 30	05 56	06 18	00 47	01 42	02 41	03 43
20	05 44	06 11	06 35	00 53	01 53	02 55	04 00
30	05 59	06 28	06 54	01 01	02 04	03 11	04 20
35	06 06	06 38	07 05	01 05	02 11	03 21	04 31
40	06 15	06 48	07 18	01 10	02 19	03 32	04 45
45	06 23	07 00	07 33	01 15	02 29	03 44	05 00
S 50	06 33	07 14	07 51	01 22	02 40	04 00	05 20
52	06 38	07 20	08 00	01 25	02 45	04 08	05 29
54	06 43	07 28	08 09	01 28	02 51	04 16	05 40
56	06 48	07 35	08 20	01 32	02 57	04 25	05 51
58	06 54	07 44	08 33	01 36	03 05	04 36	06 05
S 60	07 00	07 54	08 47	01 41	03 13	04 48	06 21

Sunset / Twilight / Moonset

Lat.	Sunset	Civil	Naut.	Moonset 15	16	17	18
N 72	□	□	□	15 35	18 10	□	□
N 70	□	□	□	15 16	17 28	20 25	□
68	□	□	□	15 01	17 00	19 11	□
66	22 30	////	////	14 50	16 39	18 34	20 27
64	21 53	////	////	14 40	16 22	18 08	19 48
62	21 26	23 12	////	14 31	16 09	17 48	19 21
60	21 06	22 23	////	14 24	15 57	17 31	19 00
N 58	20 49	21 53	////	14 18	15 47	17 18	18 43
56	20 35	21 31	23 17	14 12	15 38	17 06	18 29
54	20 23	21 13	22 32	14 07	15 31	16 55	18 16
52	20 13	20 58	22 04	14 03	15 24	16 46	18 05
50	20 03	20 45	21 43	13 59	15 18	16 38	17 55
45	19 43	20 19	21 06	13 50	15 04	16 20	17 35
N 40	19 27	19 59	20 39	13 42	14 53	16 06	17 18
35	19 14	19 43	20 18	13 36	14 44	15 54	17 04
30	19 02	19 29	20 02	13 31	14 36	15 44	16 52
20	18 43	19 07	19 35	13 21	14 22	15 25	16 31
N 10	18 25	18 48	19 15	13 13	14 10	15 10	16 13
0	18 10	18 32	18 58	13 05	13 58	14 55	15 56
S 10	17 54	18 16	18 42	12 58	13 47	14 41	15 40
20	17 37	18 01	18 28	12 49	13 35	14 25	15 22
30	17 18	17 44	18 13	12 40	13 21	14 07	15 01
35	17 07	17 35	18 06	12 35	13 13	13 57	14 49
40	16 54	17 24	17 58	12 29	13 04	13 45	14 35
45	16 39	17 12	17 49	12 21	12 53	13 31	14 18
S 50	16 21	16 58	17 39	12 13	12 40	13 14	13 58
52	16 13	16 52	17 34	12 09	12 35	13 07	13 49
54	16 03	16 45	17 30	12 05	12 28	12 58	13 38
56	15 52	16 37	17 25	12 00	12 21	12 48	13 26
58	15 40	16 28	17 19	11 55	12 13	12 37	13 12
S 60	15 25	16 18	17 13	11 49	12 04	12 24	12 55

SUN / MOON

Day	Eqn. of Time 00h	12h	Mer. Pass.	Mer. Pass. Upper	Lower	Age	Phase
	m s	m s	h m	h m	h m	d	
15	05 49	05 52	12 06	06 53	19 19	24	
16	05 55	05 58	12 06	07 45	20 13	25	◑
17	06 01	06 04	12 06	08 41	21 11	26	

1982 JULY 18, 19, 20 (SUN., MON., TUES.)

G.M.T.	ARIES G.H.A.	VENUS −3.3 G.H.A. Dec.	MARS +0.6 G.H.A. Dec.	JUPITER −1.7 G.H.A. Dec.	SATURN +1.0 G.H.A. Dec.	STARS Name S.H.A. Dec.
18 00	295 28.5	208 57.6 N22 30.4	96 13.8 S 8 43.6	86 09.6 S10 45.1	99 35.4 S 4 06.4	Acamar 315 36.4 S40 22.3
01	310 31.0	223 56.8 30.6	111 15.0 44.1	101 11.9 45.2	114 37.7 06.5	Achernar 335 44.2 S57 19.3
02	325 33.5	238 56.1 30.8	126 16.3 44.6	116 14.3 45.3	129 40.1 06.5	Acrux 173 36.1 S63 00.3
03	340 35.9	253 55.3 ·· 31.0	141 17.6 ·· 45.1	131 16.6 ·· 45.3	144 42.4 ·· 06.6	Adhara 255 31.5 S28 56.8
04	355 38.4	268 54.5 31.1	156 18.9 45.7	146 18.9 45.4	159 44.8 06.6	Aldebaran 291 16.8 N16 28.4
05	10 40.9	283 53.7 31.3	171 20.2 46.2	161 21.2 45.5	174 47.2 06.7	
06	25 43.3	298 52.9 N22 31.5	186 21.4 S 8 46.7	176 23.6 S10 45.5	189 49.5 S 4 06.7	Alioth 166 41.4 N56 03.7
07	40 45.8	313 52.2 31.7	201 22.7 47.2	191 25.9 45.6	204 51.9 06.8	Alkaid 153 17.4 N49 24.4
08	55 48.2	328 51.4 31.8	216 24.0 47.8	206 28.2 45.6	219 54.2 06.8	Al Na'ir 28 12.9 S47 02.7
S 09	70 50.7	343 50.6 ·· 32.0	231 25.3 ·· 48.3	221 30.6 ·· 45.7	234 56.6 ·· 06.9	Alnilam 276 10.6 S 1 12.7
U 10	85 53.2	358 49.8 32.2	246 26.5 48.8	236 32.9 45.8	249 58.9 06.9	Alphard 218 19.6 S 8 34.9
N 11	100 55.6	13 49.0 32.4	261 27.8 49.3	251 35.2 45.8	265 01.3 07.0	
D 12	115 58.1	28 48.3 N22 32.5	276 29.1 S 8 49.8	266 37.5 S10 45.9	280 03.7 S 4 07.1	Alphecca 126 30.8 N26 46.6
A 13	131 00.6	43 47.5 32.7	291 30.4 50.4	281 39.9 46.0	295 06.0 07.1	Alpheratz 358 07.8 N28 59.4
Y 14	146 03.0	58 46.7 32.9	306 31.6 50.9	296 42.2 46.0	310 08.4 07.2	Altair 62 30.9 N 8 49.3
15	161 05.5	73 45.9 ·· 33.0	321 32.9 ·· 51.4	311 44.5 ·· 46.1	325 10.7 ·· 07.2	Ankaa 353 38.8 S42 23.9
16	176 08.0	88 45.1 33.2	336 34.2 51.9	326 46.8 46.1	340 13.1 07.3	Antares 112 55.0 S26 23.6
17	191 10.4	103 44.4 33.4	351 35.5 52.5	341 49.1 46.2	355 15.4 07.3	
18	206 12.9	118 43.6 N22 33.5	6 36.7 S 8 53.0	356 51.5 S10 46.3	10 17.8 S 4 07.4	Arcturus 146 17.2 N19 16.6
19	221 15.4	133 42.8 33.7	21 38.0 53.5	11 53.8 46.3	25 20.1 07.4	Atria 108 17.7 S69 00.0
20	236 17.8	148 42.0 33.9	36 39.3 54.0	26 56.1 46.4	40 22.5 07.5	Avior 234 28.4 S59 27.2
21	251 20.3	163 41.2 ·· 34.0	51 40.5 ·· 54.5	41 58.4 ·· 46.5	55 24.9 ·· 07.6	Bellatrix 278 57.6 N 6 20.1
22	266 22.7	178 40.4 34.2	66 41.8 55.1	57 00.8 46.5	70 27.2 07.6	Betelgeuse 271 27.2 N 7 24.3
23	281 25.2	193 39.7 34.3	81 43.1 55.6	72 03.1 46.6	85 29.6 07.7	
19 00	296 27.7	208 38.9 N22 34.5	96 44.3 S 8 56.1	87 05.4 S10 46.6	100 31.9 S 4 07.7	Canopus 264 07.2 S52 41.0
01	311 30.1	223 38.1 34.7	111 45.6 56.6	102 07.7 46.7	115 34.3 07.8	Capella 281 09.8 N45 58.7
02	326 32.6	238 37.3 34.8	126 46.9 57.2	117 10.0 46.8	130 36.6 07.8	Deneb 49 47.1 N45 13.0
03	341 35.1	253 36.5 ·· 35.0	141 48.2 ·· 57.7	132 12.4 ·· 46.8	145 39.0 ·· 07.9	Denebola 182 57.9 N14 40.4
04	356 37.5	268 35.7 35.1	156 49.4 58.2	147 14.7 46.9	160 41.3 08.0	Diphda 349 19.5 S18 04.9
05	11 40.0	283 35.0 35.3	171 50.7 58.7	162 17.0 47.0	175 43.7 08.0	
06	26 42.5	298 34.2 N22 35.4	186 52.0 S 8 59.3	177 19.3 S10 47.0	190 46.0 S 4 08.1	Dubhe 194 20.9 N61 51.1
07	41 44.9	313 33.4 35.6	201 53.2 8 59.8	192 21.6 47.1	205 48.4 08.1	Elnath 278 42.8 N28 35.5
08	56 47.4	328 32.6 35.7	216 54.5 9 00.3	207 24.0 47.2	220 50.7 08.2	Eltanin 90 56.6 N51 29.6
M 09	71 49.9	343 31.8 ·· 35.9	231 55.7 ·· 00.8	222 26.3 ·· 47.2	235 53.1 ·· 08.2	Enif 34 10.0 N 9 47.6
O 10	86 52.3	358 31.0 36.0	246 57.0 01.4	237 28.6 47.3	250 55.5 08.3	Fomalhaut 15 49.7 S29 42.8
N 11	101 54.8	13 30.2 36.2	261 58.3 01.9	252 30.9 47.4	265 57.8 08.4	
D 12	116 57.2	28 29.5 N22 36.3	276 59.5 S 9 02.4	267 33.2 S10 47.4	281 00.2 S 4 08.4	Gacrux 172 27.5 S57 01.1
A 13	131 59.7	43 28.7 36.4	292 00.8 02.9	282 35.5 47.5	296 02.5 08.5	Gienah 176 16.8 S17 26.6
Y 14	147 02.2	58 27.9 36.6	307 02.1 03.4	297 37.9 47.6	311 04.9 08.5	Hadar 149 21.5 S60 17.5
15	162 04.6	73 27.1 ·· 36.7	322 03.3 ·· 04.0	312 40.2 ·· 47.6	326 07.2 ·· 08.6	Hamal 328 27.5 N23 22.6
16	177 07.1	88 26.3 36.9	337 04.6 04.5	327 42.5 47.7	341 09.6 08.6	Kaus Aust. 84 14.7 S34 23.6
17	192 09.6	103 25.5 37.0	352 05.9 05.0	342 44.8 47.7	356 11.9 08.7	
18	207 12.0	118 24.7 N22 37.1	7 07.1 S 9 05.5	357 47.1 S10 47.8	11 14.3 S 4 08.8	Kochab 137 18.6 N74 14.0
19	222 14.5	133 24.0 37.3	22 08.4 06.1	12 49.4 47.9	26 16.6 08.8	Markab 14 01.7 N15 06.6
20	237 17.0	148 23.2 37.4	37 09.6 06.6	27 51.8 47.9	41 19.0 08.9	Menkar 314 39.9 N 4 01.3
21	252 19.4	163 22.4 ·· 37.6	52 10.9 ·· 07.1	42 54.1 ·· 48.0	56 21.3 ·· 08.9	Menkent 148 35.5 S36 17.1
22	267 21.9	178 21.6 37.7	67 12.2 07.6	57 56.4 48.1	71 23.7 09.0	Miaplacidus 221 45.6 S69 38.8
23	282 24.3	193 20.8 37.8	82 13.4 08.2	72 58.7 48.1	86 26.0 09.0	
20 00	297 26.8	208 20.0 N22 38.0	97 14.7 S 9 08.7	88 01.0 S10 48.2	101 28.4 S 4 09.1	Mirfak 309 14.5 N49 47.7
01	312 29.3	223 19.2 38.1	112 15.9 09.2	103 03.3 48.3	116 30.7 09.2	Nunki 76 27.2 S26 19.1
02	327 31.7	238 18.4 38.2	127 17.2 09.7	118 05.6 48.3	131 33.1 09.2	Peacock 53 55.7 S56 47.5
03	342 34.2	253 17.7 ·· 38.3	142 18.4 ·· 10.3	133 08.0 ·· 48.4	146 35.4 ·· 09.3	Pollux 243 57.0 N28 04.2
04	357 36.7	268 16.9 38.5	157 19.7 10.8	148 10.3 48.5	161 37.8 09.3	Procyon 245 24.8 N 5 16.3
05	12 39.1	283 16.1 38.6	172 21.0 11.3	163 12.6 48.5	176 40.1 09.4	
06	27 41.6	298 15.3 N22 38.7	187 22.2 S 9 11.8	178 14.9 S10 48.6	191 42.5 S 4 09.4	Rasalhague 96 28.1 N12 34.5
07	42 44.1	313 14.5 38.8	202 23.5 12.4	193 17.2 48.7	206 44.8 09.5	Regulus 208 08.9 N12 03.4
08	57 46.5	328 13.7 39.0	217 24.7 12.9	208 19.5 48.7	221 47.2 09.6	Rigel 281 35.0 S 8 13.2
T 09	72 49.0	343 12.9 ·· 39.1	232 26.0 ·· 13.4	223 21.8 ·· 48.8	236 49.5 ·· 09.6	Rigil Kent. 140 23.9 S60 45.9
U 10	87 51.5	358 12.1 39.2	247 27.2 13.9	238 24.2 48.9	251 51.9 09.7	Sabik 102 39.4 S15 42.2
E 11	102 53.9	13 11.3 39.3	262 28.5 14.5	253 26.5 48.9	266 54.2 09.7	
S 12	117 56.4	28 10.5 N22 39.4	277 29.7 S 9 15.0	268 28.8 S10 49.0	281 56.6 S 4 09.8	Schedar 350 07.4 N56 26.2
D 13	132 58.8	43 09.8 39.6	292 31.0 15.5	283 31.1 49.1	296 58.9 09.8	Shaula 96 53.6 S37 05.5
A 14	148 01.3	58 09.0 39.7	307 32.2 16.0	298 33.4 49.1	312 01.3 09.9	Sirius 258 54.9 S16 41.5
Y 15	163 03.8	73 08.2 ·· 39.8	322 33.5 ·· 16.6	313 35.7 ·· 49.2	327 03.6 ·· 10.0	Spica 158 56.2 S11 04.1
16	178 06.2	88 07.4 39.9	337 34.7 17.1	328 38.0 49.3	342 06.0 10.0	Suhail 223 10.3 S43 21.7
17	193 08.7	103 06.6 40.0	352 36.0 17.6	343 40.3 49.3	357 08.3 10.1	
18	208 11.2	118 05.8 N22 40.1	7 37.2 S 9 18.2	358 42.6 S10 49.4	12 10.7 S 4 10.1	Vega 80 54.5 N38 46.1
19	223 13.6	133 05.0 40.2	22 38.5 18.7	13 44.9 49.5	27 13.0 10.2	Zuben'ubi 137 31.5 S15 58.1
20	238 16.1	148 04.2 40.3	37 39.7 19.2	28 47.3 49.5	42 15.4 10.3	
21	253 18.6	163 03.4 ·· 40.5	52 41.0 ·· 19.7	43 49.6 ·· 49.6	57 17.7 ·· 10.3	
22	268 21.0	178 02.6 40.6	67 42.2 20.3	58 51.9 49.7	72 20.1 10.4	
23	283 23.5	193 01.8 40.7	82 43.5 20.8	73 54.2 49.7	87 22.4 10.4	

	S.H.A.	Mer. Pass.
Venus	272 11.2	10 06
Mars	160 16.7	17 32
Jupiter	150 37.7	18 09
Saturn	164 04.2	17 15

Mer. Pass.	ARIES	VENUS	MARS	JUPITER	SATURN
4 13.5 (h m)	v −0.8 d 0.1	v 1.3 d 0.5	v 2.3 d 0.1	v 2.4 d 0.1	

1982 JULY 18, 19, 20 (SUN., MON., TUES.)

G.M.T.	SUN G.H.A.	SUN Dec.	MOON G.H.A.	v	MOON Dec.	d	H.P.
18 00	178 28.4	N21 07.3	220 34.0	4.5	N20 15.4	6.8	60.6
01	193 28.4	06.9	234 57.5	4.4	20 22.2	6.6	60.6
02	208 28.3	06.5	249 20.9	4.4	20 28.8	6.5	60.7
03	223 28.3 ··	06.1	263 44.3	4.3	20 35.3	6.4	60.7
04	238 28.2	05.6	278 07.6	4.1	20 41.7	6.2	60.7
05	253 28.2	05.2	292 30.7	4.1	20 47.9	6.1	60.7
06	268 28.1	N21 04.8	306 53.8	4.1	N20 54.0	5.9	60.7
07	283 28.1	04.3	321 16.9	3.9	20 59.9	5.8	60.8
S 08	298 28.0	03.9	335 39.8	3.9	21 05.7	5.6	60.8
U 09	313 28.0 ··	03.4	350 02.7	3.8	21 11.3	5.5	60.8
N 10	328 27.9	03.0	4 25.5	3.7	21 16.8	5.4	60.8
D 11	343 27.9	02.6	18 48.2	3.6	21 22.2	5.1	60.8
A 12	358 27.8	N21 02.1	33 10.8	3.6	N21 27.3	5.1	60.8
Y 13	13 27.8	01.7	47 33.4	3.5	21 32.4	4.8	60.9
14	28 27.7	01.3	61 55.9	3.5	21 37.2	4.7	60.9
15	43 27.7 ··	00.8	76 18.4	3.3	21 41.9	4.6	60.9
16	58 27.6	21 00.4	90 40.7	3.3	21 46.5	4.4	60.9
17	73 27.6	20 59.9	105 03.0	3.3	21 50.9	4.2	60.9
18	88 27.5	N20 59.5	119 25.3	3.2	N21 55.1	4.1	60.9
19	103 27.5	59.0	133 47.5	3.1	21 59.2	3.9	60.9
20	118 27.4	58.6	148 09.6	3.1	22 03.1	3.7	61.0
21	133 27.4 ··	58.2	162 31.7	3.0	22 06.8	3.6	61.0
22	148 27.3	57.7	176 53.7	3.0	22 10.4	3.4	61.0
23	163 27.3	57.3	191 15.7	2.9	22 13.8	3.3	61.0
19 00	178 27.2	N20 56.8	205 37.6	2.8	N22 17.1	3.1	61.0
01	193 27.2	56.4	219 59.4	2.9	22 20.2	2.9	61.0
02	208 27.1	55.9	234 21.3	2.7	22 23.1	2.7	61.0
03	223 27.1 ··	55.5	248 43.0	2.8	22 25.8	2.6	61.0
04	238 27.1	55.0	263 04.8	2.7	22 28.4	2.4	61.0
05	253 27.0	54.6	277 26.5	2.6	22 30.8	2.3	61.1
06	268 27.0	N20 54.1	291 48.1	2.7	N22 33.1	2.0	61.1
07	283 26.9	53.7	306 09.8	2.6	22 35.1	1.9	61.1
08	298 26.9	53.2	320 31.4	2.5	22 37.0	1.8	61.1
M 09	313 26.8 ··	52.8	334 52.9	2.6	22 38.8	1.5	61.1
O 10	328 26.8	52.3	349 14.5	2.5	22 40.3	1.4	61.1
N 11	343 26.7	51.9	3 36.0	2.5	22 41.7	1.2	61.1
D 12	358 26.7	N20 51.4	17 57.5	2.5	N22 42.9	1.0	61.1
A 13	13 26.7	51.0	32 19.0	2.4	22 43.9	0.9	61.1
Y 14	28 26.6	50.5	46 40.4	2.5	22 44.8	0.7	61.1
15	43 26.6 ··	50.1	61 01.9	2.4	22 45.5	0.5	61.1
16	58 26.5	49.6	75 23.3	2.4	22 46.0	0.3	61.1
17	73 26.5	49.2	89 44.7	2.4	22 46.3	0.2	61.1
18	88 26.4	N20 48.7	104 06.1	2.5	N22 46.5	0.0	61.1
19	103 26.4	48.2	118 27.6	2.4	22 46.5	0.2	61.1
20	118 26.4	47.8	132 49.0	2.4	22 46.3	0.4	61.1
21	133 26.3 ··	47.3	147 10.4	2.4	22 45.9	0.5	61.1
22	148 26.3	46.9	161 31.8	2.4	22 45.4	0.8	61.1
23	163 26.2	46.4	175 53.2	2.4	22 44.6	0.8	61.1
20 00	178 26.2	N20 46.0	190 14.6	2.5	N22 43.8	1.1	61.1
01	193 26.2	45.5	204 36.1	2.4	22 42.7	1.3	61.1
02	208 26.1	45.0	218 57.5	2.5	22 41.4	1.4	61.1
03	223 26.1 ··	44.6	233 19.0	2.5	22 40.0	1.6	61.1
04	238 26.0	44.1	247 40.5	2.5	22 38.4	1.7	61.1
05	253 26.0	43.6	262 02.0	2.5	22 36.7	2.0	61.1
06	268 26.0	N20 43.2	276 23.5	2.6	N22 34.7	2.1	61.1
07	283 25.9	42.7	290 45.1	2.6	22 32.6	2.2	61.1
08	298 25.9	42.2	305 06.7	2.6	22 30.4	2.5	61.1
T 09	313 25.8 ··	41.8	319 28.3	2.6	22 27.9	2.6	61.1
U 10	328 25.8	41.3	333 49.9	2.7	22 25.3	2.8	61.1
E 11	343 25.8	40.9	348 11.6	2.7	22 22.5	3.0	61.1
S 12	358 25.7	N20 40.4	2 33.3	2.8	N22 19.5	3.1	61.1
D 13	13 25.7	39.9	16 55.1	2.8	22 16.4	3.3	61.1
A 14	28 25.7	39.4	31 16.9	2.8	22 13.1	3.5	61.0
Y 15	43 25.6 ··	39.0	45 38.7	2.9	22 09.6	3.6	61.0
16	58 25.6	38.5	60 00.6	2.9	22 06.0	3.8	61.0
17	73 25.5	38.0	74 22.5	3.0	N22 02.2	4.0	61.0
18	88 25.5	N20 37.6					
19	103 25.5	37.1					
20	118 25.4	36.6					
21	133 25.4 ··	36.2					
22	148 25.4	35.7					
23	163 25.3	35.2					
	S.D. 15.8	d 0.5	S.D. 16.6		16.6		16.6

A Partial Eclipse of the Sun occurs on this date. See page 5.

Lat.	Twilight Naut.	Twilight Civil	Sunrise	Moonrise 18	19	20	21
N 72	□	□	□	□	□	□	□
N 70	□	□	□	□	□	□	□
68	////	////	00 41	□	□	□	01 28
66	////	////	01 51	23 54	24 46	00 46	02 25
64	////	////	02 26	00 04	00 33	01 30	02 59
62	////	01 13	02 51	00 24	01 00	01 59	03 23
60	////	01 57	03 11	00 42	01 21	02 22	03 43
N 58	////	02 25	03 27	00 56	01 39	02 40	03 59
56	01 07	02 46	03 40	01 08	01 54	02 55	04 12
54	01 47	03 03	03 52	01 19	02 06	03 08	04 24
52	02 13	03 18	04 02	01 29	02 17	03 20	04 35
50	02 33	03 30	04 12	01 37	02 27	03 30	04 44
45	03 09	03 55	04 31	01 56	02 48	03 51	05 03
N 40	03 35	04 15	04 46	02 11	03 05	04 09	05 19
35	03 56	04 31	05 00	02 24	03 20	04 23	05 32
30	04 12	04 44	05 11	02 35	03 32	04 36	05 44
20	04 38	05 06	05 30	02 54	03 54	04 58	06 04
N 10	04 58	05 24	05 47	03 11	04 12	05 17	06 21
0	05 15	05 41	06 03	03 27	04 30	05 34	06 37
S 10	05 30	05 56	06 18	03 43	04 47	05 52	06 54
20	05 44	06 11	06 34	04 00	05 06	06 11	07 11
30	05 58	06 27	06 53	04 20	05 28	06 32	07 30
35	06 05	06 36	07 04	04 31	05 40	06 45	07 42
40	06 13	06 46	07 16	04 45	05 55	07 00	07 55
45	06 22	06 58	07 31	05 00	06 13	07 17	08 11
S 50	06 31	07 11	07 48	05 20	06 34	07 38	08 30
52	06 35	07 18	07 57	05 29	06 45	07 49	08 39
54	06 40	07 24	08 06	05 40	06 56	08 00	08 49
56	06 45	07 32	08 16	05 51	07 10	08 13	09 00
58	06 50	07 40	08 28	06 05	07 25	08 29	09 13
S 60	06 56	07 50	08 42	06 21	07 44	08 47	09 28

Lat.	Sunset	Twilight Civil	Twilight Naut.	Moonset 18	19	20	21
N 72	□	□	□	□	□	□	□
N 70	□	□	□	□	□	□	23 51
68	23 21	////	////	□	□	23 22	23 06
66	22 18	////	////	20 27	21 50	22 24	22 36
64	21 44	////	////	19 48	21 06	21 50	22 13
62	21 21	22 55	////	19 21	20 36	21 25	21 54
60	21 00	22 13	////	19 00	20 14	21 06	21 39
N 58	20 45	21 46	////	18 43	19 55	20 49	21 26
56	20 31	21 25	23 01	18 29	19 40	20 35	21 15
54	20 19	21 08	22 23	18 16	19 27	20 23	21 05
52	20 09	20 54	21 58	18 05	19 15	20 12	20 56
50	20 00	20 41	21 38	17 55	19 05	20 03	20 48
45	19 41	20 16	21 02	17 35	18 44	19 43	20 31
N 40	19 26	19 57	20 36	17 18	18 26	19 26	20 17
35	19 12	19 41	20 16	17 04	18 11	19 12	20 06
30	19 01	19 28	20 00	16 52	17 59	19 00	19 55
20	18 42	19 06	19 34	16 31	17 37	18 40	19 37
N 10	18 25	18 48	19 14	16 13	17 18	18 21	19 21
0	18 10	18 32	18 58	15 56	17 00	18 04	19 06
S 10	17 54	18 17	18 43	15 40	16 43	17 47	18 52
20	17 38	18 02	18 32	15 22	16 23	17 29	18 35
30	17 20	17 46	18 15	15 01	16 02	17 08	18 17
35	17 09	17 36	18 07	14 49	15 49	16 55	18 06
40	16 57	17 26	18 00	14 35	15 34	16 41	17 54
45	16 42	17 15	17 51	14 18	15 16	16 24	17 39
S 50	16 25	17 01	17 42	13 58	14 54	16 03	17 21
52	16 16	16 55	17 37	13 49	14 44	15 53	17 12
54	16 07	16 48	17 33	13 38	14 32	15 42	17 02
56	15 57	16 41	17 28	13 26	14 19	15 29	16 52
58	15 45	16 33	17 23	13 12	14 03	15 14	16 39
S 60	15 31	16 23	17 17	12 55	13 44	14 56	16 24

Day	SUN Eqn. of Time 00h	12h	Mer. Pass.	MOON Mer. Pass. Upper	Lower	Age	Phase
	m s	m s	h m	h m	h m	d	
18	06 06	06 09	12 06	09 42	22 13	27	
19	06 11	06 13	12 06	10 45	23 17	28	●
20	06 15	06 17	12 06	11 49	24 21	29	

1982 JULY 21, 22, 23 (WED., THURS., FRI.)

G.M.T.	ARIES G.H.A.	VENUS −3.3 G.H.A.	Dec.	MARS +0.7 G.H.A.	Dec.	JUPITER −1.6 G.H.A.	Dec.	SATURN +1.0 G.H.A.	Dec.	STARS Name	S.H.A.	Dec.
21 00	298 26.0	208 01.1 N22	40.8	97 44.7 S 9	21.3	88 56.5 S10	49.8	102 24.8 S 4	10.5	Acamar	315 36.3	S40 22.3
01	313 28.4	223 00.3	40.9	112 46.0	21.8	103 58.8	49.9	117 27.1	10.6	Achernar	335 44.2	S57 19.3
02	328 30.9	237 59.5	41.0	127 47.2	22.4	119 01.1	50.0	132 29.5	10.6	Acrux	173 36.1	S63 00.3
03	343 33.3	252 58.7 ··	41.1	142 48.5 ··	22.9	134 03.4 ··	50.0	147 31.8 ··	10.7	Adhara	255 31.5	S28 56.8
04	358 35.8	267 57.9	41.2	157 49.7	23.4	149 05.7	50.1	162 34.1	10.7	Aldebaran	291 16.7	N16 28.4
05	13 38.3	282 57.1	41.3	172 51.0	23.9	164 08.0	50.2	177 36.5	10.8			
06	28 40.7	297 56.3 N22	41.4	187 52.2 S 9	24.5	179 10.3 S10	50.2	192 38.8 S 4	10.8	Alioth	166 41.4	N56 03.7
W 07	43 43.2	312 55.5	41.5	202 53.5	25.0	194 12.6	50.3	207 41.2	10.9	Alkaid	153 17.4	N49 24.4
E 08	58 45.7	327 54.7	41.6	217 54.7	25.5	209 14.9	50.4	222 43.5	11.0	Al Na'ir	28 12.8	S47 02.7
D 09	73 48.1	342 53.9 ··	41.7	232 55.9 ··	26.0	224 17.2 ··	50.4	237 45.9 ··	11.0	Alnilam	276 10.6	S 1 12.7
N 10	88 50.6	357 53.1	41.8	247 57.2	26.6	239 19.6	50.5	252 48.2	11.1	Alphard	218 19.6	S 8 34.8
E 11	103 53.1	12 52.3	41.9	262 58.4	27.1	254 21.9	50.5	267 50.6	11.1			
S 12	118 55.5	27 51.5 N22	41.9	277 59.7 S 9	27.6	269 24.2 S10	50.6	282 52.9 S 4	11.2	Alphecca	126 30.8	N26 46.7
D 13	133 58.0	42 50.7	42.0	293 00.9	28.2	284 26.5	50.7	297 55.3	11.3	Alpheratz	358 07.8	N28 59.5
A 14	149 00.4	57 49.9	42.1	308 02.2	28.7	299 28.8	50.8	312 57.6	11.3	Altair	62 30.9	N 8 49.3
Y 15	164 02.9	72 49.1 ··	42.2	323 03.4 ··	29.2	314 31.1 ··	50.8	328 00.0 ··	11.4	Ankaa	353 38.7	S42 23.9
16	179 05.4	87 48.4	42.3	338 04.6	29.7	329 33.4	50.9	343 02.3	11.4	Antares	112 55.0	S26 23.6
17	194 07.8	102 47.6	42.4	353 05.9	30.3	344 35.7	51.0	358 04.6	11.5			
18	209 10.3	117 46.8 N22	42.5	8 07.1 S 9	30.8	359 38.0 S10	51.1	13 07.0 S 4	11.6	Arcturus	146 17.2	N19 16.6
19	224 12.8	132 46.0	42.6	23 08.4	31.3	14 40.3	51.1	28 09.3	11.6	Atria	108 17.7	S69 00.0
20	239 15.2	147 45.2	42.6	38 09.6	31.8	29 42.6	51.2	43 11.7	11.7	Avior	234 28.4	S59 27.2
21	254 17.7	162 44.4 ··	42.7	53 10.8 ··	32.4	44 44.9 ··	51.3	58 14.0 ··	11.7	Bellatrix	278 57.6	N 6 20.1
22	269 20.2	177 43.6	42.8	68 12.1	32.9	59 47.2	51.3	73 16.4	11.8	Betelgeuse	271 27.2	N 7 24.3
23	284 22.6	192 42.8	42.9	83 13.3	33.4	74 49.5	51.4	88 18.7	11.9			
22 00	299 25.1	207 42.0 N22	43.0	98 14.6 S 9	34.0	89 51.8 S10	51.5	103 21.1 S 4	11.9	Canopus	264 07.1	S52 41.0
01	314 27.6	222 41.2	43.0	113 15.8	34.5	104 54.1	51.5	118 23.4	12.0	Capella	281 09.7	N45 58.7
02	329 30.0	237 40.4	43.1	128 17.0	35.0	119 56.4	51.6	133 25.7	12.0	Deneb	49 47.1	N45 13.0
03	344 32.5	252 39.6 ··	43.2	143 18.3 ··	35.5	134 58.7 ··	51.7	148 28.1 ··	12.1	Denebola	182 57.9	N14 40.4
04	359 34.9	267 38.8	43.3	158 19.5	36.1	150 01.0	51.8	163 30.4	12.2	Diphda	349 19.4	S18 04.9
05	14 37.4	282 38.0	43.3	173 20.7	36.6	165 03.3	51.8	178 32.8	12.2			
06	29 39.9	297 37.2 N22	43.4	188 22.0 S 9	37.1	180 05.6 S10	51.9	193 35.1 S 4	12.3	Dubhe	194 20.9	N61 51.1
T 07	44 42.3	312 36.4	43.5	203 23.2	37.6	195 07.9	52.0	208 37.5	12.3	Elnath	278 42.8	N28 35.5
H 08	59 44.8	327 35.6	43.5	218 24.4	38.2	210 10.2	52.0	223 39.8	12.4	Eltanin	90 56.7	N51 29.6
U 09	74 47.3	342 34.8 ··	43.6	233 25.7 ··	38.7	225 12.5 ··	52.1	238 42.1 ··	12.5	Enif	34 10.0	N 9 47.6
R 10	89 49.7	357 34.0	43.7	248 26.9	39.2	240 14.8	52.2	253 44.5	12.5	Fomalhaut	15 49.7	S29 42.8
S 11	104 52.2	12 33.2	43.7	263 28.1	39.8	255 17.1	52.3	268 46.8	12.6			
D 12	119 54.7	27 32.4 N22	43.8	278 29.4 S 9	40.3	270 19.4 S10	52.3	283 49.2 S 4	12.7	Gacrux	172 27.6	S57 01.1
A 13	134 57.1	42 31.6	43.9	293 30.6	40.8	285 21.7	52.4	298 51.5	12.7	Gienah	176 16.8	S17 26.6
Y 14	149 59.6	57 30.8	43.9	308 31.8	41.3	300 24.0	52.5	313 53.9	12.8	Hadar	149 21.5	S60 17.5
15	165 02.1	72 30.0 ··	44.0	323 33.1 ··	41.9	315 26.3 ··	52.5	328 56.2 ··	12.8	Hamal	328 27.5	N23 22.7
16	180 04.5	87 29.2	44.1	338 34.3	42.4	330 28.6	52.6	343 58.5	12.9	Kaus Aust.	84 14.7	S34 23.6
17	195 07.0	102 28.4	44.1	353 35.5	42.9	345 30.9	52.7	359 00.9	13.0			
18	210 09.4	117 27.6 N22	44.2	8 36.8 S 9	43.5	0 33.2 S10	52.8	14 03.2 S 4	13.0	Kochab	137 18.6	N74 14.0
19	225 11.9	132 26.8	44.2	23 38.0	44.0	15 35.5	52.8	29 05.6	13.1	Markab	14 01.6	N15 06.6
20	240 14.4	147 26.0	44.3	38 39.2	44.5	30 37.8	52.9	44 07.9	13.1	Menkar	314 39.9	N 4 01.3
21	255 16.8	162 25.2 ··	44.3	53 40.4 ··	45.0	45 40.1 ··	53.0	59 10.3 ··	13.2	Menkent	148 35.5	S36 17.1
22	270 19.3	177 24.4	44.4	68 41.7	45.6	60 42.4	53.1	74 12.6	13.3	Miaplacidus	221 45.6	S69 38.7
23	285 21.8	192 23.6	44.5	83 42.9	46.1	75 44.7	53.1	89 14.9	13.3			
23 00	300 24.2	207 22.8 N22	44.5	98 44.1 S 9	46.6	90 47.0 S10	53.2	104 17.3 S 4	13.4	Mirfak	309 14.5	N49 47.7
01	315 26.7	222 22.0	44.6	113 45.3	47.2	105 49.2	53.3	119 19.6	13.4	Nunki	76 27.2	S26 19.1
02	330 29.2	237 21.2	44.6	128 46.6	47.7	120 51.5	53.3	134 22.0	13.5	Peacock	53 55.7	S56 47.5
03	345 31.6	252 20.4 ··	44.7	143 47.8 ··	48.2	135 53.8 ··	53.4	149 24.3 ··	13.6	Pollux	243 56.9	N28 04.2
04	0 34.1	267 19.6	44.7	158 49.0	48.7	150 56.1	53.5	164 26.6	13.6	Procyon	245 24.8	N 5 16.3
05	15 36.5	282 18.8	44.7	173 50.2	49.3	165 58.4	53.6	179 29.0	13.7			
06	30 39.0	297 18.0 N22	44.8	188 51.5 S 9	49.8	181 00.7 S10	53.6	194 31.3 S 4	13.8	Rasalhague	96 28.1	N12 34.5
07	45 41.5	312 17.2	44.8	203 52.7	50.3	196 03.0	53.7	209 33.7	13.8	Regulus	208 08.9	N12 03.4
08	60 43.9	327 16.4	44.9	218 53.9	50.9	211 05.3	53.8	224 36.0	13.9	Rigel	281 35.0	S 8 13.2
F 09	75 46.4	342 15.6 ··	44.9	233 55.1 ··	51.4	226 07.6 ··	53.9	239 38.3 ··	13.9	Rigil Kent.	140 24.0	S60 45.9
R 10	90 48.9	357 14.8	45.0	248 56.4	51.9	241 09.9	53.9	254 40.7	14.0	Sabik	102 39.4	S15 42.2
I 11	105 51.3	12 14.0	45.0	263 57.6	52.5	256 12.2	54.0	269 43.0	14.1			
D 12	120 53.8	27 13.2 N22	45.0	278 58.8 S 9	53.0	271 14.5 S10	54.1	284 45.4 S 4	14.1	Schedar	350 07.4	N56 26.2
A 13	135 56.3	42 12.4	45.1	294 00.0	53.5	286 16.8	54.1	299 47.7	14.2	Shaula	96 53.6	S37 05.5
Y 14	150 58.7	57 11.6	45.1	309 01.3	54.0	301 19.1	54.2	314 50.0	14.3	Sirius	258 54.9	S16 41.4
15	166 01.2	72 10.8 ··	45.1	324 02.5 ··	54.6	316 21.3 ··	54.3	329 52.4 ··	14.3	Spica	158 56.2	S11 04.1
16	181 03.7	87 10.0	45.2	339 03.7	55.1	331 23.6	54.4	344 54.7	14.4	Suhail	223 10.3	S43 21.7
17	196 06.1	102 09.2	45.2	354 04.9	55.6	346 25.9	54.4	359 57.0	14.4			
18	211 08.6	117 08.4 N22	45.2	9 06.1 S 9	56.2	1 28.2 S10	54.5	14 59.4 S 4	14.5	Vega	80 54.5	N38 46.1
19	226 11.0	132 07.6	45.3	24 07.3	56.7	16 30.5	54.6	30 01.7	14.6	Zuben'ubi	137 31.5	S15 58.1
20	241 13.5	147 06.8	45.3	39 08.6	57.2	31 32.8	54.7	45 04.1	14.6			
21	256 16.0	162 06.0 ··	45.3	54 09.8 ··	57.8	46 35.1 ··	54.7	60 06.4 ··	14.7		S.H.A.	Mer. Pass.
22	271 18.4	177 05.2	45.4	69 11.0	58.3	61 37.4	54.8	75 08.7	14.8	Venus	268 16.9	10 10
23	286 20.9	192 04.4	45.4	84 12.2	58.8	76 39.7	54.9	90 11.1	14.8	Mars	158 49.5	17 26
Mer. Pass.	h m 4 01.7	v 0.8	d 0.1	v 1.2	d 0.5	v 2.3	d 0.1	v 2.3	d 0.1	Jupiter	150 26.7	17 58
										Saturn	163 56.0	17 04

1982 JULY 21, 22, 23 (WED., THURS., FRI.)

G.M.T.	SUN G.H.A.	SUN Dec.	MOON G.H.A.	v	MOON Dec.	d	H.P.
21 00	178 25.3	N20 34.7	174 57.7	3.4	N21 31.1	5.1	60.9
01	193 25.3	34.3	189 20.1	3.5	21 26.0	5.3	60.9
02	208 25.2	33.8	203 42.6	3.5	21 20.7	5.4	60.9
03	223 25.2 ··	33.3	218 05.1	3.6	21 15.3	5.5	60.9
04	238 25.2	32.8	232 27.7	3.7	21 09.8	5.7	60.9
05	253 25.1	32.3	246 50.4	3.8	21 04.1	5.9	60.9
W 06	268 25.1	N20 31.9	261 13.2	3.8	N20 58.2	6.0	60.8
E 07	283 25.1	31.4	275 36.0	3.9	20 52.2	6.1	60.8
D 08	298 25.0	30.9	289 58.9	4.0	20 46.1	6.3	60.8
N 09	313 25.0 ··	30.4	304 21.9	4.1	20 39.8	6.5	60.8
E 10	328 25.0	30.0	318 45.0	4.1	20 33.3	6.6	60.8
S 11	343 24.9	29.5	333 08.1	4.3	20 26.7	6.7	60.7
D 12	358 24.9	N20 29.0	347 31.4	4.3	N20 20.0	6.9	60.7
A 13	13 24.9	28.5	1 54.7	4.4	20 13.1	7.0	60.7
Y 14	28 24.8	28.0	16 18.1	4.5	20 06.1	7.1	60.7
15	43 24.8 ··	27.5	30 41.6	4.6	19 59.0	7.3	60.7
16	58 24.8	27.1	45 05.2	4.6	19 51.7	7.4	60.6
17	73 24.7	26.6	59 28.8	4.8	19 44.3	7.6	60.6
18	88 24.7	N20 26.1	73 52.6	4.8	N19 36.7	7.7	60.6
19	103 24.7	25.6	88 16.4	5.0	19 29.0	7.8	60.6
20	118 24.6	25.1	102 40.4	5.0	19 21.2	7.9	60.6
21	133 24.6 ··	24.6	117 04.4	5.2	19 13.3	8.1	60.5
22	148 24.6	24.1	131 28.6	5.2	19 05.2	8.2	60.5
23	163 24.6	23.6	145 52.8	5.3	18 57.0	8.3	60.5
22 00	178 24.5	N20 23.2	160 17.1	5.5	N18 48.7	8.4	60.5
01	193 24.5	22.7	174 41.6	5.5	18 40.3	8.6	60.4
02	208 24.5	22.2	189 06.1	5.6	18 31.7	8.7	60.4
03	223 24.4 ··	21.7	203 30.7	5.7	18 23.0	8.8	60.4
04	238 24.4	21.2	217 55.4	5.8	18 14.2	8.9	60.3
05	253 24.4	20.7	232 20.2	5.9	18 05.3	9.0	60.3
T 06	268 24.4	N20 20.2	246 45.1	6.1	N17 56.3	9.1	60.3
H 07	283 24.3	19.7	261 10.2	6.1	17 47.2	9.3	60.3
U 08	298 24.3	19.2	275 35.3	6.2	17 37.9	9.3	60.2
R 09	313 24.3 ··	18.7	290 00.5	6.3	17 28.6	9.5	60.2
S 10	328 24.3	18.2	304 25.8	6.5	17 19.1	9.5	60.2
D 11	343 24.2	17.7	318 51.3	6.5	17 09.6	9.7	60.1
A 12	358 24.2	N20 17.2	333 16.8	6.6	N16 59.9	9.8	60.1
Y 13	13 24.2	16.8	347 42.4	6.7	16 50.1	9.8	60.1
14	28 24.1	16.3	2 08.1	6.9	16 40.3	10.0	60.1
15	43 24.1 ··	15.8	16 34.0	6.9	16 30.3	10.0	60.0
16	58 24.1	15.3	30 59.9	7.1	16 20.3	10.2	60.0
17	73 24.1	14.8	45 26.0	7.1	16 10.1	10.2	60.0
18	88 24.0	N20 14.3	59 52.1	7.3	N15 59.9	10.3	59.9
19	103 24.0	13.8	74 18.4	7.3	15 49.6	10.5	59.9
20	118 24.0	13.3	88 44.7	7.5	15 39.1	10.5	59.9
21	133 24.0 ··	12.8	103 11.2	7.5	15 28.6	10.5	59.8
22	148 24.0	12.3	117 37.7	7.7	15 18.1	10.7	59.8
23	163 23.9	11.8	132 04.4	7.7	15 07.4	10.8	59.8
23 00	178 23.9	N20 11.3	146 31.1	7.9	N14 56.6	10.8	59.7
01	193 23.9	10.7	160 58.0	8.0	14 45.8	10.9	59.7
02	208 23.9	10.2	175 25.0	8.0	14 34.9	11.0	59.7
03	223 23.8 ··	09.7	189 52.0	8.2	14 23.9	11.0	59.6
04	238 23.8	09.2	204 19.2	8.3	14 12.9	11.2	59.6
05	253 23.8	08.7	218 46.5	8.4	14 01.7	11.2	59.6
F 06	268 23.8	N20 08.2	233 13.9	8.4	N13 50.5	11.2	59.5
R 07	283 23.8	07.7	247 41.3	8.6	13 39.3	11.4	59.5
I 08	298 23.7	07.2	262 08.9	8.7	13 27.9	11.4	59.5
D 09	313 23.7 ··	06.7	276 36.6	8.7	13 16.5	11.5	59.4
A 10	328 23.7	06.2	291 04.3	8.9	13 05.0	11.5	59.4
Y 11	343 23.7	05.7	305 32.2	9.0	12 53.5	11.6	59.3
12	358 23.7	N20 05.2	320 00.2	9.0	N12 41.9	11.6	59.3
13	13 23.6	04.7	334 28.2	9.2	12 30.3	11.7	59.3
14	28 23.6	04.1	348 56.4	9.3	12 18.6	11.8	59.2
15	43 23.6 ··	03.6	3 24.7	9.3	12 06.8	11.8	59.2
16	58 23.6	03.1	17 53.0	9.5	11 55.0	11.9	59.2
17	73 23.6	02.6	32 21.5	9.5	11 43.1	11.9	59.1
18	88 23.5	N20 02.1	46 50.0	9.6	N11 31.2	12.0	59.1
19	103 23.5	01.6	61 18.6	9.8	11 19.2	12.0	59.1
20	118 23.5	01.1	75 47.4	9.8	11 07.2	12.0	59.0
21	133 23.5 ··	00.6	90 16.2	9.9	10 55.2	12.1	59.0
22	148 23.5	20 00.0	104 45.1	10.0	10 43.1	12.2	58.9
23	163 23.5	19 59.5	119 14.1	10.1	10 30.9	12.2	58.9
	S.D. 15.8	d 0.5	S.D. 16.5		16.4		16.2

Moonrise

Lat.	Twilight Naut.	Civil	Sunrise	21	22	23	24
N 72	▢	▢	▢	▢	▢	05 08	07 29
N 70	▢	▢	▢	▢	03 08	05 37	07 43
68	////	////	01 11	01 28	03 52	05 59	07 54
66	////	////	02 04	02 25	04 22	06 16	08 03
64	////	////	02 35	02 59	04 43	06 29	08 11
62	////	01 29	02 58	03 23	05 01	06 41	08 17
60	////	02 06	03 17	03 43	05 15	06 51	08 23
N 58	////	02 32	03 32	03 59	05 28	06 59	08 28
56	01 21	02 52	03 45	04 12	05 38	07 06	08 32
54	01 56	03 09	03 56	04 24	05 48	07 13	08 36
52	02 20	03 22	04 06	04 35	05 56	07 19	08 39
50	02 39	03 34	04 15	04 44	06 04	07 24	08 43
45	03 14	03 59	04 34	05 03	06 19	07 36	08 50
N 40	03 39	04 18	04 49	05 19	06 32	07 45	08 55
35	03 58	04 33	05 02	05 32	06 43	07 53	09 00
30	04 14	04 46	05 13	05 44	06 53	08 00	09 05
20	04 39	05 08	05 32	06 04	07 10	08 13	09 12
N 10	04 59	05 25	05 48	06 21	07 24	08 23	09 19
0	05 15	05 41	06 03	06 37	07 37	08 33	09 25
S 10	05 30	05 55	06 18	06 54	07 51	08 43	09 31
20	05 43	06 10	06 34	07 11	08 05	08 54	09 37
30	05 57	06 26	06 52	07 30	08 21	09 06	09 45
35	06 04	06 35	07 02	07 42	08 31	09 13	09 49
40	06 11	06 44	07 14	07 55	08 42	09 21	09 54
45	06 19	06 56	07 28	08 11	08 54	09 30	10 00
S 50	06 29	07 09	07 45	08 30	09 09	09 41	10 06
52	06 33	07 15	07 53	08 39	09 17	09 46	10 09
54	06 37	07 21	08 02	08 49	09 24	09 51	10 13
56	06 42	07 28	08 12	09 00	09 33	09 57	10 16
58	06 47	07 36	08 24	09 13	09 43	10 04	10 20
S 60	06 52	07 45	08 37	09 28	09 55	10 12	10 25

Moonset

Lat.	Sunset	Twilight Civil	Naut.	21	22	23	24
N 72	▢	▢	▢	▢	23 51	23 20	22 58
N 70	▢	▢	▢	23 51	23 20	23 04	22 51
68	22 55	////	////	23 06	22 57	22 51	22 45
66	22 06	////	////	22 36	22 39	22 40	22 40
64	21 35	////	////	22 13	22 24	22 31	22 35
62	21 12	22 40	////	21 54	22 12	22 23	22 31
60	20 54	22 04	////	21 39	22 01	22 16	22 28
N 58	20 39	21 39	////	21 26	21 52	22 10	22 25
56	20 26	21 19	22 48	21 15	21 44	22 05	22 22
54	20 15	21 03	22 15	21 05	21 36	22 00	22 20
52	20 06	20 49	21 51	20 56	21 30	21 56	22 18
50	19 57	20 37	21 33	20 48	21 24	21 52	22 16
45	19 38	20 13	20 58	20 31	21 11	21 43	22 11
N 40	19 23	19 55	20 33	20 17	21 00	21 36	22 08
35	19 11	19 39	20 14	20 06	20 51	21 30	22 05
30	19 00	19 26	19 58	19 55	20 43	21 24	22 02
20	18 41	19 05	19 33	19 37	20 29	21 15	21 57
N 10	18 25	18 47	19 14	19 21	20 16	21 06	21 52
0	18 10	18 32	18 58	19 06	20 05	20 58	21 48
S 10	17 55	18 17	18 43	18 52	19 53	20 50	21 44
20	17 39	18 03	18 30	18 35	19 40	20 41	21 39
30	17 21	17 47	18 16	18 17	19 25	20 31	21 34
35	17 11	17 38	18 09	18 06	19 17	20 26	21 31
40	16 59	17 29	18 02	17 54	19 07	20 19	21 28
45	16 45	17 18	17 54	17 39	18 56	20 11	21 24
S 50	16 28	17 05	17 45	17 21	18 42	20 02	21 19
52	16 20	16 59	17 41	17 12	18 35	19 57	21 17
54	16 11	16 52	17 36	17 02	18 28	19 53	21 14
56	16 01	16 45	17 32	16 52	18 20	19 47	21 11
58	15 50	16 37	17 27	16 39	18 10	19 41	21 08
S 60	15 37	16 28	17 21	16 24	18 00	19 34	21 05

Day	SUN Eqn. of Time 00h	12h	Mer. Pass.	MOON Mer. Pass. Upper	Lower	Age	Phase
	m s	m s	h m	h m	h m	d	
21	06 19	06 20	12 06	12 52	00 21	01	
22	06 22	06 23	12 06	13 51	01 22	02	●
23	06 24	06 25	12 06	14 46	02 19	03	

Appendix

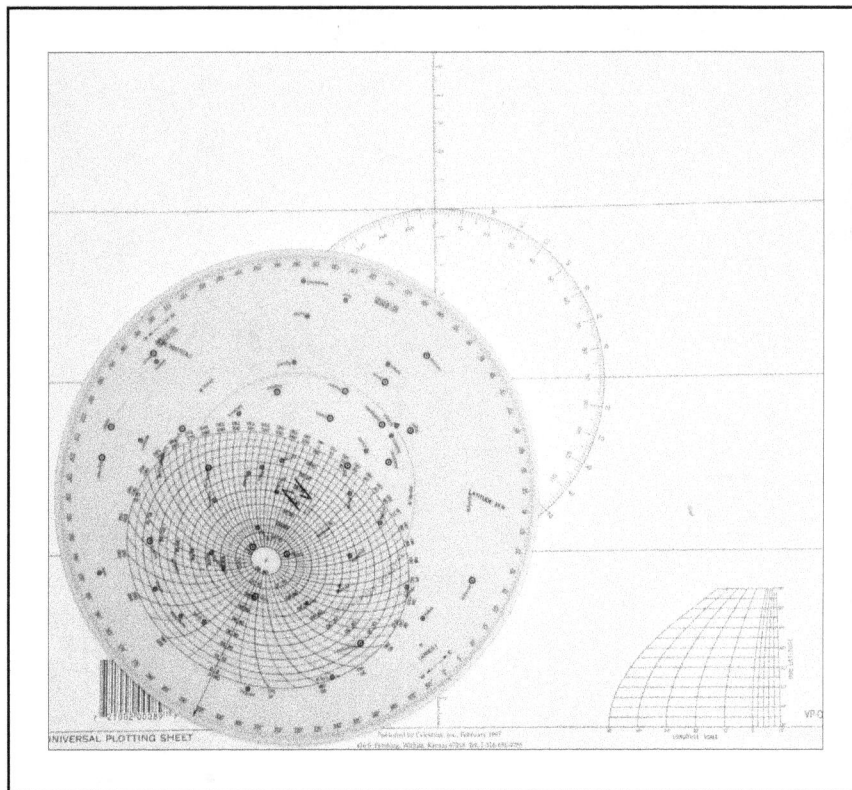

A 2102-D Star Finder and a pad of 50 Universal Plotting Sheets.
The Star Finder is nine inches in diameter.

A1. Universal Plotting Sheets

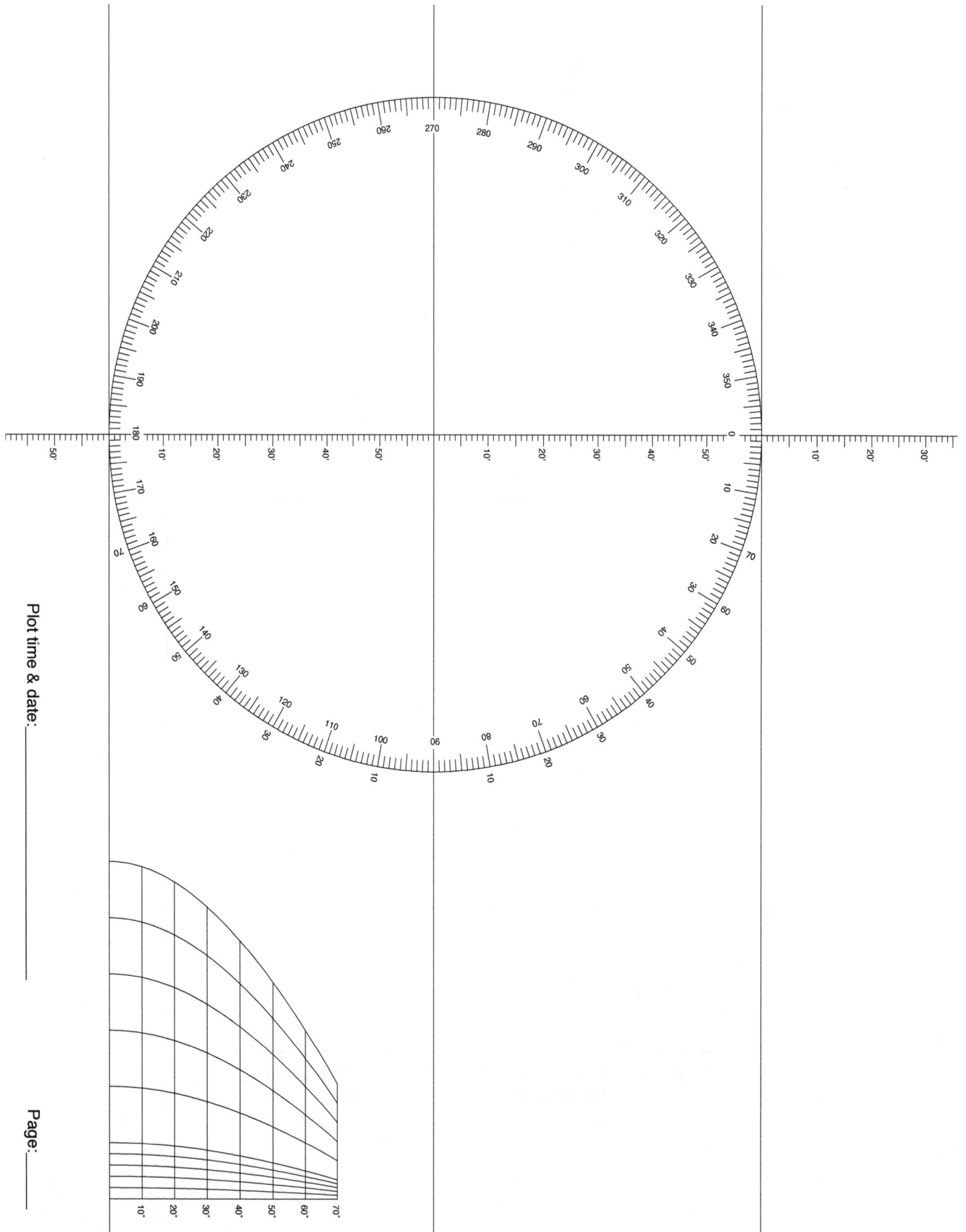

Plot time & date: _____

Page: _____

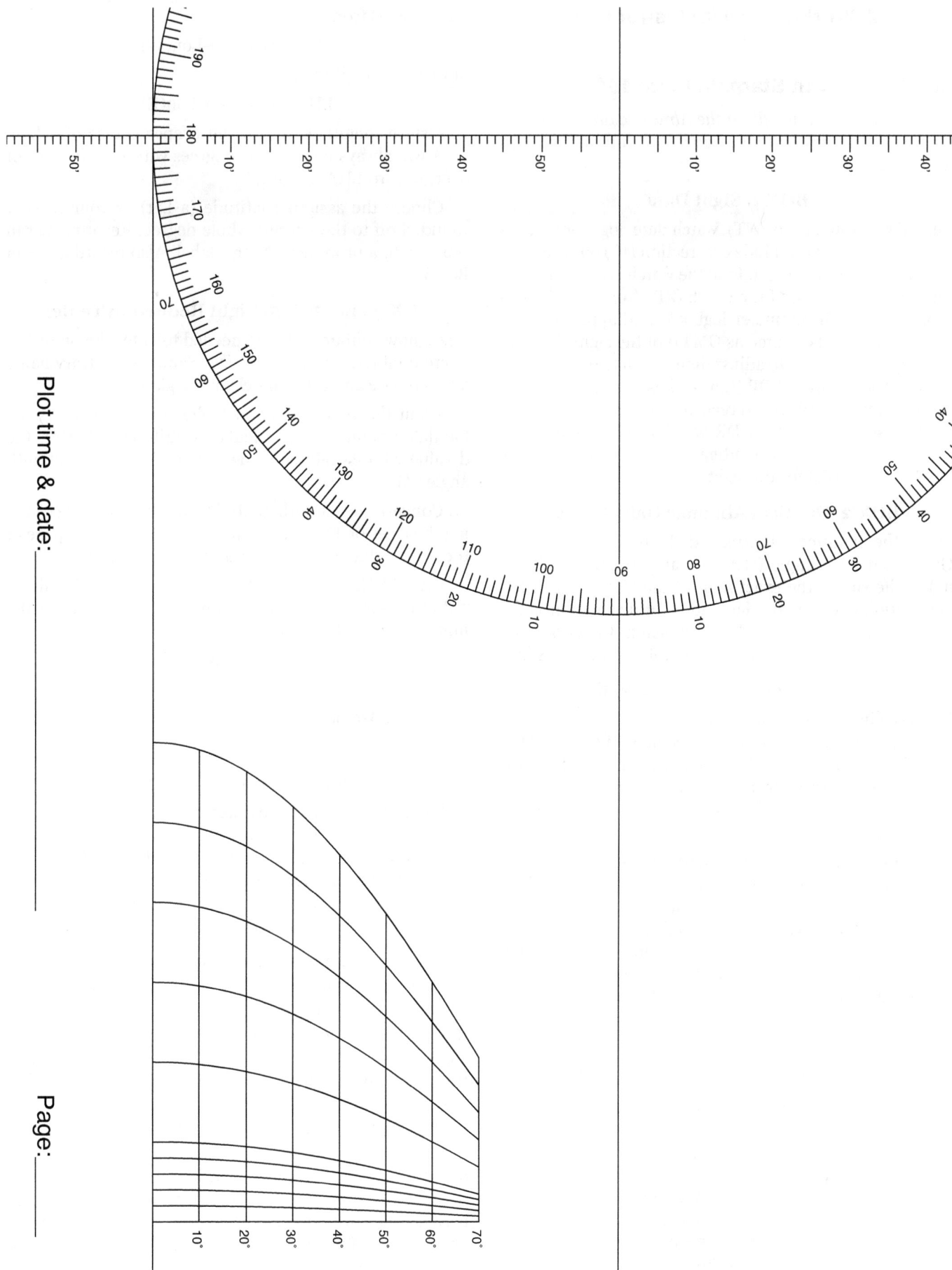

Plot time & date: _____

Page: _____

A2. Workforms with Instructions

Sun Sights with Starpath Form 104

With this form, we fill in the Almanac and Sight Reduction values first, and then do the altitude corrections to Hs to get Ho.

BOX 1. Sight Data

Record the watch time (WT), watch date, log reading, celestial body, measured index correction (IC), and sextant reading (Hs) for the sight. Find the watch error (WE) and the zone description of the watch (ZD) from WWV radio broadcasts or chronometer logbook, and apply these to WT to get the UTC (same as GMT)) of the sight. Use the extra space provided to adjust time and date if necessary. Choose and record a LOP (Line of Position) label for the sight. From your DR (dead reckoning) track on a chart or plotting sheet, figure your DR position (DR-Lat and DR-Lon) at the time and log reading of the sight. Record your height of eye (HE) for the sight.

BOX 2. Nautical Almanac Daily Pages

From the *Nautical Almanac* daily pages, record the Greenwich hour angle (GHA-hr) and declination (Dec-hr) of the sun at the exact hour of the UTC. Record the declination d-value, and label it "+" if declination is increasing with time, or "-" if decreasing. Cross out the spaces for v-value and HP; they do not apply to the sun.

BOX 3. Increments and Corrections

From the increments and corrections pages of the *Nautical Almanac*, record the sun's increment of GHA (GHA-m,s) for the minutes and seconds part of the UTC. Also record the d-correction to the declination based on the d-value given in Box 2. Cross out the SHA or v-correction space; these do not apply to the sun.

Add GHA-hr to GHA-m,s to find GHA and record it. Apply the d-corr to Dec-hr to find Dec and record it. The sign (+ or -) of d-corr is the same as that of d-value. Use the extra space provided to adjust minutes to less than 60 if necessary. You now have the GHA and Dec that apply for your precise UTC. For later use, record the degrees part of the declination (Dec-deg) in Box 4 with a prominent N or S label and also record the minutes part (Dec-min) just below Box 5.

Assumed Position and Hour Angle

Figure the assumed longitude (a-Lon) from your DR-Lon and the minutes part of GHA. In western longitudes, it should be the one longitude that lies within 30' of your DR-Lon that has the same minutes as the minutes part of GHA. In eastern longitudes, it should be the one longitude that lies within 30' of your DR-Lon that has minutes equal to 60 minus the minutes part of GHA. Record a-Lon below GHA and also in Box 6. Figure the local hour angle (LHA) from:

$$LHA = GHA - a\text{-}Lon(W)$$

in western longitudes, or

$$LHA = GHA + a\text{-}Lon(E)$$

in eastern longitudes. With the proper choice of a-Lon, LHA will always be in whole degrees with no minutes left over. Record LHA in Box 4.

Choose the assumed latitude (a-Lat) as your DR-Lat rounded off to the nearest whole degree. Record a-Lat in Box 4 with a prominent N or S label. Also record a-Lat in Box 6.

BOX 4 and BOX 5. Sight Reduction Tables

Box 4 now contains all data needed to enter the Sight Reduction tables, Pubs. 249 or 229. Same or Contrary name labels of Dec and a-Lat are clear at a glance.

From the sight reduction tables, record in Box 5 the tabulated value of the calculated altitude (tab Hc), the d-value with its tabulated sign (+ or -), and the azimuth angle (Z).

Convert the azimuth angle (Z) to the azimuth (Zn) using the rules on the work form (also given on each page of the sight reduction tables) and record it in Box 6.

CAUTION: for high-altitude sights, meaning Hc above 75° or so, you should interpolate for Z to account for the minutes part of Dec. Use:

$$Z = Z(Dec\text{-}deg) + dZ,$$

where

$$dZ = [Z(Dec\text{-}deg + 1°) - Z(Dec\text{-}deg)] \times (Dec\text{-}min)/60.$$

Pub. 249 versus Pub. 229

Although the tables are arranged differently and the values in Pub. 229 are given to a higher precision, the use of Pubs. 249 and 229 differs only in the determination of the d-correction to tab Hc. In Pub. 249 this is done in one step, whereas in Pub. 229 this must be done in several steps. The extra steps are required for the extra precision.

d-corr from Pub. 249

From Table 5 of Pub. 249, record the d-correction. It depends on the d-value and Dec-min (recorded together in Box 5 for convenience). Apply this d-corr to tab Hc to find Hc, and record it. The sign (+ or -) of d-corr is the same as the sign of the d-value given in the sight reduction tables. Also record Hc above Box 6.

The d-correction is given in Pub 249 only for whole minutes of declination. Thus you have the choice of rounding off your actual minutes of declination, or interpolating the table. The interpolation, however, will always be easy because the correction changes either by just one unit or none. (Use of Pub 229 for d-correction is given at the end of this section.)

Figure WF-1. *Sight reduction of the sun using Form 104 and Pub 249. The crossed out box is for Pub 229 only.*

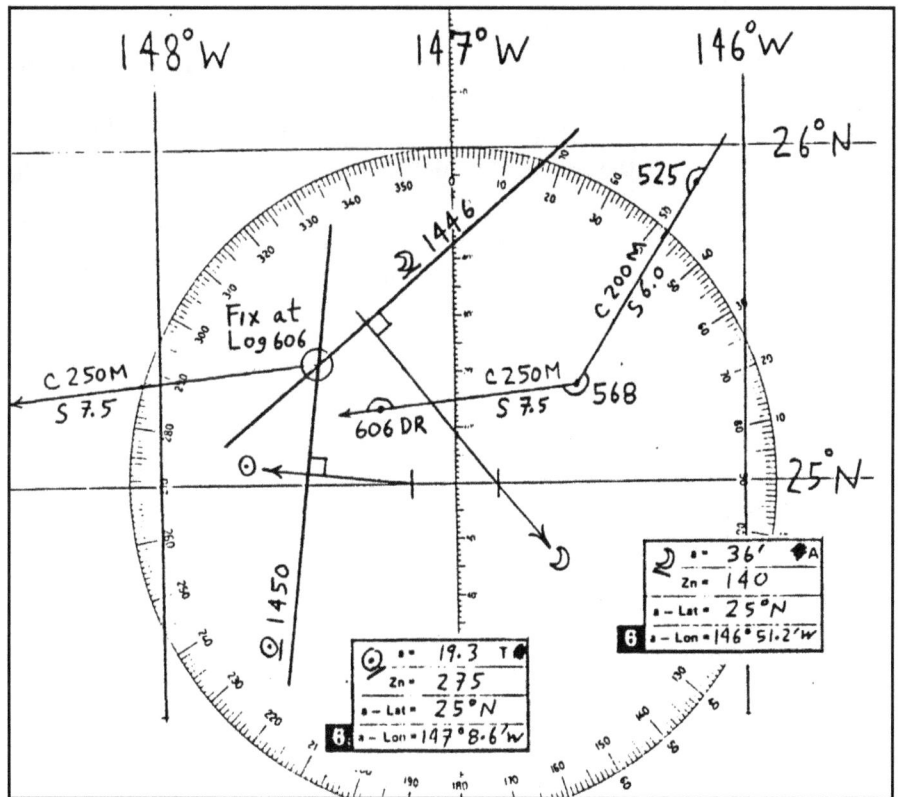

Figure WF-2. *Plot of a celestial fix from a sun and moon sight. The work form for the sun is shown in Figure WF-1. The moon sight is in Figure WF-3.*

Convert Hs to Ho

The upper right side of the work form is used to convert the sextant altitude (Hs) to the apparent altitude (Ha), and then on to the observed altitude (Ho). Altitude corrections are inside the covers of the *Nautical Almanac*. Record the Dip correction, and apply Dip corr and Index corr to Hs to get the apparent altitude (Ha).

Cross out the *additional altitude correction* (it does not apply to sun), then get the main *altitude correction*, which for the sun depends on the season, limb, and Ha of the sight.

Cross out *upper limb moon* correction, and then combine the altitude correction with Ha to get Ho.

Figure the a-value

Find the altitude intercept (a-value) as the difference between Ho and Hc (subtract smaller from larger). Extra space is provided to rewrite Ho or Hc if necessary for this subtraction. Pick the label, A for away or T for toward, that is beside the larger of Hc or Ho, and record the a-value and mark its label in Box 6.

BOX 6. Plotting the Line of Position

Box 6 now contains all data needed to plot the LOP on a plotting sheet. Plotting procedure:

(1) Set up a universal plotting sheet with mid-latitude equal to a-Lat and mid-longitude equal to a-Lon rounded off to the nearest whole degree. Plot a point at the assumed position (a-Lat, a-Lon).

(2) Draw a line (the *azimuth line*) through this point in the direction of Zn (this is the true bearing of the object at the sight time).

(3) Put a mark on the azimuth line at a distance of "a" nautical miles from the assumed position, where "a" is the a-value in Box 6 expressed in minutes of arc (get this distance from the latitude scale on the plotting sheet). Mark the azimuth line in the direction toward Zn, when "a" is labeled T; go the opposite direction along the azimuth line (away from Zn) when "a" is labeled A.

(4) Finally, draw a line perpendicular to the azimuth line passing through the point just marked. This perpendicular line is your LOP. This sight and sight reduction have told you that you are located somewhere on this line. Label the LOP with the name of the celestial body, the log reading, and the UTC.

Moon Sights with Form 104

BOX 2. *Nautical Almanac* Daily Pages

From the *Nautical Almanac* daily pages, record the Greenwich Hour Angle (GHA-hr), v-value, declination (Dec-hr), d-value, and horizontal parallax (HP) for the moon at the exact hour of the UTC. These values are simply transferred to the work form in the exact order they are listed in the *Nautical Almanac*. Figure and record the label of the d-value: label it "+" if declination is increasing with time, or "-" if decreasing. The d-value label is found from the trend in declination, not from the trend in the d-value itself.

BOX 3. Increments and Corrections

From the increments and corrections pages of the *Nautical Almanac*, record the moon's increment of GHA (GHA-m, s) for the minutes and seconds part of the GMT. Also record the d-correction to the declination (based on the d-value given in Box 2) and the v-correction (based on the v-value of Box 2). Cross out the space label "SHA"; for the moon this space is used for v-corr.

Add GHA-hr, GHA-m,s, and v-corr to find GHA and record it. Add the d-corr to Dec-hr to find Dec and record it. For the moon v-corr is always positive; d-corr has the same sign as d-value.

ALL THE REST IS THE SAME AS FOR SUN LINES except the altitude corrections for the moon are taken from the special moon tables on the back cover of the *Nautical Almanac*. Because of the way the tables are organized, the moon's additional altitude correction (needed for all moon sights) must be found after finding the altitude correction. For upper limb moon sights (and only for these) subtract 30' from the altitude corrections using the labeled space provided.

Star Sights with Form 104

BOX 2. Nautical Almanac Daily Pages

From the *Nautical Almanac* daily pages, record in Box 2 the Greenwich Hour Angle (GHA-hr) of Aries at the exact hour of the UTC. Record the declination (Dec) and sidereal hour angle (SHA) of the star in Box 3. Cross out the spaces for v-value, Dec-hr, d-value, and HP; they do not apply to stars.

BOX 3 Increments and Corrections

From the increments and corrections pages of the *Nautical Almanac*, record the Aries increment of GHA (GHA-m,s) for the minutes and seconds part of the GMT. Cross out the d-corr space; stars have no d-corr. And cross out the space label "v-corr"; for stars this space is used for SHA.

Add GHA-hr, GHA-m, s, and SHA to find the GHA of the star and record it. Use the extra space provided to adjust minutes to less than 60 and degrees to less than 360, if necessary.

ALL THE REST IS THE SAME AS FOR THE SUN-LINES except the altitude correction for stars is taken from the stars and planets table instead of the sun table.

Figure WF-3 (Form 104, Pub 249 — Moon sight reduction)

WT 14h 46m 25s	date July 11, 1986	body LL MOON	Hs 68° 35.8
WE +S-F −8	DR Lat 25°13'N	log 2606	index corr. + off, − on + 1.5
ZD +W-E +10	DR Lon 147°15'W	HE ft 9 →	DIP − 2.9
GMT 24h 46m 17s	GMT date / LOP label		Ha 68° 34.4
= 00 46 17	0046 JULY 12 / 1446 ☽		

GHA hr. 122° 37.5	v moon planets 14.3	Dec hr N9° 11.3	d/t −14.5	HP moon 56.5

GHA + m.s. 11° 2.6	d corr. ± −11.2	additional altitude corr. moon, mars, venus + +4.2
or v corr. 11.1	stars or moon, planets Dec deg N9° Dec min 0.1	altitude corr. all sights ± +31.4
GHA 133° 51.2		upper limb moon subtract 30' —
		Ho T 69° 10.0
a–Lon −W+E −146° 51.2		Hc A 69° 46.0
LHA +360 00'W/60'E		a = 36' A
= 347		

center box (crossed out — for use with Pub 229):
tens d / units d / dsd corr. + / d corr. Pub. 229
upper / lower / dsd

LHA 347	tab Hc 69° 46 d ± +48 Z 140 →	Zn = 140
Dec deg 9 N/S N	d corr (Pub. 249) + 0 Dec min. 0.1	a–Lat = 25N
a–Lat 25 N/S N	Hc 69° 46	a–Lon = 146°51.2'W

Figure WF-3. *Sight reduction of the moon using Form 104 and Pub 249. The center box crossed out is only for use with Pub 229.*

Figure WF-4 (Form 104, Pub 229 — Star sight reduction)

WT 18h 45m 02s	date SEPT 2, 1986	body Rigil Kent.	Hs 52° 42.2
WE +S-F +6	DR Lat 31°9'S	log 1253	index corr. + off, − on +2.0
ZD +W-E −11	DR Lon 157° 48'E	HE ft →	DIP − 2.8
GMT 07h 45m 08s	GMT date / LOP label		Ha 52° 41.4
	0745 SEPT 2 / 1845 ✳RK		

GHA hr. ♈ 86° 8.2	v moon planets —	Dec hr S60° 47.0	d/t —	HP moon —

GHA + m.s. ♈ 11° 18.9	d corr. ± —	additional altitude corr. moon, mars, venus + —
SHA + 140° 20.2	stars or moon, planets Dec deg S60° Dec min 47.0	altitude corr. all sights ± − 0.7
GHA 237° 47.3		upper limb moon subtract 30' —
		Ho T 52° 40.7
a–Lon −W+E +158° 12.7		= 51 100.7
LHA 396° 00'W/60'E		Hc A 51° 59.9
− 360		a = 40.8 T

center box (Pub 229):
d	tens 30	23.5	upper —
	units 4.2	3.3	lower —
dsd corr. +	—	dsd ←	
d corr. (Pub. 229)	26.8		

LHA 36	tab Hc 52° 26.7 d ± −34.2 Z 28.8 →	Zn = 208.8
Dec deg 60 N/S S	d corr. Pub. 229 −26.8 Dec min. 47.0	a–Lat = 31°S
a–Lat 31 N/S S	Hc 51° 59.9	a–Lon = 158°12.7'E

Figure WF-4. *Sight reduction of a star (Rigil Kentarus) using Form 104 and Pub 229. The only difference between Pub 229 and Pub 249 for this form is the box in the middle of the form used to figure the d correction to Hc.*

Planet Sights with Form 104

BOX 2 Nautical Almanac Daily Pages

From the *Nautical Almanac* daily pages, record the Greenwich Hour Angle (GHA-hr) and declination (Dec-hr) of the planet at the exact hour of the UTC. Record the declination d-value, and label it "+" if declination is increasing with time, or "-" if decreasing. Record the v-value, it is positive for all planets except Venus, which can sometimes be negative. If it is negative, it is listed as such, and the v-corr found from it should be subtracted. Cross out the space for HP; it is only used for the moon.

BOX 3 Increments and Corrections

From the increments and corrections pages of the *Nautical Almanac*, record the planet's increment of GHA (GHA-m,s) for the minutes and seconds part of the GMT. Also record the d-correction to the declination (based on the d-value of Box 2) and the v-correction to the GHA (based on the v-value in Box 2). Cross out the space label "SHA"; for planets this space is used for v-corr. Add GHA-hr, GHA-m,s, and v-corr to find GHA and record it.

If v-value is negative for Venus, the v-corr is negative. Apply d-corr to Dec-hr to find Dec and record it. The sign of d-corr is the same as that of d-value.

ALL THE REST IS THE SAME AS FOR SUN LINES except the altitude correction for planets is taken from the stars and planets table instead of the sun table. Also there is a small additional altitude correction in the *Nautical Almanac* for the nearby planets Mars and Venus. A labeled space is provided for this additional correction.

d-corr from Pub. 229

Pub 229 can be used to reduce any sight. It provides a higher precision of result (0.1' on Hc and Zn) compared to Pub 249 (1'), but it takes a few extra steps to obtain this.

In Form 104, we use the middle box for these extra steps to finding the d-correction to Hc. The star and planet sights shown in Figures WF-4 and WF-5 use Pub 229 for the d-correction.

First record the tens and units parts of the d-value in the spaces above Box 5. From the Interpolation Table on the inside covers of Pub. 229, record the tens and units corrections with their tabulated signs (+ or -) in the spaces next to the d-value parts. These corrections depend on the d-value parts and on Dec-min, which is called the *declination increment* in Pub. 229. Add the tens and units corrections to get the d-corr and then apply this correction to tab Hc to get the final Hc Also record Hc in the space above Box 6.

If (when first recording tab Hc, d, and Z) the d-value is listed in italics with a dot beside it, a further correction is needed for maximum precision. Proceed as above, but also record the d-values just above and just below (d-upper and d-lower) the tabulated d-value. These are the d-values that correspond to Dec values 1° above and below the Dec-deg recorded in Box 4. Next figure the double second difference (dsd), which equals the difference between d-upper and d-lower, and record it. Find the dsd-correction in the small table, inset next to the tens and units corrections table. Record this small dsd correction and add it to the tens and units correction to find the final d-corr. The dsd-corr is always positive, regardless of the sign of the tens and units corrections.

dsd corrections are only needed for higher-altitude sights, and for these you must interpolate for the azimuth angle Z as explained in the caution note. Hence the italics and dot signaling a dsd correction is also your signal to interpolate for Z. Pub 249 does not have this built-in warning.

Pub 229 includes illustrated examples of the use of dsd and other sight reduction procedures.

A blank sample of the workform is at the end of this section.

A hi-res pdf version of the Starpath workforms suitable for printing is available at
starpath.com/HBS

1

WT	18ʰ 37ᵐ 18ˢ	date SEPT 2, 1986	body Venus	Hs	39° 59.6
WE +S−F	+6	DR Lat 31° 9′ S	log 1252	index corr. + off, − on	+2.0
ZD +W−E −11		DR Lon 157° 48′ E	HE ft 8 →	DIP	−2.8
GMT 07ʰ 37ᵐ 24ˢ		GMT date / LOP label 0737 SEPT 2 / 1837 ♀		Ha	39° 58.8

2

| GHA hr. | 243° 36.4′ | v moon planets +0.4 | Dec hr S 12° 21.3′ | d ± +1.1 | HP moon —— |

3

GHA + m.s.	9° 21.0′		d corr. ± +0.7		additional altitude corr. moon, mars, venus + +0.2
or v corr.	0° +0.3′	stars or moon, planets	Dec deg S 12° Dec min 22.0		altitude corr. all sights ± −1.2
GHA	252° 57.7′				upper limb moon subtract 30′ ——
a−Lon −W+E	+158° 2.3′	tens d 30 11.0 units d 0.1 0.0 dsd corr. + —— d corr. Pub. 229 11.0	d upper —— d lower —— dsd ← ——	Ho T	39° 57.8
LHA	411° 00′ W/60′ E −360			Hc A	39° 35.0

4 / 5 / 6

LHA	51		**5** tab Hc 39° 24.0	d ± +30.1 z/00.3 →	a = 22.8 T Zn = 280.3
Dec deg	12 N S		d corr. Pub 249 +11.0	Dec min. 22.0	a−Lat = 31 S
a−Lat	31 N S		Hc 39° 35.0		**6** a−Lon = 158° 2.3′ E

Figure WF-5. *Sight reduction of a planet (Venus) using Form 104 and Pub 229. The only difference between Pub 229 and Pub 249 for this form is the box in the middle of the form used to figure the d correction to Hc.*

1	WT	h	m	s	date		body		Hs		°	'
	WE +S -F				DR Lat		log		index corr. + off - on			
	ZD +W -E				DR Lon		HE ft	→	DIP -			
	GMT	h	m	s	GMT date / LOP label				Ha		°	'

| 2 | GHA hr. | ° | ' | v moon planets | Dec hr | ° | ' | d + - | HP moon | |

3	GHA + m.s.	°	'		d corr.	+ -	'	additional altitude corr. moon, mars, venus
	SHA + or v corr.	°	'	stars or moon, planets	Dec	°	Dec min	'	altitude corr. all sights
	GHA	°							upper limb moon subtract 30'
			tens d			d upper		Ho	°	'
			units d			d lower		
	a-Lon -W+E	°	'	dsd corr.	+	dsd ←		Hc	°	'
	LHA	00' W / 60' E	d. corr.	**Pub. 229**				

T A

4	LHA	°		5	tab Hc	°	'	d + -	Z	a =	TA
	Dec deg	° N S			d. corr.	**Pub. 249**	'	Dec min		Zn =
	a-Lat	° N S			Hc	°				6	a - Lat =
											a - Lon =

North Latitudes	South Latitudes
LHA greater than 180° .... Zn = Z	LHA greater than 180° .... Zn = 180° - Z
LHA less than 180° .... Zn = 360° - Z	LHA less than 180° .... Zn = 180° + Z

1	WT	h	m	s	date		body		Hs		°	'
	WE +S -F				DR Lat		log		index corr. + off - on			
	ZD +W -E				DR Lon		HE ft	→	DIP -			
	GMT	h	m	s	GMT date / LOP label				Ha		°	'

| 2 | GHA hr. | ° | ' | v moon planets | Dec hr | ° | ' | d + - | HP moon | |

3	GHA + m.s.	°	'		d corr.	+ -	'	additional altitude corr. moon, mars, venus
	SHA + or v corr.	°	'	stars or moon, planets	Dec	°	Dec min	'	altitude corr. all sights
	GHA	°							upper limb moon subtract 30'
			tens d			d upper		Ho	°	'
			units d			d lower		
	a-Lon -W+E	°	'	dsd corr.	+	dsd ←		Hc	°	'
	LHA	00' W / 60' E	d. corr.	**Pub. 229**				

T A

4	LHA	°		5	tab Hc	°	'	d + -	Z	a =	TA
	Dec deg	° N S			d. corr.	**Pub. 249**	'	Dec min		Zn =
	a-Lat	° N S			Hc	°				6	a - Lat =
											a - Lon =

A3. Twilight Skies at Sight Times

The following pages show the sky plotted out as a radar screen, with the vessel position in the center of the screen. The circumference is the horizon; each range ring is an altitude of 15°; the center of the diagram is overhead. North is on the top; East is on the right.

The brightness of the stars have been limited to those with magnitudes brighter than 2.5. The smaller the magnitude the brighter the object. In this scale planets generally have negative magnitudes.

Also shown for comparison is the triad of best sights, based on standard criteria, namely the three bodies closest to 120° apart, bright as possible, and closest to same altitude. The angular separation is the dominant criterion. In several cases the rigorous application of the algorithm used clearly failed, and even though the criteria was maximized, the best choices were not found by that method.

We do not always use these choices in many cases, because we have to take what is available in clear sky and not behind sails, but these can serve as at least one answer to what would be the best bodies to use for a fix.

The star charts are presented for each day that star or planet sights were taken. The time used to compute the sky was the time of the first sight taken. The DR position used is the position from the last sight taken. This is not really consistent, but it does not materially affect what we see or how we might use it.

The table below each chart is the magnitude (Mag), calculated altitude (Hc), and azimuth (Zn) for each body shown, along with the official number of the star from the *Nautical Almanac*.

Normally we would take sights only for bodies above 15° (to rule out effects of abnormal refraction) and below 75° (to rule out the need for special analysis of high sights), but we show them all here so the full sky of mag 2.5 and brighter objects are shown.

Celestial Navigation Data for 1982 Jul 5 at 12:03:50 UT

For Assumed Position:　Latitude　N 46 29.3
　　　　　　　　　　　　　Longitude　W 127 42.9

Object	GHA		Dec		Hc		Zn	Refr	SD	PA	Sum
	°	'	°	'	°	'	°	'	'	'	'
SUN	359	50.5	N22	47.5	− 6	14.6	47.1	---	---	---	---
MOON	189	25.5	S22	32.3	+ 1	20.5	234.4	−27.3	14.7	54.0	41.4
VENUS	33	34.6	N20	48.7	+12	11.7	72.5	−4.4	0.1	0.1	−4.2
ALDEBARA	35	23.8	N16	28.4	+10	18.5	76.9	−5.2	0.0	0.0	−5.2
ALIOTH	270	48.3	N56	03.7	+17	07.0	339.5	−3.2	0.0	0.0	−3.2
ALKAID	257	24.3	N49	24.4	+15	20.6	328.7	−3.5	0.0	0.0	−3.5
ALPHECCA	230	37.8	N26	46.6	+10	54.9	297.6	−4.9	0.0	0.0	−4.9
ALPHERAT	102	14.9	N28	59.4	+63	32.1	122.4	−0.5	0.0	0.0	−0.5
ALTAIR	166	37.9	N 8	49.3	+39	50.1	233.9	−1.2	0.0	0.0	−1.2
CAPELLA	25	16.9	N45	58.8	+24	44.4	48.3	−2.1	0.0	0.0	−2.1
DENEB	153	54.2	N45	12.9	+71	47.9	275.6	−0.3	0.0	0.0	−0.3
DIPHDA	93	26.6	S18	04.9	+18	24.4	145.7	−2.9	0.0	0.0	−2.9
DUBHE	298	27.8	N61	51.1	+18	35.7	355.4	−2.9	0.0	0.0	−2.9
ELNATH	22	49.9	N28	35.5	+11	03.5	59.8	−4.9	0.0	0.0	−4.9
ELTANIN	195	03.6	N51	29.6	+47	06.5	302.4	−0.9	0.0	0.0	−0.9
ENIF	138	17.1	N 9	47.6	+52	12.9	197.2	−0.8	0.0	0.0	−0.8
FOMALHAU	119	56.8	S29	42.8	+13	28.5	173.1	−4.0	0.0	0.0	−4.0
HAMAL	72	34.6	N23	22.6	+40	28.0	98.1	−1.2	0.0	0.0	−1.2
KOCHAB	241	25.3	N74	14.0	+38	31.0	341.5	−1.2	0.0	0.0	−1.2
MARKAB	118	08.7	N15	06.5	+57	37.0	162.6	−0.6	0.0	0.0	−0.6
MENKAR	58	47.0	N 4	01.2	+17	19.3	102.8	−3.1	0.0	0.0	−3.1
MIRFAK	53	21.6	N49	47.7	+42	21.4	57.3	−1.1	0.0	0.0	−1.1
NUNKI	180	34.2	S26	19.1	+ 2	55.8	225.7	−13.8	0.0	0.0	−13.8
RASALHAG	200	35.1	N12	34.4	+20	50.6	266.4	−2.6	0.0	0.0	−2.6
SCHEDAR	94	14.6	N56	26.1	+67	11.8	51.9	−0.4	0.0	0.0	−0.4
VEGA	185	01.5	N38	46.1	+48	04.6	280.8	−0.9	0.0	0.0	−0.9
POLARIS	70	46.6	N89	10.7	+46	55.9	1.0	−0.9	0.0	0.0	−0.9
ARIES	104	07.0									

Moon phase is waxing gibbous, 99% illuminated

Star data from USNO. *Data like this is available at the link starpath.com/usno that takes you to the Naval Observatory (we make a link because the original changes frequently). In our text we call this page the celestial navigator's dream machine. It has everything we want.*

Problem 1 – July 5th, 05:03:50, 46° 29.3'N, 127° 42.9'W

Triad: 1/112
Weight: 2.44

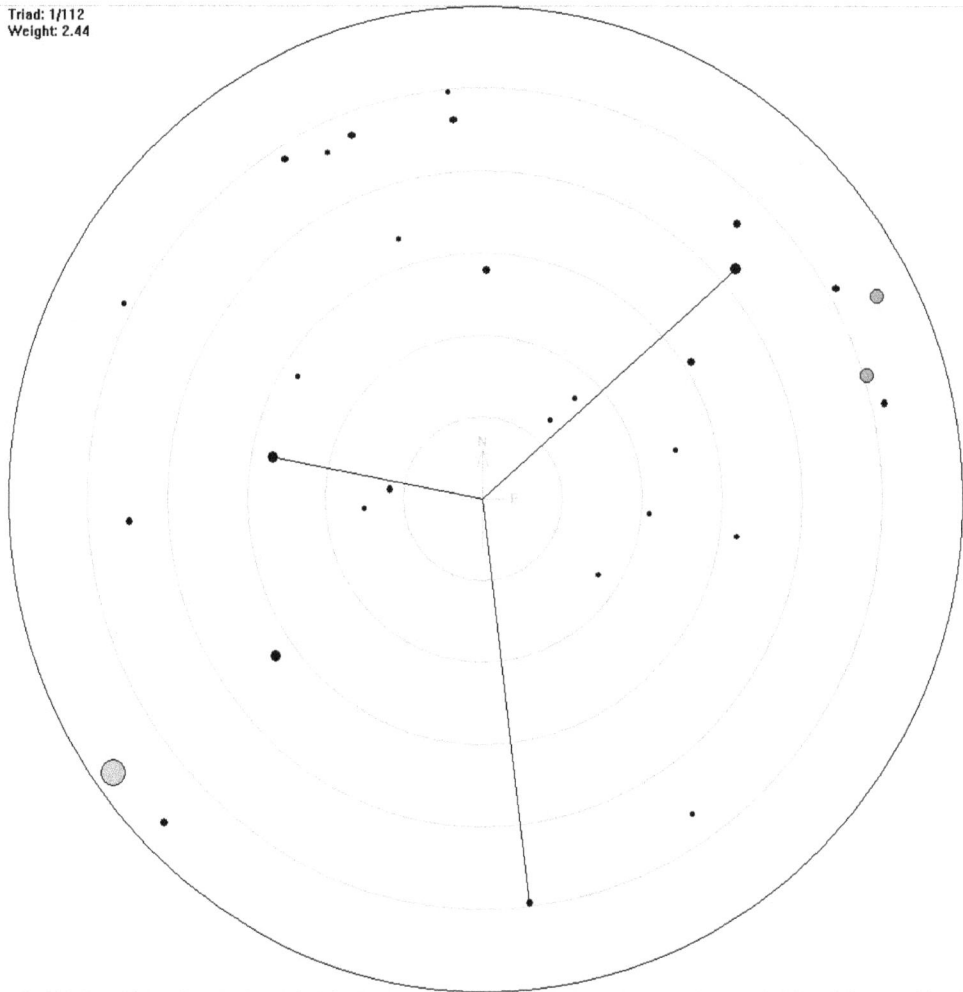

Body	Mag	Hc	Zn
Moon		001°19.3'	234.5°
1: ALPHERATZ	2.2	063°33.4'	122.5°
4: DIPHDA	2.2	018°25.3'	145.7°
6: HAMAL	2.2	040°29.5'	098.1°
9: MIRFAK	1.8	042°22.7'	057.3°
10: ALDEBARAN	1.1	010°20.0'	076.9°
12: CAPELLA	0.2	024°45.5'	048.4°
14: ELNATH	1.7	011°04.8'	059.9°
27: DUBHE	2	018°35.6'	355.4°
32: ALIOTH	1.7	017°06.5'	339.5°
34: ALKAID	1.8	015°19.8'	328.7°
40: KOCHAB	2.2	038°30.5'	341.5°
41: ALPHECCA	2.2	010°53.6'	297.6°
46: RASALHAGUE	2	020°49.1'	266.4°
47: ELTANIN	2.4	047°05.2'	302.4°
49: VEGA	0.1	048°03.2'	280.9°

Body	Mag	Hc	Zn
50: NUNKI	2	002°54.7'	225.7°
51: ALTAIR	0.8	039°48.9'	234.0°
53: DENEB	1.2	071°46.4'	275.6°
56: FOMALHAUT	1.2	013°28.6'	173.1°
58: POLARIS	2	046°56.0'	001.0°
59: Caph	2.4	070°15.7'	041.2°
62: Gamma Casiopeiae	2.2	064°10.0'	043.2°
63: Mirach	2.4	057°46.3'	095.1°
67: Almak	2.2	051°44.8'	076.1°
84: Menkalinan	2	018°43.7'	043.4°
108: Merak	2.4	013°13.9'	355.0°
121: Mizar	2.2	018°11.1'	335.0°
164: Gamma Cygni	2.2	066°44.2'	265.6°
Mercury	-2	004°51.3'	063.4°
Venus	-4.2	012°13.0'	072.5°

Problem 7 – July 9th, 21:44:32, 36° 56.5'N, 132° 32'W

Triad: 1/186
Weight: 2.59

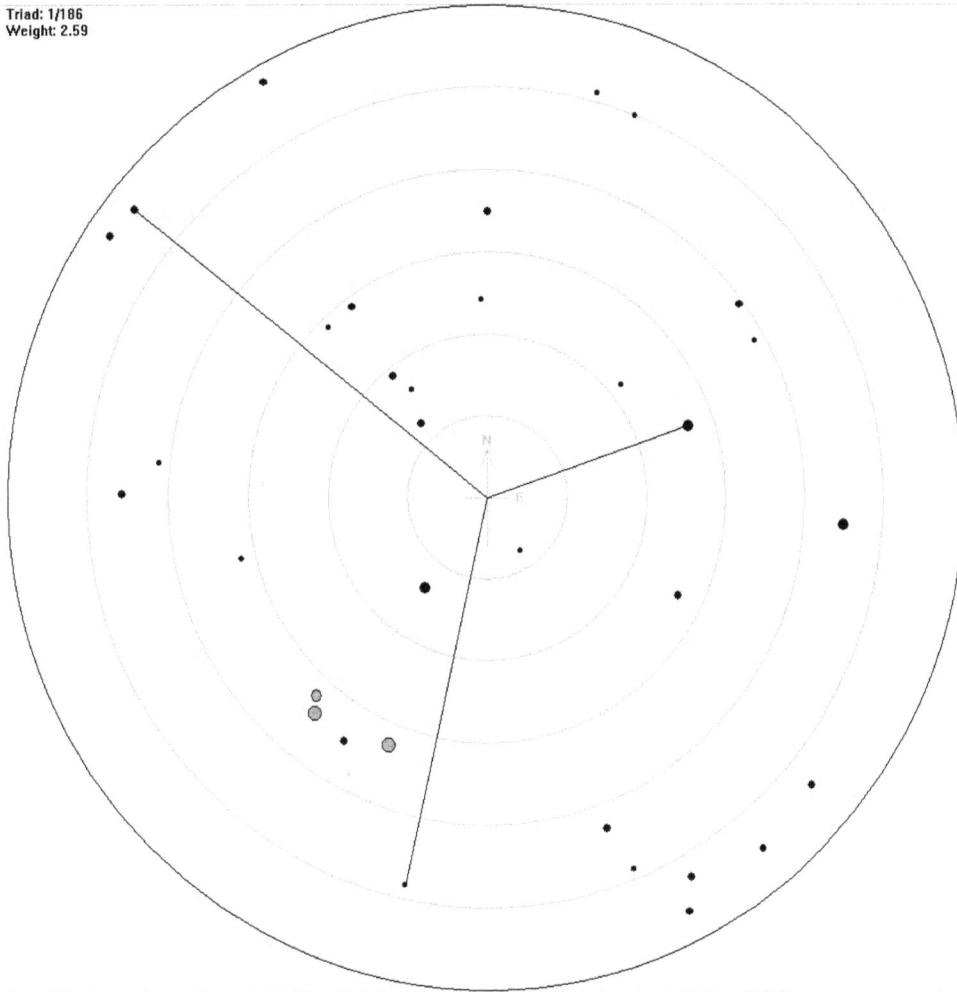

Body	Mag	Hc	Zn
21: POLLUX	1.2	002°09.4'	304.1°
26: REGULUS	1.2	019°30.3'	270.6°
27: DUBHE	2	045°34.8'	324.0°
28: DENEBOLA	2.2	040°59.1'	256.5°
32: ALIOTH	1.7	060°45.1'	321.4°
33: SPICA	1.2	036°24.8'	211.4°
34: ALKAID	1.8	071°05.6'	317.4°
36: MENKENT	2.2	015°28.0'	192.5°
37: ARCTURUS	0.2	069°08.3'	215.6°
40: KOCHAB	2.2	052°39.9'	358.3°
41: ALPHECCA	2.2	078°11.5'	147.4°
42: ANTARES	1.2	023°44.4'	159.8°
45: SHAULA	1.7	008°32.7'	151.2°
46: RASALHAGUE	2	048°49.3'	116.5°
47: ELTANIN	2.4	056°44.5'	050.3°
48: KAUS AUSTR	2	005°09.9'	141.0°
49: VEGA	0.1	048°55.9'	070.8°

Body	Mag	Hc	Zn
50: NUNKI	2	007°00.7'	130.6°
51: ALTAIR	0.8	020°22.0'	094.3°
53: DENEB	1.2	029°09.2'	053.3°
58: POLARIS	2	036°08.4'	000.2°
59: Caph	2.4	012°47.3'	021.6°
62: Gamma Casiopeiae	2.2	011°07.2'	015.6°
84: Menkalinan	2	000°41.0'	331.0°
95: Castor	1.6	003°00.4'	308.5°
105: Algeiba	2.2	026°12.0'	276.1°
108: Merak	2.4	045°32.1'	316.3°
121: Mizar	2.2	064°55.0'	324.3°
145: Epsilon Scorpii	2.4	014°50.1'	158.1°
152: Theta Scorpii	2	003°03.1'	153.4°
164: Gamma Cygni	2.2	030°16.9'	060.3°
Mars	-0.1	037°23.9'	219.6°
Jupiter	-2.1	039°43.7'	202.5°
Saturn	0.9	040°03.3'	221.8°

Problem 9 – July 11th, 05:37:48, 35° 17.7'N, 134° 09.3'W

Triad: 1/241
Weight: 2.93

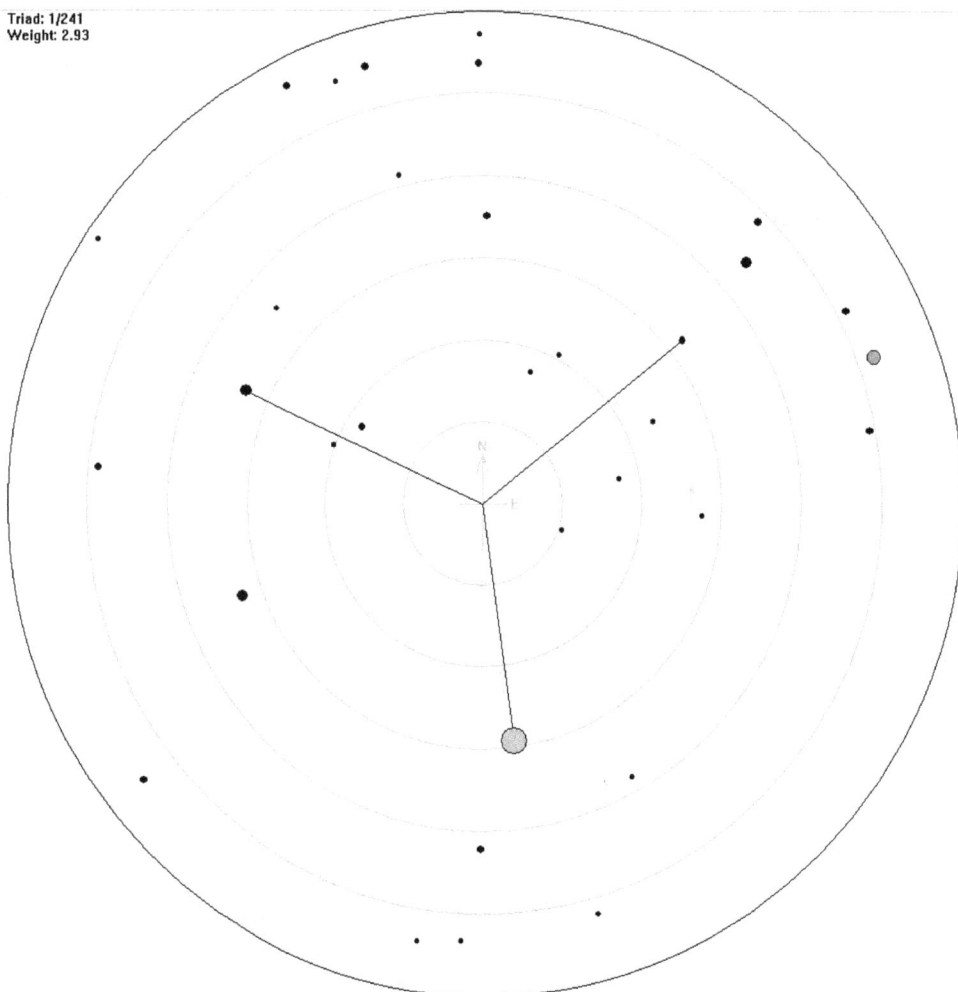

Body	Mag	Hc	Zn
Moon		044°56.2'	172.1°
1: ALPHERATZ	2.2	073°56.8'	108.2°
2: ANKAA	2.4	009°45.2'	163.7°
4: DIPHDA	2.2	031°05.3'	150.6°
6: HAMAL	2.2	047°37.7'	093.1°
9: MIRFAK	1.8	040°43.9'	051.3°
10: ALDEBARAN	1.1	013°57.5'	079.5°
12: CAPELLA	0.2	021°48.7'	048.3°
14: ELNATH	1.7	010°59.0'	062.6°
27: DUBHE	2	007°09.1'	359.4°
32: ALIOTH	1.7	004°37.0'	344.3°
34: ALKAID	1.8	002°38.3'	334.0°
40: KOCHAB	2.2	026°04.4'	345.1°
41: ALPHECCA	2.2	000°01.0'	303.5°
46: RASALHAGUE	2	014°36.8'	275.2°
47: ELTANIN	2.4	035°30.3'	312.3°
49: VEGA	0.1	038°52.8'	294.5°

Body	Mag	Hc	Zn
50: NUNKI	2	005°45.1'	231.9°
51: ALTAIR	0.8	039°45.8'	249.8°
53: DENEB	1.2	062°20.5'	301.5°
55: AL NAIR	2.2	006°53.2'	188.6°
56: FOMALHAUT	1.2	024°59.5'	180.2°
58: POLARIS	2	035°49.9'	000.8°
59: Caph	2.4	063°34.3'	020.5°
62: GammaCasiopeiae	2.2	058°25.5'	027.5°
63: Mirach	2.4	063°23.9'	079.8°
67: Almak	2.2	053°41.5'	064.7°
84: Menkalinan	2	014°54.1'	045.0°
108: Merak	2.4	001°46.8'	359.6°
121: Mizar	2.2	005°33.6'	340.0°
164: GammaCygni	2.2	059°02.1'	290.9°
171: Beta Gruis	2.2	007°39.2'	182.7°
Venus	-4.2	009°28.8'	069.9°

Problem 12 – July 13th, 06:00:18, 33° 11'N, 136° 27.3'W

Triad: 1/165
Weight: 2.68

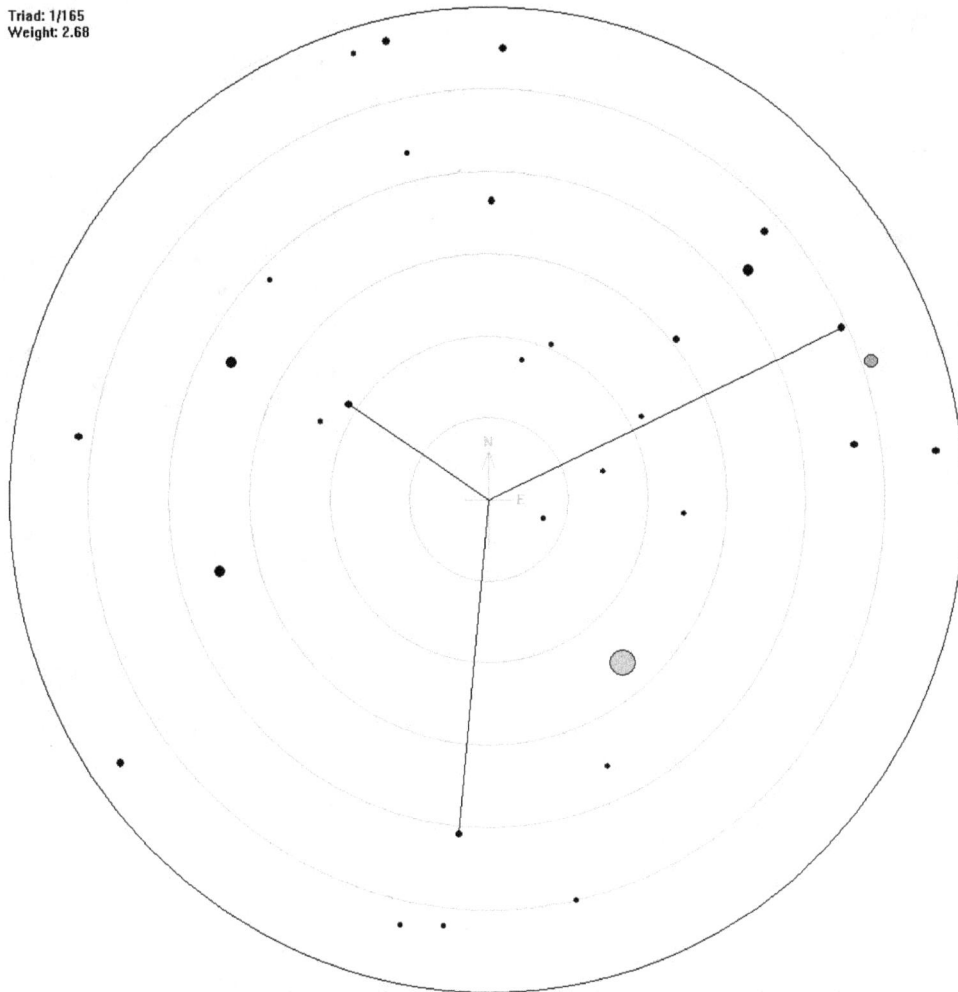

Body	Mag	Hc	Zn
Moon		049°53.7'	140.0°
1: ALPHERATZ	2.2	078°46.8'	108.7°
2: ANKAA	2.4	012°53.4'	167.5°
4: DIPHDA	2.2	034°57.7'	155.5°
6: HAMAL	2.2	052°08.5'	093.9°
9: MIRFAK	1.8	042°48.3'	050.3°
10: ALDEBARAN	1.1	017°56.8'	081.7°
12: CAPELLA	0.2	023°43.7'	049.4°
13: BELLATRIX	1.7	002°21.1'	084.0°
14: ELNATH	1.7	013°59.1'	064.8°
27: DUBHE	2	005°05.5'	001.9°
32: ALIOTH	1.7	001°29.1'	347.1°
40: KOCHAB	2.2	022°56.6'	346.4°
46: RASALHAGUE	2	010°00.1'	278.6°
47: ELTANIN	2.4	030°51.7'	314.3°
49: VEGA	0.1	034°00.5'	297.5°
50: NUNKI	2	003°28.3'	235.2°

Body	Mag	Hc	Zn
51: ALTAIR	0.8	036°12.0'	255.4°
53: DENEB	1.2	057°30.3'	303.5°
55: AL NAIR	2.2	008°10.1'	192.2°
56: FOMALHAUT	1.2	026°53.1'	185.4°
58: POLARIS	2	033°46.6'	000.7°
59: Caph	2.4	062°51.3'	014.0°
62: Gamma Casiopeiae	2.2	058°22.2'	022.6°
63: Mirach	2.4	067°16.1'	076.4°
67: Almak	2.2	056°40.7'	062.1°
84: Menkalinan	2	016°34.9'	046.7°
121: Mizar	2.2	002°09.5'	342.8°
164: Gamma Cygni	2.2	054°10.2'	294.3°
171: Beta Gruis	2.2	009°24.4'	186.4°
Venus	-4.1	011°02.1'	070.7°

Problem 17 – July 16th, 06:55:50, 28° 34.5'N, 142° 43'W

Triad: 1/263
Weight: 2.62

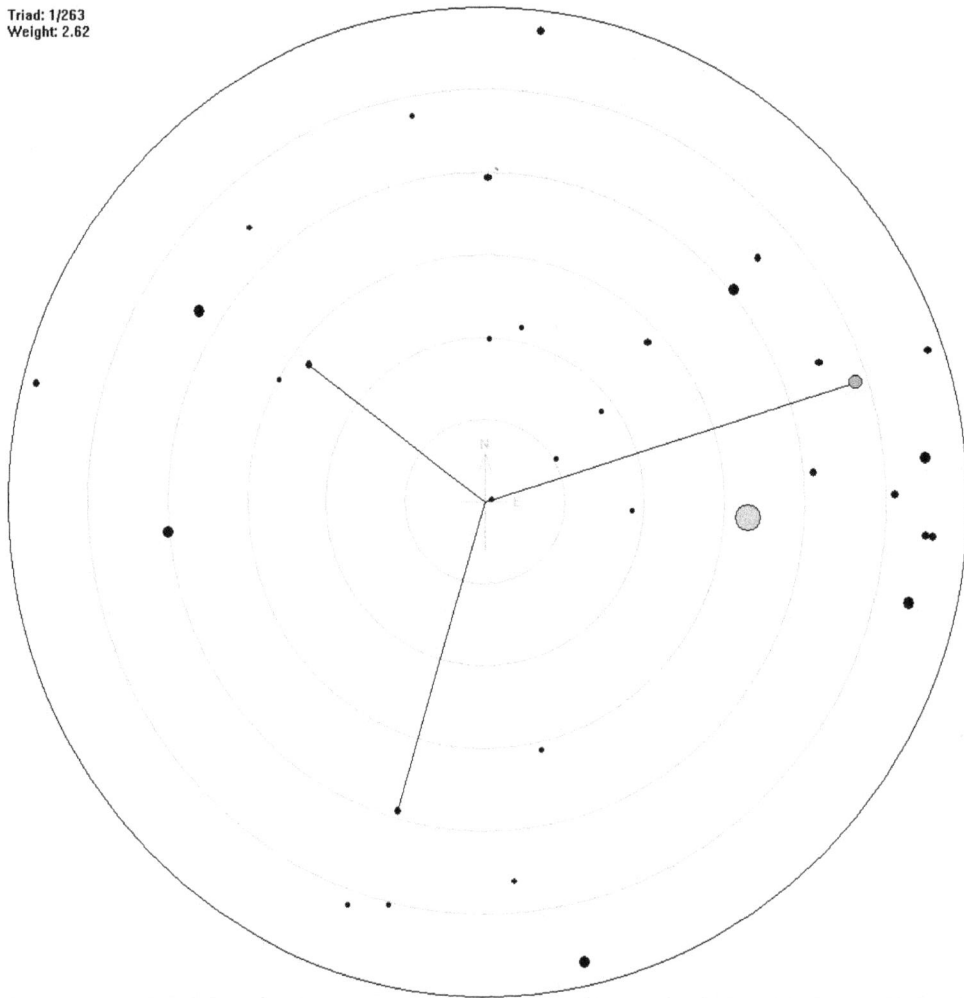

Body	Mag	Hc	Zn
Moon		039°04.8'	093.3°
1: ALPHERATZ	2.2	088°34.9'	072.6°
2: ANKAA	2.4	018°48.6'	175.3°
4: DIPHDA	2.2	042°16.9'	166.6°
5: ACHERNAR	0.6	001°45.8'	167.3°
6: HAMAL	2.2	061°32.4'	093.2°
9: MIRFAK	1.8	046°35.0'	046.4°
10: ALDEBARAN	1.1	026°28.0'	084.9°
11: RIGEL	0.3	006°22.2'	103.0°
12: CAPELLA	0.2	027°44.4'	050.3°
13: BELLATRIX	1.7	011°09.7'	088.8°
14: ELNATH	1.7	020°29.3'	067.8°
15: ALNILAM	1.7	005°07.3'	094.2°
16: BETELGEUSE	0.3	005°05.1'	084.3°
27: DUBHE	2	001°12.0'	006.9°
40: KOCHAB	2.2	016°30.0'	349.0°
46: RASALHAGUE	2	000°09.6'	284.3°

Body	Mag	Hc	Zn
47: ELTANIN	2.4	021°14.2'	318.1°
49: VEGA	0.1	023°49.3'	302.6°
51: ALTAIR	0.8	028°00.3'	264.7°
53: DENEB	1.2	047°24.7'	307.0°
55: AL NAIR	2.2	010°07.0'	199.3°
56: FOMALHAUT	1.2	029°42.3'	196.1°
58: POLARIS	2	029°15.8'	000.5°
59: Caph	2.4	059°30.2'	001.8°
62: Gamma Casiopeiae	2.2	056°40.8'	012.1°
63: Mirach	2.4	074°08.3'	059.7°
67: Almak	2.2	061°56.2'	052.7°
82: Alnitak	1.8	003°46.2'	094.3°
84: Menkalinan	2	020°15.6'	049.0°
87: Alhena	1.8	000°19.5'	071.4°
164: Gamma Cygni	2.2	043°58.0'	299.7°
171: Beta Gruis	2.2	012°20.4'	193.8°
Venus	-4.1	015°11.4'	072.4°

Problem 18 – July 16th, 21:53:55, 27° 23.3'N, 144° 20'W

Triad: 1/246
Weight: 2.64

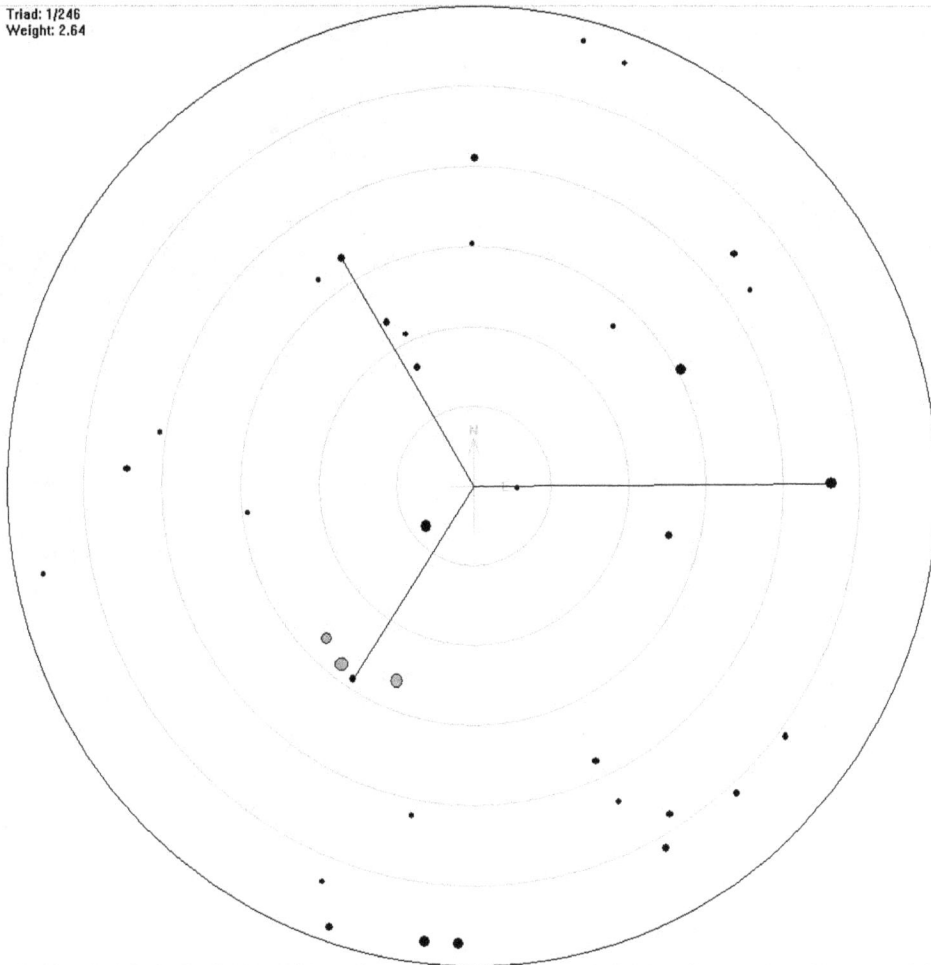

Body	Mag	Hc	Zn
25: ALPHARD	2.2	002°55.4'	258.8°
26: REGULUS	1.2	021°22.8'	272.9°
27: DUBHE	2	038°47.1'	329.0°
28: DENEBOLA	2.2	044°47.0'	263.6°
31: GACRUX	1.6	000°12.6'	198.8°
32: ALIOTH	1.7	053°57.8'	331.2°
33: SPICA	1.2	045°39.2'	212.9°
34: ALKAID	1.8	064°20.8'	333.7°
35: HADAR	0.8	001°39.2'	186.5°
36: MENKENT	2.2	025°15.5'	191.1°
37: ARCTURUS	0.2	077°40.0'	231.0°
38: RIGIL KENT	0.1	001°46.6'	182.1°
40: KOCHAB	2.2	043°09.0'	359.6°
41: ALPHECCA	2.2	081°23.5'	091.9°
42: ANTARES	1.2	031°45.4'	155.4°
45: SHAULA	1.7	015°43.1'	148.4°
46: RASALHAGUE	2	050°05.1'	103.7°
47: ELTANIN	2.4	048°32.4'	041.9°

Body	Mag	Hc	Zn
48: KAUS AUSTR	2	011°04.5'	138.6°
49: VEGA	0.1	043°03.0'	061.2°
50: NUNKI	2	011°23.5'	127.9°
51: ALTAIR	0.8	018°31.1'	089.5°
53: DENEB	1.2	021°28.4'	049.1°
58: POLARIS	2	026°34.8'	000.2°
59: Caph	2.4	003°05.5'	020.1°
62: Gamma Casiopeiae	2.2	001°20.1'	014.2°
105: Algeiba	2.2	027°02.5'	279.6°
108: Merak	2.4	039°41.2'	322.2°
115: Muhlifain	2.4	008°00.8'	201.6°
121: Mizar	2.2	057°42.4'	335.2°
145: Epsilon Scorpii	2.4	022°44.0'	154.8°
152: Theta Scorpii	2	010°31.3'	151.3°
164: Gamma Cygni	2.2	023°21.3'	055.4°
Mars	0	046°40.5'	217.5°
Jupiter	-2.1	049°20.7'	202.3°
Saturn	1	048°31.6'	225.0°

Problem 20 – July 18th, 07:40:22, 26° 56'N, 148° 48'W

Triad: 1/287
Weight: 2.49

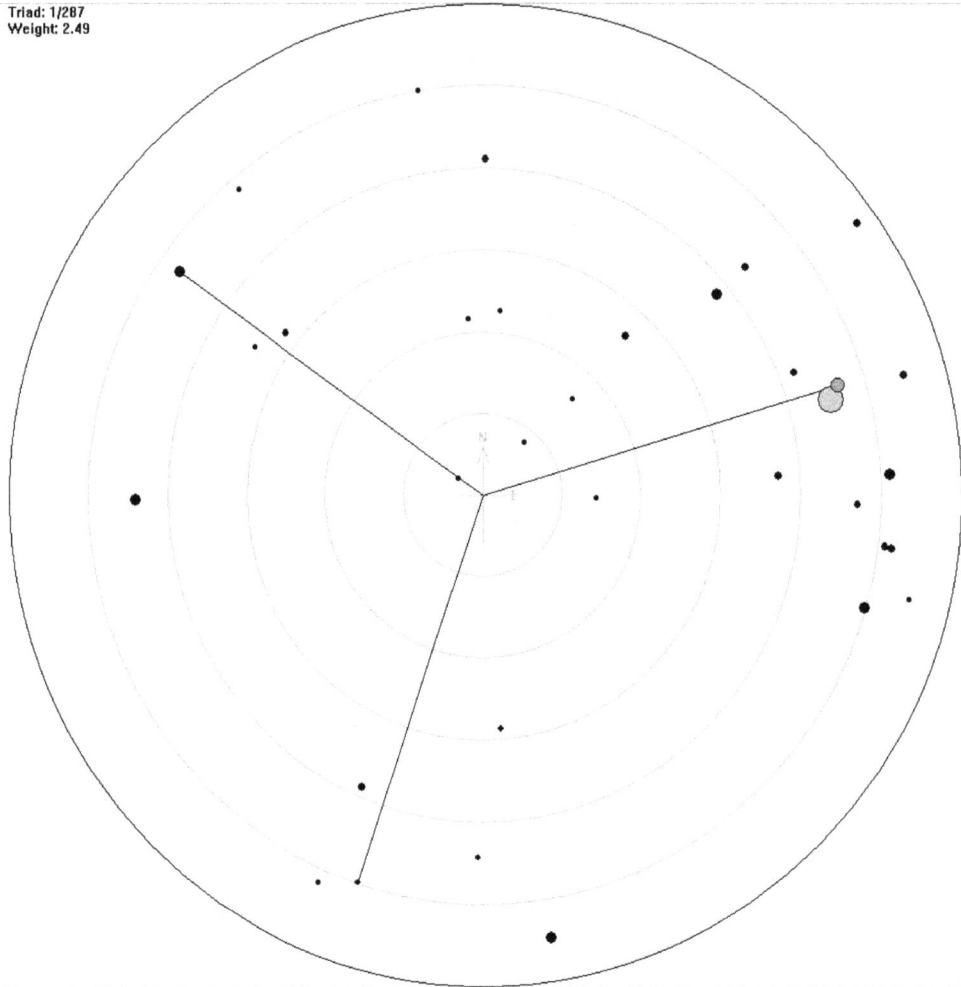

Body	Mag	Hc	Zn
Moon	020°17.4'	075.0°	
1: ALPHERATZ	2.2	084°14.3'	303.3°
2: ANKAA	2.4	021°39.7'	180.8°
4: DIPHDA	2.2	045°52.1'	175.5°
5: ACHERNAR	0.6	005°32.3'	170.9°
6: HAMAL	2.2	067°55.1'	091.4°
9: MIRFAK	1.8	049°06.3'	042.6°
10: ALDEBARAN	1.1	032°31.0'	086.3°
11: RIGEL	0.3	013°05.9'	106.0°
12: CAPELLA	0.2	030°52.4'	050.1°
13: BELLATRIX	1.7	017°26.2'	091.4°
14: ELNATH	1.7	025°20.9'	069.0°
15: ALNILAM	1.7	011°37.2'	097.1°
16: BETELGEUSE	0.3	011°08.4'	087.1°
40: KOCHAB	2.2	012°47.8'	350.7°
47: ELTANIN	2.4	015°08.6'	320.3°
49: VEGA	0.1	017°09.0'	305.4°

Body	Mag	Hc	Zn
51: ALTAIR	0.8	021°52.8'	269.3°
53: DENEB	1.2	040°50.4'	308.5°
55: AL NAIR	2.2	010°16.2'	203.8°
56: FOMALHAUT	1.2	030°04.5'	203.3°
58: POLARIS	2	026°40.3'	000.4°
59: Caph	2.4	056°40.7'	355.0°
62: Gamma Casiopeiae	2.2	055°01.8'	005.6°
63: Mirach	2.4	077°14.6'	038.9°
67: Almak	2.2	064°52.2'	043.7°
82: Alnitak	1.8	010°16.3'	097.3°
83: Kappa Orionis	2.2	005°11.1'	103.4°
84: Menkalinan	2	023°18.2'	049.8°
87: Alhena	1.8	005°32.7'	074.4°
95: Castor	1.6	001°12.5'	054.7°
164: Gamma Cygni	2.2	037°14.0'	302.1°
171: Beta Gruis	2.2	013°08.0'	198.5°
Venus	-4.1	018°13.7'	073.2°

Problem 21 – July 18th, 22:23:10, 25° 04.5'N, 150° 20'W

Triad: 1/241
Weight: 2.83

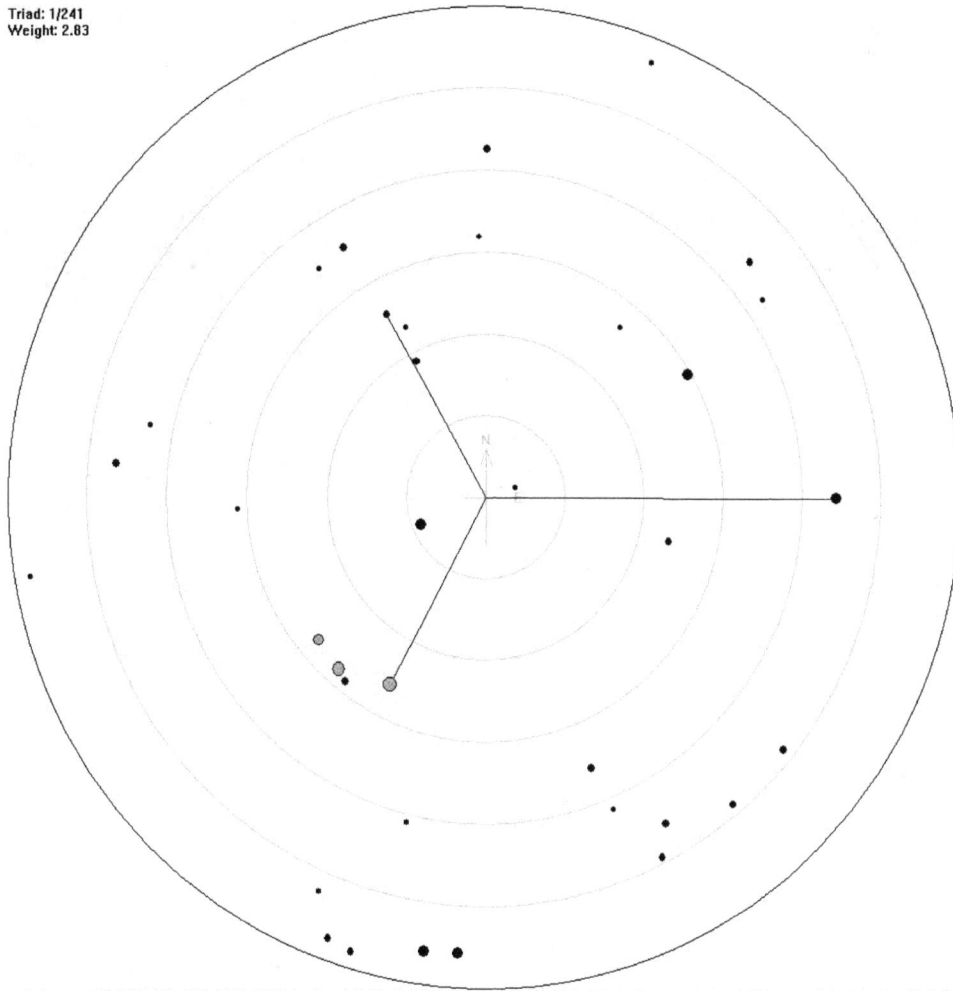

Body	Mag	Hc	Zn
25: ALPHARD	2.2	000°25.7'	260.3°
26: REGULUS	1.2	018°15.8'	275.1°
27: DUBHE	2	035°16.9'	329.5°
28: DENEBOLA	2.2	042°00.6'	267.4°
31: GACRUX	1.6	001°23.9'	200.3°
32: ALIOTH	1.7	050°30.1'	330.7°
33: SPICA	1.2	045°48.5'	218.2°
34: ALKAID	1.8	060°56.2'	332.1°
35: HADAR	0.8	003°34.2'	188.1°
36: MENKENT	2.2	026°52.0'	194.2°
37: ARCTURUS	0.2	076°17.0'	247.7°
38: RIGIL KENT	0.1	003°56.2'	183.7°
40: KOCHAB	2.2	040°47.1'	358.4°
41: ALPHECCA	2.2	084°02.9'	072.0°
42: ANTARES	1.2	035°03.1'	158.1°
45: SHAULA	1.7	019°13.2'	150.3°
46: RASALHAGUE	2	053°30.4'	103.2°
47: ELTANIN	2.4	048°42.2'	039.1°

Body	Mag	Hc	Zn
48: KAUS AUSTR	2	014°45.6'	140.2°
49: VEGA	0.1	044°28.8'	059.4°
50: NUNKI	2	015°09.0'	129.3°
51: ALTAIR	0.8	021°28.5'	090.1°
53: DENEB	1.2	022°11.8'	049.0°
58: POLARIS	2	024°16.6'	000.2°
59: Caph	2.4	001°58.7'	021.4°
105: Algeiba	2.2	023°41.9'	281.9°
108: Merak	2.4	036°02.9'	322.9°
115: Muhlifain	2.4	009°00.4'	203.6°
117: Mimosa	1.5	000°26.7'	197.1°
121: Mizar	2.2	054°20.8'	334.1°
145: Epsilon Scorpii	2.4	026°03.3'	157.0°
152: Theta Scorpii	2	013°56.9'	153.1°
164: Gamma Cygni	2.2	024°28.6'	055.3°
Mars	0	046°46.8'	221.4°
Jupiter	-2.1	050°10.8'	207.9°
Saturn	1	047°54.8'	230.4°

Problem 22 – July 19th, 07:26:19, 24° 39'N, 151° 15'W

Triad: 1/262
Weight: 2.66

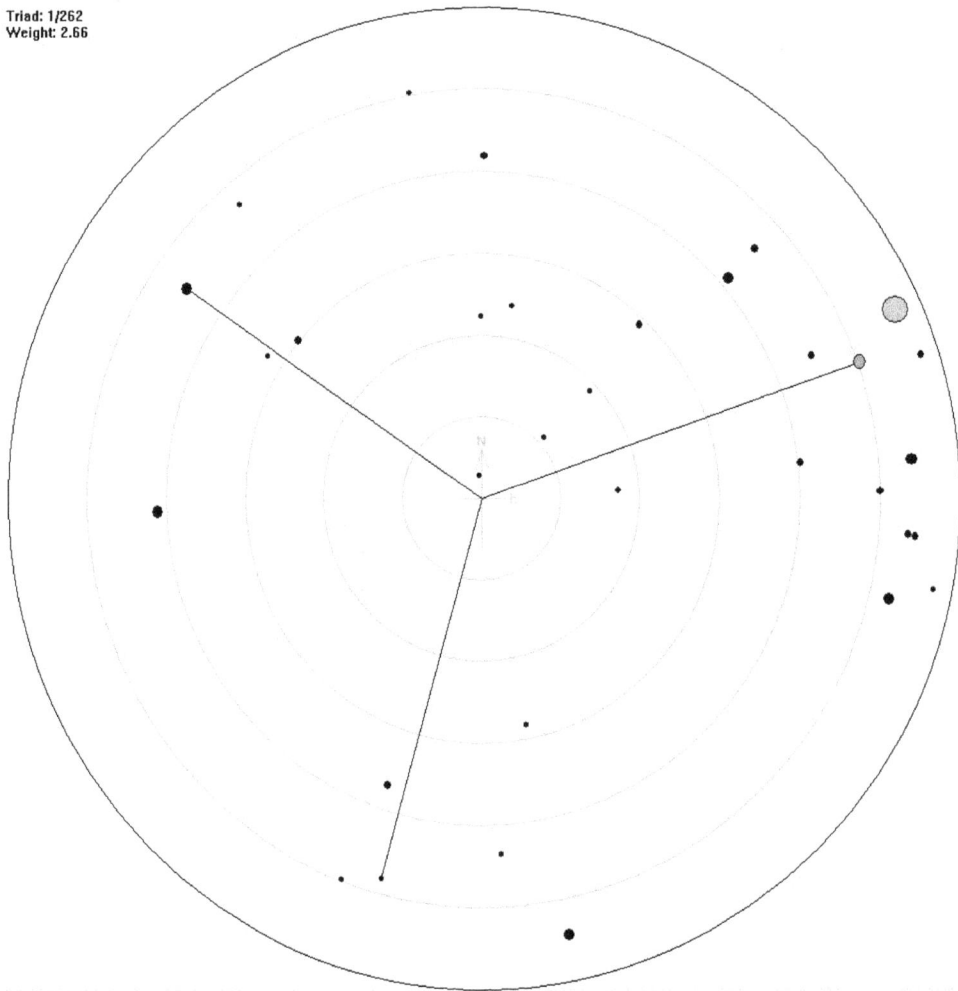

Body	Mag	Hc	Zn
Moon		002°19.9'	066.0°
1: ALPHERATZ	2.2	085°38.1'	354.0°
2: ANKAA	2.4	022°51.1'	176.8°
4: DIPHDA	2.2	046°30.7'	168.5°
5: ACHERNAR	0.6	005°59.3'	168.3°
6: HAMAL	2.2	063°23.3'	086.6°
9: MIRFAK	1.8	045°05.7'	043.1°
10: ALDEBARAN	1.1	027°54.8'	083.7°
11: RIGEL	0.3	009°03.9'	103.4°
12: CAPELLA	0.2	026°36.5'	049.1°
13: BELLATRIX	1.7	012°55.8'	088.9°
14: ELNATH	1.7	020°41.2'	067.1°
15: ALNILAM	1.7	007°16.1'	094.7°
16: BETELGEUSE	0.3	006°33.2'	084.8°
40: KOCHAB	2.2	012°18.1'	349.6°
47: ELTANIN	2.4	017°04.0'	319.4°
49: VEGA	0.1	020°06.9'	304.4°

Body	Mag	Hc	Zn
51: ALTAIR	0.8	026°25.2'	267.7°
53: DENEB	1.2	043°31.5'	309.9°
55: ALNAIR	2.2	013°10.2'	200.9°
56: FOMALHAUT	1.2	032°53.6'	198.9°
58: POLARIS	2	025°21.2'	000.5°
59: Caph	2.4	055°36.1'	359.7°
62: Gamma Casiopeiae	2.2	053°10.0'	009.4°
63: Mirach	2.4	073°14.3'	046.1°
67: Almak	2.2	060°46.7'	046.0°
82: Alnitak	1.8	005°55.5'	094.9°
83: Kappa Orionis	2.2	001°03.1'	101.1°
84: Menkalinan	2	019°03.4'	048.4°
87: Alhena	1.8	000°51.5'	072.3°
164: Gamma Cygni	2.2	040°21.0'	302.8°
171: Beta Gruis	2.2	015°40.5'	195.4°
Venus	-4.1	012°27.7'	070.6°

Problem 23 – July 19th, 22:18:54, 23° 49'N, 152° 25'W

Triad: 1/235
Weight: 2.74

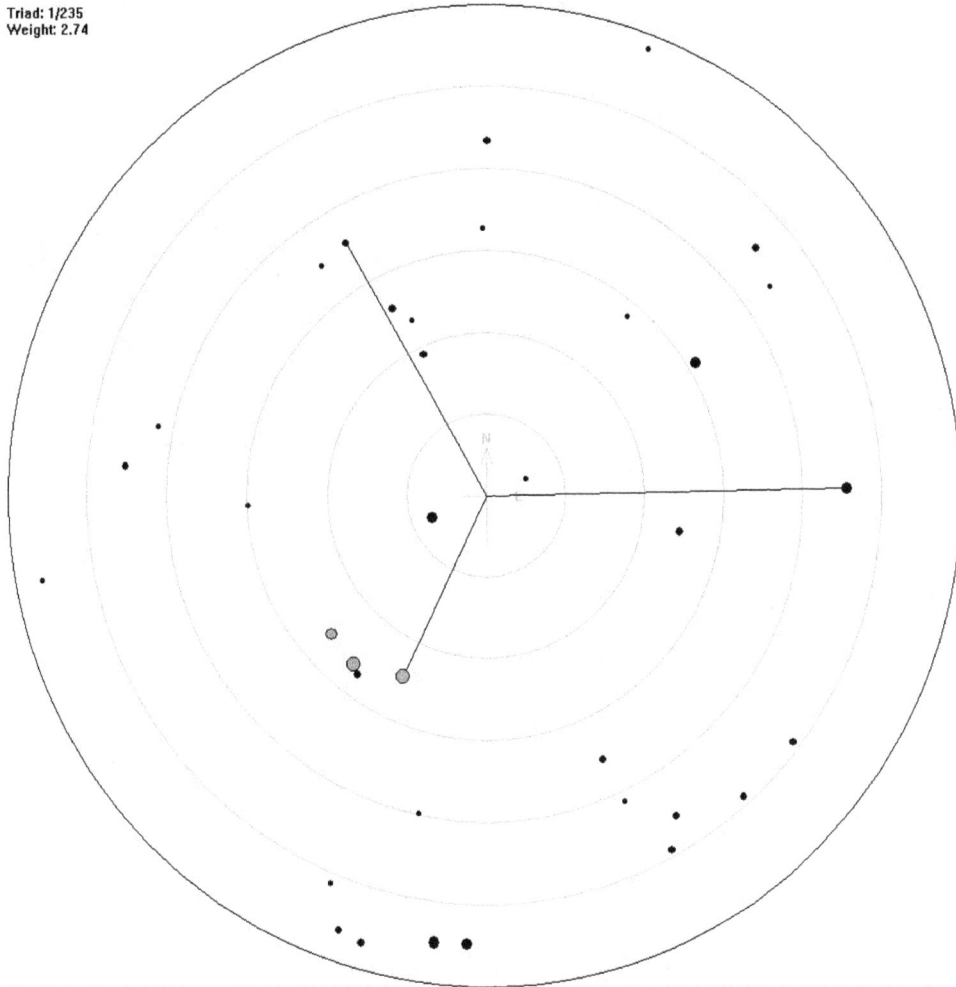

Body	Mag	Hc	Zn
25: ALPHARD	2.2	002°35.4'	259.4°
26: REGULUS	1.2	020°07.3'	274.7°
27: DUBHE	2	035°11.5'	330.2°
28: DENEBOLA	2.2	044°02.1'	267.6°
31: GACRUX	1.6	003°14.6'	199.4°
32: ALIOTH	1.7	050°20.2'	332.7°
33: SPICA	1.2	047°60.0'	216.5°
34: ALKAID	1.8	060°41.3'	335.4°
35: HADAR	0.8	005°04.2'	187.1°
36: MENKENT	2.2	028°32.3'	192.4°
37: ARCTURUS	0.2	078°34.8'	248.7°
38: RIGIL KENT	0.1	005°17.6'	182.7°
40: KOCHAB	2.2	039°34.6'	359.2°
41: ALPHECCA	2.2	081°45.8'	067.2°
42: ANTARES	1.2	035°25.4'	155.6°
45: SHAULA	1.7	019°17.5'	148.5°
46: RASALHAGUE	2	051°49.7'	100.2°
47: ELTANIN	2.4	046°29.4'	039.0°

Body	Mag	Hc	Zn
48: KAUS AUSTR	2	014°25.6'	138.7°
49: VEGA	0.1	042°08.7'	058.4°
50: NUNKI	2	014°23.3'	127.9°
51: ALTAIR	0.8	019°29.4'	088.8°
53: DENEB	1.2	019°53.4'	048.3°
58: POLARIS	2	023°01.2'	000.2°
59: Caph	2.4	000°06.3'	020.5°
105: Algeiba	2.2	025°22.5'	281.7°
108: Merak	2.4	036°13.4'	323.7°
115: Muhlifain	2.4	010°55.8'	202.5°
117: Mimosa	1.5	002°12.4'	196.1°
121: Mizar	2.2	054°02.2'	336.4°
145: Epsilon Scorpii	2.4	026°23.7'	155.0°
152: Theta Scorpii	2	014°08.5'	151.6°
164: Gamma Cygni	2.2	022°08.6'	054.4°
Mars	0	049°07.4'	219.0°
Jupiter	-2.1	052°11.0'	205.4°
Saturn	1	050°14.5'	229.1°

Problem 26 – July 20th, 22:03:59, 22° 39.5'N, 153° 59'W

Triad: 1/271
Weight: 2.8

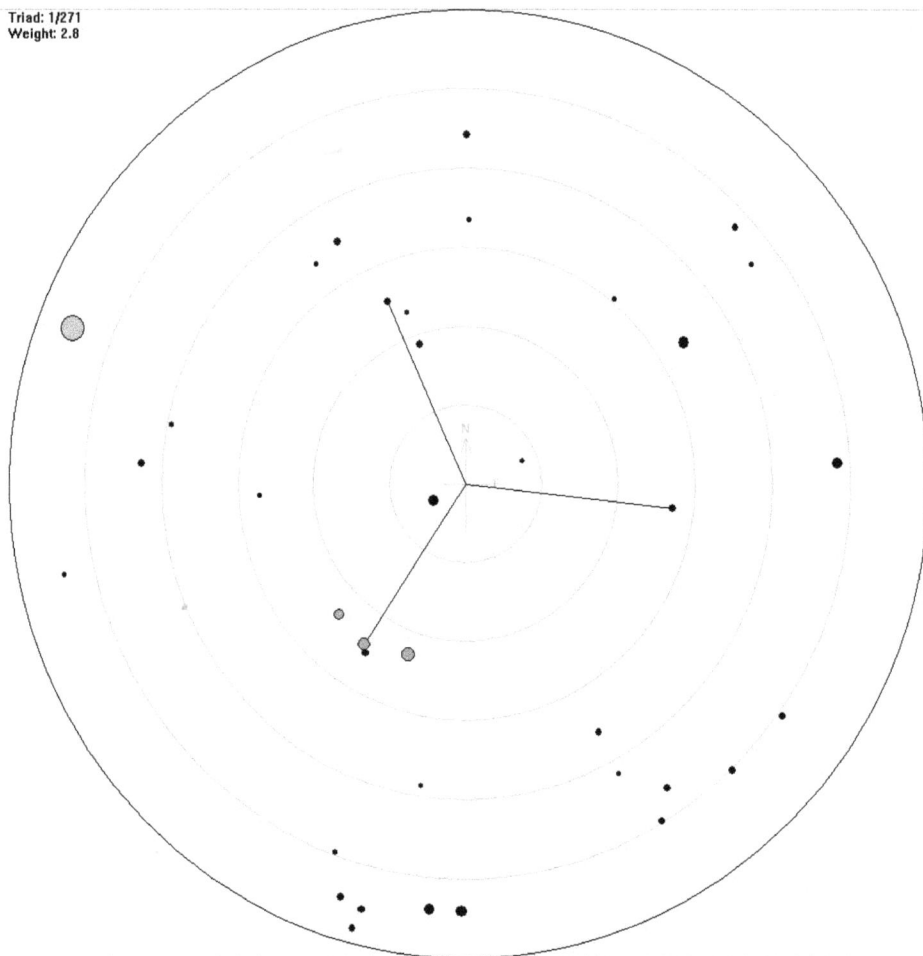

Body	Mag	Hc	Zn
Moon		004°39.3'	290.9°
25: ALPHARD	2.2	006°42.7'	257.8°
26: REGULUS	1.2	023°59.9'	273.5°
27: DUBHE	2	036°06.6'	331.4°
28: DENEBOLA	2.2	048°03.4'	266.9°
30: ACRUX	1.1	000°10.1'	194.8°
31: GACRUX	1.6	005°36.1'	197.4°
32: ALIOTH	1.7	051°00.5'	335.9°
33: SPICA	1.2	051°11.5'	211.7°
34: ALKAID	1.8	061°04.7'	341.1°
35: HADAR	0.8	006°38.8'	185.0°
36: MENKENT	2.2	030°24.7'	188.6°
37: ARCTURUS	0.2	082°41.1'	243.8°
38: RIGIL KENT	0.1	006°34.2'	180.5°
40: KOCHAB	2.2	038°24.8'	000.7°
41: ALPHECCA	2.2	077°38.8'	067.9°
42: ANTARES	1.2	034°40.8'	151.0°
45: SHAULA	1.7	018°06.5'	145.5°
46: RASALHAGUE	2	048°04.0'	096.4°

Body	Mag	Hc	Zn
47: ELTANIN	2.4	043°04.4'	039.6°
48: KAUS AUSTR	2	012°35.9'	136.1°
49: VEGA	0.1	038°09.6'	057.7°
50: NUNKI	2	011°53.8'	125.4°
51: ALTAIR	0.8	015°28.6'	086.7°
53: DENEB	1.2	016°10.1'	047.2°
58: POLARIS	2	021°50.6'	000.1°
105: Algeiba	2.2	029°02.3'	281.0°
108: Merak	2.4	037°35.5'	325.0°
115: Muhlifain	2.4	013°27.6'	200.1°
117: Mimosa	1.5	004°22.4'	194.2°
121: Mizar	2.2	054°24.6'	340.5°
145: Epsilon Scorpii	2.4	025°38.5'	151.3°
152: Theta Scorpii	2	013°11.2'	148.9°
164: Gamma Cygni	2.2	018°15.1'	053.2°
Mars	0	052°29.9'	213.4°
Jupiter	-2.1	054°46.1'	199.2°
Saturn	1	053°57.4'	224.9°

Problem 27 – July 21st, 07:51:02, 22° 04.5'N, 153° 12.5'W

Triad: 1/241
Weight: 2.59

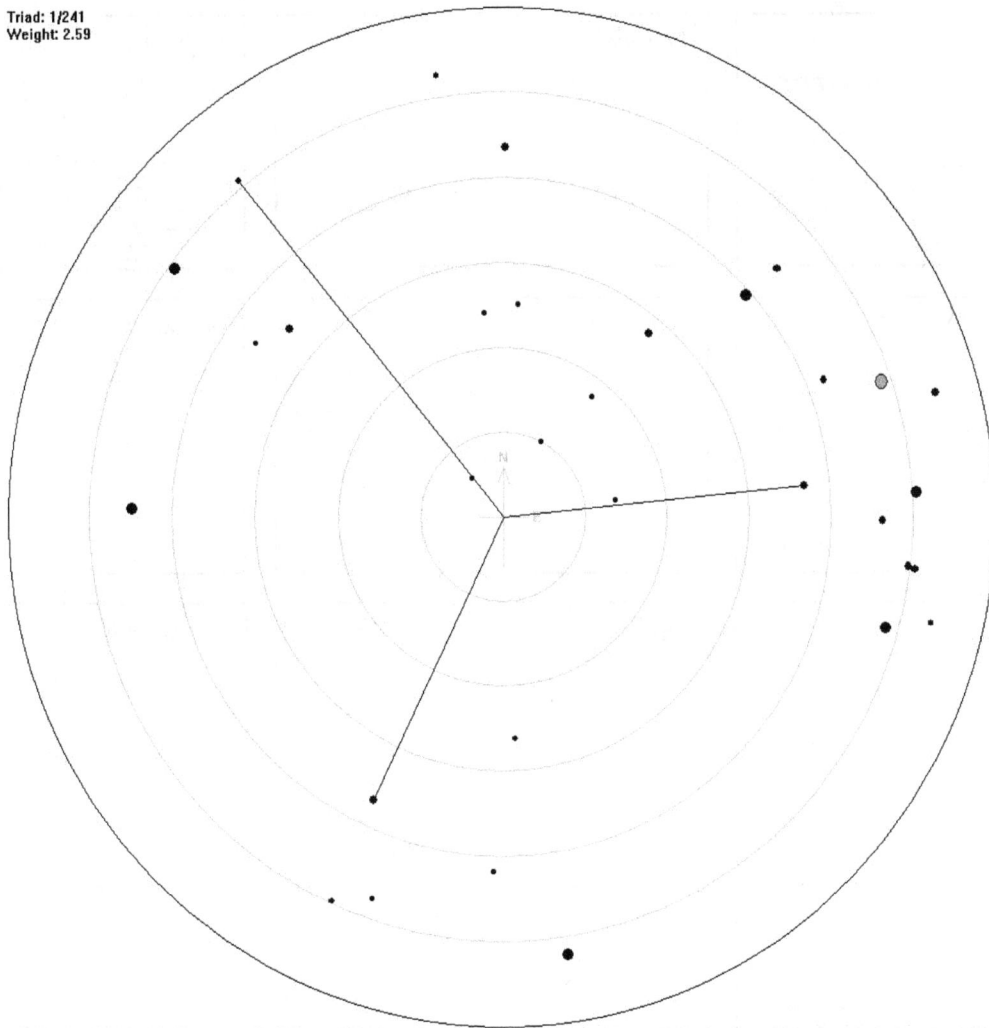

Body	Mag	Hc	Zn
1: ALPHERATZ	2.2	080°48.2'	320.1°
2: ANKAA	2.4	025°29.6'	181.8°
4: DIPHDA	2.2	049°47.5'	176.9°
5: ACHERNAR	0.6	009°31.3'	171.5°
6: HAMAL	2.2	068°49.1'	082.0°
9: MIRFAK	1.8	046°55.4'	039.4°
10: ALDEBARAN	1.1	033°18.8'	084.3°
11: RIGEL	0.3	015°13.7'	105.7°
12: CAPELLA	0.2	029°12.4'	048.5°
13: BELLATRIX	1.7	018°37.3'	090.6°
14: ELNATH	1.7	024°57.5'	067.6°
15: ALNILAM	1.7	013°11.9'	096.8°
16: BETELGEUSE	0.3	012°03.1'	086.8°
40: KOCHAB	2.2	008°48.6'	351.1°
47: ELTANIN	2.4	011°26.8'	321.2°
49: VEGA	0.1	013°58.8'	306.5°

Body	Mag	Hc	Zn
51: ALTAIR	0.8	020°44.4'	271.3°
53: DENEB	1.2	037°30.9'	310.9°
55: AL NAIR	2.2	013°19.7'	204.8°
56: FOMALHAUT	1.2	033°07.8'	205.4°
58: POLARIS	2	022°49.2'	000.4°
59: Caph	2.4	052°44.0'	354.5°
62: Gamma Casiopeiae	2.2	051°16.8'	004.2°
63: Mirach	2.4	074°36.3'	027.2°
67: Almak	2.2	062°39.4'	037.3°
82: Alnitak	1.8	011°51.7'	097.0°
83: Kappa Orionis	2.2	007°10.2'	103.5°
84: Menkalinan	2	021°37.9'	048.8°
87: Alhena	1.8	005°35.3'	074.5°
164: Gamma Cygni	2.2	034°10.8'	304.5°
171: Beta Gruis	2.2	016°24.9'	199.6°
Venus	-4.1	014°45.5'	071.1°

A4. Computer Solutions Plotted

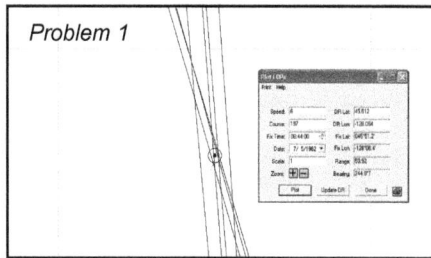

Problem 1

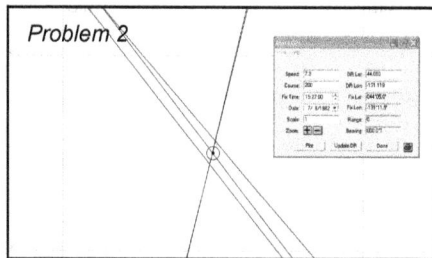

Problem 2

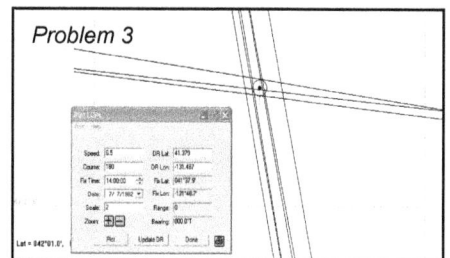

Problem 3

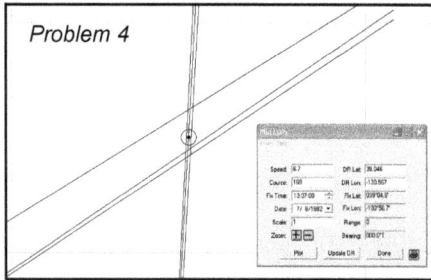

Problem 4

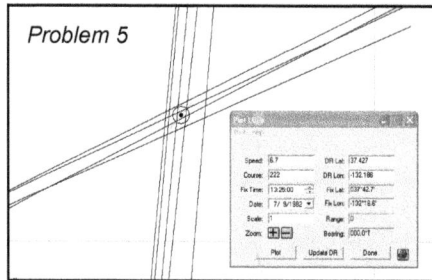

Problem 5

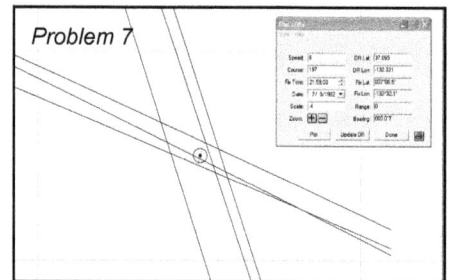

Problem 7

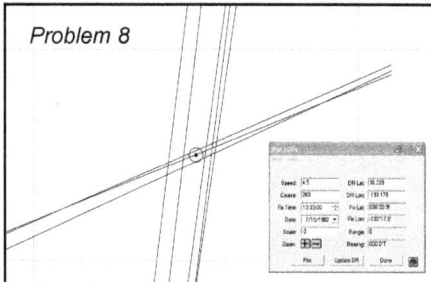

Problem 8

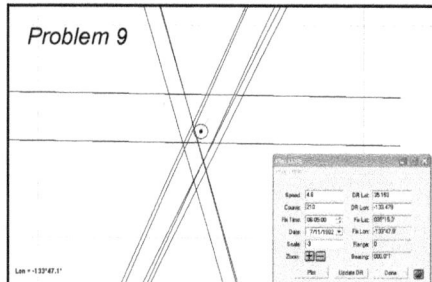

Problem 9

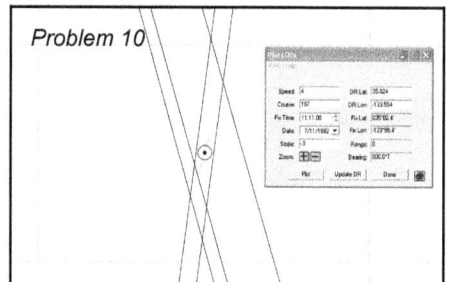

Problem 10

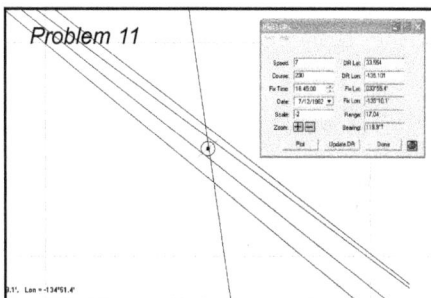

Problem 11

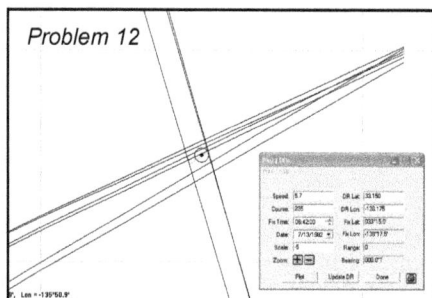

Problem 12

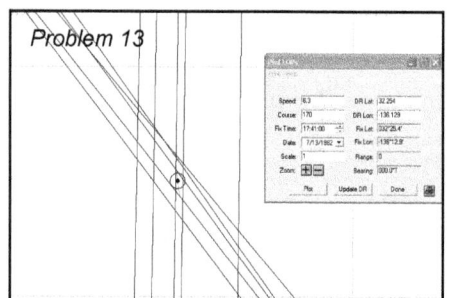

Problem 13

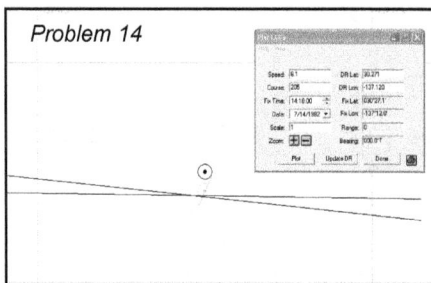

Problem 14

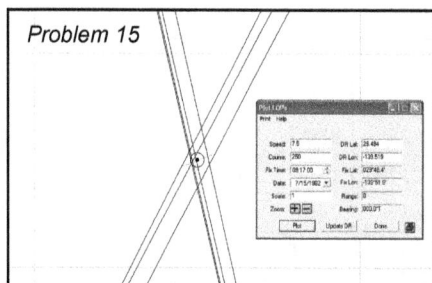

Problem 15

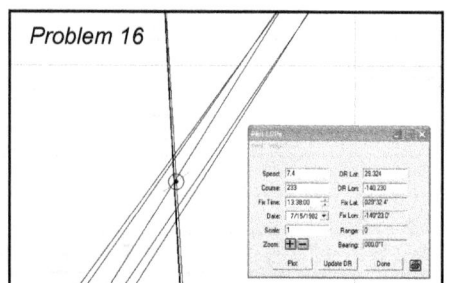

Problem 16

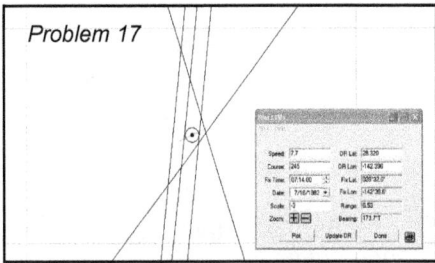

Problem 17

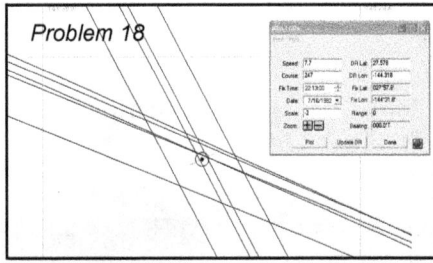

Problem 18

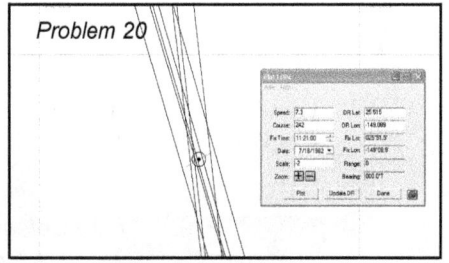

Problem 20

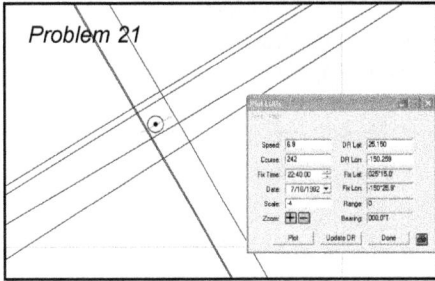

Problem 21

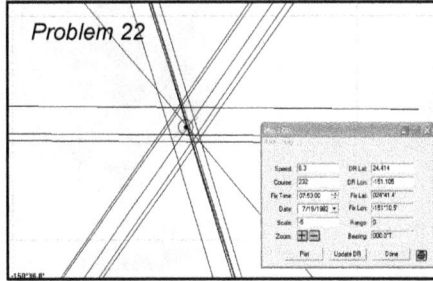

Problem 22

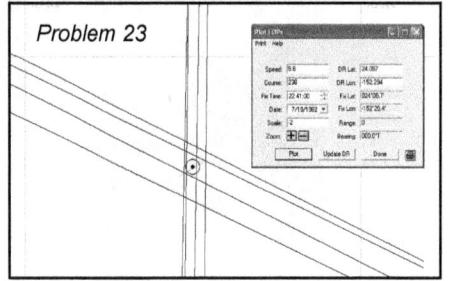

Problem 23

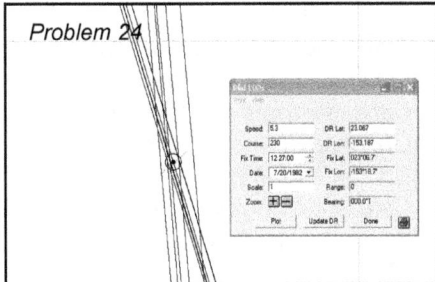

Problem 24

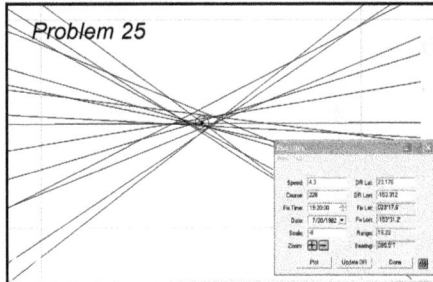

Problem 25

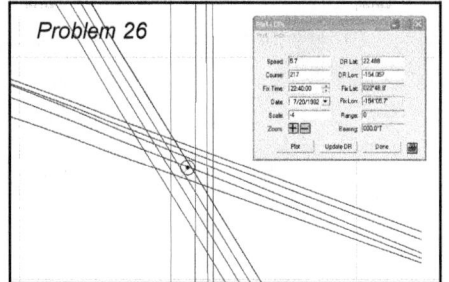

Problem 26

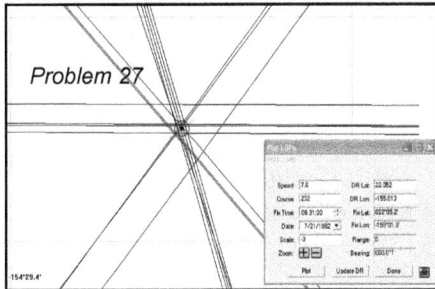

Problem 27

The a-values and DR positions used for these computations are listed in the Computed Solutions section.

A5. Resources for Celestial Navigation

Books

These books are available at nautical bookstores nationwide, or they can be ordered online at starpath.com–also available as Kindle and Apple Books.

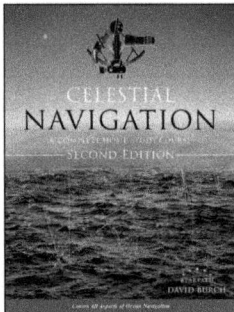

Celestial Navigation – A Complete Home Study Course, Second Edition, David Burch (Starpath Publications, 1978, 2021).

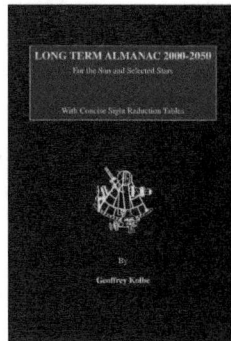

Long Term Almanac 2000-2050 – For the Sun and Selected Stars with Concise Sight Reduction Tables, Geoffrey Kolbe (2nd edition, Starpath Publications, 2008).

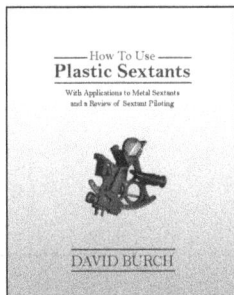

How to Use Plastic Sextants – With Applications to Metal Sextants and a Review of Sextant Piloting, David Burch (Starpath Publications, 2010).

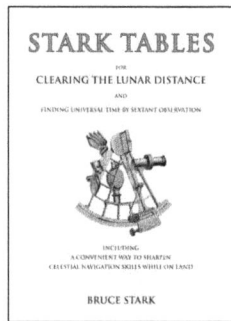

Stark Tables for Clearing the Lunar Distance – and Finding Universal Time by Sextant Observation Including a Convenient Way to Sharpen Celestial Navigation Skills While On Land, Bruce Stark (Revised 3rd edition, Starpath Publications 2010).

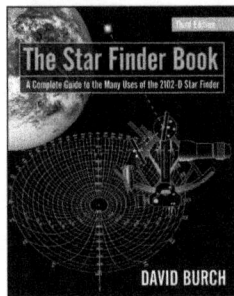

The Star Finder Book – A Complete Guide to the Many Uses of the 2102-D Star Finder, David Burch (2nd edition, Starpath Publications, 2008).

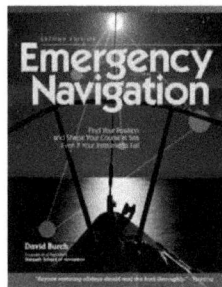

Emergency Navigation, David Burch. Covers navigation without instruments using basic principles of cel nav. (2nd edition, McGraw Hill, 2008)

Online

aa.usno.navy.mil	US Naval Observatory (shortcut to cel nav data: starpath.com/usno)
celestialnavigation.net	A wonderful source for all things celestial
starpath.com/HBS	News, updates, and resources related to this book
time.gov	Online source of UTC, resources and history of timekeeping, and information on time tic broadcasts.

Index

Celestial body references listed below are for their location in the Navigation Sights Section, which in turn provides the Sight Session and Problem number for finding them in other parts of the book.

David and Steve on the bow of the world's most advanced warship, the Destroyer USS Spruance (DDG 111). The authors were invited to the commissioning of the ship in Key West, FL as guests of the Commanding Officer, CDR Tate Westbrook, in recognition of the Starpath training in celestial and coastal navigation provided to officers of the ship.

About the authors

David Burch is Director of Starpath School of Navigation. He is fellow of the Institute of Navigation and the Royal Institute of Navigation and received the former's Superior Achievement Award for outstanding performance as a practicing navigator. He has navigated eleven Hawaii races in boats from 36 ft to 73 ft, including an elapsed time record for boats under 38 ft that lasted for 16 years, two division wins, and two Gabriella III Navigator's Trophies for first to finish.

Stephen Miller is the Starpath Lead Instructor in Coastal and Celestial Navigation. He holds a USCG Masters License, and was previously the Dean of Professional Mariner Training at Chapman School of Seamanship in Stuart, FL, where he taught all levels of navigation in the classroom and underway. He is a former Navy Quartermaster, with more than 25 years of sailing experience in his own boat on the East Coast. He is the author of *The Captain's Moon*, a book on moon photography.

www.ingramcontent.com/pod-product-compliance
Lightning Source LLC
Chambersburg PA
CBHW050413110426

42812CB00006BA/1883